Martin Röhricht

Advanced Signaling Support for IP-based Networks

Advanced Signaling Support for IP-based Networks

by
Martin Röhricht

Dissertation, Karlsruher Institut für Technologie (KIT)
Fakultät für Informatik
Tag der mündlichen Prüfung: 8. Februar 2013
Referenten: Prof. Dr. Martina Zitterbart, Prof. Dr. Hannes Hartenstein

Impressum

Karlsruher Institut für Technologie (KIT)
KIT Scientific Publishing
Straße am Forum 2
D-76131 Karlsruhe
www.ksp.kit.edu

KIT – Universität des Landes Baden-Württemberg und
nationales Forschungszentrum in der Helmholtz-Gemeinschaft

KIT Scientific Publishing 2013
Print on Demand

ISBN 978-3-7315-0037-7

Advanced Signaling Support
for IP-based Networks

zur Erlangung des akademischen Grades eines

Doktors der Ingenieurwissenschaften

von der Fakultät für Informatik
des Karlsruher Instituts für Technologie (KIT)
genehmigte

Dissertation

von

Martin Röhricht

aus Karlsruhe

Tag der mündlichen Prüfung: 8. Februar 2013

Erster Gutachter: Professor Dr. Martina Zitterbart

Zweiter Gutachter: Professor Dr. Hannes Hartenstein

Meinen Eltern Gudrun und Michael gewidmet

Acknowledgments

Die Entstehung dieser Arbeit wäre nicht ohne die Hilfe und Unterstützung einiger Personen möglich gewesen, denen ich auf diesem Wege meinen Dank hierfür aussprechen möchte. An erster Stelle möchte ich meiner Betreuerin Prof. Dr. Martina Zitterbart dafür danken, dass sie mir die Möglichkeit geboten hat, am Institut für Telematik als wissenschaftlicher Mitarbeiter zu arbeiten und während dieser Zeit die vorliegende Dissertation zu erstellen. Ebenso danke ich meinem Zweitgutachter, Herrn Prof. Dr. Hannes Hartenstein dafür, dass er sich trotz umfangreicher dienstlicher Verpflichtungen die Zeit genommen hat, mir als Korreferent zur Verfügung zu stehen.

Während meiner Zeit am Institut hatte ich das Glück, mit einer Vielzahl von liebenswerten und hilfsbereiten Kollegen zusammen zu arbeiten. Meinem langjährigen »Mentor« Roland Bless möchte ich in besonderer Weise meinen Dank aussprechen. Er war es, der mich an die Welt der IETF heranführte. Das schier endlose Wissen und die unbändige Wissbegierde unseres »Silberrückens« prägten meine Zeit am Institut nachhaltig und waren ein steter Quell der Inspiration. Mit Christian Hübsch habe ich einen großartigen Menschen und Freund kennengelernt, der mir auch in schwierigen Zeiten immer zur Seite stand. Mit meinen ehemaligen Kollegen Jochen Furthmüller, Thomas Gamer, Christian Haas, Christoph Mayer und Hans Wippel hatte ich das Vergnügen, viel Zeit zu verbringen und dabei eine ganze Menge zu lernen. Ich danke ihnen hierfür herzlich. Ebenso möchte ich meinen zahlreichen Studenten dafür danken, dass ich mit ihnen zusammen arbeiten durfte, besondere Erwähnung verdienen hierbei die Herren Matthias Dettling, Max Laier, Micha Lenk und Patric Marschall. Mein alter Schulfreund David Talbott war mir in sprachlichen Fragestellungen eine enorme Stütze. Ich werde ihm nie vergessen, wie er sich bei einer Dienstreise, die mich nach Japan führte, um mein Wohlergehen kümmerte. Danke David.

Ein ganz besonderer Dank richtet sich an meine Eltern und meine Familie, ohne deren Unterstützung und Rückhalt ich niemals so weit gekommen wäre. Sie haben mir stets ein unerschütterliches Maß an Vertrauen und Liebe entgegengebracht und standen mir zu jeder Zeit zur Seite. Ihnen ist diese Arbeit gewidmet. Meinem letzten Dank gebührt eigentlich die erste Stelle: Meiner Frau Karin danke ich für die großartige Unterstützung, die sie mir zu jeder Zeit hat zukommen lassen. Sie ist das größte Glück, das mir in meinem Leben begegnen konnte.

Stuttgart im Juni 2013

Zusammenfassung

In heutigen Kommunikationsnetzen bildet *Signalisierung* bereits eine zentrale Komponente. Sie ermöglicht es, Dienste innerhalb dieser Netze, wie beispielsweise Telefonie, dynamisch und auf Anforderung hin zu steuern. Signalisierungsprotokolle erlauben somit – unabhängig von der eigentlichen Nutzdatenübertragung – das Etablieren und die Verwaltung von Multimediasitzungen. Sollen die Signalisierungsprotokolle jedoch zukünftigen Anforderungen im Internet gerecht werden, so sehen sie sich drei wesentlichen Herausforderungen gegenübergestellt: die Signalisierung muss vor Missbrauch durch unberechtigte Nutzer geschützt werden (*Sicherheit*); Signalisierung muss von mobilen Endsystemen aus genutzt werden können (*Mobilität*); und Signalisierung im Internet muss skalierbar durchgeführt werden können (*Skalierbarkeit*). Das Ziel dieser Dissertation ist es daher, fortgeschrittene Signalisierung für IP-basierte Netze unter Berücksichtigung der drei genannten Herausforderungen zu ermöglichen.

Das Thema Sicherheit spielt gerade in einem nicht-vertrauenswürdigen Umfeld wie dem Internet eine entscheidende Rolle. Im ersten Teil dieser Dissertation wird daher ein Sicherheitskonzept für Signalisierungsprotokolle entworfen. Die entwickelten Verfahren erlauben es, eine sichere Authentifizierung und Autorisierung eines Nutzers durchzuführen. Das Konzept dieser Arbeit beruht auf dem Einsatz feingranularer und leichtgewichtiger Sicherungsmechanismen und sieht vor, die Nutzeridentität sowie den Inhalt einer Signalisierungsnachricht eng an das Autorisierungsobjekt zu koppeln. Die Verzahnung des Autorisierungsobjekts mit der Nutzeridentität ermöglicht, dass ein einzelnes Autorisierungsobjekt nicht von einem Angreifer für eigene Zwecke missbraucht werden kann. Die Kopplung mit der Signalisierungsnachricht erlaubt es, in feingranularer Weise einen Integritätsschutz über schützenswerte Teile einer Signalisierungsnachricht durchzuführen, während andere Teile der Nachricht weiterhin von Zwischensystemen verändert werden dürfen bzw. verändert werden müssen. Das entwickelte Konzept umfasst hochauflösende Zeitstempel, um sog. Replay-Attacken zu verhindern, Möglichkeiten zur sog. Krypto-Agilität zum dynamischen Austausch eingesetzter kryptografischer Algorithmen und bietet eine einheitliche Lösung für verschiedenste Signalisierungsprotokolle, d. h. sie ist unabhängig von der tatsächlich verwendeten Signalisierungsanwendung.

Eine weitere grundlegende Herausforderung für Signalisierungsprotokolle stellt heutzutage die zunehmende Mobilität von Endsystemen im Internet dar. Eine Signalisierungssitzung, die an einen festen Ort gebunden ist, kann ohne explizite

Mobilitätsunterstützung nicht mehr von einem mobilen Nutzer in Anspruch genommen werden, sobald dieser an einen neuen Ort gewechselt ist. Im zweiten Teil dieser Arbeit wird daher das Ziel verfolgt, Mobilität für Signalisierungssitzungen im Internet zu ermöglichen. Hierfür wurde zum einen eine Lösung für das im Internet derzeit am weitesten verbreitete Mobilitätsmanagementprotokoll Mobile IP entwickelt. Die Lösung setzt auf ein eigens entwickeltes Flow Information Service Element, mittels dessen Mobilitätsinformationen mit den Signalisierungsinstanzen ausgetauscht werden können und wodurch auch ein stationärer Kommunikationspartner über Mobilität seines Gegenübers in Kenntnis gesetzt werden kann. Da eine angepasste Signalisierung unter Nutzung von Mobile IP erst *nach* erfolgtem Wechsel des Zugangspunktes durchgeführt werden kann, wurden in dieser Arbeit zum anderen auch Lösungen entwickelt, die es erlauben, *unabhängig* von einem Mobilitätsmanagementprotokoll Signalisierung bereits im Vorfeld entlang eines *antizipierten* Pfads vornehmen zu können. Unter der Voraussetzung, dass das mobile Endsystem seinen zukünftigen (antizipierten) Zugangspunkt ermitteln kann, ermöglicht dies, dass Ressourcen für Dienste sofort zur Verfügung stehen, sobald das mobile Endsystem zu diesem Zugangspunkt gewechselt ist. Hierzu mussten die bestehenden Signalisierungsprotokolle um verschiedene Funktionalitäten erweitert werden. Diese umfassen Möglichkeiten, einen antizipierten Wechsel vorzubereiten, die neue Signalisierungssitzung nach dem Wechsel zu aktivieren und die alte Signalisierungssitzung nach dem erfolgten Wechsel abbauen zu können.

Da die Durchführung von Ressourcenreservierungen mithilfe von Signalisierungsprotokollen auch dann noch eine akzeptable Leistungsfähigkeit aufweisen soll, wenn sich die Anzahl seiner Nutzer – wie im Internet möglich – signifikant erhöht, widmet sich der dritte Teil dieser Dissertation der Skalierbarkeit von Ressourcenreservierungen. Hierzu wurden zum einen bestehende Signalisierungsprotokolle um Unterstützung für IP Multicast erweitert und zum anderen Konzepte entwickelt, die gleichartige Ressourcenreservierungen zu einer einzelnen Aggregatreservierung zusammenfassen können. Gruppenbasierte Kommunikation ist bereits heute bei der Bereitstellung von IPTV weltweit im Einsatz und wird mittels IP Multicast realisiert. Signalisierungsunterstützung für gruppenbasierte Kommunikation ermöglicht es somit, die Vorteile dieser Kommunikationsform für den Einsatz von Signalisierung hinsichtlich einer effizienten Datenauslieferung auszunutzen. Mithilfe der entwickelten Mechanismen ist durch den Einsatz von IP Multicast die Zustandshaltung auf den Zwischenknoten und dem Wurzelknoten nicht mehr abhängig von der Gesamtanzahl der Blattknoten, sondern nur noch von der Anzahl der direkten Nachbarknoten gemäß des jeweiligen Verzweigungsgrads. Die weiteren in dieser Arbeit entwickelten Mechanismen zur Verbesserung der Skalierbarkeit zielen nicht auf die Verwendung von IP Multicast ab, sondern erlauben es, gleichartige Ressourcenreservierungen in IP-basierten Netzen zu größeren, zusammengefassten Reservierungen zu aggregieren. Die Konzepte sind so ausgelegt, dass die Aggregationsmechanismen vollständig verteilt und auch über die Grenzen verschiedener administrativer Domänen hinweg durchgeführt werden können. Eine wesentliche Herausforderung bestand in der effizienten Bestimmung von Aggregationseingangs- und -endpunkten, die ein a priori Wissen über den Verlauf der jeweiligen Datenpfade und die Dienstklassenabbildungen der Reservierungen voraussetzen. Die hierzu entwickelten Lösungen sehen vor, die benötigten Informationen über die Route einer Signalisierungsnachricht beim initialen Signalisierungsaustausch aufzuzeichnen und dieses Wissen für die Bestimmung der Aggregationsendpunkte zu verwenden. Für die Zustandsverwaltung innerhalb des Aggregats muss eine eigene Signalisierungssitzung zwischen dem Aggregationseingangs- und -endpunkt etabliert werden. Um auf dynamische Routingänderungen reagieren zu können, wird der Signalisierungspfad periodisch auf Veränderungen überprüft und das Aggregat daraufhin angepasst. Die Anpassung des Aggregats erfolgt einer berechneten Heuristik zufolge nur in größeren Intervallen. Die Anwendbarkeit der entwickelten Konzepte wurde mittels Simulationen in einer Internet-ähnlichen Topologie analysiert. Die Evaluationsergebnisse zeigen, dass die Anzahl an zu verwaltenden Zuständen im Kernbereich des Internets hierdurch signifikant reduziert werden kann. Selbst unter einer stark zunehmenden Zahl an Einzelreservierungen bleibt die Anzahl an Aggregatreservierungen auf einem nahezu konstanten Niveau.

Contents

List of Figures

List of Tables

List of Acronyms

Acronym	Definition
A-MRM	Aggregate Message Routing Method
A-MRI	Aggregate Message Routing Information
AF	Assured Forwarding
AHO	Anticipated Handover
API	Application Programming Interface
AR	Access Router
AS	Autonomous System
ATM	Asynchronous Transfer Mode
BE	Best Effort
BGP	Border Gateway Protocol
BGRP	Border Gateway Reservation Protocol
CASP	Cross-Application Signaling Protocol
CN	Correspondent Node
CoA	Care-of-Address
CRN	Crossover Node
DARIS	Dynamic Aggregation of Reservations for Internet Services
DiffServ	Differentiated Services
DMSP	Domain Manager Signaling Protocol
DSCP	DiffServ Code Point
DSDM	Differentiated Services Domain Manager
EAP	Extensible Authentication Protocol
EF	Expedited Forwarding
EST-MRI	Explicit Signaling Target Message Routing Information
EST-MRM	Explicit Signaling Target Message Routing Method
FIB	Forwarding Information Base

GIST	General Internet Signaling Transport
HA	Home Agent
HMAC	Keyed-Hashing for Message Authentication
HMIPv6	Hierarchical Mobile IPv6
HO	Handover
HoA	Home Address
HOT	Heuristically Optimal Topology
IANA	Internet Assigned Numbers Authority
ICMP	Internet Control Message Protocol
IDL	Intermediate Deaggregation Location
IETF	Internet Engineering Task Force
IGMP	Internet Group Management Protocol
IntServ	Integrated Services
IP	Internet Protocol
IPTV	Internet Protocol Television
ISDN	Integrated Services Digital Network
ITU-T	International Telecommunication Union – Telecommunication Standardization Sector
KDC	Key Distribution Center
LRM	Local Resource Manager
MA	Messaging Association
MAC	Message Authentication Code
MANETs	Mobile Ad-hoc Networks
MARSP	Mobility-Aware Reservation Signaling Protocol
MIB	Management Information Base
MN	Mobile Node
MPLS	Multi-Protocol Label Switching
MRI	Message Routing Information
MRM	Message Routing Method

NAT	Network Address Translation
NLI	Network Layer Information
NSIS	Next Steps in Signaling
NSLP	NSIS Signaling Layer Protocol
NTLP	NSIS Transport Layer Protocol
OSPF	Open Shortest Path First
P2P	Peer-to-Peer
PC-MRI	Path-coupled Message Routing Information
PC-MRM	Path-coupled Message Routing Method
PDU	Protocol Data Unit
PHB	Per-Hop Behavior
PIM-DM	Protocol Independent Multicast – Dense-Mode
PIM-SM	Protocol Independent Multicast – Sparse-Mode
PSTN	Public Switched Telephone Network
QN	Querying Node
QNE	QoS NSLP Entity
QNI	QoS NSLP Initiator
QNR	QoS NSLP Responder
QoS	Quality-of-Service
QSPEC	Quality-of-Service Specification
RAO	Router Alert Option
ReaSE	Realistic Simulation Environments for OMNeT++
RES	Reservation Mode Bit
RIB	Routing Information Base
RII	Request Identification Information
RIP	Routing Information Protocol
RMF	Resource Management Function
RSA	Rivest, Shamir, and Adleman
RSN	Reservation Sequence Number

Rspec	Reservation Specification
RSVP	Resource ReSerVation Protocol
RTCP	RealTime Control Protocol
RTP	Real-Time Transport Protocol
SAML	Security Assertion Markup Language
SCMP	Stream Control Message Protocol
SCTP	Stream Control Transmission Protocol
SICAP	Shared-Segment Inter-Domain Control Aggregation Protocol
SII	Source Identification Information
SIP	Session Initiation Protocol
SNMP	Simple Network Management Protocol
SS7	Signaling System 7
ST-II	Internet Stream Protocol Version 2
ST2+	Internet Stream Protocol Version ST2+
TCP	Transmission Control Protocol
TGS	Ticket Granting Server
TGT	Ticket Granting Ticket
TLP	Type-Length-Position
TLS	Transport Layer Security
TLV	Type-Length-Value
Tspec	Traffic Specification
UDP	User Datagram Protocol
ULA	Unique Local Address
USAGI	UniverSAl playGround for Ipv6
VoIP	Voice-over-IP
YESSIR	YEt another Sender Session Internet Reservations

List of Symbols

Symbol	Definition
α	*Mobility*: number of signaling hops between MN and AR_N
	Aggregation: factor for additional amount of reserved resources
β	*Mobility*: number of signaling hops between AR_N and CN
	Aggregation: smoothing factor for the estimated utilization
γ	*Mobility*: number of signaling hops between AR_O and CRN
	Aggregation: threshold for a lower-bound factor upon which an aggregate should be reduced
δ	*Multicast*: artificially added delay for a GIST RESPONSE message
Δ	*Multicast*: lowest accumulated delay between adjacent signaling entities
Δt	*Aggregation*: interval size upon which an aggregate's utilization is re-calculated
d	*Multicast*: multicast tree depth
e_j^i	*Multicast*: jth signaling entity at level i of multicast tree
f_{RSV}	Processing time to forward a QoS NSLP RESERVE
f_{RSP}	Processing time to forward a QoS NSLP RESPONSE
f_{QUERY}	Processing time to forward a QoS NSLP QUERY
f_{NOTIFY}	Processing time to forward a QoS NSLP NOTIFY
F	*Multicast*: multicast tree fanout
k	*Aggregation*: aggregation threshold
l	*Multicast*: number of opportunities per signaling peer to respond to a GIST QUERY
o	Time between incoming trigger and outgoing GIST QUERY
p	Time between incoming GIST QUERY and outgoing GIST RESPONSE
q	Time between incoming GIST RESPONSE and outgoing QoS NSLP RESERVE
r	Time between incoming GIST RESPONSE and outgoing QoS NSLP QUERY
RTT_i	Round trip time between signaling entity i and signaling entity $i+1$

s	Time between incoming GIST RESPONSE and outgoing QoS NSLP NOTIFY
t_i	Propagation delay between signaling entity i and signaling entity $i+1$
u	Time between incoming QoS NSLP QUERY and outgoing QoS NSLP RESERVE
v	Time between incoming QoS NSLP RESERVE and outgoing QoS NSLP RESPONSE
w	Time between incoming QoS NSLP NOTIFY and outgoing QoS NSLP QUERY
x	Time between incoming GIST RESPONSE and outgoing QoS NSLP RESPONSE
y	Time between incoming QoS NSLP NOTIFY and outgoing QoS NSLP RESERVE
z_{NOTIFY}	Time between incoming trigger and outgoing QoS NSLP NOTIFY
z_{RSV}	Time between incoming trigger and outgoing QoS NSLP RESERVE

Chapter 1

Introduction

The Internet has certainly revolutionized the world of communications and has already become an indispensable part of today's life. In the future, its importance, both in societal and economic terms, will increase further, since telecommunication providers have already introduced a shift to an "all-IP" paradigm used in "Next Generation Networks". Within these networks, all services that are offered, for example Internet telephony (Voice-over-IP, VoIP) or Internet television (IPTV) are carried over the Internet Protocol (IP), instead of being carried over dedicated circuit-switched transmission lines.

Internet users already take the use of video and other real-time demanding applications over the Internet for granted. For instance, according to a recent Sandvine report [San12] the American video-on-demand service provider Netflix already accounts for approximately 60% of the total Internet traffic in the U.S. during peak time. This trend will continue over the next few years, according to a Cisco report [Cis12a] which states that Internet video-on-demand traffic will triple by 2016 with 79% being videos in high-definition. Multimedia applications, such as VoIP or IPTV, typically require low latency or a low packet loss rate. Unfortunately, the Internet only provides a *best-effort* packet delivery service where competing resource demands may conflict which leads to congestion and packet loss in the network.

In order to control scarce resources in a network, *Quality-of-Service* (QoS) mechanisms must be used. QoS support cannot increase the amount of available network resources, it can, however, be used to allocate resources, an provide mechanisms for a differentiation amongst a set of flows. While network resources are always controlled by a network operator's policy, they can be admitted either statically or dynamically. *Signaling* allows users to request resources from a network on-demand

and to interact with a network operator's resource control function. Network signaling protocols allow for admission control, an on-demand negotiation of QoS parameters, and a corresponding reservation of required resources in the network.[1] Signaling has been subject to a number of research and standardization activities in the past. Recently, the Internet Engineering Task Force (IETF) standardized the *Next Steps in Signaling* (NSIS) protocol framework, which provides a generic network signaling protocol suite for the Internet.

1.1 Problem Statement and Objectives

This dissertation aims at providing an integrated solution for on-demand resource reservations in today's and upcoming IP-based networks. Since signaling builds a key component in order to allow for an on-demand negotiation and establishment of resource reservations, an advanced signaling solution is required. Therefore, this dissertation assumes an underlying IP-based network with an Internet-like structure composed of different administrative domains and Internet routers as well as end systems acting as signaling entities. The design of an advanced signaling solution must consider the following aspects (cf. Figure 1.1):

Figure 1.1: *Requirements for signaling in IP-based networks*

Security builds an essential prerequisite for signaling protocols, since only authorized users should be allowed to access and request network resources, i.e., unauthorized use by third parties must be prevented. Potential security threats include, for instance, the modification or replay of signaling messages. This would allow an attacker to request resources on behalf of another user or manipulate another user's reservation request upon which this user may get charged for much more resources than were originally requested. Therefore, the authenticity and

---

[1]As opposed to *application signaling protocols* which are usually only meaningful to the end systems.

integrity of signaling messages must be preserved by a signaling protocol. Otherwise, it is very unlikely that this protocol will experience widespread deployment in untrusted networks like the Internet.

In addition, a strong trend toward the use of mobile devices can also be observed in the Internet. According to a Cisco report [Cis12b] this trend will only accelerate going forward, since global mobile data traffic is expected to increase 18-fold between 2011 and 2016. Signaling protocols must therefore provide support for *mobility* of end users. For instance, in case an already established resource reservation is not automatically adapted to the mobile device's new location, a mobile user cannot use its previously established resource reservation anymore. The user would then have to establish an entirely new reservation. This can, however, not be considered an adequate solution, due to the fact that the user would be accounted for an additional reservation or his new reservation request may even be rejected since he already reached his limit of permitted resource reservations.

Since signaling protocols being deployed in the Internet may be used by a potentially very large number of users, *scalability* is a major concern. Scalable and efficient delivery of data toward a group of receivers can already be employed in many of today's networks in form of group communication. While *IP multicast* is often used in today's networks in order to deliver data flows toward a group of receivers, supporting high bandwidth streams across larger networks, e.g., for live multimedia events, requires corresponding QoS guarantees for these IP multicast flows. However, resources can only be reserved for IP multicast flows if the resource reservations being managed by signaling protocols fit to the actual data flow delivery.

A further scalability problem affecting QoS signaling protocols is concerned with the maintenance of state for resource reservations. Since each reservation requires per-flow reservation state to be maintained on the corresponding signaling entities, an increasing number of resource reservations—that would have to be maintained especially in the core domains of the Internet—eventually leads to scalability issues. It would be much more effective to bundle "similar" resource reservations into aggregate reservations, such that signaling entities in the Internet's core domains would only maintain state for one aggregate reservation.

1.2 Contributions and Assumptions

In order to fulfill the identified requirements for an advanced signaling solution, this dissertation makes the following contributions:

- *Security mechanisms* form an essential part of protecting signaling messages from being misused by unauthorized entities. The security mechanisms applied must be cryptographically strong and provide means to dynamically exchange cryptographic algorithms, i.e., provide methods for crypto-agility, on demand.

  Since signaling entities have only limited computational resources in terms of CPU and memory, the security functions developed in this dissertation are light-weight and do not impose a significant computational overhead.

  Furthermore, despite applying a protection mechanism for signaling messages, signaling entities along the path must still be able to process these signaling messages and even modify certain parts of it. Therefore, this dissertation developed a fine-grained protection mechanism which can be applied to only selected parts of a given signaling message.

- *Signaling support for mobile users* represents another important requirement for signaling protocols, since mobility is becoming increasingly popular and signaling protocols can no longer assume an always fixed location of end systems. Resource reservations established by a QoS signaling protocol should therefore be automatically adapted to a mobile user's new location, i.e., a signaling protocol must be aware of a mobile user's current location.

  However, the main challenge in using QoS signaling in mobile environments is to create a linkage between the signaling protocol's control path and the data path in order to adapt an already established resource reservation to the new user's location, under the constraint that an existing mobility management protocol's operation should remain unmodified. This is difficult to achieve, since a mobility management protocol usually hides the mobility aspect from its applications. This dissertation developed concepts to allow for location-independent signaling services if the mobile user and its communication partner make use of a mobility management protocol.

  A further challenge arises under the constraint that the mobile node's stationary communication partner does not use a mobility management protocol but controls the resource reservation. In this case, the stationary signaling entity cannot be aware of the mobile user's new location and hence, cannot adapt the corresponding resource reservation, while the mobile node cannot adapt the reservation on its own, since it does not control the reservation. In order to solve this problem, this dissertation developed concepts that allow a mobile user to transfer the required information toward its communication partner upon which a resource reservation can be adapted.

Furthermore, in mobile environments it is desirable for users to have a resource reservation been established for a newly, *anticipated* data path just before they actually change their point of attachment. This dissertation allows for an anticipated handover concept of signaling sessions. This allows users to use signaling services seamlessly and without intervals of interruptions of the signaling session while being mobile.

- *Scalability* constitutes another major requirement for signaling protocols that are used in IP-based networks. While IP multicast provides a scalable and efficient data delivery service, an IP unicast-based QoS signaling protocol cannot simply be employed in IP multicast environments. Challenges in adapting unicast-based QoS signaling protocols are mainly concerned with group membership dynamics that may occur in IP multicast environments. New members may join or leave a multicast group at any time and a QoS signaling protocol must be able to adapt resource reservations for dynamic multicast groups.

Another challenge is concerned with the scope of signaling messages. In order to allow for scalable resource reservations in IP multicast environments it must be ensured that the resource initiator is not "flooded" by signaling messages that are returned from an entire group of signaling responders. This dissertation provides concepts to adapt IP unicast-based QoS signaling protocols to be used in IP multicast environments.

Furthermore, in order to allow for scalable resource reservations in IP-based networks, "similar" resource reservations can be aggregated to a single aggregate reservation. The main challenges that must be resolved by a resource reservation aggregation concept are the following. The actual single reservation's path cannot be known by a signaling protocol instance a priori. This is, however, necessary in order to decide which reservations can be replaced by an aggregate reservation. Since each reservation request is independently mapped to a specific service class on each intermediate signaling entity, a reservation's service class mappings must also be taken into account. A further challenge that must be resolved is concerned with potential conflicts that may arise when aggregates are established by independently operating signaling entities.

The aggregation concept developed in this dissertation resolves these challenges and allows multiple single resource reservations to be replaced by one aggregate reservation. Information about a reservation's path and its service class mappings are collected at the beginning of a signaling session. Strategies are employed that allow for the detection and resolution of conflicts between competing aggregates. The developed aggregation concepts provide the potential for a significant reduction of signaling state that must be maintained at signaling entities, especially at the highly utilized Internet's core domains.

Furthermore, the concepts developed in this dissertation fulfill the following additional requirements:

- Signaling operates in a *decentralized* fashion, i.e., it is not controlled by a centralized entity, such as a bandwidth broker or domain resource manager. A decentralized approach can be expected to achieve a more robust and scalable solution.

- Signaling can be used in *inter-domain* wide scenarios, i.e., from end-to-end across different administrative domains, rather than being limited to intra-domain scenarios only.

The NSIS protocol suite builds the basis for this work. The decision to use these protocols as a basis are due to the fact that NSIS is a recently standardized signaling protocol framework which already provides a large amount of the necessary base functionality.

The evaluation of the different signaling concepts focuses on different evaluation parameters and performance metrics. In cases where the signaling concepts developed provide additional *functionality*, the evaluation focuses on measurements regarding a potentially imposed overhead. For instance, while the exact benchmark numbers obtained in the evaluation testbed are subject to change on different hardware and software, the evaluation should justify that the processing costs imposed by the signaling protocol are only marginal compared to the time needed to transfer data across the network. All concepts proposed by this dissertation were implemented prototypically for the NSIS protocol suite [Ble+12a] and evaluated within a dedicated router testbed or within the OMNeT++ simulation framework.

1.3 Structure

The structure of this dissertation is as follows. Chapter 2 provides the background and the fundamentals of signaling in IP-based networks. It includes an overview of the most important QoS signaling protocols.

Chapter 3 provides a detailed analysis of security threats for signaling protocols in IP-based networks and presents security concepts that can be used in order to allow for authentic signaling. The design outlined in this chapter proposes a light-weight and fine-grained protection mechanism for signaling messages that can be bound to signaling sessions and users. This chapter also outlines a use-case scenario for the developed concepts in a Kerberos-based environment.

Since mobility plays an important role in today's networks, Chapter 4 shows how signaling can be used for mobile users either in cooperation with an existing mobility management protocol like Mobile IP or even without being tied to a mobility management protocol and by providing support for anticipated handovers.

Chapter 5 provides an analysis of the requirements and the design for advanced QoS signaling in IP multicast environments. The chapter discusses the challenges that arise when signaling protocols designed for IP unicast environments are used in multicast environments.

Chapter 6 deals with aggregation mechanisms that can be applied to signaling protocols in large IP networks. It focuses especially on the case of inter-domain wide aggregation mechanisms. This chapter presents a thorough analysis of different problem areas and provides a design for dynamic inter-domain aggregation of resource reservations.

The dissertation concludes in Chapter 7, which gives a summary of contributions, and provides an outlook on future work in the context of this dissertation.

Chapter 2

Background and Fundamentals

This chapter presents the background and the fundamentals of signaling in IP-based networks. Section 2.1 begins with an overview of what is broadly termed the *Internet architecture*, reviews some important aspects of the Internet's "design philosophy", and describes relevant parts of the Internet's structure and components with respect to the operation of signaling protocols.

Since most of the signaling mechanisms developed in this dissertation are exemplified or are specifically designed for the establishment of resource reservations, Section 2.3 provides a brief overview of Quality-of-Service support in the Internet.

Section 2.4 deals with *signaling protocols*. This section explains why signaling is needed, how signaling protocols conceptually operate, and provides some typical examples of signaling protocols, especially with respect to Internet-based Quality-of-Service signaling protocols.

The *Next Steps in Signaling* (NSIS) framework provides a recently standardized, feature-rich Internet signaling protocol suite and is used throughout this dissertation to prototypically exemplify the concepts designed in this dissertation. Therefore, Section 2.4.9 provides the necessary background information about the NSIS framework and its protocol operation.

2.1 IP-based Networks and the Internet Architecture

This section provides a brief overview of the Internet architecture by putting special emphasis on those parts relevant for the operation of Internet-based signaling protocols. The original objectives of the Internet architecture and its so-called "design philosophy" are discussed by Clark [Cla88] while Carpenter [RFC1958], as well as Bush and Meyer [RFC3439], outline some architectural principles of the Internet.[1]

One of the most fundamental design goals of the Internet architecture was to *interconnect different networks*. Different here refers to varying underlying network technologies—such as Ethernet-based local area networks or packet radio networks—and in terms of the administrative responsibilities. Each single network that is administrated independently by its network operator constitutes a dedicated domain. The Internet can therefore be considered to constitute a so-called "network of networks".

This early design goal is still provided by the operation and interconnection of *Autonomous Systems* (AS). While ASes are interconnected to each other via *core routers* (also known as *border routers*) and routing between ASes is accomplished by an exterior gateway protocol (e.g., BGP), each AS administrates its network independently of any other AS and accomplishes internal routing by using an interior gateway protocol (e.g., RIP or OSPF).

The *AS-level hierarchy* conceptually consists of a small set of transit providers (constituting so-called transit ASes) and a large set of access providers (constituting so-called stub ASes) as illustrated in Figure 2.1. While a transit AS usually only interconnects different networks through itself, a stub AS is located at the edge of the AS-level hierarchy and does usually not serve as transit network for two other ASes. In this sense, end systems are usually connected to stub ASes.

The router-level topology can be conceptually separated into *core, gateway*, and *edge* routers, as illustrated in Figure 2.2. A relatively low number of core routers has a low node degree in a meshed topology, whereas the number of gateway routers toward the edge is high with a high node degree. End systems are connected to the Internet via edge routers which have a node degree of one.

Another major design goal of the Internet architecture was to provide a *robust* communication service. Unlike many other networks, e.g., the public switched telephone network (PSTN), the Internet does not rely on a circuit-switched network, but rather relies on a *packet-switched network* which provides a stateless *datagram service*.[2] That is, forwarding of data is accomplished on the granularity of packets each of which are routed toward their destination based on the address information contained in the packet itself. A stream of packets logically belonging together

---

[1]Note, that the Internet's architecture and its principles were documented retrospectively, not in advance.

[2]As opposed to packet-switched networks which use virtual circuits instead, like *Asynchronous Transfer Mode* (ATM).

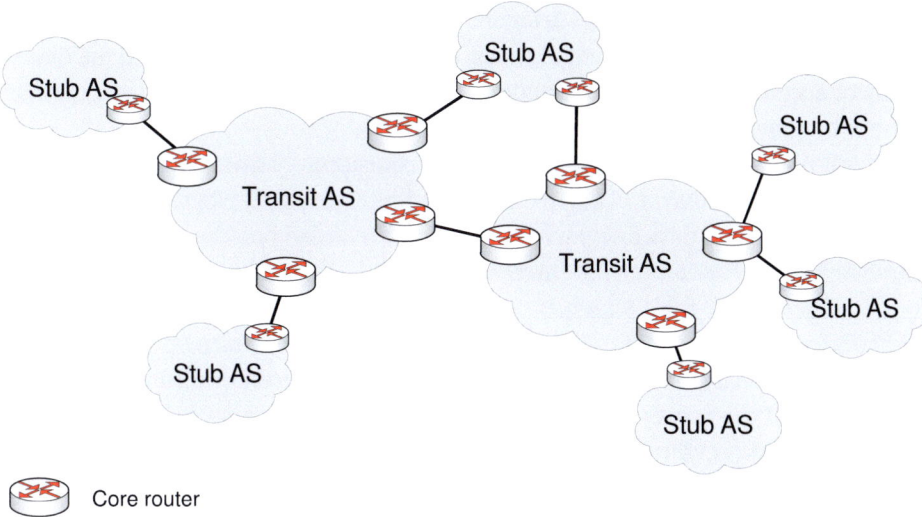

Figure 2.1: *AS-level hierarchy used in the Internet*

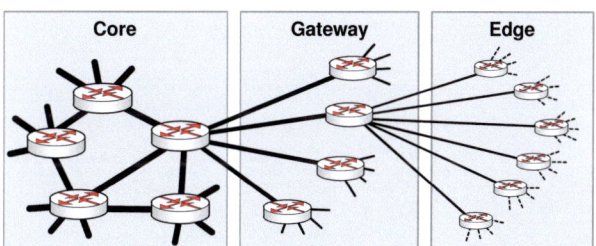

Figure 2.2: *Hierarchical structure of the router level topology within an AS (as illustrated by Gamer and Scharf [GS08])*

is commonly referred to as *data flow*. Blake et al. [RFC3260] use the following definition to characterize a microflow, which is a particular data flow:

> *Microflow: a single instance of an application-to-application flow of packets which is identified by source address, source port, destination address, destination port and protocol id.*

The design decision to use a datagram service allows for the following important properties: packets are routed *stateless* along the corresponding data path, i.e., routers do not have to keep *state* about individual data flows. This lowers the complexity and provides a more robust service against failures in the network.

However, the Internet was only designed to provide a communication service on a *best effort* basis. More advanced services, e.g., targeting at a guaranteed maximum delay or a guaranteed minimum data rate over the course of a data flow's lifetime, cannot be provided by the core Internet protocols.

An Internet router's functionalities can be conceptually divided into a so-called *Data Plane* and a *Control Plane*, as illustrated in Figure 2.3. Normal data packets are processed in the data plane where they are forwarded based on the information contained in the *Forwarding Information Based* (FIB). FIBs are optimized forwarding tables which allow for a stateless operation in the data plane. IP forwarding is only performed in *downstream* direction. That is, the forwarding decision is only based on an IP packet's destination address and the information contained in the FIB, such that the router selects an outgoing interface for a packet. Even though a router knows on which interface a packet has arrived, it has however no route in the packet's *upstream* direction. Therefore, it is important to note that paths taken by data packets between two end systems may be asymmetric and do not necessarily cross the same intermediate routers.

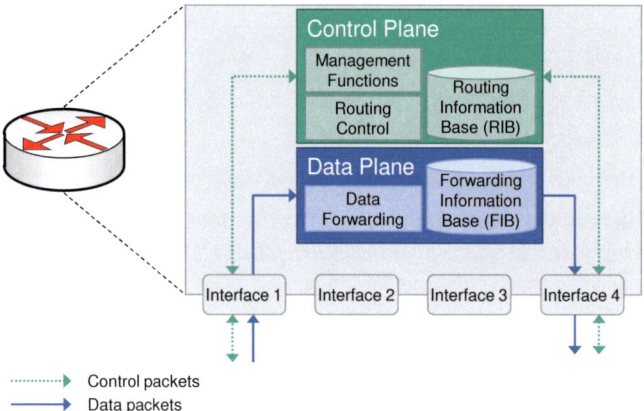

Figure 2.3: *Abstract view of an Internet router model with separated control and data planes*

Management functionality and routing control functions are processed within the control plane. A *Routing Information Base* (RIB) serves as routing table on which a dedicated routing protocol operates. The information contained in a RIB is then used to generate a FIB. In Figure 2.3 IP packets used by routing and management protocols are termed *control packets*. In order to be passed to the control plane, these control packets must therefore be taken out of the router's "fast path". This can be either accomplished by directly addressing packets toward a router or by specific interception mechanisms such as a *Router Alert Option* (RAO) [RFC2113; RFC2711] where an IP option is used to instruct a router along the path to more closely examine a packet that has not been addressed toward the router itself.

Despite the fact that the Internet "only just works" [Han06], the Internet's remarkable success within the last decade led to great demands for more advanced network services. Due to its basic design principles the Internet architecture is still evolving in a sense that new extensions must be created in order to satisfy these demands. Therefore, routers are nowadays expected to do more than just routing and forwarding. This can be observed by the wide adoption of *Network Address Translator* (NAT) gateways, firewalls, and caches, even though some of these extensions may sometimes require state to be installed on routers or may even violate the end-to-end principle [SRC84]. Amongst services that do not constitute an integral part of the Internet architecture are an integrated *security* concept, *mobility* support, a *group communication* model, or *Quality-of-Service* (QoS) mechanisms.

2.2 Mobility Support in IP-based Networks with Mobile IPv6

In IP-based networks a system's interface is identified by its IP address, and a system's transport connections are usually identified by a five-tuple of IP addresses, transport protocol port numbers, and the corresponding transport protocol number. However, the IP address does not only serve as a system's identifier but also as its locator. That is, as soon as a mobile node moves to a different location, not only does its IP address change but also its identifier. That makes mobility support in IP-based networks conceptually hard to handle. In order to allow for mobility support in IP-based networks, Mobile IP [Per02] in form of Mobile IPv4 [RFC5944] and Mobile IPv6 [RFC6275] were proposed by the IETF as an extension to the base IPv4 and IPv6 protocols.

This section provides a brief overview of the basic operation of Mobile IPv6. This dissertation focuses on Mobile IPv6 as opposed to its predecessor Mobile IPv4, mainly because Mobile IPv6 provides integrated support for route optimization and has no need for special routers acting as "foreign agents", making support for

IPv6 a necessity for any currently developed Internet protocol. Therefore, if not otherwise stated, the term "Mobile IP" refers to Mobile IPv6.

2.2.1 Mobile IPv6 Terminology

Since different entities interact with each other when Mobile IPv6 is used and a set of Mobile IPv6-specific terms is used throughout this dissertation, the following terminology summarizes and briefly describes the most important terms and roles.

Mobile Node (MN) A mobile node is a node that moves to a different network point of attachment. In order to make use of Mobile IP as mobility management protocol, the mobile node must support Mobile IP.

Correspondent Node (CN) A node to which a mobile node communicates. It is important to note, that a correspondent node itself can also be a mobile node whenever two mobile nodes communicate with each other. A stationary correspondent node does not necessarily need Mobile IP support in order to communicate with a mobile node.

Home Agent (HA) A dedicated router in the mobile node's home network which serves as proxy for the mobile node in case the mobile node is temporarily located in a foreign network. The home agent is therefore responsible for redirecting data packets from the mobile node's home address to the mobile node's actual care-of-address.

Home Address (HoA) A stable IP address within the mobile node's home network under which the mobile node is reachable by correspondent nodes when located at home or when located in a foreign network. The home address is used by applications on the mobile node and the correspondent nodes, respectively.

Care-of-Address (CoA) A normal IPv6 unicast address that is assigned to the mobile node when located in a foreign network. The care-of-address identifies the actual current location of the mobile node.

Binding A logical association between the mobile node's home address and its current care-of-address. A binding is only valid for a certain period of time and must be periodically refreshed. The binding allows the home agent to forward packets to the mobile node's current care-of-address that were destined for the mobile node's home address.

Binding Cache A set of bindings between home addresses of mobile nodes and their corresponding care-of-addresses. A binding cache is maintained by the home agent and possibly also used by the correspondent node if the correspondent node supports Mobile IP.

Binding Update List A list of binding entries with home agents and correspondent nodes being maintained by the mobile node. The list is used by the mobile node to refresh actively used bindings before expiration and to select the right care-of-address when communicating directly with a correspondent node.

2.2.2 Mobile IPv6 Operation

Mobile IP's goal is to keep a device's mobility transparent from its applications. This is accomplished by means of a dedicated HoA which serves as a permanent address of the MN, independent of the MN's current location. The HoA belongs to the MN's *home network*, i.e., in case the MN is located in its home network, it operates as an ordinary system within this network. In case the MN moves to a *foreign network* it eventually acquires a CoA of the foreign network's address space. In order for the MN to still be reachable by its HoA, an HA serves as proxy within the MN's home network. Mobile IP is then used by the MN to inform the HA about its movement and in order to establish a *binding* on the HA between the HoA and the current CoA.

Mobile IPv6 supports two modes of operation: *tunnel mode* and *route optimized mode*. Tunnel mode is used initially and whenever the CN does not support Mobile IPv6. Figure 2.4 gives a conceptual overview of Mobile IPv6's basic operations.

The MN is first located in foreign network *A* and attached to an access router AR_0. In case tunnel mode is used, the HA serves as proxy for the HoA and a bi-directional IPv6-in-IPv6 tunnel is established between the HA and the MN. Since the MN is always identified by its HoA, the *logical flow* in tunnel mode exists between the HA and the CN, whereas the *tunneled flow* is located between the HA and the MN.

Figure 2.5 illustrates how data packets are exchanged between the CN and the MN across the HA in tunnel mode. In case data packets are sent from the CN toward the MN, the original data packet is addressed toward the MN's HoA and intercepted by the HA. The HA then encapsulates the original data packet into an outer IPv6 packet which is addressed toward the MN's actual CoA.

Whenever the MN sends a data packet toward the CN, it encapsulates the designated original data packet into an outer tunnel IPv6 packet destined to the HA. In this case the MN encodes its HoA as source address and the CN's IP address

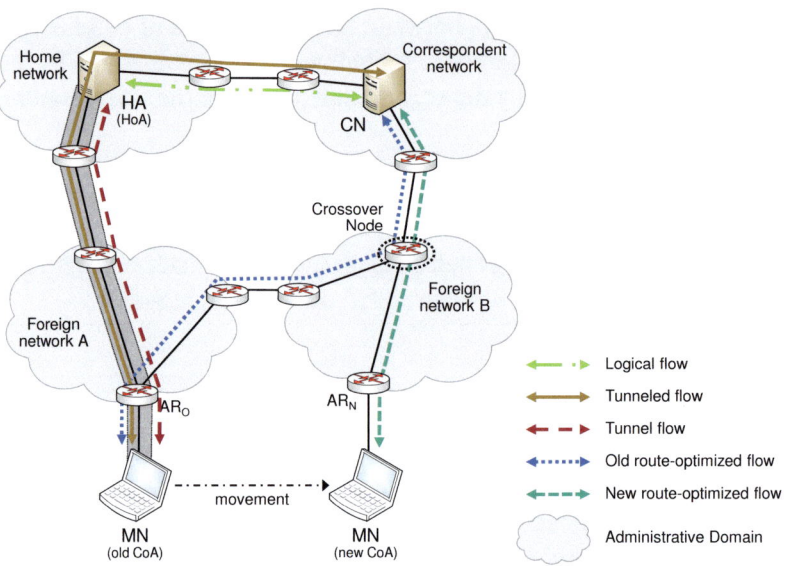

Figure 2.4: *Conceptual overview of tunnel mode and route optimized mode operation with Mobile IPv6*

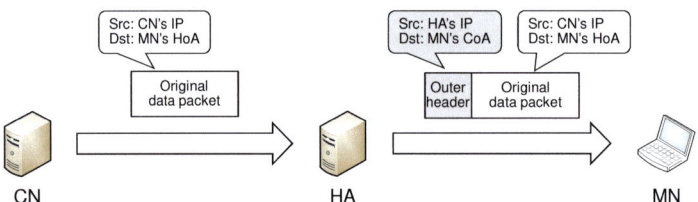

(a) Addressing schemes used when data packets are sent from the CN toward the MN across the HA

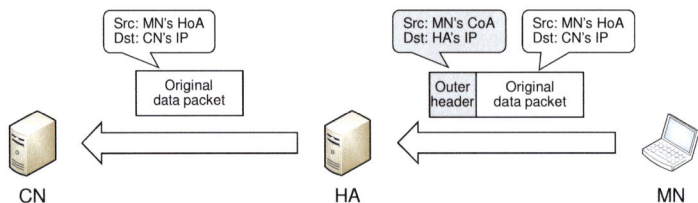

(b) Addressing schemes used when data packets are sent from the MN toward the CN across the HA

Figure 2.5: *Data forwarding in Mobile IPv6's tunnel mode operation (as illustrated by Soliman [Sol04])*

as destination address into the "original" data packet. The outer header is, however, addressed toward the HA's IP address and contains the MN's CoA as source address.

Even though tunnel mode preserves the end-to-end transparency between MN and CN, it also produces some overhead in terms of bytes per packet and in terms of latency, since every data packet exchanged between the CN and the MN must be encapsulated and forwarded by the HA, even if the CN and the MN are topologically located close to each other.

Route optimization was introduced by Mobile IPv6 in order to allow for a more efficient communication between the MN and the CN and can be used whenever the CN is Mobile IPv6-aware. In this case the MN and the CN establish a binding between the MN's current CoA and its corresponding HoA, which can then be used to send traffic directly from one endpoint to another, instead of redirecting it through the MN's home network. As soon as the MN moves to another location it obtains a new CoA which in turn causes the MN to update existing bindings, including bindings belonging to tunnel flows. This way all connected CNs will know where to send their traffic. It is important to note, that the applications on both endpoints still use the HoA in order to communicate with each other, i.e., the translation mechanism between the HoA and the actual CoA is kept transparent from the applications. If a data packet is sent from the CN, the MN's HoA is exchanged by the actual MN's CoA in the destination cache and the HoA is appended in a corresponding IPv6 extension header in order to allow the MN to find the right binding context for this data packet. Hence, these IPv6 extension headers can be used to differentiate route-optimized packets from normal packets.

In order to establish and maintain bindings between the different entities involved in Mobile IP, dedicated Mobile IP signaling messages are exchanged between these entities. Figure 2.6 illustrates the "return routability procedure" and the binding update process in Mobile IPv6.

Before a MN can update bindings toward a CN, a return routability procedure must be performed. This procedure allows a CN to assure that the MN is in fact reachable at the claimed CoA and at its HoA. This is accomplished by using a cryptographic token exchange between the MN and the CN where so-called "keygen tokens" must be combined by the MN into a "binding management key" which can then be used for subsequently sent binding updates. The four Mobile IPv6 signaling messages `Home Test Init`, `Care-of-Test Init`, `Home Test`, and `Care-of-Test` are used for this return routability procedure. After that, the actual binding between a MN's current CoA, its HoA, and the CN can be updated. A binding is eventually updated by using the two Mobile IPv6 signaling messages `Binding Update` and `Binding Acknowledgement`.

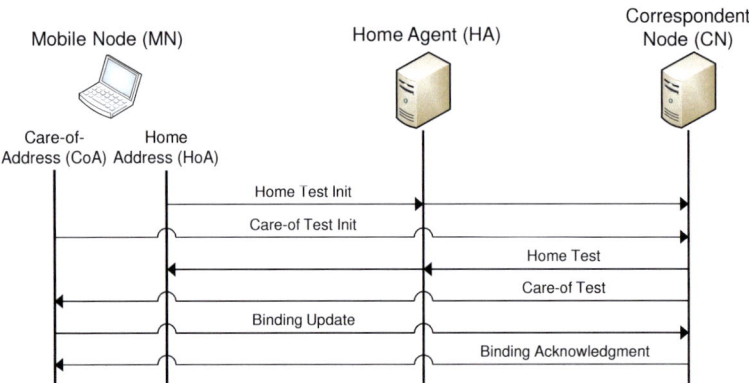

Figure 2.6: *Message sequence diagram of the return routability procedure and binding update process using Mobile IPv6*

2.3 Quality-of-Service Support in the Internet

Despite the Internet's immense success during the last decades, it was only designed to provide a best effort service upon which more advanced services should be realized. The raising need for these advanced services, e.g., as being required by real-time applications, imposes a number of challenges on the actually perceived quality of the offered services. Therefore, providing *Quality-of-Service* (QoS) in the Internet plays an important role for researchers and network engineers.

The term Quality-of-Service is defined differently by different standards bodies. Within the Internet Engineering Task Force (IETF), QoS is defined as follows [RFC2386]:

> *Quality-of-Service (QoS): A set of service requirements to be met by the network while transporting a flow.*

The Internet's best effort service works just "good enough" for the majority of today's applications. It can, however, not provide any guarantees about the quality that a service will actually receive. If there is no differentiation between different flows, all data packets are treated equally. Hence, in case of congestion in the network, all applications served with a best effort delivery service will suffer proportionally the same, no matter whether the users use Peer-to-Peer (P2P) file sharing applications, watch video streams, or make an emergency call over Voice-over-IP (VoIP).

QoS support cannot increase the amount of available network resources. It can, however, be used to allocate resources, provide policing and mechanisms for a differentiation amongst a set of flows. In this sense, QoS support is said to provide a "managed unfairness" between flows, where one flow is served a better quality than a competing flow. For instance, in case of congestion, a specified set of flows receives a guaranteed QoS, while the remaining set of flows is only served on a best-effort basis. One of the most important aspects, when resources are reserved in order to provide QoS guarantees, is a corresponding *admission control* functionality which validates whether sufficient resources are available.

Different applications and telecommunication services exhibit different network traffic characteristics and demand for a specific type of QoS. An application's traffic can be broadly categorized into elastic and inelastic, as well as interactive and non-interactive traffic [SCJ11]. While elastic applications are able to adjust their network traffic to the current network conditions (e.g., TCP-based applications would lower their throughout in response to network congestion), inelastic applications cannot easily adjust their network traffic. Examples for applications that generate elastic traffic are email or P2P file sharing which can both be regarded as elastic applications but non-interactive, whereas web browsing or network control applications generate elastic but interactive traffic. Examples for applications generating inelastic traffic are video-on-demand or live TV which are both inelastic but also non-interactive, while VoIP or online gaming can be both considered inelastic and interactive.

QoS can be quantitatively measured by specific "performance metrics", e.g., *throughput, end-to-end delay*, or *jitter*. Different applications have different demands according to their traffic characteristics outlined above, i.e., an elastic, non-interactive file transfer wants to achieve a high throughput but can easily cope with a high delay or jitter, whereas a VoIP call aims primarily at being served with low delay and jitter, and requires only a steady but low throughput rate.

Based on these parameters QoS can be guaranteed either *statistically* or *deterministically* [FV90]. While deterministic guarantees provide data flows with an exclusively reserved amount of resources, statistical guarantees reserve resources only based on a statistical bound with a certain probability that the QoS parameter will be met. Even though conflicts may occur between competing data flows, statistical guarantees prove to be much more efficient in terms of resource utilization.

There exists a wide variety of approaches on how QoS can be actually achieved in IP-based networks and ranges—according to the Internet's layered architecture— from the lowest layers up to the application layer. In the past, various overlays have been proposed by which QoS could be achieved, e.g., OverQoS [Sub+04] or QRON [LM04]. However, Crowcroft et al. [Cro+03] argue that, while overlays are perfectly valid in order to deploy novel qualitative services, they are not useful to deploy quantitative services. This is basically due to the fact that overlays exhibit their own topologies and routing which often contradicts a network operator's traffic engineering strategies. Furthermore, overlays impose additional per-packet encapsulation and routing overhead, such that the use of multiple overlays eventually results in an even worse situation. Finally, overlays are only re-active to network conditions by nature, i.e., they can't actually provide any QoS guarantees by reserving resources in a network on demand.

Another commonly used technology which is often used in today's networks in order to control forwarding of data traffic is *Multi-Protocol Label Switching* (MPLS) [RFC3031]. While MPLS allows network operators to perform traffic engineering, it is, however, usually limited to a single provider's domain and not used in an end-to-end fashion across different administrative domains. Even though MPLS allows to control forwarding of data traffic, it does not provide means to realize a fine-grained control of transmission resources on a per-class level. This can only be accomplished by relying on some additional QoS-specific mechanisms, such as Diffserv-aware MPLS Traffic Engineering [RFC3564; RFC4124]. Note, however, that traffic engineering performed by MPLS cannot be influenced in any way by an end-user, but is instead only controlled by the network operator. Furthermore, MPLS itself does not provide support for admission control or resource reservations along an MPLS path.

2.3.1 QoS Components and Mechanisms

An on-demand provisioning of QoS guarantees in IP-based networks requires the use of specific components and mechanisms. According to an IP router's separation into a control plane and a data plane, some of the QoS functionalities are realized within the control plane, while others are part of the data plane. Basically, differentiation of data packets is achieved in the data plane by classification in forwarding classes and traffic conditioning of incoming data, while a resource-based admission control is part of the control plane. Figure 2.7 gives a conceptual overview of a QoS router and its functional blocks (based on [RFC3290]).

Whenever data packets enter a QoS router, the following QoS control functions are usually performed:

Classifying Since QoS mechanisms are logically applied to data flows, incoming packets must be classified according to a set of rules. These rules can be based on traffic profiles or reservation data, e.g., in form of a multi-field classifier (cf. a data packet's "five-tuple") or an aggregate classifier (cf. a packet's DiffServ code point).

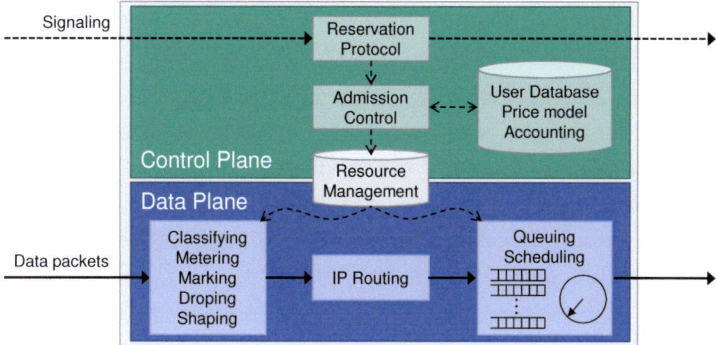

Figure 2.7: *Conceptual overview of a QoS router and its functional blocks*

Classification of data packets builds a necessary precondition for the differentiation of data flows.

Metering Data flows selected by a classifier are metered against a given traffic profile. That is, a meter verifies whether the traffic originating from a data flow conforms to its corresponding traffic conditioning agreement. A well-known example of a meter used in QoS models is the token bucket.

Marking If necessary, packets may get marked (e.g., with a DiffServ code point) in order to determine their subsequent treatment within this router or on routers residing along the data path.

Shaping Packets of a data flow may be delayed in order to bring the data flow into conformance to its traffic profile.

Dropping In case a data flow does not conform to a given traffic profile, all or some of the data flow's packets may be dropped.

Classifying and metering can be regarded as monitoring resource usage, while marking, shaping, and dropping can be considered traffic conditioning mechanisms. The term *policing* refers to the process of comparing incoming data packets against a traffic profile and apply traffic conditioning on the data flow in order to make the output stream conformant to the traffic profile.

Once packets of a data flow were monitored and policing mechanisms have been applied on them, they are inserted into different *queues* on which specific *scheduling algorithms* are performed. The scheduler strategy determines how resources are actually assigned, i.e., which queue (and therefore which packet) is served next.

Well-known scheduling strategies being used by QoS routers are *Simple Priority Queueing*, or *Weighted Fair Queueing*.

Before data flows can be treated with a specific QoS, the corresponding QoS parameters must be signaled and negotiated between the communicating entities. This can be accomplished basically in two different ways. Resource provisioning can be configured manually in order to be used over a long period of time. Alternatively, a resource reservation can be established dynamically and *on-demand* which requires the use of a dedicated *signaling protocol*.

A policy-based admission control is used to determine which reservation request can be granted. Requests must be rejected if the requesting user is not permitted to use the requested resources or if the amount of requested resources exceeds the amount of available resources. The admission control's decision is based on predefined policies and uses existing user databases and pricing models. In case a reservation request can be granted, the reserved resources are subsequently accounted. The *Resource Management* provides an interface between the QoS's control plane functionality and the QoS's data plane functionality. That is, based on the information carried by a reservation protocol, reservation state for a data flow is installed on that router and appropriate QoS parameters are configured in the data plane.

2.3.2 QoS Architectures in the Internet

In the mid-1990's an increasing use of real-time demanding applications raised the need for QoS support in the Internet. In order to address those application's concerns and meet their requirements, the IETF came up with two different proposals for QoS models, first the *Integrated Services* (IntServ) and as successor the *Differentiated Services* (DiffServ) architectural model.

2.3.2.1 The Integrated Services (IntServ) Architectural Model

IntServ [RFC1633] was designed to fit into the existing Internet architecture and required the use of an IP multicast-capable reservation protocol. Its QoS mechanisms operate on data flows, i.e., in order to provide a data flow with QoS support, state must be kept on the intermediate routers along a data flow's path in the network. In this sense, IntServ introduced a fundamental shift away from the paradigm of a stateless router.

The IntServ model is based on the QoS components outlined in Section 2.3.1 and specifies two service categories in addition to a basic best effort service: *Guaranteed Service* [RFC2212] and *Predictive Service* [RFC2211] (also named *Controlled Load*).

A guaranteed service is in conformance with a deterministically guaranteed QoS, e.g., by specifying a lower bound for an end-to-end latency. It is designed to serve inelastic real-time applications for which resources, such as bandwidth or buffers in queues, are reserved exclusively.

The predictive service, on the other hand, is less restrictive and only provides statistical QoS guarantees. It only uses admission control and policing but does not rely on specific scheduling algorithms. By offering a predictive service, the amount of resources being "reserved" may exceed the amount of resources being available. This strategy is based on the assumption, that not each user requests its reserved resources at the same time, which allows for a statistical multiplexing of available resources. In case this assumption does not hold at a moment in time, QoS cannot be provided due to the lack of available resources.

The Resource ReSerVation Protocol (RSVP) signaling protocol was designed to be used within IntServ domains. Wroclawski [RFC2210] provides an overview on how RSVP is supposed to be used with IntServ. RSVP's design and operation are further investigated in Section 2.4. The IntServ model faces, however, a number of challenges affecting its deployment, as already outlined by Mankin et al. [RFC2208]. First and foremost, the IntServ model poses severe *scalability* problems.

Since scalability builds an important aspect not only for Internet applications and services, but for system design in general, Weinstock and Goodenough [WG06] provide an in-depth analysis of how the term scalability is defined in the literature. Based on this analysis and on a definition provided by Bless [Ble02], this dissertation uses the term scalability as follows:

> *Scalability: The ability of a system to remain functional and provide acceptable performance even under the consideration of a significant increase of specific system parameters, i.e., a growth rate that exceeds several orders of magnitude.*

IntServ's scalability problems stem from the fact, that each RSVP-capable router maintains reservation state on a per-flow granularity, i.e., QoS parameters, timers, and addresses must be kept in memory and processed individually by the router's CPU for each single data flow. This unnecessarily increases complexity on forwarding and classification of data packets, especially in highly utilized routers such as in the Internet's core domains. Second, services are not classified into more coarse-grained QoS classes, but instead each individual data flow is free to

choose its own set of QoS parameters. This requires an IntServ router to support a
dynamically changing set of services.

2.3.2.2 The Differentiated Services (DiffServ) Architectural Model

The Differentiated Services (DiffServ) architectural model [RFC2475] was designed
in order to provide scalable service differentiation in the Internet. Scalability is
achieved by a two-fold approach: traffic is aggregated into distinct *service classes*
which prevents routers from having to maintain per-flow state. Furthermore, more
complex functionality, such as classification, marking, or policing, is only performed
at network boundary nodes.

DiffServ strictly separates QoS forwarding mechanisms in the data plane from
QoS management functionality in the control plane, i.e., DiffServ was designed
without a corresponding QoS signaling protocol. Instead of specifying a fixed set of
pre-defined services, DiffServ rather provides a set of building blocks which can be
used to offer high-quality, but still application-independent, services. These building
blocks provide functional elements in the form of so-called *Per-Hop Behaviors* (PHB),
packet classification functions, and traffic conditions functions.

The DiffServ concept works basically as follows: Instead of identifying data flows
at each router separately by their *multi-field classifier*, data flows are classified
into a fixed set of service classes and are afterwards identified by bits being set
in the IP header, a so-called *DiffServ code point* (DSCP) [RFC2474]. The complex
operation of classifying data flows is performed at network *Boundary Nodes*, where
the number of flows entering the network is still manageable by a single router.
The DSCP selects the PHB and therefore controls how a data packet is forwarded
within the core of a DiffServ network, i.e., at *Interior Nodes*. Each PHB specifies
how resources are allocated for a behavior aggregate, e.g., by allocating a specific
amount of the available bandwidth of a link for a specific aggregate.

Within the DiffServ model a DiffServ domain is specified as a set of DiffServ-
capable routers which provide a common set of PHB group implementations.
Boundary nodes act both as *Ingress Nodes* and *Egress Nodes*. Figure 2.8 gives
an overview of the DiffServ architectural model. Once traffic originating from
a data sender enters a DiffServ domain, data packets are classified and possibly
conditioned at the domain's ingress node, e.g., by choosing a DSCP for a given
multi-field classifier in order to enforce the use of a specific PHB.

The next DiffServ-capable router along the path must then only inspect a packet's
DSCP upon which the corresponding PHB can be applied. Therefore, all data packets being marked with the same DSCP are bundled to the same behavior aggregate

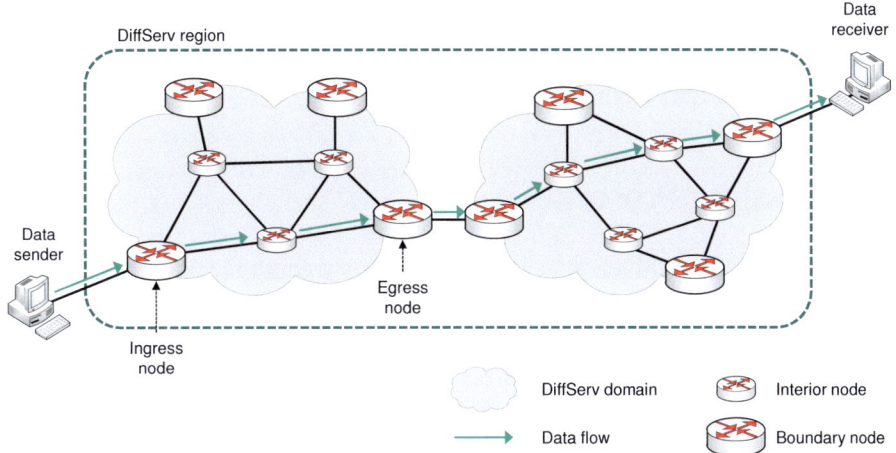

Figure 2.8: *Conceptual overview of DiffServ's architectural model*

and receive the same forwarding behavior along their path. Currently, there are two PHBs specified by the IETF, the *Expedited Forwarding* (EF) PHB [RFC3246; RFC3247] and the *Assured Forwarding* (AF) PHB [RFC2597; RFC3260].

The EF PHB can be seen as a "premium" service which aims at achieving low delay, low jitter, and low loss of data packets. In order to achieve these difficult goals, the EF PHB provides packets being suitably marked short or empty queues. Therefore, ingress nodes are responsible to ensure that an aggregate's maximum arrival rate is less than an aggregate's minimum departure rate. Traffic not conforming to this requirement must be dropped. If this requirement can be satisfied, interior nodes should observe minimized queueing delays on EF traffic. Since EF traffic is served with highest priority or a large weight in the scheduler, it is a very valuable service and intended to be used by interactive real-time demanding applications, such as VoIP.

The AF PHB provides different levels of forwarding assurances for data traffic. It defines independent service classes within which each packet receives a particular drop precedence. For each AF class, a specific amount of resources, in terms of bandwidth and buffer space, is allocated. Currently, there are four different AF classes and three different drop precedence values specified. The AF PHB guarantees data flows to be served with a specific amount of bandwidth as long as the sender's data rate stays below a pre-defined threshold. A sender can, however, also use more bandwidth if resources permit. In case the sender sends at a data rate above the pre-defined threshold and resources are scarce, data packets are dropped according to the configured drop precedence value. Therefore, while the AF PHB can also be used for applications with a high amount of traffic bursts, long lasting bursts receive a higher drop probability.

2.4 Signaling Protocols

Signaling protocols build a key component in many communication networks, such as the Internet. Signaling can be used in order to install, maintain, and remove states in a network or on end systems. This allows for a *dynamic* and *on-demand* management of network and system resources and services.

Within telephone networks, signaling protocols have always been used for the exchange of control information, e.g., in order to control network resources, and maintain telephone connections. For instance, signaling protocols are used in telephone networks and the Internet to discover the callee, to establish a corresponding connection, to alert the callee via a ringing tone, and to control the telecommunication circuit. Regarding IP-based networks, Internet telephony (VoIP) and multimedia sessions are usually established and maintained by the *Session Initiation Protocol* (SIP) [RFC3261].

Signaling protocols are usually used for the transport of control information, rather than for the transport of the application data itself. In terms of SIP, the actual communication data is mostly transferred by the *Real-time Transport Protocol* (RTP). *Mobile IP* [RFC6275] can be considered a signaling protocol for the support of mobile users in the Internet and the *Internet Group Membership Protocol* (IGMP) [RFC3376] is used to maintain group memberships in IP multicast environments.

In general, signaling in IP-based networks can be categorized into *application layer signaling* (e.g., SIP) and *network layer signaling* (e.g., IGMP). While the former is only interpreted by end systems or dedicated application level gateways, the latter directly interacts with components inside the network, e.g., routers or NAT gateways. Furthermore, signaling can be either performed *in-band* or *out-of-band*. By using in-band signaling, the signaling information is embedded into the actual application data, whereas out-of-band signaling transports its signaling information on behalf of a dedicated signaling protocol which operates decoupled from the application data's protocol.

Another important aspect when dealing with signaling is the way how state is maintained along the lifetime of a signaling session. That is, a signaling session can either rely on a *hard-state* or a *soft-state* paradigm [Ji+07]. In a hard-state based approach state remains established until it is explicitly released, whereas in a soft-state based approach state is released automatically upon the expiration of a soft-state timer which has not been refreshed on time. While the former was often used in public switched telephone networks, the latter is usually applied in today's IP-based networks. This is mainly due to the fact, that the overhead incurred by the requirement to periodically refresh soft-states can be considered justifiable, compared to a hard-state approach which requires reliable signaling and where resources may be blocked unnecessarily in time of failures. In case a signaling protocol relies on a soft-state approach, the synchronization of signaling state in multi-hop signaling systems can be either realized on an *end-to-end* or a *hop-by-hop* basis.

One of the primary signaling applications in IP-based networks builds QoS signaling. Manner and Fu [RFC4094], as well as Vali et al. [Val+04], provide overviews of existing QoS signaling protocols. Brunner [RFC3726] provides a detailed discussion about requirements for signaling protocols by strongly focusing on QoS signaling. Since this dissertation exemplifies most of its concepts for a recently standardized QoS signaling protocol suite, the most commonly used protocols in this area are briefly discussed in the following.

2.4.1 The Internet Stream Protocol ST2+

In the late 1970's the *Internet Stream Protocol* (ST) was proposed as one of the first protocols in the Internet, that was explicitly designed for the transportation of real-time data over the Internet. In 1990 ST was replaced by a new protocol version 2 (ST-II) [RFC1190] and in 1995 the protocol was further revised within the IETF upon which a refined version was specified, called ST2+ [RFC1819].

ST2+ is a hard-state signaling protocol, that was designed to be used for real-time data transfer and provides means for the establishment of corresponding resource reservations. Its protocol functionality operates at the same layer as IP, i.e., it was designed to be used complementary to IP's best effort data delivery service (in fact, ST2+ was assigned the Internet protocol number 5, i.e., it can be considered IPv5). This does, however, also imply, that ST2+ must be supported by end systems and all intermediate routers along a data flow's path.

ST2+ was designed as an entire architecture, consisting of different components. These components comprise a data transfer protocol (simply called ST), a dedicated signaling protocol, called *Stream Control Message Protocol* (SCMP) which can be considered a counterpart to IP's ICMP, and a flow specification (*FlowSpec*) data structure which holds the data flow's QoS characteristics. Furthermore, ST2+'s architecture considers the FlowSpec to be interpreted by a router's *Local Resource Manager* (LRM) and a routing function which selects the appropriate routes. Both, the LRM and the routing function have, however, not been specified by ST2+.

The communication model follows a two step approach where real-time channels (so-called "*streams*") are established first via SCMP by selecting routes and reserving resources along the path, upon which the real-time data can be actually transferred via ST. Reservations are established from a single source toward one or more receivers in form of routing trees. ST2+ even allows receivers to later join an existing reservation.

Despite the fact that ST2+ was standardized by the IETF, it did never gain greater deployment. This can be mainly attributed to some technical shortcomings. The most critical aspect in this regard is that ST2+ doesn't build upon IP's existing functionality, but instead had to provide some of the same functionality again. In order to be used for the actual transfer of the real-time application's data, it requires full implementation of its protocols within the end systems and all routers. Being designed as a hard state protocol and relying on per-flow reservation state has severe impacts on ST2+'s scalability. Furthermore, security aspects were not explicitly considered in ST2+'s design.

2.4.2 The Resource ReSerVation Protocol (RSVP)

The *Resource ReSerVation Protocol* (RSVP) is one of the most commonly used QoS signaling protocols in the Internet. It was first proposed by Zhang et al. [Zha+93] before its specification was later standardized by the IETF [RFC2205]. RSVP focuses on a close integration into the IntServ model [WC97]. Even though RSVP is nowadays used with certain extensions in order to perform traffic engineering, this section focuses on its QoS signaling capabilities.

RSVP can be used to establish resource reservations for unidirectional data flows. It follows a soft-state approach and decouples the actual QoS semantics transported within signaling messages from the signaling operation's logic. RSVP operates independently from an underlying routing protocol and establishes reservations along a routing protocol's path. This allows to automatically adapt to potential route changes in the network.

RSVP's design was mainly driven by the need to provide resource reservations for group communications. Therefore, support for IP multicast played a major role in its design process. Since QoS requests from receivers in a multicast group may be heterogeneous and only receivers know their capacity limitations, it was felt that the provisioning of scalable resource reservations can only be achieved by relying on receiver-initiated reservations. That is, the receiver is responsible for actually maintaining a resource reservation toward the sender of the data packets.

RSVP was designed to operate from end-to-end, i.e., it is triggered by an end system in order to establish a reservation toward another end system. Its protocol mechanisms rely on two basic message types, PATH and RESV messages. Since a receiver-initiated reservation must be established in the data flow's upstream direction, the data flow sender triggers the establishment of a reservation by sending a PATH message toward its receivers. In order to be intercepted and interpreted by each intermediate RSVP-capable router, this message carries a RAO. The PATH message contains the desired QoS characteristics by using a so-called *FlowSpec* object. The FlowSpec object is opaque to RSVP and contains information about the reservation specification (*RSpec*), the service class, and the data flow's traffic specification (*TSpec*). A data flow is identified in RSVP by a *Session*—which consists of the flow's destination IP address, destination port number, and IP protocol identifier—and a *FilterSpec* which consists of the data flow's source IP address and source port number.

The PATH message can be either sent toward a unicast receiver or a group of receivers by using an IP multicast destination address and is therefore sent in the data flow's downstream direction upon which it installs reverse-path state on all intermediate RSVP-capable routers. When a receiver receives a PATH message, it issues a corresponding RESV message with a potentially adapted FlowSpec, in order to actually reserve resources along the data flow's path. Reservations being established along a multicast distribution tree are automatically merged by RSVP.

The data sender is responsible to periodically sending refreshing PATH messages, whereas a data flow's receiver is responsible for periodically sending refreshing RESV messages. Even though RSVP relies on a soft-state paradigm where reverse-path state and reservation state times out if not being actively refreshed, RSVP provides also explicit tear down functionalities for PATH and RESV messages.

Despite RSVP's great adoption by the research community and even router vendors, it has been criticized for a number of reasons. Since RSVP is tightly coupled to the IntServ model, its per-flow control state provides only poor scalability. Although aggregation concepts for RSVP [RFC3175] were later proposed, these mechanisms are usually not applicable within inter-domain scenarios (see Section 6.3.1 for a detailed discussion). Furthermore, the original RSVP design does not provide means for hop-by-hop reliability of signaling message exchange and does not take security concerns into account.

RSVP was also not designed with mobility support in mind. In case a mobile node changes its location, it also usually obtains a new IP address. RSVP's reservations are, however, tightly bound to the data flow identifier, and therefore also to the mobile node's former IP address. A signaling session should therefore rather be identified by a location-independent identifier which may encompass several data flow identifiers. Furthermore, a re-establishment of a reservation can only be triggered by the entity emitting the PATH message. However, RSVP provides no means for a mobile node to trigger the emission of a PATH message by its communication partner.

RSVP's integrated IP multicast support introduced a high level of complexity. Especially RSVP's design decision to rely on receiver-initiated reservations, which was driven by the intention to support heterogeneous receivers in multicast environments, is disputable. Multimedia applications do rarely rely on codecs that allow for such a fine-grained level of QoS demands. For such scenarios *Layered Multicast* as being proposed by McCanne et al. [MJV96], should be used instead. RSVP's missing support for sender-initiated reservations proves also to be less advantageous, since charging and pricing is more likely to affect the data senders, rather than the receivers.

In response to RSVP's multicast dependency, Fu et al. [FKT02] provide an analysis on RSVP's multicast support and propose the use of a so-called RSVP-Lite derivative, which only supports unicast reservations. Westberg et al. [Wes+02], as well as Greco et al. [GDB03] proposed the design of an updated version of RSVP which also provides sender-initiated reservations and a dedicated reservation's session identifier. However, none of these proposals have been addressed by an updated specification.

2.4.3 YESSIR

The establishment of resource reservations for multimedia flows by means of in-band signaling is proposed by Pan and Schulzrinne [PS99]. The so-called *YEt another Sender Session Internet Reservations* (YESSIR) protocol focuses primarily on reduced processing costs at routers and aims at achieving a light-weight reservation mechanism for real-time applications.

Instead of providing a dedicated out-of-band signaling protocol, the authors argue that a substantial fraction of multimedia applications relies on the use of the *Real-Time Transport Protocol* (RTP) [RFC3550], such that YESSIR's control information can be embedded into RTP's control protocol (RTCP). According to RTCP's operation, YESSIR follows a soft-state approach. In order to be intercepted and interpreted by intermediate routers, YESSIR messages are sent with a RAO.

YESSIR follows a sender-initiated approach, since it was felt that RSVP's support for heterogeneous receivers introduced an unnecessarily high amount of complexity. YESSIR was, however, designed to be compatible with the IntServ model and even considered a combined signaling approach with RSVP. YESSIR introduces the notion of *partial reservations*, where a reservation can be used by a sender, even if only a fraction of the intermediate routers committed the requested amount of resources. It is then up to the sender to decide whether he would like to use this partial reservation or cancel the entire reservation request. Furthermore, YESSIR provides a *shared* reservation style, where resources being allocated can be used by all senders of an RTP session.

Even though YESSIR can be considered a light-weight signaling alternative to conventional out-of-band signaling protocols, protocol overhead introduced in terms of bandwidth consumption can be considered negligible compared to the huge amount of data that traverses a router anyway. YESSIR does, unfortunately, not provide means to support mobile users, nor does it provide any advanced security mechanisms that go beyond IP layer security. Furthermore, YESSIR does not provide mechanisms to allow for scalable resource reservations. The most imminent drawback of the proposed approach is, that YESSIR's signaling mechanisms are tightly coupled to RTP. That is, an application and the intermediate network routers must support RTP. A generic signaling protocol which operates independently from a specific application is more advantageous.

2.4.4 Boomerang

Boomerang [Feh+99] provides a light-weight and simplified resource reservation protocol which operates independently of the underlying QoS model, i.e., IntServ or DiffServ. The protocol aims at establishing bi-directional reservations and can be either initiated by the sender or the receiver of the data flow.

In case a user wants to establish a resource reservation, a Boomerang message is sent by the so-called *Initiating Node* toward the designated receiver. A reservation is established for a data flow which is specified by the flow's multi-field classifier. In the current implementation Boomerang messages are simply embedded into ICMP ECHO and REPLY messages which are expected to be intercepted by intermediate Boomerang-aware routers. These routers reserve the requested amount of resources and forward the message hop-by-hop further along the path. As soon as a Boomerang message reached its receiver (in both directions for the ECHO and REPLY messages), the resource reservation in this direction was successfully established, otherwise a router rejects a reservation request by using an ERROR message.

The signaling logic is primarily maintained at the initiating node—even the responding node is not required to be aware of the actual Boomerang's signaling logic. Since Boomerang follows a soft-state approach, the initiating node is responsible for sending periodic refreshes from end-to-end. The authors argue, that this approach eliminates the need for keeping signaling state on intermediate routers. However, since the responder does not participate in the signaling operation, Boomerang does not provide an end-to-end negotiation of signaling parameters.

Although the approach taken by Boomerang provides indeed a light-weight signaling alternative, a lot of questions regarding the feasibility of the chosen approach remain unanswered. For instance, it remains unclear how resource reservations are handled if responses do not reach the initiator (e.g., due to dropped ICMP messages on the return path). Even though the authors claim that no signaling state on intermediate routers must be kept, Boomerang still requires per-flow reservation state to be maintained at those routers—otherwise no effective admission control can be provided. Furthermore, Boomerang lacks a fair amount of more sophisticated signaling mechanisms, especially with respect to mobility or security support and does not provide means for scalable resource reservations. Internet-Drafts for Boomerang's protocol specification [ABC99] and a Boomerang framework [BCA00] provide some more details about Boomerang's anticipated operation but have not been further refined.

2.4.5 INSIGNIA

Lee et al. [Lee+00] propose an IP-based QoS signaling framework, called *INSIGNIA*, which aims at providing QoS guarantees within mobile ad-hoc networks (MANETs). In order to be highly responsive to changes within the network—especially due to mobility events—INSIGNIA's design focuses strongly on light-weight signaling mechanisms and small signaling overhead. INSIGNIA is therefore based on in-band signaling and follows a soft-state approach.

QoS control information is embedded by a reservation initiator into IP header options of multimedia data packets. The reservation initiator sets a *reservation mode bit* (RES) in the data packets of the corresponding multimedia flow and expresses the required amount of resources in terms of a minimum and maximum bandwidth request in a 19 bit long IP option field. Intermediate routers are then expected to intercept and interpret these packets, perform admission control, and reserve the requested amount of resources, if permitted. In case a router cannot grant the requested amount of resources, the router changes the RES bit to reflect a *best effort mode* (BE). Otherwise, if the receiver receives a data packet with RES bit set, it acknowledges this end-to-end reservation by means of a QoS report. Like YESSIR, INSIGNIA also allows for partial reservations where the initiator must decide whether it wants to use an established reservation across a partial set of routers, or if it tears down the entire reservation.

INSIGNIA does not consider existing QoS models, such as IntServ or DiffServ. Its reservations are only expressed in terms of a minimum and maximum bandwidth range which does not provide very flexible and fine granular means to express QoS requirements of an application. By being based on an in-band signaling approach, INSIGNIA requires applications to be INSIGNIA-aware. INSIGNIA performs very well in terms of low overhead, fast operation, and adaptive service offering which builds one of the most important requirements in order to be used in MANETs. However, security aspects are not considered by the INSIGNIA approach. This proves to be particularly problematic with respect to the authentication of reservation requests and protection against attackers. Furthermore, by focusing on MANETs only, INSIGNIA does not provide mechanisms to allow for scalable resource reservations, which are required in Internet-like scenarios. Lee et al. [Lee+99] also published an Internet-Draft which was, however, not further refined.

2.4.6 BGRP

The *Border Gateway Reservation Protocol* (BGRP) [PHS99; PHS00b] was designed as an inter-domain QoS signaling protocol which specifically aims at achieving scalability by aggregating resource reservations. BGRP was not designed to be used as an end-to-end QoS signaling protocol, but rather aggregates reservations between border routers of different administrative domains.

In order to do so, BGRP establishes aggregate reservations along "sink trees" which are formed according to BGP routing. That is, a destination domain's border router acts as the tree's root and border routers of different source domains are used as the tree's leaves. BGRP assumes DiffServ to be used in the data plane and follows a soft-state signaling approach. By being based on an aggregation concept the number of signaling states that must be maintained at a border router corresponds to the number of destination domains for the aggregate reservations. This allows BGRP to perform very well in terms of scalability. However, BGRP does not explicitly address security concerns and since BGRP acts only between border routers it does not operate in an end-to-end manner. Therefore, BGRP does not provide support for mobile end users.

The BGRP concept was also brought to the IETF in form of an Internet-Draft by Pan et al. [PHS00a]. More details about BGRP's operation and a discussion about the proposed approach are provided in Section 6.3.2.

2.4.7 SICAP

The *Shared-Segment Inter-Domain Control Aggregation Protocol* (SICAP) [SGV03; Sof03] was also designed as a QoS signaling protocol which set a strong focus on scalability. Just like BGRP, SICAP performs also aggregation of resource reservations between border routers of different administrative domains. It even supports BGRP's sink tree-based approach and uses the same set of signaling messages. However, SICAP also introduces the notion of shared segment-based aggregations. Following this approach resource reservations being established along shared segments of a data path can be aggregated.

Routers functioning as so-called *Intermediate Deaggregation Locations* (IDLs) serve as aggregation points, where single reservations are merged into aggregates or aggregate reservations are split into single aggregates. Therefore, aggregates are established between different IDLs. Once a new single reservation request reaches an IDL, this reservation is automatically incorporated into an existing aggregate. In order to prevent such IDLs from having to keep track of each single reservation identifier, IDLs in SICAP only maintain a list of destination prefixes that can be accessed by this particular aggregate. Section 6.3.3 provides more details about SICAP's operation.

2.4.8 DARIS

The *Dynamic Aggregation of Reservations for Internet Services* (DARIS) [Ble02; Ble04] architecture provides another signaling framework for inter-domain aggregations of resource reservations. Different from BGRP and SICAP, it relies on the use of central domain resource managers.

DARIS also follows a shared segment-based approach, i.e., aggregates are established only once a pre-defined threshold of reservations share a common data path segment. This allows all intermediate routers along a given aggregate to remove signaling state for single reservations contained in this aggregate. Only the aggregator node and the deaggregator node must still be aware of the single reservations.

DARIS introduces some very sophisticated signaling mechanisms. For instance, the signaling load can be significantly reduced by reserving an additional amount of resources for aggregates which must not instantaneously be adapted with every added or removed reservation. Furthermore, DARIS also introduces the notion of message waiting conditions and hierarchical aggregates where longer aggregates can be nested in shorter ones. The DARIS architecture even provides support for group communication by IP multicast. DARIS is discussed in more detail in Section 6.3.4.

2.4.9 The Next Steps in Signaling (NSIS) Framework

Within the past, a large amount of research and engineering effort went into the design of different QoS models and signaling protocols. However, since none of the proposals reached significant deployment or was even standardized, RSVP remained the only standardized QoS signaling protocol at hand. In response to the lack of a widely deployed QoS infrastructure in the Internet, Geoff Huston [RFC2990] highlighted a set of outstanding architectural issues and the NSIS working group was formed in the IETF. NSIS's protocol design was deeply influenced by the *Cross-Application Signaling Protocol* (CASP) [FTH06].

The NSIS framework [RFC4080] provides a standardized network signaling protocol suite which can be used to install, maintain, and manipulate state in network nodes. Its architecture and protocols are based on the most recent findings in the development and operation of Internet signaling protocols. A strong focus was set to the *extensibility* of the NSIS protocol suite. Inspired by a proposal for a two-level architecture for Internet signaling [BL02], one of the most important design decisions was concerned with a generic *two-layered architecture* which decouples the routing and transport of signaling messages from the actual signaling application's logic. This provides enough flexibility to easily create new signaling applications on top of a common signaling transport protocol.

This separation of concerns was motivated from experiences with RSVP which lacks the flexibility to allow for a signaling application other than for resource reservations. The two-layered architecture is illustrated in Figure 2.9 with a lower-layer *NSIS Transport Layer Protocol* (NTLP) part and an upper-layer *NSIS Signaling Layer Protocol* (NSLP) part.

Currently, there are three different protocols specified by the IETF. The *General Internet Signaling Transport* (GIST) protocol [RFC5971] fulfills the requirements of an NTLP, the *Quality-of-Service NSIS Signaling Layer Protocol* (QoS NSLP) [RFC5974] acts as a QoS signaling protocol for resource reservations, and the *NAT/FW NSIS Signaling Layer Protocol* (NAT/FW NSLP) [RFC5973] can be used to dynamically manage and configure NAT gateways and firewalls.

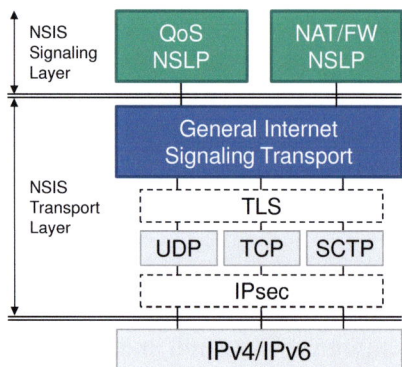

Figure 2.9: *Architectural overview of the Next Steps in Signaling (NSIS) framework*

One of the main objectives of the NSIS protocols is to *re-use* existing protocols and mechanisms instead of re-designing them from scratch. For instance, the NTLP runs above existing transport protocols, such as UDP, TCP, TCP with TLS, or SCTP. The QoS NSLP protocol can be seen as successor of RSVP.

The following sections provide an overview of the GIST and QoS NSLP protocols. Some details about the NAT/FW NSLP, as well as some implementation experiences and performance studies are presented by Steinleitner, Peters, and Fu [SPF06]. Furthermore, Fu et al. [Fu+05] provide a comprehensive overview of the NSIS framework and compare it with RSVP.

2.4.9.1 The General Internet Signaling Transport (GIST) Protocol

The GIST protocol serves as concrete realization of an NTLP and therefore provides a general routing and transport service for signaling applications. GIST works on behalf of a signaling application (i.e., a specific NSLP) and is responsible for the detection of the next signaling entity along the data path which actually supports the required NSLP. An NSLP is identified by a dedicated *NSLP-ID*.

Figure 2.10 illustrates the signaling relationship between different routers and signaling entities along a data path. In this scenario a signaling application is realized by NSLP *A* (e.g., QoS NSLP) and signaling for NSLP *A* takes place along a data path with five different routers. Router ① supports GIST and signaling application *A*, router ② is not NSIS-aware and therefore neither supports GIST, nor any NSLP. Router ③ supports GIST, as well as NSLP *A* and another NSLP *B* (e.g., NAT/FW NSLP). Router ④ does only support GIST and NSLP *B*, and router ⑤ supports GIST and NSLP *A*.

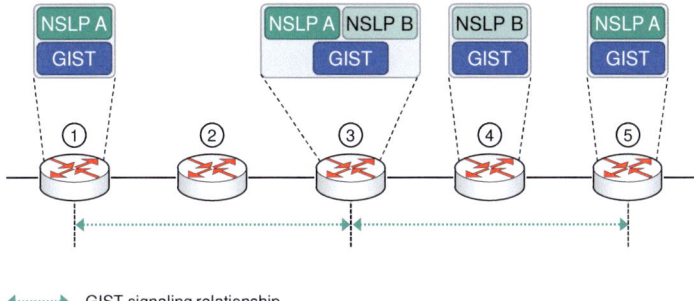

Figure 2.10: *Signaling relationship between different routers and signaling entities along a data path*

GIST has no notion of an end-to-end signaling session and operates only on a hop-by-hop basis. However, signaling routing state between any routers or end systems is only established in case this router supports GIST, as well as the particular requested NSLP. In the example provided above, a GIST signaling relationship is established between router ① and router ③. Even though each signaling message along this path is routed across router ②, this router is kept transparent for the signaling session, since it does neither support GIST, nor the requested NSLP.[3]

The next GIST signaling relationship is established between router ③ and router ⑤. In this case router ④ is kept transparent for this signaling session. Even though it supports GIST, it does not provide support for the requested NSLP. In the following, this dissertation refers to a router or end system which is NSIS-aware—in the sense that it supports GIST and the required NSLP—as *signaling entity* consistently.

Since a signaling entity is not aware of its directly adjacent signaling peer in advance, it must probe the network by employing an initial GIST three-way handshake as illustrated in Figure 2.11. The first message in this sequence is a GIST QUERY which is sent via UDP, carries a RAO, and is addressed toward the data flow's IP destination address. Each NSLP is identified by a specified RAO value. The RAO allows intermediate routers along the path to pre-filter IP packets of interest, i.e., intercept a GIST QUERY message in case this router supports GIST and the requested NSLP. Hence, the RAO is used to push messages from a router's normal data forwarding path into the router's control plane. In case a QUERY message remains unanswered, GIST uses an exponential backoff timer to retransmit the QUERY.

---

[3]It must, however, still take the RAO into account.

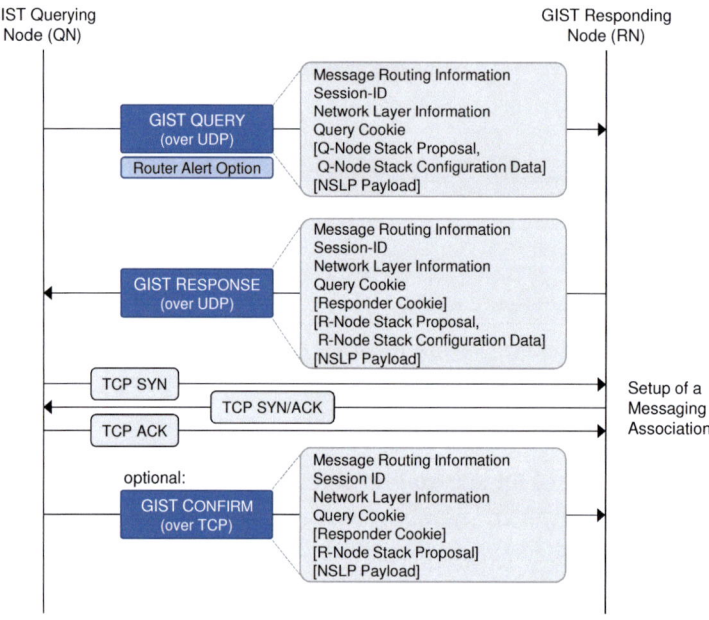

Figure 2.11: *Message sequence of a GIST three-way handshake for the initial establishment of signaling routing state between two adjacent signaling entities*

The signaling entity emitting the initial GIST QUERY message is called GIST *Querying Node* (QN) and the signaling entity that becomes the adjacent signaling peer is called GIST *Responding Node* (RN). After receiving an initial QUERY message, the RN's signaling application decides whether it wants to peer with the QN. If the peering decision is positive, the RN replies with a GIST RESPONSE message which in turn can be answered by a (optional) GIST CONFIRM message.

Once signaling routing state has been established between a QN and a RN, messages from the NSLP signaling application are sent via GIST DATA messages. Internally, GIST uses two modes of message delivery operation. GIST signaling messages being sent via UDP are sent in *Datagram Mode* (D-mode)—a special case of this D-mode operation is the Q-mode which is enabled for the very first QUERY message whenever no signaling routing state has been established yet. The second mode of operation is called *Connection Mode* (C-mode) and is used to transfer large signaling messages, can use underlying security mechanisms, and provides congestion control for signaling messages. DATA messages can therefore either be transmitted in D-mode via UDP or reliably in C-mode by a dedicated

Messaging Association (MA). An MA is established during the three-way handshake (cf. TCP connection setup after GIST's RESPONSE message in Figure 2.11). The used transport protocol is negotiated between the QN and the RN during the handshake by using stack proposal objects.

The actually used mode of operation can differ between any two signaling entities along a signaling path. That is, signaling sessions which are expected to be used over a long period of time, e.g., at the Internet's core, are likely to use C-mode connections, while signaling sessions with a shorter lifetime, e.g., at the network's edge, are likely to use D-mode connections. Note, however, that while each signaling flow requires the use of a dedicated GIST signaling routing state, GIST messages for each signaling routing state can be multiplexed across an already established TCP connection. This proves especially advantageous if this transport connection is secured, e.g., by using TLS.

GIST is flexible and extensible since it allows to use different *Message Routing Methods* (MRMs). An MRM is used to discover signaling messages' routes. The default MRM is the *Path-Coupled MRM* (PC-MRM) which routes signaling messages along the actual data path. This is an important property for resource reservations, since a reservation refers to a particular data flow such that state needs to be established on routers along this data path.

The information which describes a signaling flow's path is encapsulated in a *Message Routing Information* (MRI) object. For the PC-MRM a corresponding PC-MRI contains a flow identifier and additional control information. The flow is identified by the network layer version (IPv4 or IPv6), source address, destination address, the used transport protocol and ports, and a DiffServ code point. This does basically correspond to the multi-field classifier which identifies micro-flows in the Internet (cf. Section 2.1).

Whenever routes change in the underlying IP network, a QN's directly adjacent signaling peer may change upon which an existing GIST peering relationship is no longer valid. GIST is able to automatically detect route changes by relying on a soft-state approach and periodically probing the network, i.e., by repeating the GIST handshake in order to discover a new signaling peer. In case the same RN responds to the initial GIST QUERY, a CONFIRM can be omitted. If the RN changed, the signaling application is notified about the detected route change and can react accordingly, e.g., adapting a resource reservation.

In order to detect, whether the next peer along a path changed, the *Network Layer Information* (NLI) object plays an important role. The NLI contains detailed information about a signaling peer's identity in terms of an individually chosen interface-independent identifier which has a high probability of uniqueness, and an

IP address through which the signaling entity can be reached. A changed NLI can therefore be used as indication of a changed peer in downstream direction.

Besides identifying signaling flows by means of MRIs, NSIS also introduces the notion of a *Session Identifier* (Session ID). A Session ID is a 128 bit long location-independent identifier for signaling sessions which is chosen by the session's initiator. It must be cryptographically random in order to be (probabilistically) globally unique. The Session ID allows for an association of several signaling flows to one signaling session. This is an important property in order to realize signaling for mobile end systems and also a significant difference compared to RSVP which only has a notion of signaling flows.

Different from RSVP, GIST does already provide a number of inherent security features at the signaling transport layer. GIST employs an optional denial-of-service protection by providing a cookie-based three-way handshake. This so-called *delayed state installation* mechanism works as follows. In case a RN receives an initial QUERY message from a QN it is usually supposed to install signaling routing state for a new signaling session. By relying on the delayed state installation mode, the RN does not immediately setup signaling routing state. Instead, the RN encapsulates and integrity protects the context data into a *Responder Cookie* which is sent back to the QN in the subsequent RESPONSE. This responder cookie must then be returned by the QN which allows the RN to defer signaling routing state to be installed until it receives a CONFIRM message with an authentic responder cookie. This prevents attackers flooding NSIS signaling entities from exhausting context state at a RN (cf. TCP SYN flooding). The QN can also use a *Query Cookie* which prevents a QN from processing blindly injected RESPONSE messages.

Another level of protection is achieved by the 128 bit long Session ID which protects against blindly injected signaling messages and off-path attackers. Furthermore, existing security protocols like TLS or IPsec can be used by GIST if a secure message transport was requested by the NSLP.[4] This allows GIST to exchange signaling messages authenticated, integrity protected and confidentially between any two directly adjacent signaling entities.

The strong presence of Network Address Translators (NATs) imposes some major challenges on network signaling layer protocols like NSIS. NAT gateways perform transparent translations on address information contained in the IP and transport layer headers. Signaling routing state on signaling entities is, however, maintained based on address information contained in the payload of GIST data packets. In case a NAT gateway merely adapts the address information contained in the IP and

---

[4]Which protocol is actually used is determined by GIST and not by the signaling application.

transport layer headers, but not in the GIST packet, inconsistent signaling routing state will be installed on the different signaling entities, eventually terminating the GIST handshake process.

Therefore, any protocol that carries address information in its payload must be explicitly supported by a NAT gateway. In order to be used even across NAT gateways, GIST provides a so-called *NAT Traversal Object*. This object carries the necessary translation information and needs to be included into GIST QUERY messages by a GIST-aware NAT gateway. A prototypical implementation of such a GIST-aware NAT gateway demonstrated, that NSIS signaling can safely be performed across such NAT gateways [BR10a].

In comparison to RSVP, GIST provides a set of important improvements. Signaling message routing can be realized by different MRMs and is not restricted to a "path-coupled" variant only. This allows for a much greater flexibility especially with respect to future signaling application's needs. By relying on already standardized underlying transport protocols, GIST avoids a re-implementation of existing functionality. Furthermore, the use of TCP or SCTP allows for the transport of large signaling messages, as opposed to RSVP which relies on the use of UDP only. The use of a dedicated Session ID allows for a differentiation between signaling sessions and signaling flows which proves useful for signaling scenarios with mobile end systems. GIST does also address security by an optional use of underlying security functionalities such as TLS or IPsec, as well as Cookie mechanisms. Fu et al. [Fu+09] provide some more details about GIST and offer some first hand implementation experiences by providing an overhead and performance study of the GIST protocol.

2.4.9.2 The Quality-of-Service Signaling Layer (QoS NSLP) Protocol

The QoS NSLP protocol is a QoS signaling protocol which can be used to establish resource reservations in the network. In combination with GIST, it can be regarded as successor of RSVP.

QoS NSLP is based on a soft-state approach, i.e., actively used resource reservations must be periodically refreshed. Established reservations can also actively be torn down, if requested. Opposed to RSVP, which was limited to receiver-initiated reservations only, QoS NSLP provides support for sender- and receiver-initiated reservations. This allows for a much greater flexibility with respect to the signaling entity that can be accounted for a resource reservation request.

QoS NSLP supports different QoS models by employing a dedicated QoS specification object, called QSPEC template [RFC5975]. The QSPEC template specifies its

QoS requirements independently of the used QoS provisioning approach and can specify parameter ranges. It therefore allows for end-to-end resource reservations across different administrative domains which rely on the use of different QoS models, such as DiffServ or IntServ.

Figure 2.12 illustrates the use of sender-initiated reservations across a set of three signaling entities. For sender-initiated reservations the signaling procedure is started with a GIST three-way handshake between the *QoS NSLP Initiator* (QNI) and its next QoS NSLP-capable signaling entity in downstream direction, called *QoS NSLP Entity* (QNE). Once signaling routing state has been established, the QNI emits a QoS NSLP RESERVE message, carrying a QSPEC object, toward the QNE.

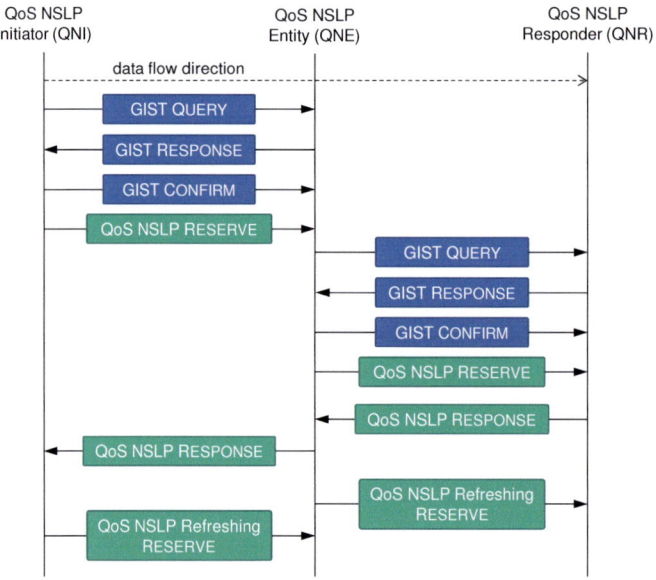

Figure 2.12: *Message sequence for a sender-initiated reservation with QoS NSLP across a set of three signaling entities*

Upon reception of a RESERVE message, the QNE inspects the QSPEC object and performs admission control. In case the resource reservation request can be fulfilled, state is installed and resources are reserved. If resources can only be partly granted, the QSPEC can also be modified (if permitted by a parameter range) before the reservation request is forwarded further along the path.

The QNE is then responsible to forward this RESERVE toward the final RESERVE's destination which acts as *QoS NSLP Responder* (QNR). If requested by an optional *Request Identification Information* (RII) object, the QNR replies to a reservation request with a RESPONSE message. This can be used to provide information about the result of a reservation request back to the QNI in form of an *Information Object* (INFO-SPEC). A RESPONSE is then sent back to the QNI in the data flow's upstream direction.

In case receiver-initiated reservations are used, as depicted in Figure 2.13, the data flow sender triggers the establishment of a resource reservation by emitting a QoS NSLP QUERY message with a RESERVE-INIT flag set. The QUERY is used to install reverse-path state on all intermediate signaling entities since the corresponding reservation should be established for the data flow from the sender to the receiver, i.e., in downstream direction. A QUERY message must carry a QSPEC and can already be used in the admission control process but does, however, not actually reserve the requested resources.

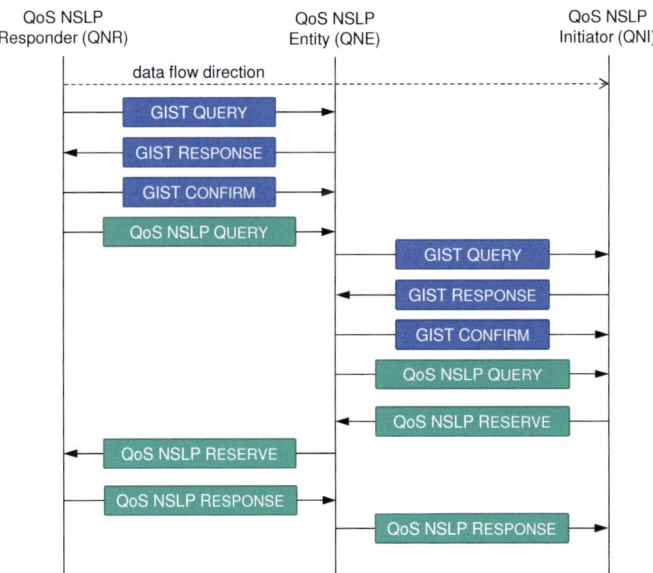

Figure 2.13: *Message sequence for a receiver-initiated reservation with QoS NSLP across a set of three signaling entities*

As soon as the last signaling entity along the path receives the QUERY, the resource reservation can be actually established by a corresponding RESERVE. According to the QoS NSLP specification, the signaling entity emitting the initial RESERVE always acts as QNI. Therefore, in the receiver-initiated case the data flow sender acts as QNR and the data flow receiver as QNI of the resource reservation.

Even though QoS NSLP follows a soft-state approach, resource reservations can also be actively torn down. This is accomplished by using a TEAR flag which must be set in a RESERVE message. Each RESERVE message carries a *Reservation Sequence Number* (RSN). A change of reservation parameters can be signaled by an incremented RSN. An RSN value has, however, only local significance between a QNE and the next signaling entity in downstream direction.

QoS NSLP provides an additional NOTIFY message which can be sent by a QNE asynchronously in order to convey information to another QNE. A NOTIFY message is therefore used for notifications, e.g., to signal a detected route change or specific error conditions, and carries an INFO-SPEC object with more detailed information about the notification.

In order to allow a router's packet classifier to identify data flows for which a specific QoS policy should be applied, QoS NSLP provides a dedicated PACKET-CLASSIFIER object. This object basically indicates which of the information contained in the MRI should be used for packet classification.

Furthermore, QoS NSLP provides protocol mechanisms which allow to enforce a relationship between different signaling sessions or signaling messages. A BOUND-SESSION-ID can be used to express a dependency relation between two or more signaling sessions, either for unidirectional signaling sessions which logically belong together, or for bidirectional resource reservations. Binding of signaling messages can be realized by using the MSG-ID and BOUND-MSG-ID objects. This message binding is particularly useful in order to allow for more efficient simultaneous signaling exchanges which can then later be synchronized by means of these two objects.

In comparison to RSVP, QoS NSLP provides the following set of improvements. RSVP was designed with a strong focus on being used in conjunction with IP multicast. Since it was argued that sender-initiated reservations won't scale well in scenarios with heterogeneous receivers (in terms of QoS demands), RSVP only supports receiver-initiated reservations. Multicast support set therefore a strong limitation on RSVP's protocol design. QoS NSLP was designed with support for sender- and receiver-initiated reservations. Different from RSVP, the NSIS protocol suite introduces the notion of a session identifier, complementary to the commonly used flow identifier (GIST's MRI). This allows QoS NSLP to be prepared for mobility support where one signaling session may be comprised of more than one signaling flows. Finally, RSVP was designed as a QoS signaling protocol that can be used within the IntServ model. QoS NSLP abstracts from the actual QoS model being used underneath by providing a dedicated QSPEC template which can be used across IntServ and DiffServ domains, for instance. Just like GIST, QoS NSLP was designed to be easily extensible. Arumaithurai et al. [Aru+08] provide further information about implementation experiences and offer a performance study of the QoS NSLP protocol. The flexible design of the QoS NSLP protocol also allows for a coupling with SIP [RB12] in order to reserve resources for SIP-based services, such as VoIP telephony.

2.4.10 Summary

In order to allow for dynamic resource reservation and admission control in IP-based networks, a large number of QoS signaling protocols and frameworks were proposed by the research community in the past. Table 2.1 on pages 46–47 compares the QoS signaling approaches that were discussed in this section.

   Signaling protocols follow nowadays usually a soft-state based approach. ST2+ is the only signaling protocol of the ones being discussed, that relies on a hard-state mechanism. Some signaling protocols use in-band signaling where control information is directly embedded into an application's data packets. Such a design is usually well-suited to provide a very light-weight signaling alternative and hence, was mostly motivated by performance considerations. However, in-band signaling does not provide a clear separation of functionalities from an architectural point of view and requires the application to be adapted, too.

   Mobility support is concerned with the question whether an established QoS signaling session is automatically adapted once a mobile user changes its location. While INSIGNIA was explicitly designed to be used in mobile environments, only the NSIS protocol suite provides basic mobility support.[5] At the time RSVP was designed, multicast was considered to play an important role when it comes to the provisioning of QoS support for real-time demanding applications. However, only RSVP and DARIS provide inherent multicast support.

   The analyzed signaling protocols also provide different capabilities with respect to scalability and security. While both attributes play an important role, in order to be deployed in the Internet, only few signaling protocols addressed these properties. Scalability was only explicitly addressed by BGRP, SICAP, and DARIS, which all

---

[5]This is further investigated in Chapter 4.

Mechanisms and Features	ST2+ [RFC1819]	RSVP [RFC2205]	YESSIR [PS99]	Boomerang [Feh+99]	INSIGNIA [Lee+00]
State Maintenance	Hard-state	Soft-state	Soft-state	Soft-state	Soft-state
Signaling Approach	Out-of-band	Out-of-band	In-band in RTP data packets	In-band in ICMP data packets	In-band in IP data packets
Initiation Mode	Sender-initiated	Receiver-initiated	Sender-initiated	Sender-initiated	Sender-initiated
Supported QoS Models	None	IntServ; DiffServ only partly covered [RFC2998]	None	None	None
Signaling Scope	End-to-end	End-to-end	End-to-end	End-to-end	End-to-end
Mobility	Not supported	Not supported	Not supported	Not supported	Inherently supported
Security	Not considered	Partly covered by extensions	Not considered	Not considered	Not considered
Multicast	Partly, realized via IP unicast routing	Inherently supported	Not supported	Not supported	Not supported
Scalability	Weak, per-reservation state	Weak, but partly improved by aggregation extension [RFC3175]	weak, per-reservation state	Weak, per-reservation state	Weak, per-reservation state
Signaling Architecture	Distributed	Distributed	Distributed	Distributed	Distributed

Table 2.1: *Functional comparison of different QoS signaling protocols and frameworks*

Mechanisms and Features	BGRP [PHS00b]	SICAP [SGV03]	DARIS [Ble04]	NSIS [RFC4080]
State Maintenance	Soft-state	Soft-state	Soft-state	Soft-state
Signaling Approach	Out-of-band	Out-of-band	Out-of-band	Out-of-band
Initiation Mode	Receiver-initiated	Receiver-initiated	Sender- and receiver-initiated	Sender- and receiver-initiated
Supported QoS Models	DiffServ	DiffServ	DiffServ	IntServ, Diff-Serv
Signaling Scope	Edge-to-edge	Edge-to-edge	End-to-end	End-to-end, Edge-to-edge, End-to-edge
Mobility	Not supported	Not supported	Not supported	Basically supported
Security	Not considered	Not considered	Not explicitly considered, but controlled by domain manager	Use of TLS or IPsec for hop-by-hop protection
Multicast	Not supported	Not supported	Supported	Not supported
Scalability	Strong through aggregation	Strong through aggregation	Strong through aggregation	Weak, per-reservation state
Signaling Architecture	Distributed	Distributed	Centralized	Distributed

Table 2.1: *Functional comparison of different QoS signaling protocols and frameworks (continued)*

relied on the aggregation of resource reservations. Security, on the other hand, was usually not explicitly discussed. While RSVP provides some security extensions, only the NSIS protocol suite was designed to provide more sophisticated security capabilities.

2.5 Conclusion

This dissertation aims at providing advanced signaling support for IP-based networks. This chapter presented the background and fundamentals of signaling in IP-based networks. It analyzed important aspects of the Internet architecture, such as its design goals, which aim at a robust and stateless operation, and the separation between an Internet router's control and data plane.

QoS support in the Internet is also concerned with this separation, since QoS control functions are performed in a router's data plane, whereas signaling protocols operate in a router's control plane. While a number of QoS signaling protocols has already been designed and standardized for the Internet, none of them can be considered a comprehensive solution. Almost none of the existing signaling protocols provides support for advanced security mechanisms, only few were designed to support mobile end users, and nearly none of them provides mechanisms to allow for scalable resource reservations. Even NSIS, which is the most recently standardized signaling protocol suite and already provides many sophisticated signaling mechanisms, lacks appropriate mechanisms to allow for authenticated signaling, support for mobile users, or support for scalable resource reservation.

## Chapter 3

Authentic Signaling
in IP-based Networks

Security builds one of the most important non-functional aspects when network protocols are designed. This holds especially true for network signaling protocols which allow for an on-demand control of network services and resources. In this chapter the challenges in designing secure signaling protocols are analyzed and security concepts for authentic signaling in IP-based networks are proposed.

The requirements for secure signaling protocols are outlined in Section 3.1. In order to allow for authentic signaling, the security mechanisms should be *generic and flexible* enough to be applicable by different signaling applications and *lightweight* to not incur too much processing overhead. Since non-critical parts of a signaling message should still be modifiable by untrusted signaling entities, the protection of signaling messages should be *fine-grained*. In order to achieve a scalable solution with respect to the number of cryptographic session keys that need to be maintained by a signaling entity the protection should provide *user-based authentication* mechanisms.

Based on these requirements Section 3.2 specifies the objectives for secure signaling protocols, outlines existing security mechanisms, and evaluates their applicability to signaling protocols. Related work regarding existing security mechanisms for signaling protocols are discussed in Section 3.3. The concepts developed for authentic signaling are presented in Section 3.4.

One important goal of this dissertation is to rely on standardized protocols and mechanisms as much as possible. The concepts outlined in this chapter are therefore conceptually based on an existing proposal for a so-called *Session*

Authorization Object which was introduced within the IETF's NSIS working group as a dedicated authorization object for signaling messages. Since the working group's proposal [MST07] did not fulfill the aforementioned requirements, this dissertation presents security mechanisms for signaling protocols. Section 3.5 presents an extended version of the Session Authorization Object. This extended version was first proposed in [BR09b] upon which most of these extension have been incorporated into the resulting Internet Standard [RFC5981].

Since signaling protocols are often used within networks that use an underlying authentication service such as Kerberos, Section 3.6 shows how the extended Session Authorization Object can interact with the Kerberos network authentication service.

A prototypical implementation of the Session Authorization Object was integrated into the NSIS-ka suite [Ble+12a]. Important design aspects of this implementation are presented in Section 3.7. Based on this implementation the performance achieved and the overhead induced by the Session Authorization Object are evaluated in Section 3.8. Section 3.9 summarizes the achievements and concludes this chapter.

3.1 Problem Statement and Requirements

In order to gain a better understanding of how signaling protocols can be secured, the signaling protocol's security requirements must be identified and existing approaches to satisfy these requirements must be analyzed. According to ITU-T Recommendation X.800 [ITU91] a security architecture for data communication networks can be logically grouped into the following components:

Security Threats — potential violations of security and possible danger for a communication system

Security Services — abstract communication services that must be realized in order to protect communication systems from security threats

Security Mechanisms — concrete building blocks that can be used in order to realize security services

The following sections discuss these three components in more detail with a focus on the applicability with respect to signaling protocols.

3.1.1 Security Threats for Signaling Protocols

Since signaling protocols allow for the installation and manipulation of state in the network, signaling protocols must be protected from an unauthorized use and are subject to a number of security attacks. This section provides an overview of the most important security threats for signaling protocols. Usually these security threats stem from attacks that are used in combination in order to compromise specific signaling protocol features.

3.1.1.1 Modification of Messages

Modification of messages means that a legitimate message is altered, delayed, or messages are being reordered by an adversary which usually acts as a *Man-in-the-Middle*. In terms of signaling protocols, service requests can get modified by an adversary in order to gain unauthorized access to resources. For instance, a signaling service request to install a NAT binding for a specific IP address and transport protocol port pair can get modified to an adversary's needs. Insertion of new messages and deletion of existing messages fall into the same category.

3.1.1.2 Eavesdropping

Eavesdropping is a form of a passive attack that can be used by an adversary in order to gain information from transmitted communication messages. This information, which may be potentially confidential, can then be used for traffic analysis or further active attacks, such as replay attacks. For instance, a signaling flow's QoS parameters, NAT bindings, firewall policy rules, user identities, network configuration information, authentication or authorization information may be collected by an adversary.

Eavesdropping is very difficult to detect and this attack can usually only be prevented by means of encryption. However, regarding signaling protocols, the encryption of signaling messages between two end systems may be challenging, since certain parts of a signaling message should still be accessible by intermediate signaling entities whereas other parts of the message should only be accessible by the end systems.

3.1.1.3 Replay of Messages

Replay attacks are based on the aforementioned eavesdropping attacks. In this case data captured from communication messages is replayed by an adversary at a later time. Note, that this affects also authenticated messages which can be replayed by an adversary. This replay attack can then be used for further attacks, such as Man-in-the-Middle or Denial-of-Service attacks, and eventually results in an unauthorized effect. Timestamps and message sequence numbers in conjunction with integrity protection mechanisms provide means against simple replay attacks.

3.1.1.4 Masquerade

A masquerade occurs when an entity pretends to be another entity and therefore uses a different entity's identity. Regarding signaling protocols, this attack may be used by an adversary to gain unauthorized access to resources. For instance, if the messages of an authentication sequence are captured and replayed, an adversary may use signaling protocols for resource reservations for itself on behalf of someone else. Masquerading therefore usually includes further forms of active attacks, such as replay attacks. While these types of attacks cannot be prevented, proper authentication and integrity protection mechanisms provide means against masquerade attacks.

3.1.2 Security Services for Signaling Protocols

As described above signaling protocols are threatened by a wide range of different security attacks. This section provides an overview of services that can be used in order to protect signaling protocols against these security threats. Definitions of these security services and the aforementioned security threats can also be found in the Internet Security Glossary [RFC4949].

3.1.2.1 Confidentiality

Confidentiality provides a security service that is used to protect information contained in transmitted data such that only authorized entities are able to obtain the information. The level of protection, i.e., which parts of the transmitted data are protected, can vary. In terms of signaling protocols, for instance, the entire transport connection can be protected, a single signaling message can be protected, or only specific parts of a signaling message can be protected. While an end-to-end encryption provides a viable way for the protection of application-layer signaling protocols, it can principally not be applied to network-layer signaling protocols, since certain parts of a signaling message must be interpreted by intermediate signaling entities.

Note, that the term protection in terms of confidentiality does not prevent a third party from modifying, inserting, or deleting a message—instead, it only protects the content of the message from unauthorized disclosure.

3.1.2.2 Authentication

Authentication describes the ability to prove the identity of the communicating entity (peer entity authentication) or the source of a message (data-origin authentication). It is important, that the authentication service should not be limited to the initial connection establishment, but instead also be available for the lifetime of this connection, such that there exists a binding between the peer's identity and all its subsequently sent messages. Note, that authentication mechanisms do not prevent from duplication or modification of messages.

3.1.2.3 Data Integrity

Data integrity provides a security service that allows a receiver to detect unauthorized alteration of transmitted data. This includes modification, insertion, or re-ordering of messages. Data integrity can be provided on different levels—for example the entire connection can be integrity-protected, only single messages, or just parts of single messages can be integrity-protected. Different from a confidentiality service, data integrity does not protect the content of a message from being disclosed to a third party. Note, that integrity protection does not prevent message alteration by an unauthorized third party, but it provides detection in case of modification by an unauthorized party. Data integrity is usually combined with proper authentication mechanisms, such that data authenticity can be verified.

3.1.3 Security Mechanisms for Signaling Protocols

In order to design secure signaling protocols with respect to the aforementioned security services, concrete protocol mechanisms must be applied. This section provides an overview of existing security building blocks that can be used by IP-based signaling protocols. More detailed information on these available security components and mechanisms are discussed by Stallings [Sta11] and Bless et al. [Ble+05].

3.1.3.1 Digital Signature

A digital signature provides means to cryptographically protect the source and the *integrity* of a message. Furthermore, it can also be used to prove the *authenticity* of a given message such that a recipient can use the digital signature to verify the originator. There exists a wide variety of ways how digital signatures can be constructed. Usually this is accomplished by means of asymmetric cipher models (*public-key cryptography*) and hash functions as depicted in Figure 3.1.

At first, a cryptographic hash function H is used to retrieve a fixed-length *message digest* d of a message m (step ①). After that, the message digest is encrypted by the sender's private key $k_{private}$ (step ②). The resulting encrypted message digest is used as the message's digital signature s and can be verified through a third party by means of the sender's public key k_{public}. Both, the original plain text message m and the digital signature s are now transmitted toward the receiver. In order to verify the digital signature, the receiver uses the same hash function H as the sender to get the message digest d from the message m (step ③). Furthermore, the receiver uses the sender's public key to decrypt the digital signature s (step ④). Finally, the decrypted equal the receiver can be assured that the message m it received was not modified during transit.

3.1.3.2 Encryption

Encryption can be used to provide *confidentiality* of a message. It cryptographically transforms the original *plain text* message m into a *cipher text* form c that cannot be interpreted by an unauthorized third party. The encryption function E, which returns the cipher text c, uses a *key* k and the plain text message m as input parameters, e.g., $c = E(m, k)$. Based on the keys and the transformation process being used, this can be either accomplished by means of asymmetric cryptography with a public-private key pair, symmetric cryptography with a shared key, or a combination of both. An example for asymmetric cryptography is the RSA algorithm [RSA78]; an example for symmetric cryptography is AES [DR01].

Figure 3.2 exemplifies the use of public-key encryption and decryption between a sender and a receiver. In this case the sender intends to send an encrypted message toward a receiver. At first, the sender encrypts the plain text message m by using an encryption algorithm and the receiver's public key as an input parameter (step ①). The resulting cipher text c is transmitted subsequently (step ②), upon which the receiver uses the corresponding decryption algorithm with its private key as input parameter in order to retrieve the original message m (step ③).

In case symmetric cryptography is used by both parties, the encryption and decryption algorithms work on the same shared symmetric key instead of a public and private key, respectively.

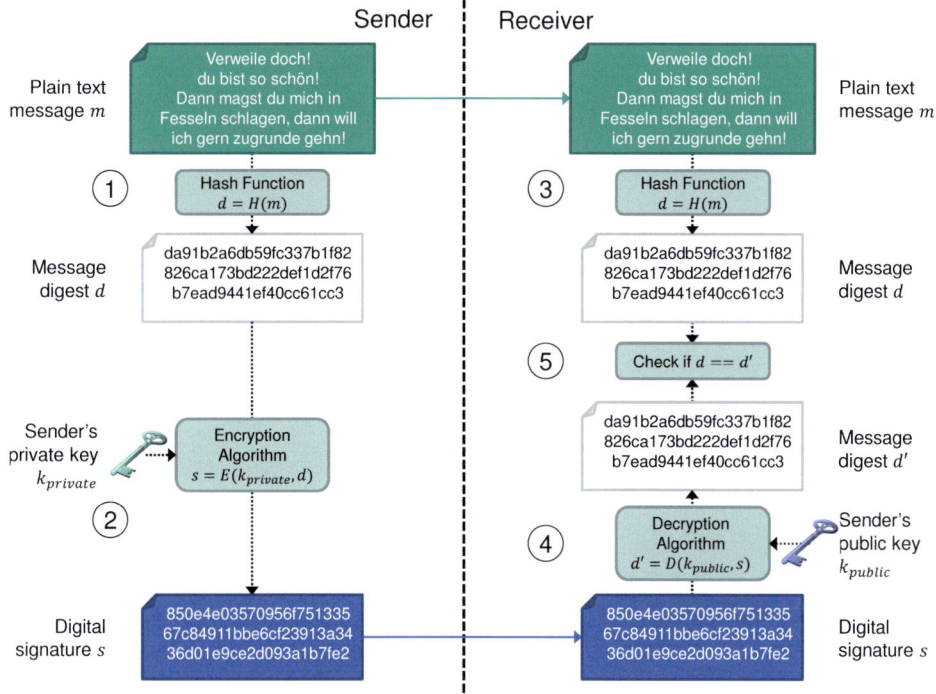

Figure 3.1: *Creation and verification of a digital signature*

3.1.3.3 Cryptographic Hash Function

A cryptographic hash function $H(a) = b$ describes a one-way function which is easy to compute but computationally very hard to reverse. That means for every $b \in B$ the probability is low to find an $a \in A$ in polynomial time. It transforms a message of arbitrary length into a fixed-length message digest. Examples of cryptographic hash functions are MD5 [RFC1321] or SHA-2 [NIS08].

3.1.3.4 Message Authentication Code

A message authentication code (MAC) is a cryptographic checksum of a message that can be used to verify the *integrity* and the *authenticity* of a message and is therefore usually appended to the plain text message. Different from a message digest, a MAC algorithm takes two input parameters—a message and a secret key. It uses a secret key k to transform a plain text message m into a fixed-length MAC d. The secret key is a necessary component of a message authentication code to

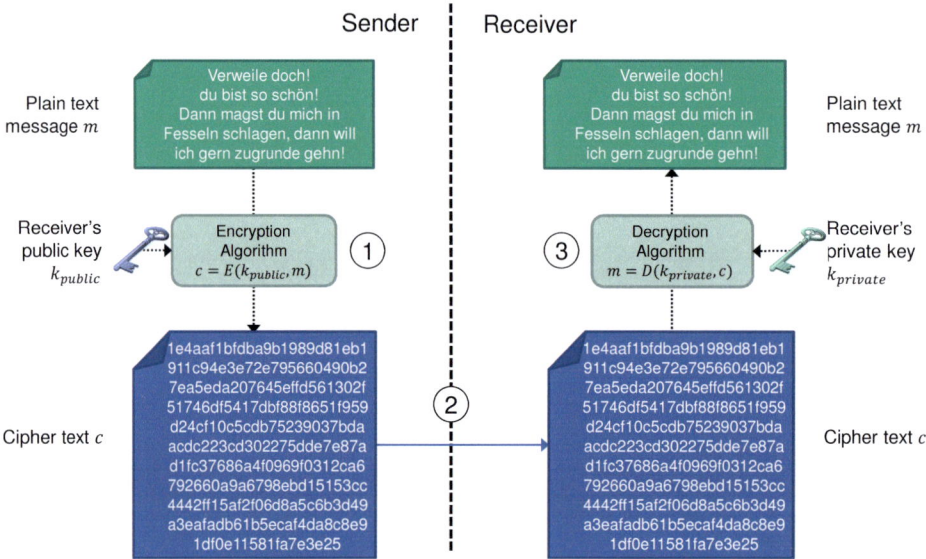

Figure 3.2: *Encryption and decryption of a message using public key cryptography*

secure the message digest such that an attacker is not able to calculate a valid MAC d' after having altered the plain text message from m to m'.

MACs are usually built either by using symmetric block ciphers (e.g., DES or AES) or by using cryptographic hash functions (e.g., MD5 or SHA). A specific form of the latter is called HMAC (*keyed-hashing for message authentication*) [RFC2104]. An HMAC uses a cryptographic hash function H in combination with a secret key k in order to transform a plain text message m into a fixed-length message authentication code d. Even though the cryptographic strength of the HMAC depends on the properties of the particular cryptographic hash function being used, the calculation operates conceptually independent of the hash function.

The HMAC's hash function operates on blocks of data. In the following B denotes the length of such blocks in bytes and L denotes the hash function's output length in bytes. The calculation of an HMAC on a data block *text* works as follows:

$$HMAC(text) = H(k \oplus opad | H(k \oplus ipad | text))$$

ipad and *opad* are both bit strings of size B and contain only the characters 0x36 and 0x5c, respectively. In a first step, key k is concatenated with *ipad* using an XOR-operation, upon which the data block *text* is appended to this bit string. Then the hash of this value is calculated using the hash function H. After that, the key k

is concatenated with *opad* using an XOR-operation and the value of the preceding operation is appended, upon which the hash function is calculated on the new value.

The HMAC provides the significant property to not allow an unauthorized entity to simply extend *m* by still retrieving the same message authentication code. Furthermore, it can be implemented in software quite efficiently, and the hash functions being used can be easily replaced in case more efficient or more secure hash functions are available or required.

3.1.3.5 Summary

Figure 3.3 summarizes the potential security threats, security services and security mechanisms that are relevant to signaling protocols. Based on the analysis of existing services and mechanisms, the following section elaborates the concrete objectives for secure signaling protocols.

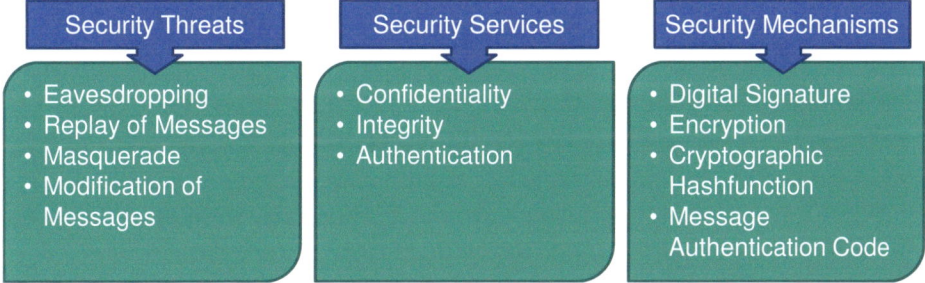

Figure 3.3: *Signaling protocols can use a specific set of security mechanisms in order to realize security services and protect from security threats*

3.2 Objectives for Secure Signaling Protocols

The level and granularity in which existing security mechanisms can be applied in order to protect from security threats can differ. Likewise, security services that must be realized do often depend on the particular application scenario. With respect to signaling protocols the following security objectives can be identified:

- *User-based authentication*

  The Next Steps in Signaling framework's GIST protocol already provides support for encrypted channels between two directly adjacent signaling entities by means of existing security protocols like the *Transport Layer Security* (TLS) protocol, for instance. An encrypted channel does, however, not differentiate between single users and sessions but rather multiplexes all signaling associations over one single encrypted connection. Instead, a signaling protocol's security model should provide means for *user-based authentication of signaling messages*.

- *Integrity protection*

  Signaling messages can be subject to manipulation during transit, either intentionally or simply by accident. The signaling message's data integrity plays, however, an important role, since state in network entities is adjusted accordingly. For instance, Quality-of-Service reservations or firewall pinholes could be changed wrongly on behalf of a manipulated signaling message. Even though manipulation of signaling messages itself cannot be guaranteed to be prevented, a signaling protocol's security model should provide means to detect any manipulation by *integrity-protecting every single signaling message*.

- *Fine-grained protection*

  Integrity protection of signaling messages builds an important security objective for signaling protocols in order to verify that the signaling message was not manipulated during transit. It may, however, be desirable that certain parts of a signaling message should also be modifiable by intermediate signaling entities that are not part of the trust relationship. For instance, consider a Quality-of-Service reservation request issued by a signaling initiator where two parameters specify the minimum and the available resources to be reserved. While the minimum parameter for this request should not be changed by any untrusted signaling entity, the available parameter must be changed by every signaling entity that participates in this signaling session, even if it is not part of the trust relationship. Therefore, a signaling message's integrity protection should not simply cover the entire message but rather provide means for a *fine-grained protection of a signaling message*.

- *Light-weight protection*

  Adding security capabilities to signaling protocols imposes additional costs and may lead to significant processing and forwarding delays. These costs become even more significant when a potentially high amount of signaling messages reaches a signaling entity within a short period of time. In order to keep the processing time and latency for signaling messages small, the security model should provide *light-weight security mechanisms for signaling messages*.

- **Binding between authorization token and signaling message**

  Service requests that are issued due to signaling messages must be authorized, otherwise the service request cannot be accepted by the receiving entity. The authorization for a specific service must be provided by means of an authorizing entity which can issue a dedicated authorization token to the initiator of the request. However, if this authorization token is not directly related in any way to this particular service request and signaling message, the service request may be changed or an attacker may use the same authorization token for its own needs. Therefore, a requirement for secure signaling is to establish a *binding between the authorization token and the signaling message that transports this token*.

- **Crypto agility**

  The level of security that can be achieved is tightly coupled with the particular cryptographic mechanisms and algorithms that are used. It is therefore important to provide means to dynamically *exchange these cryptographic mechanisms and algorithms during the lifetime of a signaling session*.

3.3 Related Work

The IETF published a comprehensive glossary for information system security by Shirey [RFC4949]. The RFC provides a detailed set of terms, definitions, and abbreviations for the terminology of information system security which are also used as a basis for the security requirements identified by this dissertation.

A thorough analysis on the security threats faced by stateful protocols, especially with respect to potential denial-of-service attacks is provided by Aura and Nikander [AN97]. The document gives generic advise on how stateful protocols can be securely transformed into stateless protocols. While some of the proposed mechanisms, like the use of secure cookies for authentication, are already present in modern signaling protocols like GIST, some others should also be applied by

signaling protocols as well. For example, an integrity protection via message authentication codes or means against replay attacks like timestamps and periodically
changing signature keys.

3.3.1 Security Enhancements for RSVP

One of the most important and actually deployed QoS signaling protocols in the
Internet is the Resource ReSerVation Protocol (RSVP). However, the design of
RSVP did, unlike NSIS, not set a strong focus on security requirements from the
beginning.

RFC 2747 and RFC 3097 introduced an RSVP specific so-called INTEGRITY object
which can be used between two RSVP signaling entities in order to provide authentication, integrity protection, and replay protection of signaling messages [RFC2747;
RFC3097]. The two signaling entities maintain a security association which may be
either initialized by means of an integrity handshake or which exists permanently
between peering domain routers. Therefore, the achieved security is based on
a chain-of-trust between neighboring RSVP entities. While the proposed object
adds a useful level of security to RSVP, it has no notion of an end-to-end security
protection and does not provide means for a fine-grained integrity protection since
the integrity protection covers always the entire signaling message. Furthermore, it
does not work on a session-based concept but rather multiplexes different signaling
associations over one security association.

In order to allow for a policy-based admission control and user-based authentication in RSVP, RFC 2750 defines a set of corresponding protocol extensions [RFC2750]. A so-called POLICY_DATA object is used to transport policy information. This object can also use an INTEGRITY object for integrity protection of
the policy data. RFC3182 specifies the identity representation in the POLICY_DATA
element for admission control [RFC3182].

This POLICY_DATA object was used for a further refinement of a Session Authorization Policy Element [RFC3520]. This element is used as an authorization
token for a signaling session that is issued by an authorizing entity. It is, however,
tightly coupled to RSVP and hence, to resource reservations. Even though it carries
a specific attribute that characterizes the authorized session, e.g., the bandwidth
allocated or the used RSVP flow spec specification, the element itself is not directly
associated with the contents of the signaling message, since the authentication data
is computed only over all the data contained in the policy element itself. Therefore,
it does not provide integrity protection of the signaling message itself, especially not
a fine-grained integrity protection of non-mutable objects. Furthermore, an RSVP

message must only contain at most one policy element which can cause problems regarding the authorization of signaling sessions that span multiple administrative domains.

A concrete utilization of the session authorization policy element is provided in RFC 3521, which specifies a comprehensive framework for session setup with media authorization [RFC3521]. The document describes how the setup of multimedia sessions can be linked against subsequent resource reservations in order to verify the authorization and validity of service requests. According to the trust relationship in a network, three different models for session setup can be used. Within each of these models an authorizing entity generates a session authorization policy element—as defined in RFC 3520—which is used to exchange authorization information between the network entities. While the authors leave some of the detailed mechanisms open to the implementations, such as the integrity protection of the authorization token, the document gives a good advise on the different entities that are involved in a session authorization process.

Wu et al. [Wu+99] analyzed potential threats to RSVP messages and proposed solutions in order to protect them from insider and outsider attackers. The authors focused especially on the challenge to provide integrity protection for mutable objects of a signaling message. They propose an RSVP extension called SDS/CD (Selective Digital Signature with Conflict Detection) where a responder piggybacks the digitally signed mutable objects that it received. This allows all intermediate signaling entities to verify whether the values in the received objects are equivalent to or where adjusted in accordance with the values they forwarded. If they are not in accordance with locally stored values a conflict is detected and a policy server can take appropriate actions.

Based on this approach, Talwar and Nahrstedt proposed a scalable QoS protection for RSVP messages, called RSVP-SQoS [TN00]. Later Talwar et al. [TNN01] presented an enhanced version of RSVP-SQoS. RSVP-SQoS is based on two processing phases, one for being applied within subnetworks and one for being applied across subnetworks. Digital signatures are used to sign every signaling message sent from the signaling's initiator or from the responder. Relying on digital signatures and therefore a public-key-based security mechanism allows for proper authentication and can guarantee non-repudiation in case it is used in conjunction with time stamps and a trusted third party. Just as in SDS/CD, this approach uses dedicated feedback signaling messages which can be used to check the integrity of RSVP QoS parameters within subnetworks upon reception of the original signaling message. Different from SDS/CD this design relies on a hierarchical network design. Following this approach, the feedback signaling messages are solely used within a subnetwork in order to detect malicious router attacks. Once a signaling message reaches an egress entity, this entity constructs a feedback message that signs the mutable objects of the original signaling message and sends this feedback message back in upstream direction. This allows intermediate signaling entities up to the ingress entity to check whether a malicious router caused a conflict in the reservation request. In case a conflict is detected, the session can be torn down subsequently. The authors claim that the scalability of the proposed approach is preserved since these delayed integrity checks are only used within subnetworks. However, the paper does not provide a quantitative evaluation or measurements, especially with respect to the duration of the delayed integrity checks. Furthermore, relying on digital signatures can be considered quite computing-intensive, especially if additionally being applied for reverse integrity checks for every single feedback signaling message.

Tschofenig and Graveman [RFC4230] provide a comprehensive analysis and summary of RSVP's currently specified security properties. This document is also meant to present some lessons learned from RSVP's security design considerations in order to be used for the design of future signaling protocols. The authors give a detailed overview of the INTEGRITY or the POLICY_DATA objects, discuss the corresponding security properties, and name some remaining issues.

3.3.2 Security Enhancements for NSIS

The NSIS protocol suite can be seen as successor of RSVP, but in contrast to RSVP one of the most important design goals from the beginning were built-in security mechanisms. As already outlined in Chapter 2 NSIS provides an optional denial-of-service protection by employing a cookie-based three-way handshake for a delayed-state-installation of signaling routing state. Furthermore, the 128 bit long Session ID offers additional protection against blindly injected messages by off-path attackers.

Another level of protection for signaling messages in NSIS can be achieved by letting the signaling layer application (NSLP) request a secure transport service via GIST. Upon such a request, two adjacent GIST signaling entities employ a TLS protected transport connection between each other. This allows an authenticated, integrity protected, and confidential transport of signaling messages. Furthermore, each NSLP can perform its own peering decision based on identities or data contained in the QUERY.

However, even though NSIS already provides these basic security mechanisms the signaling protocols are still subject to security threats. For this reason, RFC 4081 provides a comprehensive list of potential security threats for the NSIS protocol suite [RFC4081]. The document describes potential security attacks in detail by focusing on the existing GIST, QoS NSLP, and NAT/FW NSLP protocols. According to RFC 4081, protection of signaling protocols can be logically separated into two distinct steps. Within the first step a *security association* must be established between two signaling entities in order to provide secure authentication and key establishment. As soon as a security association is established, subsequent message protection can be provided within a second step. This message protection can consist of different protection mechanisms such as integrity, confidentiality, or replay protection. The document does, however, only focus on a comprehensive analysis of potential security threats for the NSIS protocols, but it does not provide concrete solutions for the identified threats, e.g., how existing protocol security mechanisms could be used to resolve the identified issues.

Although security threats were intensely analyzed and some basic security mechanisms were already built-in in NSIS, authentication and authorization mechanisms were not designed as integrated parts of the NSIS protocol suite. Tschofenig and Fu [TF06] systematically analyze the security options currently provided by NSIS and give a detailed overview of potential security threats for the NSIS protocols. They categorize adversaries regarding on-path, off-path, or insider attacks. However, the authors do not propose any new functionalities that should be added to the NSIS protocols in order to address the remaining security issues.

In subsequent work Tsenov et al. [Tse+05] propose an integrated solution of the Extensible Authentication Protocol (EAP) [RFC3748] with QoS NSLP in order to achieve authentication and authorization capabilities. In this approach, EAP messages are encapsulated into QoS NSLP messages by means of a newly defined EAP_DATA element and exchanged between QoS NSLP entities and policy aware entities. In order to transmit EAP messages reliably between different entities, dedicated messaging associations have to be established. In order to permit a cryptographic binding between EAP and GIST's TLS protection, the authors propose to derive GIST's TLS session key for the secured messaging association from the established EAP session. However, binding of EAP methods to QoS NSLP messages leads to extensive modifications of the existing QoS NSLP state machine and it requires all participating network elements to be aware of this modification. Since the proposed approach relies only on GIST's security mechanisms, it does not provide any integrity protection for the QoS NSLP message. Relying on GIST's security protection only results, however, in the problems already discussed above and does, for instance, not allow for inter-domain wide security protection of NSLP messages. Instead of providing dedicated integrity protection of the NSLP message, the proposed solution rather focuses on providing authentication credentials only by means of EAP. Furthermore, the paper does not closely elaborate error handling and does not discuss re-routing events.

Polito and Schulzrinne [PS07a] propose a token-based approach for call-authorization which relies on a consortium-based trust model between providers. A home provider issues authorization tokens for users which are then shared between service providers following a logical ring structure and are transmitted over dedicated encrypted channels. The tokens contain a digital signature in order to guarantee integrity, data origin, and non-repudiation and are described using the Security Assertion Markup Language (SAML) protocol. The authors also briefly sketch the use of a potential new NSIS signaling application, called remote authorization application which, however, would require the QoS NSLP state machine to be adapted significantly. Since the content of NSLP messages is not included into authenticity checks, there is no binding between the token and the NSLP message content. Furthermore, the approach proposed is relatively heavy-weight since it uses backend communication to policy servers and public-key cryptography for verification of authentication requests.

While most of the signaling protocols discussed above are related to QoS signaling, Felis and Stiemerling [FS07] propose a security solution for the NSIS path-coupled NAT and firewall signaling protocol. The approach is based on a hop-by-hop channel encryption where shared secret keys between any two directly adjacent signaling entities are obtained from a Diffie-Hellman key exchange. In order to protect signaling messages from end-to-end, the signaling initiator generates a dedicated public-private key pair per signaling session and signs all subsequently sent signaling messages accordingly. The Session ID acts as a handle for intermediate signaling entities to correlate signaling messages with a signaling session and is derived by hashing the public key. The public key must be distributed amongst the different signaling entities either in form of a public key infrastructure or must be included into one of the signaling messages itself. Since the signaling initiator digitally signs the entire signaling message, this approach does not allow certain parts of the signaling message to be adapted by intermediate signaling entities. By heavily relying on asymmetric cryptography and its session-orientation, this solution can be considered less scalable and introduces a potentially high overhead. The approach does also not discuss how authorization tokens from policy servers could be used in order to verify signaling service requests.

RFC 5981 specifies an NSIS specific Session Authorization Object that can be used to authenticate and authorize a signaling session [RFC5981]. The design of this Session Authorization Object is closely related to RSVP's POLICY_DATA object. While the solution presented in this dissertation relies on this Session Authorization Object definition, some of its key elements were first introduced in [BR09b] and then incorporated into the resulting Internet standard, such as user- and session-based authentication, fine-grained protection mechanisms, crypto-agility, or a necessary binding between the signaling message and the authorization token. The following section discusses the design decisions that were used to create this object and lead to the necessary extensions and modifications of the originally proposed object format. Section 3.5 then presents the Session Authorization Object.

3.4 Authentic QoS Signaling with NSIS

As already outlined above the NSIS protocol suite provides some basic security mechanisms in order to protect channels between two adjacent signaling entities. In fact, the GIST specification explicitly requires support for Transport Layer Security (TLS) by every NSIS signaling entity. However, whether two NSIS entities actually use a TLS-secured messaging association is open to the participating signaling entities.

Since it is GIST's responsibility to establish and maintain messaging associations, they are only meaningful to directly adjacent NSIS entities and do not provide end-to-end semantics. Figure 3.4 illustrates how NSIS PDUs are exchanged across four signaling entities in case secured messaging associations are only used between some of them.

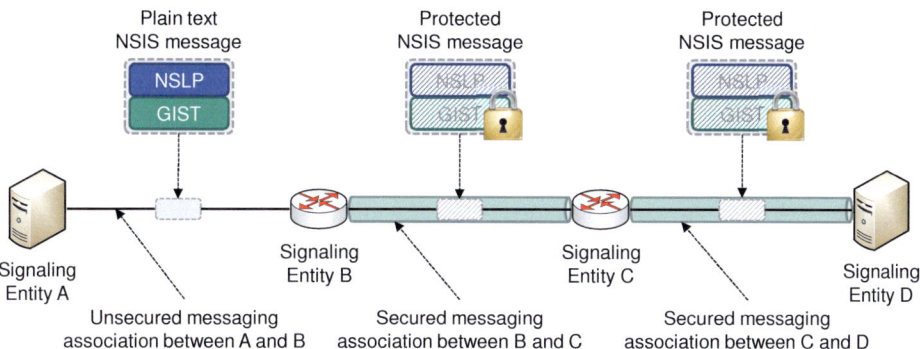

Figure 3.4: *Secured messaging associations between signaling entity B and C, as well as between signaling entity C and D protect NSIS messages along these path segments*

In this case the signaling entities *A* and *B* make no use of a secured messaging association and hence the NSIS PDU is transmitted unprotected between these two entities. The signaling entities *B* and *C*, as well as *C* and *D*, use a secured messaging association between each other. This results in the transmission of encrypted and integrity protected NSIS PDUs between these entities.

This approach has, however, three significant drawbacks in order to realize a secure signaling protocol suite. First, it does not provide user- or session-based authentication mechanisms since all NSIS PDUs between any two adjacent signaling entities are multiplexed across the very same secured messaging association. Second, by relying on a TLS-encrypted channel the integrity protection has no end-to-end semantics and does, furthermore, not allow for a fine-grained integrity protection by always covering the entire signaling message. Finally, a secured messaging association between two signaling entities provides only a GIST peer authorization but does not correlate the protection of the signaling messages to an actual authorization process on application level.

Based on this analysis and the objectives outlined in Section 3.2 the following sections present concepts for authentic signaling which fulfill these requirements:

- User- and session-based authentication mechanisms

- Light-weight integrity protection of signaling messages

- Binding between the authorization information and the signaling message

- Fine-grained protection mechanisms

- Crypto-agility

3.4.1 User- and Session-based Authentication Mechanisms

In order to allow for a policy-based per-session authorization of service requests that are issued due to signaling messages, it is necessary to provide a dedicated *Session Authorization Policy Element*. Usually, a trusted third party, e.g., a AAA server, issues this element which contains information that may be used by a signaling entity to verify a service request's validity and to prove its authenticity.

The channel security offered by GIST is not appropriate, since the protection is not provided on a per-session or per-user level. Instead, all signaling sessions are multiplexed across the same protected channel. Hence, this approach is insufficient for a secure accounting and proper authorization of service requests.

Figure 3.5 illustrates how a signaling protocol can conceptually use a Session Authorization Policy Element. At first, the signaling entity A requests a Session Authorization Policy Element for a given service S_A from a trusted AAA server (step ①). In case the service request is valid and can be granted, the AAA server issues a Session Authorization Policy Element P_A for this particular service request (step ②). After that, signaling entity A can use P_A in order to transmit a signaling message toward signaling entity B (step ③). In this example, the Session Authorization Policy Element is appended to a QoS NSLP signaling message which carries some typical QoS NSLP message objects. Finally, the receiving signaling entity B verifies P_A's validity upon which it processes the information contained in the actual signaling message.

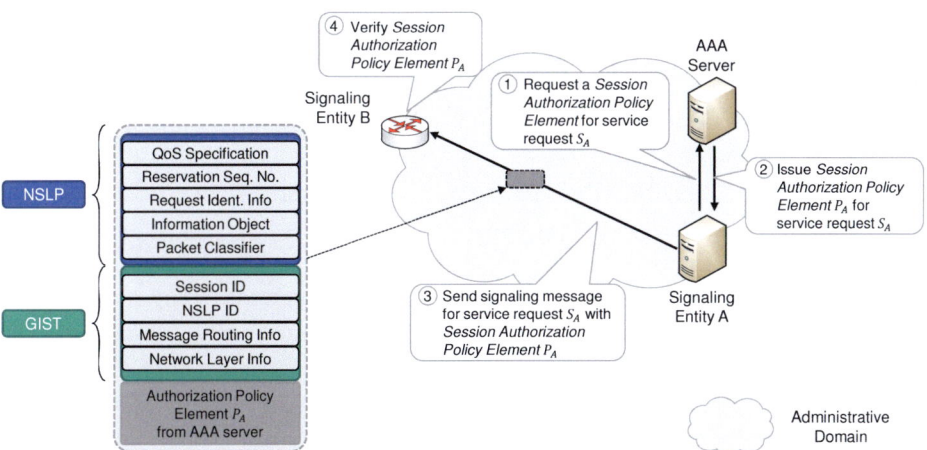

Figure 3.5: *A AAA server issues a Session Authorization Policy Element in order to authenticate and authorize a service request*

3.4.2 Light-weight Integrity Protection of Signaling Messages

One of the most fundamental requirements, as discussed in Section 3.2, is to provide a *light-weight integrity protection* for signaling protocols with respect to computational resources. Since the computational overhead introduced by processing signaling messages should be kept as small as possible, processing costs play an important role regarding the signaling protocol's scalability characteristics. For this reason, additional security mechanisms should not significantly degrade the performance of signaling message processing. Integrity protection of signaling messages can be basically achieved via digital signatures which are based on public-key cryptography or by using a keyed-hashing for message authentication (HMAC) code which is based on shared symmetric keys.

Since the computational overhead imposed by asymmetric cryptography is much higher than by symmetric cryptography, an efficient integrity protection of signaling messages can be achieved much better by using an HMAC based protection as opposed to digital signatures. Therefore, the protection mechanism used for the Session Authorization Object in this dissertation relies on HMACs. Which specific hash algorithm should be used is, however, open to implementations. RFC 4270 describes the use of hash algorithms in network protocols and discusses known attacks [RFC4270]. This document can be used as a guideline in order to decide which algorithm can be considered appropriate for integrity protecting signaling messages.

3.4.3 Binding between the Authorization Information and the Signaling Message Content

In order to allow a signaling application to commit resources as being requested by an incoming service request, the use of these resources must haven been authorized in advance. This can usually be accomplished by means of a dedicated authorization token that was issued by a third party, such as a AAA server. However, if this authorization token is merely an opaque element whose information is not tightly bound to the information contained in the service request itself, the service request may get changed or the authorization token may get misused by an attacker.

Therefore, the authorization token should be cryptographically bound to the information contained in the signaling message. This can be accomplished by means of a digital signature or a message authentication code which is computed over the signaling message's content *and* the authorization token as illustrated in Figure 3.6.

As shown on the left hand side of this example, an opaque authorization token is simply appended to the signaling message without any further protection mechanism and therefore potentially subject to be misused by an attacker. In order to protect the authorization token from being misused, the information contained in the token itself should be coupled with the information contained in the signaling

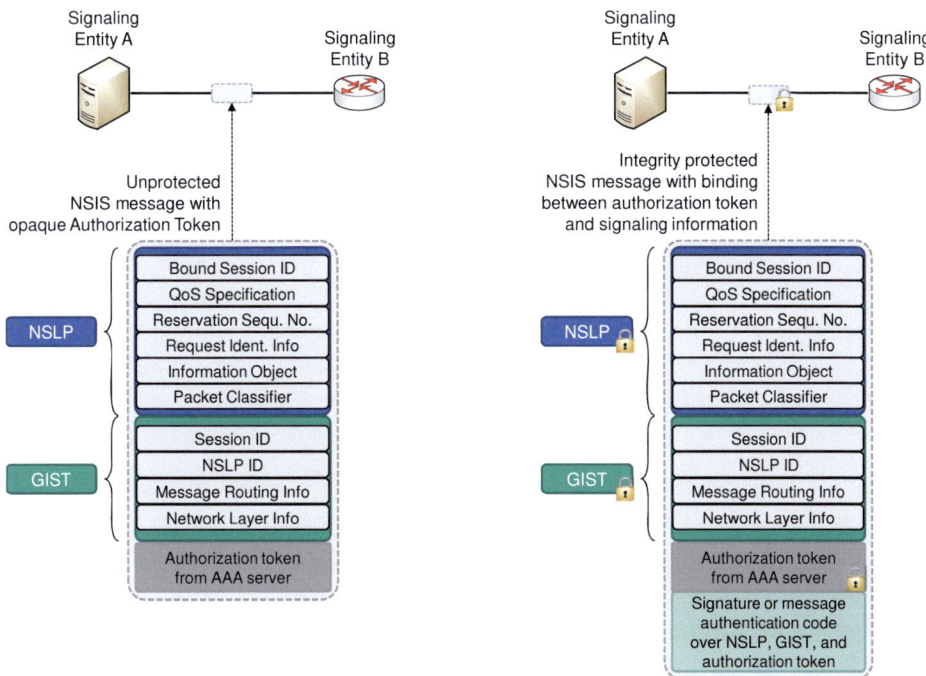

Figure 3.6: *A cryptographic binding between the authorization token and the signaling message's content can be provided if the integrity protection is
computed over the signaling message's content and the authorization
token (as shown on the right)*

message as shown on the right hand side of Figure 3.6. In this example, a digital
signature or a message authentication code is computed over the content of the
signaling message and the authorization token. Since this signature can only be
issued by an authorized entity, such as the owner of the digital signature's private
key, the authorization token cannot be corrupted or misused by an outside attacker.

3.4.4 Fine-grained Protection

Integrity protection of signaling messages is important to protect the information
contained in a signaling message from being manipulated by an unauthorized
entity. However, in some circumstances, intermediate network elements should
be explicitly allowed to modify specific parts of a signaling message. For instance,
consider a signaling message for a resource reservation request where the QoS

parameters, such as the available bandwidth for a reservation, are carried in a dedicated information element. Since this information is subject to differ between distinct signaling entities, it must be collected along the reservation path and hence should also be allowed to be modified by each intermediate signaling entity.

This can be conceptually accomplished by explicitly specifying those elements of a signaling message that are covered by the integrity protection, e.g., in form of a *list of protected information elements*. This list must be determined by the same signaling entity that computes the digital signature or message authentication code. Furthermore, the information elements contained in this list must be uniquely identifiable amongst the information elements contained in the signaling message and the sequential order of these elements must be preserved, so that the receiving signaling entity performs the computation over the identical content.

Figure 3.7 illustrates how a fine-grained security protection for signaling messages can be realized. The left-hand side of the figure shows how an unprotected NSIS signaling message, containing a number of QoS NSLP and GIST objects, is transferred from signaling entity *A* to signaling entity *B*. Since this signaling message is entirely unprotected, its content may get modified by an unauthorized entity. A fine-grained integrity protection of an NSIS signaling message is shown on the right-hand side of this figure.

Different from the example illustrated in Figure 3.6, where the entire NSLP and GIST content of the signaling message is included into the computation of the digital signature, this time only specific parts, such as the QoS Specification object or the Reservation Sequence Number, are included into the digital signature's computation.[1]

While the protection of signaling messages builds an inherent security requirement per se, the protection mechanism itself must be fine-grained enough to allow the specification of distinct parts of a signaling message that should remain modifiable. The presented approach allows for a fine-grained integrity protection of those parts of a signaling message that should not be modified by anyone else than the creator of the message, while still allowing the rest of the message to be modified by intermediate signaling entities.

---

[1]Special rules may apply to the QoS Specification object which should itself only be partially protected. Since specific parts of the QoS Specification object are open to be adapted by intermediate signaling entities, the fine-grained protection should only cover those parts of this object that are not subject to be changed by unauthorized entities.

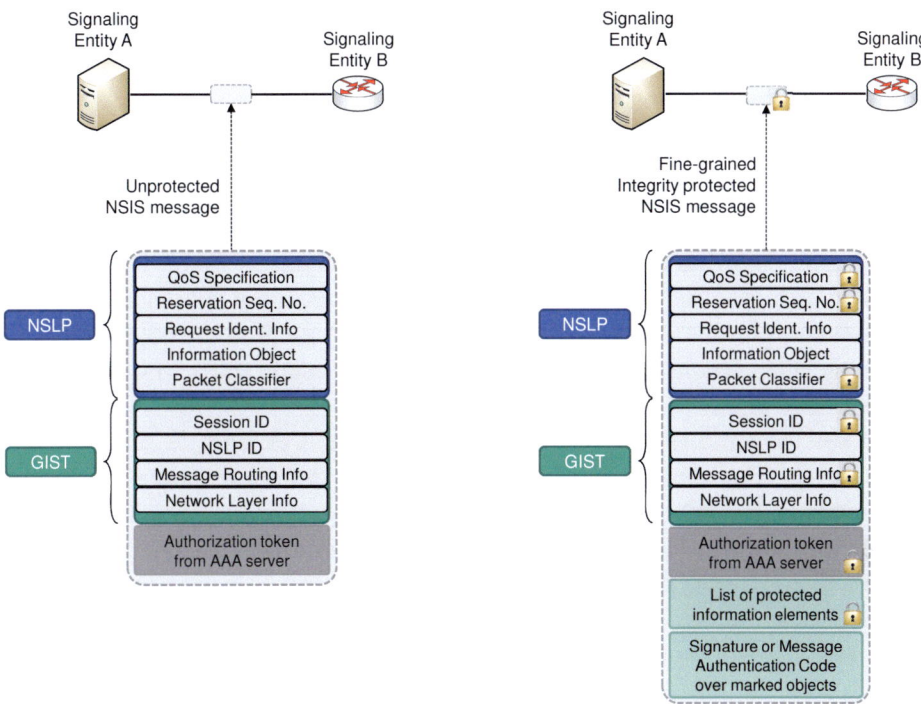

Figure 3.7: *A fine-grained security protection covers only those parts of a signaling messages that are contained in a list of protected information elements*

3.4.5 Crypto-agility

The level of security that can be achieved by a specific security mechanism highly depends on the strength of the cryptographic algorithm and the key lengths being used. The term *crypto-agility* denotes the protocol's ability to adapt to evolving security requirements by applying new cryptographic mechanisms without having to change the protocol specification. For example, in case a signaling message is protected by means of a SHA-1-based HMAC and it is felt that SHA-1 does not provide the needed level of security anymore, crypto-agility provides the flexibility to exchange SHA-1 against a stronger hash function, such as SHA-256.

In order to support crypto-agility for the integrity protection mechanisms outlined above, an identifier for the used hash function should be used. For interoperability reasons this identifier should be chosen from a standardized registry, e.g., IANA's "Transform Type 3 - Integrity Algorithm Transform IDs" of the "Internet Key Exchange Version 2 (IKEv2) Parameters"[2] registry. This dissertation does not provide means to negotiate which cryptographic mechanisms are available to signaling entities at a given moment in time.

3.5 The Session Authorization Object

This section describes the format of a *Session Authorization Object* for the NSIS signaling protocols and proposes extensions that are necessary to fulfill the security requirements presented in Section 3.1. In order to accomplish the objectives for a secure signaling protocol outlined in Section 3.2 this section starts with an analysis of the particular mechanisms that must be applied.

The Session Authorization Object was introduced as an opaque authorization token for signaling sessions within the NSIS protocol suite. It therefore follows the same common object header and attribute notation in a type-length-value (TLV) bit level format as any other NSIS object. The Session Authorization Object starts with an object header as depicted in Figure 3.8.

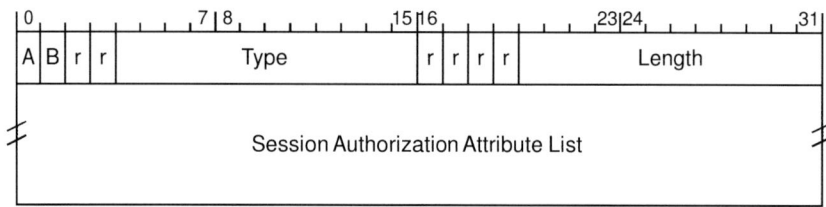

Figure 3.8: *The Session Authorization Object's object header definition*

The Type represents the type of this object and holds the IANA registered value 0x016 (SESSION_AUTH_OBJECT). The Length field specifies the length of the object's Session Authorization Attribute List in 32-bit words. The bits marked with r are reserved for future use, whereas the bits denoted with A and B are extensibility flags that specify how a receiver should act in case it is not aware of this particular object. Possible values are to reject the message and subsequently return an error message (AB=00), to delete and ignore this object (AB=01), to forward the message unchanged (AB=10), or to incorporate the object into the local signaling application state for further refresh or repair messages (AB=11).

---

[2]see http://www.iana.org/assignments/ikev2-parameters/ikev2-parameters.xml

The following Session Authorization Attribute List is a collection of attributes that describe the session and provide further information for verification of service requests. Each of these Session Authorization Attribute objects contains four different fields, namely the length, its type and subtype, and the attribute's specific information, as depicted in Figure 3.9.

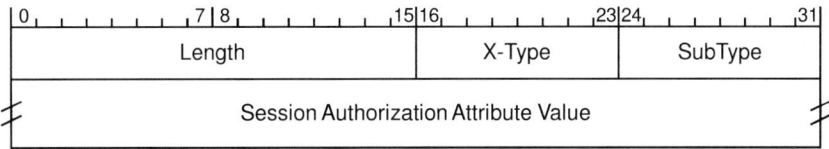

Figure 3.9: *The Session Authorization Object's attribute header definition*

RFC 5981 specifies eight possible attribute types of which two were newly introduced in [BR09b], namely a *Session Identifier* and an *NSLP Object List*. The currently defined attribute types (X-Type) are as follows:

Authorizing Entity Identifier: identifies the authorizing entity that created the Session Authorization Object and authorized the service request. Possible SubTypes include, for instance, an IPv4 or IPv6 address, a fully qualified domain name, or a distinguished name of an X.509 certificate.

Furthermore, a new SubType called HMAC_SIGNED was introduced in [BR09b]. This HMAC subtype indicates that the authentication data attribute (see below) contains a self-signed HMAC signature. In case this attribute is used, the newly introduced NSLP Object List attribute (see below) must also be present. For this subtype the attribute's value contains the algorithm identifier that was used to calculate the HMAC according to the Transform ID from Transform Type 3 of the IKEv2 registry [RFC5996].

Source Address: identifies the source of the signaling session initiator and can contain IPv4 or IPv6 addresses, a list of UDP or TCP ports, or a security parameter index. This information usually corresponds to the flow information contained in the Message Routing Information object.

Destination Address: identifies the destination of the authorized signaling session and can contain the same subtypes as the source address attribute.

Start Time: identifies the start time of the authorized session. This information is important to prevent replay attacks and can be used in order to reject service requests that have not been received within a few seconds. The value currently consists of a 64 bit wide NTP time stamp [RFC5905].

End Time: identifies the end time of the authorized session in order to explicitly limit the time until a service can be used. The value consists of a 64 bit wide NTP time stamp.

Authentication Data: contains the authentication data as being specified by the authorizing entity identifier and must be the last attribute in the attribute list. The authentication data contains the signature over all objects listed in the NSLP Object List.

Session Identifier: used by the authorizing entity to uniquely identify the authorized service request. The information contained in this attribute can help to detect replay attacks or to correlate service requests with specific policy decision entries. This Session Identifier is not to be confused with GIST's session identifier. Since the content of its value is only meaningful to the authorizing entity, no subtypes are specified and the format is implementation specific.

NSLP Object List: contains a list of NSLP objects that should be integrity protected and are therefore included into the keyed-hash computation. In case an NSLP Object List attribute is used for fine-grained integrity protection of NSLP PDUs, an attribute of type Authentication Data must also be present which contains the result of the keyed-hash computation.

The format of an NSLP Object List attribute is illustrated in Figure 3.10. The attribute's X-Type field contains the IANA registered value 0x07 (NSLP_OBJECT_LIST). Since no subtypes are used, the SubType field contains all zeros. After that, the number of signed NSLP objects is specified and then all NSLP objects that are included into the HMAC computation are listed according to their unique NSLP 12-bit object type identifier.

This design allows for a variable length, extensible, and generic form of a fine-grained protection for NSLP signaling messages.

```
0               7 8              15 16            23 24             31
+-------------------------------+-----------------+-----------------+
|            Length             | NSLP Object List|      zero       |
+-------------------------------+--+--+--+--+------------------------+
|   Number of signed NSLP objects = n  |r |r |r |r |  NSLP Object Type (1) |
+--+--+--+--+---------------------------+-----------------------------+
|r |r |r |r |   NSLP Object Type (2)    |            ...              |
+--+--+--+--+---------------------------+-----------------------------+
|r |r |r |r |   NSLP Object Type (n)    |    (padding if required)    |
+--+--+--+--+---------------------------+-----------------------------+
```

Figure 3.10: *The Session Authorization Object's newly introduced NSLP Object List attribute*

3.5.1 Example of a Complete Session Authorization Object

An example of a complete Session Authorization Object that uses a hash-based message authentication code is depicted in Figure 3.11. In this example all Session Authorization attributes are highlighted in color.

The example starts with an authorizing entity identifier of subtype HMAC_SIGNED that indicates that this Session Authorization Object contains a self-signed HMAC signature. The corresponding hash algorithm identifier is specified afterwards. After that, the authorizing entity's 32 bit wide IPv4 source address and the 64 bit wide start time of the authorized session are specified. The fine-grained integrity protection is subsequently provided by means of the NSLP object list which denotes the number of the NSLP objects that are included into the HMAC computation and a list of the corresponding NSLP object types. Finally, the authentication data itself is provided which contains an implementation specific key identifier as well as the actual message authentication code—in this case the HMAC data.

Although the Session Authorization Object supports a variety of different integrity protection mechanisms only the ones based on shared symmetric keys provide a light-weight form of integrity protection. For this reason, this dissertation concentrates on an HMAC-based integrity protection for signaling messages. Note, however, that security mechanisms that are based on shared symmetric keys cannot be used to provide *non-repudiation*, since the originator's service request and the corresponding authentication data can be modified by each entity that shares the same secret.

The shared symmetric keys must, however, be securely distributed in advance. The keys can be exchanged by means of a pre-shared manual installation or, for example, by means of a Kerberos Ticket in a Kerberos-based domain. Since Kerberos is a widely used authentication protocol in today's networks, such as Windows

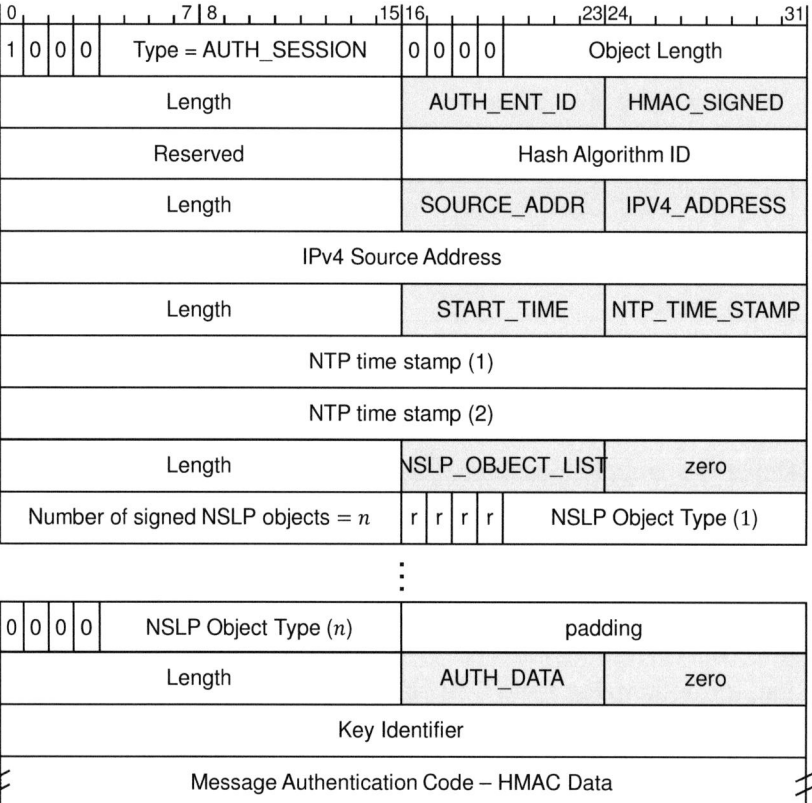

Figure 3.11: *Example of a complete Session Authorization Object containing a hash-based message authentication code*

Domain Controller, the following section conceptually elaborates how the Session Authorization Object can be used in a Kerberos-based domain.

3.6 Using the Session Authorization Object in a Kerberos-based Domain

The *Kerberos Network Authentication Service* [RFC4120] provides a distributed authentication service based on shared symmetric keys. It can be used for a secured mutual authentication service between a client and a server over a non-secured network. Some of the most important functionalities that Kerberos provides is a secure key distribution and a so-called single-sign-on solution. Based on this mechanism a login session is established once a user authenticates itself, which allows the user to gain access to specific resources without being prompted to login again for every single service request at this resource.

3.6.1 The Kerberos Authentication Process

Kerberos relies on a dedicated *Authentication Server* (AS) which maintains a user database and has pre-shared keys with each user. The AS is responsible for generating session keys and distributing these keys to the service requesting user and the requested resources. Therefore, it is not necessary that the user and the resources initially share a key. However, in order to be used by the Kerberos authentication service, the resources in a Kerberos domain must be "kerberized" resources, i.e., share a common secret with the *Ticket Granting Server* (TGS).

The authentication service conceptually consists of three steps. First, a user authenticates itself against an authentication server during an authentication exchange. After being authenticated, the user requests a ticket from a TGS during a ticket granting service exchange. Once the user retrieved the ticket for this particular resource from the TGS, he can access the requested resource.

Figure 3.12 illustrates the authentication process and shows the Kerberos messages that are exchanged between the different entities. The authentication server and the TGS are usually combined by means of one *Key Distribution Center* (KDC).

First of all, the user U initiates an authentication exchange by sending an Authentication Request with the user's identity toward the authentication server. The authentication server replies with an Authentication Response message which holds a session key $Key_{U,TGS}$ for the communication between the user and the TGS, and a *Ticket Granting Ticket* (TGT). The session key $Key_{U,TGS}$ is encrypted with the shared key between the user and the AS:

$$[Key_{U,TGS}]Key_{U,AS}$$

The TGT contains the user's identity U, a validity time, and also the session key $Key_{U,TGS}$. However, the TGT is encrypted with a key that is shared between the TGS and the AS, and can therefore not be extracted by the user:

$$[TGT(U, validity, Key_{U,TGS})]Key_{AS,TGS}$$

In order to gain access to a resource R, the user sends a Ticket Request toward the TGS which holds the encrypted TGT from the AS and an authenticator $Auth(U, t)$

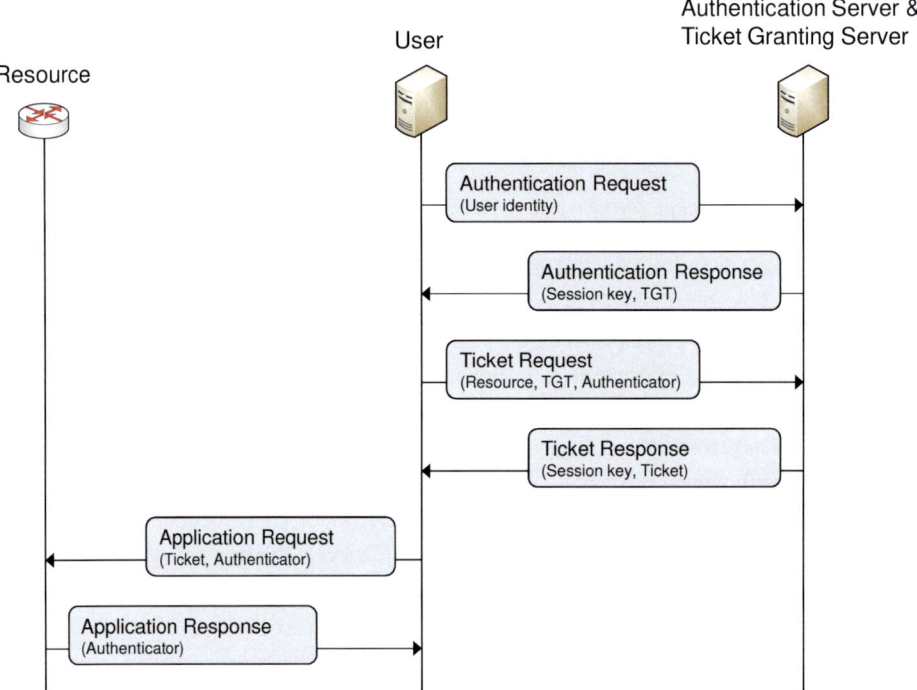

Figure 3.12: *Exemplified data flow using the Kerberos Network Authentication Service (taken from [Ble+05])*

which contains the user's identity U and a time stamp t. This authenticator is encrypted with the session key $Key_{U,TGS}$:

$$[Auth(U,t)]Key_{U,TGS}$$

The TGS replies with a Ticket Response which holds a ticket T for the requested resource and a session key $Key_{U,R}$ that can be used for the communication with the resource. The ticket T is encrypted with a shared secret $Key_{TGS,R}$ between the TGS and the resource and hence, cannot be decrypted by the user. The session key, however, is encrypted with the shared key between the TGS and the user $Key_{U,TGS}$ and hence, can be extracted by the user.

The resource can then be accessed by means of an Application Request message which holds the ticket T and an authenticator $Auth(U,t)$ which is encrypted with the session key $Key_{U,R}$:

$$[Auth(U,t)]Key_{U,R}$$

The resource then verifies the ticket T and extracts the session key $Key_{U,R}$ from the ticket. After that, it can use this session key to verify the encrypted authenticator $Auth(U,t)$ upon which the resource replies with an Application Response and a corresponding authenticator $Auth(R,t)$. This authenticator must then be verified by the user and in case the authenticator is valid, the mutual authentication between the user and the resource is completed.

3.6.2 Integration of the Session Authorization Object in a Kerberos Environment

This section illustrates how the Kerberos authentication service can be used in conjunction with the Session Authorization Object to permit for a user-based authentication of NSIS signaling sessions. In this context, the user acts as an NSLP signaling initiator, whereas the resource is usually an NSLP signaling entity. The NSLP entities are assumed to be kerberized resources, i.e., they have a shared key with the TGS and can therefore decode tickets from the TGS for their own resource or service.

Figure 3.13 gives an overview of an initial signaling session authorization with the Session Authorization Object in a Kerberos-based domain. The procedure consists of five steps of which the first three are based on standard Kerberos upon which in a fourth step QoS NSLP signaling is used:

① The NSLP initiator requests a Kerberos resource ticket T from the TGS. This step corresponds to the Ticket Request in a Kerberos authentication process illustrated in Figure 3.12.

② The TGS replies with a Ticket Response message that contains the Kerberos resource ticket T and a session key $Key_{A,B}$.

③ Since the session key $Key_{A,B}$ is encrypted with the shared key between the user and the TGS it must be decrypted and can then be used for the HMAC computation of HMAC-signed Session Authorization Objects. In order for the session key to be used for subsequent signaling messages it must be stored locally and must be indexed under an implementation specific key identifier. The key identifier can then be transmitted in the Session Authorization Object's Authentication Data (AUTH_DATA) attribute (cf. Figure 3.11).

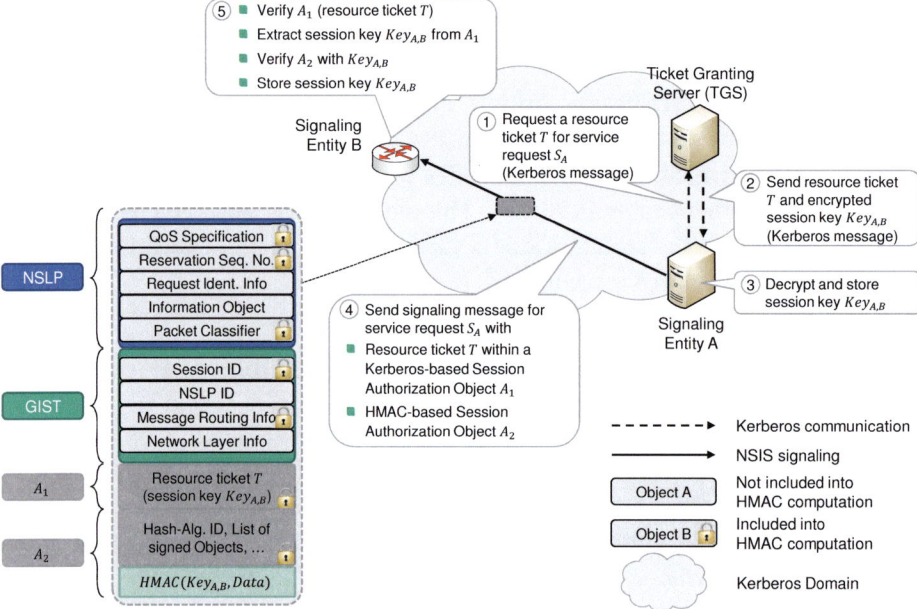

Figure 3.13: *Overview of an initial session authorization with the Session Authorization Object in a Kerberos-based environment*

④ The NSLP initiator sends a signaling message toward its next hop NSLP entity that contains two Session Authorization Objects. The first one, called A_1, carries the Kerberos resource ticket T and therefore implicitly contains the session key $Key_{A,B}$. The authorizing entity identifier of A_1 is set to `KRB_PRINCIPAL` as depicted in Figure 3.14. The second one, called A_2 is a Session Authorization Object that contains the HMAC of signed NSLP objects and has an authorizing entity identifier of type `HMAC_SIGNED`.

⑤ Once the NSLP signaling message reaches an NSLP entity, the Kerberos resource ticket T from Session Authorization Object A_1 is verified and the session key $Key_{A,B}$ is extracted from T. After that, $Key_{A,B}$ can be used to verify the integrity of A_2. The session key is then also stored locally for any further signaling requests.

Figure 3.14 shows the object format of the Session Authorization Object that contains a Kerberos resource ticket. In this case the authorizing entity identifier is of type `KRB_PRINCIPAL` and contains the Kerberos principal name of the authorizing entity. The resource ticket T is then transparently included into the authentication data together with a key identifier, that is used as a key index for the exchanged and locally stored session key.

Integrating the Kerberos ticket into an NSLP signaling message by means of the Session Authorization Object proves especially useful in order to avoid an additional exchange of Kerberos messages between the signaling entities. By relying on this dedicated Kerberos-based Session Authorization Object the session key for the keyed hash algorithm can be securely exchanged between the different signaling entities.

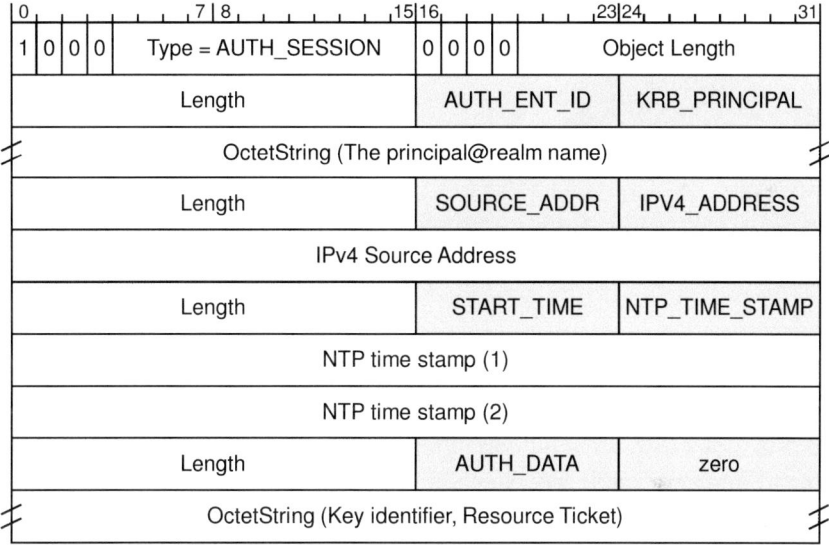

Figure 3.14: *An exemplified Session Authorization Object for a Kerberos ticket*

For subsequent signaling between the signaling initiator A and the signaling entity B of Figure 3.13 it is not necessary to request another Kerberos resource ticket. Instead, according to the Kerberos single sign-on principle the signaling initiator A and the signaling entity B both locally store the session key $Key_{A,B}$ in order to use it for subsequently secured communication as depicted in Figure 3.15.

In this example, the signaling entity A uses a formerly extracted session key $Key_{A,B}$ to send a signaling message with an HMAC-based Session Authorization Object toward signaling entity B. The session key can even be changed seamlessly at any time by simply sending a new Kerberos resource ticket toward signaling entity B.

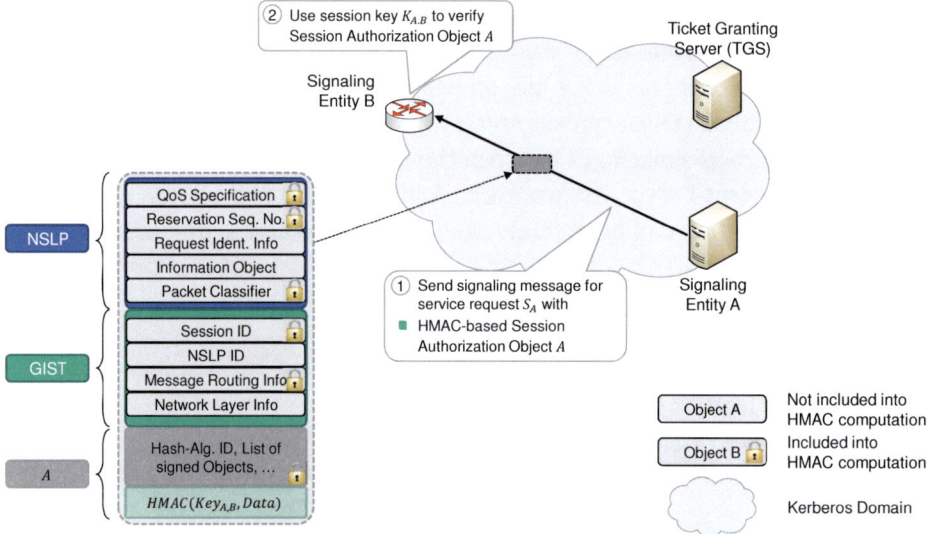

Figure 3.15: *Overview of a subsequent session authorization request with the Session Authorization Object in a Kerberos-based environment*

In this case, the new key can be used at any point in time later by simply changing the key identifier in the HMAC signed object.

This provides a *user-based authorization* where a shared key does not have to be exchanged for every single new signaling session or flow. Instead, one session key can be used for a secured communication between two signaling entities across multiple signaling sessions. Furthermore, this session key is also available for integrity protecting signaling messages in the opposite direction.

3.7 Implementation

The Session Authorization Object was prototypically implemented for the NSIS-ka suite [Ble+12a] by Akbaba [Akb09]. This section describes how an HMAC-based Session Authorization Object is created by a signaling initiator, how it is verified by a receiver, and presents the design of a so-called TLP_List data structure that is used to improve the performance of the creation and verification process.

3.7.1 The `TLP_List` Data Structure

The most important design decisions regarding the implementation of the Session Authorization Object are concerned with the logical placement of a Session Authorization Object module and good performance characteristics, i.e., mechanisms that induce low computational overhead.

According to the Internet standard [RFC5981] the Session Authorization Object belongs logically to the NSLP layer and is therefore also specified as an NSLP object. However, as already outlined above, the signaling message's integrity protection should cover a specified set of NSLP and NTLP objects. Since the content of the NTLP layer's objects cannot be known by the NSLP layer in advance once a signaling message is created, the actual calculation of the signaling message's authentication code must be deferred until the byte stream of the NSLP and the NTLP layer is complete. On the other hand, in case an integrity protected signaling message is received from the network, the authentication code's verification process should happen as soon as possible in order to avoid unnecessary resource consumption from parsing and decoding message objects, updating state machines, routing tables and session contexts, even though the signaling message's signature was finally considered to be invalid.

Therefore, a dedicated data structure was introduced into the NSIS-ka's Protocol Library which allows an efficient access to all NSLP and NTLP message objects at an early stage. This *Type-Length-Position* data structure, called `TLP_List`, holds a list of all NSIS objects in the message byte stream which contains the object's type, its length, and its position in the `NetMsg` buffer. Since all NSIS message objects share a common header format that follows a *Type-Length-Value* (TLV) structure, creating the `TLP_List` is quite convenient. The `TLP_List` is implemented as a hash map (`std::unordered_map`) which uses the NSIS object's unique `Type` and `SubType` values as its key. The key points to a linked list data structure, where the object's positions are stored relative to the `NetMsg`'s buffer begin. This hash table can then be used for unifying the `NSLP_OBJ_LIST` in order to retrieve all objects which are included into the message authentication code's calculation in $O(1)$ instead of in $O(n)$ in case the entire `NetMsg` buffer would have to be parsed again.

The `TLP_List` is also used in case an NSIS signaling message is created. In this case the position of the NSLP and NTLP objects in the `NetMsg` buffer is stored in the data structure once an object is serialized. This prevents from re-iterating over the entire message buffer at the very end in order to collect all NSIS message objects that are specified in the `NSLP_OBJ_LIST`. Instead, this information can then directly by retrieved through the `TLP_List` again in constant time.

Figure 3.16 exemplifies how the `TLP_List` data structure is used to calculate the HMAC over specific objects of an NSIS signaling message. In this example a `NetMsg` buffer contains the serialized byte stream of the NTLP and the NSLP PDUs with their respective signaling message objects. A hexadecimal number indicates each object's position in the `NetMsg` buffer, e.g., `0x0013` for the Session ID. For each object a dedicated entry is inserted into the `TLP_List`'s hash table. The object's unique 16 bit wide type and subtype fields, as specified by IANA's registry, are concatenated to a 32 bit wide value that serves as key, e.g., `0x00010004` for GIST's Session ID. The corresponding value is a list that contains the object's length (e.g., 20 bytes in case of the Session ID) and the aforementioned position in the `NetMsg` buffer.

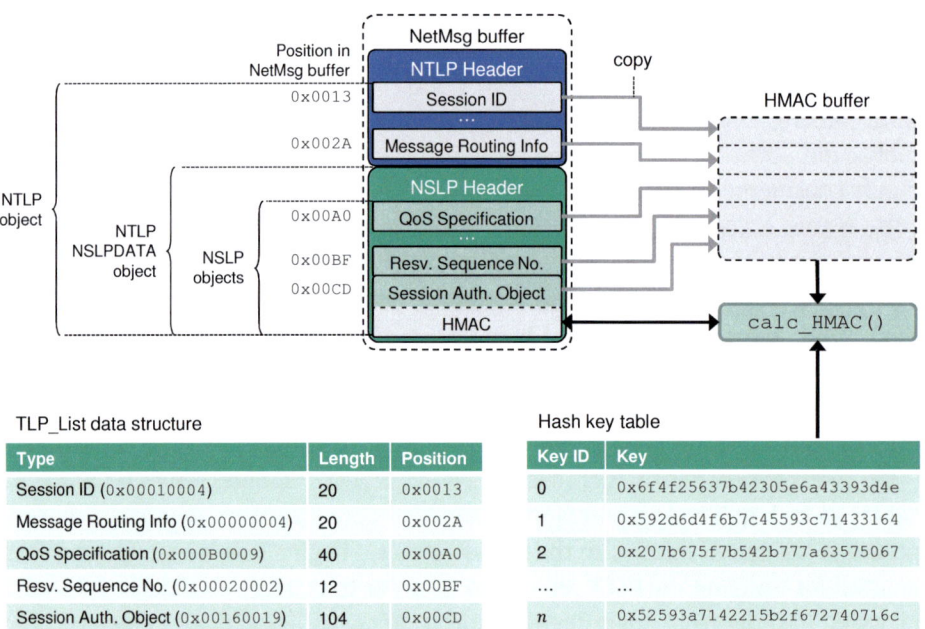

Figure 3.16: *Exemplified usage of the TLP_List data structure*

With this data structure, the positions of all those objects that must be integrity protected, can now be easily retrieved from the `TLP_List` without having to reiterate over all NSLP objects. The content of each of those objects is then copied into a temporary HMAC buffer, upon which the HMAC can be calculated by means of a `calc_HMAC()` function. This copy is necessary to obtain a continuous byte stream on which the HMAC calculation can be performed. The `calc_HMAC()` function uses the HMAC buffer and the necessary cryptographic key from its hash key table as input parameters. Depending on whether this is used for the creation or the verification of an integrity protected signaling message, the calculated HMAC value is stored in the Session Authorization Object's corresponding HMAC field or is compared to the value in such a field.

In case more than one Session Authorization Object is used within one NSIS signaling message, the `TLP_List` proves again to be very efficient, since the `TLP_List`'s content can be used by all Session Authorization Objects in order to access specific signaling objects in the `NetMsg` buffer.

3.7.2 HMAC-based Session Authorization Object Creation

The creation of an HMAC-based Session Authorization Object is depicted in Figure 3.17 and works as follows:

① An external signaling application triggers a signaling request toward the NSIS-ka instance which is conceptually separated into an NSLP and an NTLP layer, according to the NSIS framework. This request is passed as an application message (of type `QoS_Appl_Msg`) toward the NSLP `ProcessingModule` which triggers and reacts on events and processes internal messages. In this case, the `ProcessingModule` analyzes the signaling application's request and creates C++ objects for the corresponding NSIS signaling message and all of its signaling message objects. An internal signaling message of type `SignalingMsg` is used as a container for these C++ objects.

② Since the signaling message should be protected by means of a Session Authorization Object, the `Session Authorization Object` module is used to create a corresponding C++ object for the NSIS signaling message.

③ The internal signaling message of type `SignalingMsg` is then passed via an internal message queue to the NSLP's `StateModule`. The `StateModule`'s responsibility is to implement the NSLP protocol logic and state machine, and to create and manage the signaling session's context. In this case a new session context is established, lifetime and retransmission timers are started, and the NSLP PDU is finally serialized from the C++ objects into byte code by means of a `NetMsg` buffer as container.

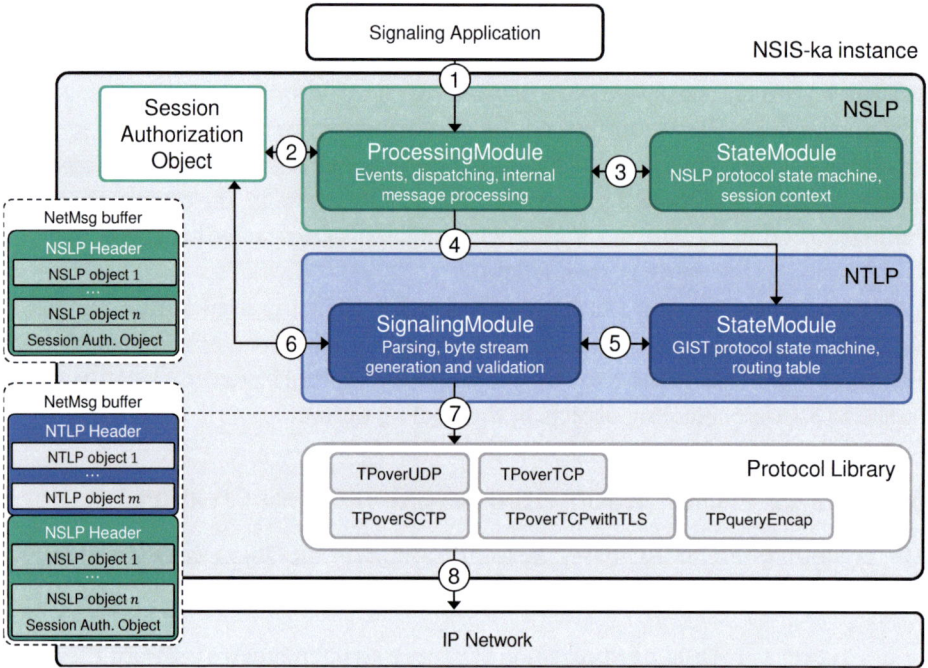

Figure 3.17: *Serialization process of an NSIS PDU with a Session Authorization Object in the NSIS-ka suite*

④ Once the serialized NSLP PDU was returned to the NSLP `ProcessingModule`, the PDU is passed via the GIST API and a corresponding internal message of type `APIMsg` to the NTLP layer. The NTLP layer's `StateModule` receives the serialized NSLP PDU from the NSLP layer. The `StateModule` implements GIST's protocol logic and state machine, manages GIST's routing table and corresponding timers. According to the signaling application's request and the NSLP PDU, the `StateModule` checks, whether routing state is already established, creates C++ objects for the GIST PDU objects and constructs the GIST PDU accordingly.

⑤ The C++ objects of this GIST PDU are encapsulated into an internal signaling message of type `SignalingMsg` and passed toward GIST's `SignalingModule`. This module is responsible for the serialization of C++ objects into a byte stream and further message exchange with underlying transport modules.

⑥ In case a Session Authorization Object is used, it is necessary that the HMAC is calculated over the specified NSLP and NTLP objects. Therefore, it is the SignalingModule's responsibility to create the corresponding HMAC by means of the Session Authorization Object module's `calc_HMAC()` function after every single object of the entire NSIS PDU was serialized.

⑦ Once the HMAC was inserted into the serialized NSIS PDU the `NetMsg` buffer is passed as an internal signaling message of type `TPMsg` to the Protocol Library's transport modules. These transport modules provide a generic interface that can be used to create and manage underlying network connections according to the signaling protocol's needs.

⑧ Finally, the NSIS signaling message is passed to the IP network.

Since the HMAC must cover a set of NSLP and NTLP objects, its calculation must be deferred until all those objects are finally serialized. Hence, even though the Session Authorization Object is logically part of the NSLP layer, the `calc_HMAC()` function must be called from the NTLP layer just before the serialized NSIS PDU is passed to the network.

3.7.3 HMAC-based Session Authorization Object Verification

The verification of an HMAC-based Session Authorization Object is depicted in Figure 3.18 and works as follows:

① The Protocol Library's transport modules receive a signaling message from the IP network. The byte stream is stored in a `NetMsg` buffer and a `TLP_list` is created accordingly. This happens in the transport module of the corresponding transport connection, e.g., TPoverUDP in case the signaling message was transmitted over UDP.

② The transport module, e.g., TPQueryEncap, passes the byte stream to the GIST SignalingModule. Before every single object is deserialized from the `NetMsg` buffer, the `TLP_List` data structure is used to check whether the NSIS signaling message contains a Session Authorization Object, at all.

③ In case a Session Authorization Object is in place, which has an `AUTH_ENT_ID` attribute of type `HMAC_SIGNED` and an NSLP object list attribute, the corresponding PDU objects are copied into a temporary buffer (cf. Section 3.16) upon which the HMAC is calculated by means of the Session Authorization

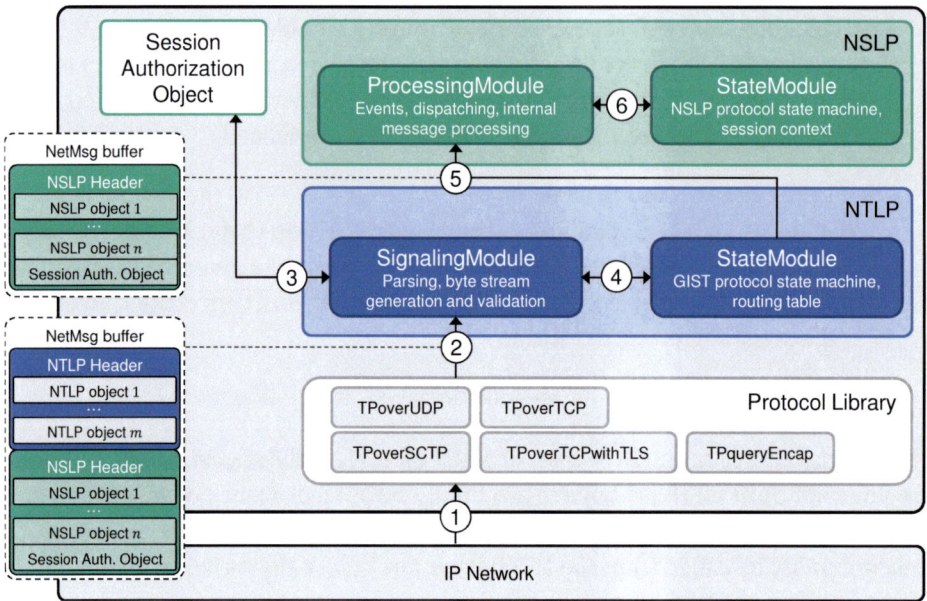

Figure 3.18: *Deserialization process of an NSIS PDU an verification of a Session Authorization Object in the NSIS-ka suite*

Object module's `calc_HMAC()` function. The result is compared with the value contained in the Session Authorization Object's `AUTH_DATA` attribute. GIST's `SignalingModule` will continue with the deserialization process only, if the HMAC verification was successful. This allows a signaling message to be discarded as soon as possible in case its signature is invalid.

④ After the `SignalingModule` completed the deserialization of the NSIS PDU's NTLP objects, the corresponding C++ objects are passed toward GIST's `State-Module`. The `StateModule` updates the routing table, session-specific timers, and processes the signaling message according to its current state in the protocol state machine.

⑤ The NTLP payload is then passed toward the registered NSLP instance by means of an `APIMsg` which contains a `NetMsg` buffer that is filled with the serialized NSLP objects. Once the NSLP `ProcessingModule` receives this internal signaling message, its content gets deserialized into NSLP C++ objects.

⑥ Finally, the C++ objects are passed toward NSLP's StateModule by means of a SignalingMsg upon which the NSLP protocol state machine and session context is updated.

3.8 Evaluation

This section provides an evaluation of the signaling performance and associated costs of the Session Authorization Object's integrity protection. The evaluation aims at demonstrating that the processing overhead imposed by the session authorization mechanisms is small compared to the already existing time required to establish a resource reservation from end to end.

The topology used for the evaluations consisted of three signaling entities as illustrated in Figure 3.19. Whenever the Session Authorization Object had to be used, the NSIS signaling initiator created a Session Authorization Object which integrity protected specific parts of the RESERVE signaling message by means of an HMAC. The intermediate NSIS signaling entity participated in the NSIS signaling message processing, but did not interpret the Session Authorization Object. This was done in order to simulate an end-to-end protection that still permits intermediate signaling entities to actively participate in the signaling session. At the NSIS signaling responder the integrity of the incoming RESERVE message was finally verified upon which an integrity protected RESPONSE message was returned.

As illustrated in Figure 3.19 the NSIS signaling for a resource reservation request consists of a GIST three-way handshake between each directly adjacent signaling entities in order to set up signaling routing state for the signaling session. This is subsequently followed by a GIST DATA message carrying a QoS NSLP RESERVE message. Once the final signaling destination of this signaling request has been reached, the NSIS signaling responder replies with a QoS NSLP RESPONSE message which is forwarded back to the initiator of the original request.

In case a signaling session has to be torn down, the NSIS signaling initiator sends a tearing RESERVE toward the NSIS signaling responder upon which a subsequent tearing RESPONSE tears down signaling routing state for this particular session on each of the involved signaling entities. In this case, no additional GIST three-way handshake has to be performed, since signaling routing state for this signaling session has already been established.

The time required to establish a resource reservation, d_{setup}, consists of the following components: the parameter o which denotes the time required between

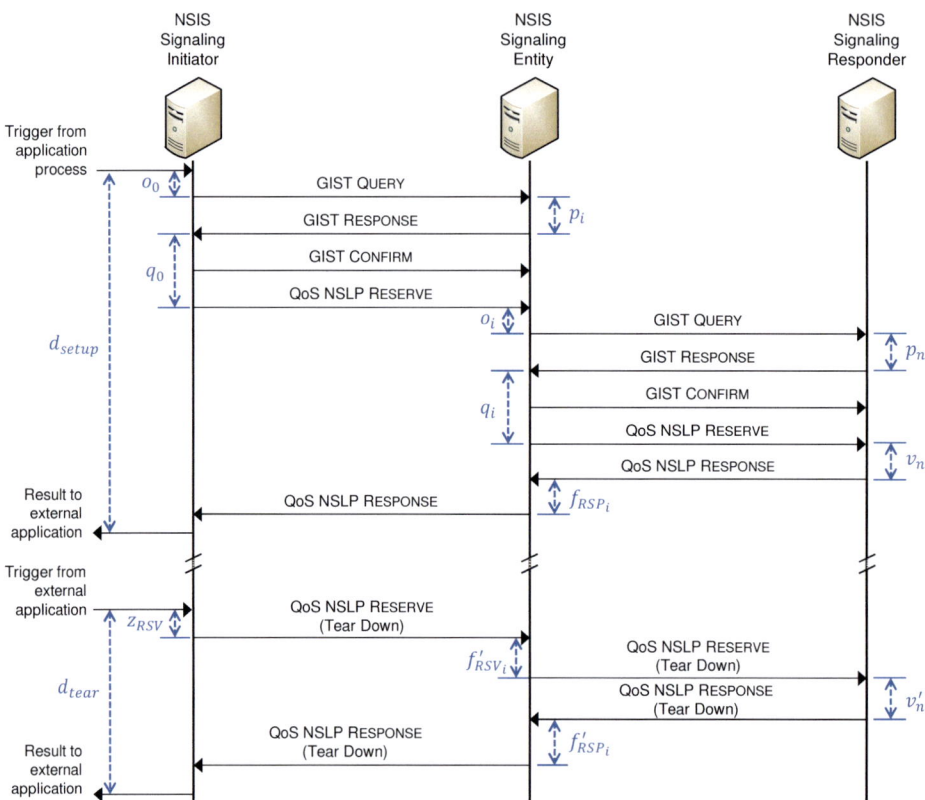

Figure 3.19: *Message sequence diagram of the evaluation scenario*

receiving an incoming trigger and sending a subsequent GIST QUERY message.[3] The
parameter p denotes the time required on a signaling entity to reply to an incoming
GIST QUERY with a subsequent GIST RESPONSE, the parameter q denotes the time
required between receiving a GIST RESPONSE message and sending a QoS NSLP
RESERVE, the parameter v corresponds to the time required between receiving an incoming QoS NSLP RESERVE and replying with a corresponding QoS NSLP RESPONSE,
and the time f_{RSP} is required for forwarding a QoS NSLP RESPONSE message on each
intermediate signaling entity. Furthermore, each signaling message transmitted
over the wire requires an additional propagation delay t_i with $t_i = \frac{1}{2}\text{RTT}_i$.

---

[3]Note, that the NSIS-ka implementation uses an external application process for the initial
reservation request o_0 which is passed toward the NSIS-ka instance over a UNIX Domain Socket
interface.

Given this set of parameters, the total duration for establishing a resource reservation across n signaling hops (i.e., for $n+1$ signaling entities) can be expressed by equation 3.1:

$$d_{setup} = \left(\sum_{i=1}^{n} o_i + p_i + q_i + \frac{3}{2}\text{RTT}_i \right) + v + \frac{1}{2}\text{RTT} + \left(\sum_{i=1}^{n-1} f_{RSP_i} + \frac{1}{2}\text{RTT}_i \right) \quad (3.1)$$

Equation 3.2 estimates the time required to tear down a reservation. In this case parameter z_{RSV} is used to denote the time required between the initial trigger and the outgoing QoS NSLP tearing RESERVE message. The parameter v' is used to denote the time required between receiving a tearing RESERVE and replying with a QoS NSLP RESPONSE, and the parameters f'_{RSV} and f'_{RSP} are used to denote the time required to forward a tearing RESERVE or forward a corresponding QoS NSLP RESPONSE, respectively.

$$d_{tear} = z_{RSV} + \text{RTT} + v' + \left(\sum_{i=1}^{n-1} f'_{RSV} + f'_{RSP} + \text{RTT}_i \right) \quad (3.2)$$

A router testbed was used to perform measurement-based evaluations. The testbed consisted of three standard PCs which acted as signaling entities and were equipped with the same hardware and software.[4] The round trip time between any two signaling entities averaged to 0.24 ms. The evaluation consisted of 100 distinct measurements where a resource reservation was established and two seconds later torn down by means of a tearing reservation request. The measurements were then repeated with the use of the Session Authorization Object.

Figure 3.20 shows the measurement results for the time required to establish and subsequently tear down a QoS NSLP signaling session with and without using a Session Authorization Object. The measured values correspond to the total signaling duration d_{setup} and d_{tear} and therefore include the creation and communication of the request from the application process toward the NSIS instance of the NSIS the signaling initiator.

---

[4]Each signaling entity was equipped with an Intel Xeon X3430 quad-core CPU running at 2.40 GHz, 4 GB RAM, and Intel 82580 Gigabit Ethernet network interfaces which were interconnected by a Cisco Catalyst switch 6500 running CatOS. All signaling entities used an Ubuntu 10.10 server installation with a Linux 2.6.35 kernel and an instance of the NSIS-ka implementation at revision 6443.

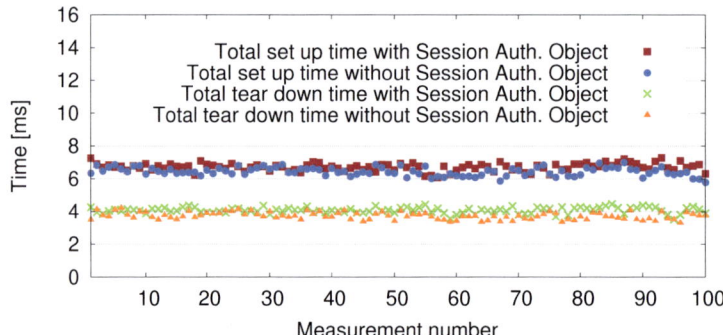

Figure 3.20: *Signaling cost comparison of a QoS NSLP reservation request with and without using a Session Authorization Object*

The time required to establish a signaling session across three signaling entities in this setup accounts for 6.72 ms on average when a Session Authorization Object is used as opposed to 6.43 ms on average when no Session Authorization Object is used. In case a tearing reservation request is protected by means of a Session Authorization Object, the entire signaling time accounts for 4.09 ms on average, as opposed to 3.71 ms when no Session Authorization Object is used.

The Session Authorization Object therefore accounts for an overhead of approximately 4.5% for establishing a signaling session and 10.2% for tearing down a reservation request in this particular setup. Table 3.1 summarizes the message sizes of RESERVE and RESPONSE messages with and without a Session Authorization Object. Since the RESERVE's and RESPONSE's message sizes for tear down requests are smaller than the ones for a setup request, an additionally used Session Authorization Object imposes relatively more overhead for tear down requests.

Table 3.2 summarizes the processing times obtained in the testbed based measurements, according to the parameters introduced in Figure 3.19. From these measurement numbers can be derived, that the overhead imposed by the Session Authorization Object is relatively small. Note, that this overhead factor only affects the signaling message's processing times. That is, the round trip times are not affected by the Session Authorization Object and especially in Internet-like scenarios the round trip times can be expected to be significantly larger than in this testbed scenario. Therefore, the percentage of the total signaling time that can be attributed to the use of the Session Authorization Object depends fundamentally on the number of involved signaling entities and the round trip times between each adjacent signaling entities.

Signaling message	with Session Auth. Object	without Session Auth. Object	size of Session Auth. Object
RESERVE	260 Byte	160 Byte	100 Byte
Tearing RESERVE	216 Byte	112 Byte	100 Byte
RESPONSE	216 Byte	148 Byte	68 Byte
Tearing RESPONSE	212 Byte	144 Byte	68 Byte

Table 3.1: *Different message sizes for* RESERVE *and* RESPONSE *messages with and without an additional Session Authorization Object*

Definition	Symbol	w/o session authorization	with session authorization
Time between incoming trigger and outgoing GIST QUERY	o	1.08	1.12
Time between incoming GIST QUERY and outgoing GIST RESPONSE	p	0.54	0.55
Time between incoming GIST RESPONSE and outgoing QoS NSLP RESERVE	q	0.44	0.43
Time between incoming QoS NSLP RESERVE and outgoing QoS NSLP RESPONSE	v	0.87	0.93
Time between incoming QoS NSLP RESERVE (Tear) and outgoing QoS NSLP RESPONSE	v'	0.75	0.88
Processing time to forward a QoS NSLP RESPONSE message	f_{RSP}	0.65	0.69
Processing time to forward a QoS NSLP RESERVE (Tear) message	f'_{RSP}	0.77	0.81
Processing time to forward a QoS NSLP RESPONSE (Tear) message	f'_{RSP}	0.72	0.74
Total reservation setup duration	d_{setup}	6.43	6.72
Total reservation tear down duration	d_{tear}	3.71	4.09

Table 3.2: *Average time in milliseconds for the establishment and the removal of a resource reservation of 100 measurements with and without the use of a Session Authorization Object*

Since the Session Authorization Object provides an integrity protection of the signaling message by means of an HMAC, it is important to evaluate the costs that are associated with the creation and verification of the HMAC itself. Table 3.3 summarizes the evaluation results from fine-grained internal measurement benchmarks and Figure 3.21 illustrates the results.[5]

	Avg [μs]	Min [μs]	Max [μs]	StdDev [μs]
HMAC creation (Initiator)	26.2	18.2	72.8	7.1
HMAC creation (Responder)	24.5	21.1	31.5	1.7
HMAC verification (Initiator)	24.2	19.6	73.0	5.2
HMAC verification (Responder)	24.3	21.7	50.5	3.6

Table 3.3: *Evaluation results for HMAC generation and verification for 100 runs*

Since the HMAC is based on symmetric cryptography the times needed for the creation of an HMAC should conceptually not differ from the times needed for the verification of an HMAC. This is the case for the measurements of this evaluation where the creation and the verification of the HMAC accounts for approximately $25\,\mu s$ on average. The HMAC creation and verification presented in this evaluation also contain the creation of the TLP_List, deserialization and decoding of the Session Authorization Object and finally the cryptographic HMAC calculation itself.

Compared to the times needed for the processing of the signaling messages itself, the HMAC computation can be considered negligible and therefore provides a viable way to integrity-protect signaling messages.

3.9 Conclusion

This chapter developed concepts for secure and authentic signaling. The solution achieves the following objectives: signaling entities along a data path are always able to interpret protected signaling messages. This is a necessary precondition for network layer signaling protocols where intermediate signaling entities must be able to interpret a signaling message's content. The concepts provide a *fine-grained*

---

[5]SHA1 was used as cryptographic algorithm for the HMAC and the OpenSSL library (version 0.9.8o) was used for the calculation of the HMACs.

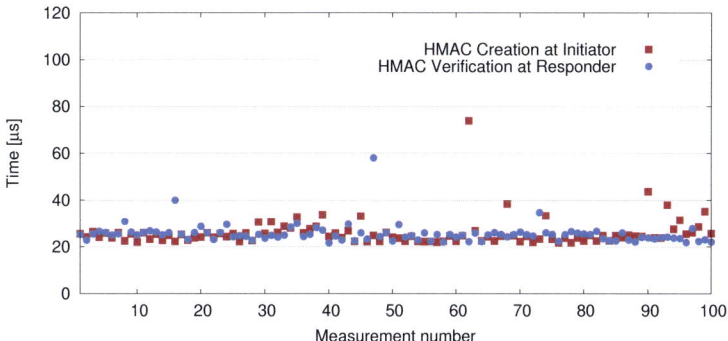

Figure 3.21: *Measurement results for the HMAC creation and verification at the signaling initiator and responder*

authentication mechanism which allows to integrity-protect pre-defined parts of a signaling message, while the remaining parts are still modifiable by intermediate signaling entities. The developed concepts rely on a *user-based* authentication mechanism where a signaling message's protection refers to a user. This allows for good *scalability* properties, since cryptographic keys are used on the granularity of signaling users, rather than on single signaling sessions. The proposed concepts ensure that the authorization information is tightly coupled with the corresponding signaling message in order to prevent authorization information from being used by an unauthorized entity. Furthermore, the concept focuses on the use of security mechanisms that allow for a *light-weight* integrity protection of signaling messages by relying on an HMAC-based protection. Finally, the security concepts outlined allow for *cryptographic agility*, such that cryptographic algorithms can be dynamically exchanged during a signaling session's lifetime.

## Chapter 4

QoS Signaling Support
for Mobile Users

Internet services are nowadays accessed more and more via mobile devices. In order to allow established resource reservations to be automatically adapted to the current mobile user's location, the QoS signaling protocol must be prepared for being used in mobile environments.

This chapter analyzes challenges that arise when resource reservations are used by mobile users in IP-based networks. It sets requirements for mobility-aware QoS signaling and proposes a set of design principles. Since mobility in IP-based networks is nowadays usually accomplished by means of dedicated mobility management protocols, Section 4.4 elaborates how QoS signaling can be used in conjunction with Mobile IPv6. In order to allow for seamless handovers of resource reservations, Section 4.5 provides the design of an anticipated handover signaling mechanism for QoS signaling sessions.

4.1 Problem Statement and Requirements

The use of mobile devices allows users to dynamically change their location and therefore switch between different points of attachment. However, in case a resource reservation has been established from the mobile device's previous location, this reservation will not be automatically adapted to the mobile device's new location. Hence, the mobile user cannot use its previously established resource reservation anymore.

After changing to a new point of attachment a *Mobile Node* (MN) would therefore have to establish an entirely new reservation. However, this cannot be considered an adequate solution since it leads to a number of subsequent problems. First, for each additional reservation request the user may also get accounted additionally. This imposes unnecessary costs since the user can only use one resource reservation at a time. Second, an additional reservation request can also be rejected if the user already reserved its maximum amount of resources with its previous reservation request. Therefore, an already established reservation should rather be adapted to the MN's new location instead of establishing an additional reservation.

Figure 4.1 illustrates a mobility scenario for a QoS signaling session. In this scenario a MN is attached to an Access Router, called AR_O, and has a resource reservation established toward a *Correspondent Node* (CN) along a corresponding data path, denoted *old data path* in Figure 4.1. At that time, the QoS signaling session consists of a single signaling flow, denoted *old signaling flow*.

In case the MN changes its point of attachment from the old access router AR_O toward a new access router AR_N, the data path from the MN toward the CN also changes. Hence, in order to provide the MN with QoS guarantees also along the new data path, the QoS signaling protocol is responsible to adapt the resource reservation accordingly, i.e., a *new signaling flow* must be subsequently established along the *new data path* which belongs to the same *signaling session*. Once this new signaling flow was successfully established, the signaling session comprises two signaling flows, the new and the old one. Both signaling flows cross each other eventually at a so-called *Crossover Node* (CRN). Depending on the resource availability at the new access router and along the new data path, it may then also be necessary to adapt the reservation along the path segment between the CRN and the CN.

In order to allow signaling applications in IP-based networks to be used by mobile users, the following set of requirements must be met by a modern signaling protocol suite:

- *Interaction with Mobility Management Protocols*

  Mobility in IP-based networks is usually accomplished by means of a dedicated mobility management protocol, such as Mobile IPv6 in order to transparently retain the data connectivity for transport protocols and applications. A signaling protocol should therefore be able to interact with an existing mobility management protocol. In particular, it should be aware of and actively react on any changes that affect the data path between the MN and the CN.

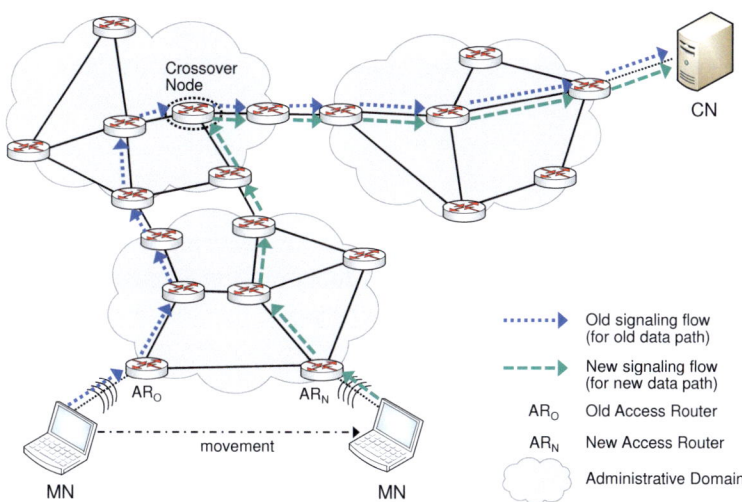

Figure 4.1: *Signaling scenario for a mobile user where a signaling session comprises an old and a new signaling flow*

- *Anticipated QoS Signaling*

  A QoS signaling protocol should provide means for anticipated signaling along an anticipated data path. Most of the existing approaches where signaling is used in mobile environments are usually based on a *hard handover* where the resource reservation is adapted to the new data path after the MN changed its location. However, it is desirable for users to have a resource reservation been established for a newly, anticipated data path just before they actually change their point of attachment. This allows users to use QoS seamlessly and without intervals of interruptions of the signaling session when being mobile.

  Furthermore, additional requirements that should be fulfilled by a QoS signaling solution are the following: the signaling protocol should rely on a decentralized session management in order to operate independently of a centralized management entity. Resource reservations should work from end-to-end across multiple administrative domains, rather than being based on "micro-mobility" QoS solutions which are only meaningful within the MN's current access network. The QoS signaling protocol should provide support for sender- and receiver-initiated reservations in order to be more flexible to the user's needs. Furthermore, once a handover has been performed, resources along the obsolete path should be released as soon as possible in order to reduce reservation blocking for new reservation requests.

4.2 Related Work

Mobility can be supported in the Internet in a variety of ways [RFC6301]. Mobile IP [RFC6275] represents a standardized mobility management protocol in the Internet. Prior work on providing mobility support for QoS resource reservations therefore focused mainly on Mobile IP as mobility management protocol and RSVP as QoS signaling protocol. As one of the first, Awduche and Agu [AA97] proposed some mobile extensions for RSVP. The suggested approach introduces a number of additional RSVP message types that must be supported by an RSVP-capable router and relies on so-called virtual receivers that act as proxies on behalf of mobile nodes in order to setup resource reservations from new access points. Terzis et al. [TSZ99] proposed to use RSVP tunnels with Mobile IP. This *RSVP Tunnel* approach is based on Mobile IP and relies on extensions for RSVP and Mobile IP. The applied tunneling mechanism introduces some additional overhead and is limited to hard handovers only. By being based on RSVP it is also limited to IntServ as QoS model and provides support for receiver-initiated reservations only.

RSVP mobility support was also introduced by Chen and Huang [CH00] in a *Multicast RSVP* approach. This approach takes advantage of RSVP's multicast capability which is then used in order to reserve resources in mobile environments. A mobile proxy acts as mobility agent on behalf of a mobile node and establishes reservations to its subnet and all neighboring subnets. This approach therefore results in a huge amount of over-reservations toward subnets that are never visited by the mobile node. Huang and Chen [HC03] further extended Multicast RSVP in order to work in conjunction with Hierarchical Mobile IPv6 (HMIPv6) [RFC5380]. However, this approach still relies heavily on special mobile proxy agents, introduces a number of new RSVP message types that must be supported by intermediate signaling entities, and does not provide support for sender-initiated reservations or a QoS model independence.

A protocol called *MRSVP* was proposed by Talukdar et al. [TBA01]. This protocol works also in conjunction with Mobile IP but also supports anticipated handovers for mobile nodes. However, these advanced resource reservations are simply established along *all* neighboring subnets that were specified in a newly introduced MSPEC object, which leads to an unnecessarily high amount of resource reservations. The approach also relies on dedicated proxy agents that must be discovered using a dedicated proxy discovery protocol. In order to overcome this excessive use of resource reservations, Tseng et al. [TLL01] proposed a hierarchical mobile RSVP protocol called *HMRSVP*. This approach is based on MRSVP but extends it to make use of HMIPv6. It still comes with the same weaknesses as MRSVP and also relies on using special purpose mobile proxies and excessively uses tunneling thereby adding a significant overhead to the signaling operation.

Lai et al. [LMD06] presented a protocol called *HO-RSVP* which also extends RSVP to support mobile nodes. HO-RSVP is, however, based on Mobile IPv4 and depends on a number of new RSVP message types that must be supported by all intermediate RSVP signaling entities. A proposal called *Fast RSVP* was presented by Sun et al. [Sun+11]. This approach focuses again on the interaction of Mobile IPv6 and RSVP. It provides support for anticipated handovers and focuses especially on reducing the handover latency for mobile nodes. This is achieved by so-called "guard channels" which are established with an appropriate resource reservation between neighboring access routers once a mobile node anticipates to move to a new access router. Once the mobile node moves to its new access router, the guard channel is used as an entry for Mobile IPv6's tunnel across the HA toward the CN. Since both, the guard channel and the tunnel itself are equipped with QoS, the mobile node will experience a seamless handover. The mobile node can then subsequently establish a route optimized data path and a corresponding resource reservation toward the CN. The proposed approach only requires few additional protocol extensions for RSVP but still suffers from RSVP's weaknesses. Furthermore, the additional resource reservation for the guard channel may not be granted.

An evaluation of mobility and QoS interaction is provided by Manner [Man+02] where a set of different micro- and macro-mobility solutions are discussed in greater detail. The ITSUMO project [Che+00] proposed the design of an entire QoS architecture for future wireless IP networks. However, this design is entirely based on one global server which works as a DiffServ bandwidth broker. It does not consider end-to-end QoS provisioning across different administrative domains and may suffer from scalability issues. In more recent work, Lampropoulos et al. [LSP08] presented a proposal for a media-independent handover for seamless service provisioning. This work focuses, however, only on the link layer and a minimization of the handover delay. It does not consider end-to-end QoS support or QoS signaling at all. Similar, Moon and Aghvami [MA04] presented Quality-of-Service mechanisms in all-IP wireless access networks that are restricted to micro-mobility solutions using RSVP.

A promising approach for a Quality-of-Service management architecture in IP-based networks that also supports anticipated handovers was introduced by Hillebrand et al. [Hil+05; Ble+07]. A dedicated Mobility-Aware Reservation Signaling Protocol (*MARSP*) was proposed which also acts independently from the underlying QoS model. MARSP was designed to support hard handovers, anticipated handovers, or even combinations of both. It is independent of the radio access technologies being used and also provides support for inter-domain handovers. A significant difference to the approach presented in this dissertation is that the corresponding signaling architecture is based on central domain managers, whereas the approach provided by this dissertation follows a fully decentralized approach.

The design presented in this dissertation works fully distributed and independently of any central domain managers. It is not restricted to one administrative domain but provides an end-to-end signaling solution. The QoS signaling concepts developed in this dissertation provide support for sender- and receiver-initiated reservations and abstract from the actual QoS model being used, e.g., IntServ or DiffServ. Furthermore, this approach can be used in conjunction with Mobile IP (cf. Section 4.4) but provides also means to automatically adapt QoS signaling sessions to a user's new location independent of the underlying mobility management protocol (cf. Section 4.5.3)[1] and supports anticipated handovers (cf. Section 4.5.2).

Table 4.1 summarizes the most important proposals and compares their functionality. Since the MARSP QoS signaling is carried out by means of a centralized domain resource manager, there exists no notion of sender- or receiver-initiated reservations in this case. These two reservation types are, however, also supported by MARSP since the domain resource manager establishes the resources reservations no matter whether they were initiated by the data flow receiver or the data flow sender. The last column of Table 4.1, denoted *NSIS-Mobility*, reflects the functional capabilities of the solution provided in this thesis.

4.3 Challenges for QoS Signaling Protocols in Mobile Environments

The main challenge in using QoS signaling in mobile environments is to create a linkage between the control path and the data path in order to adapt an already established resource reservation to the new user's location, under the constraint that an existing mobility management protocol's operation should remain unmodified. This is difficult to achieve, since a mobility management protocol, such as Mobile IP, hides the mobility aspect from its applications.

---

[1]Under the constraint that the mobility management protocol instance informs the signaling protocol instance about mobility-related IP address information and handovers.

Provided functionality	RSVP Tunnel [TSZ99]	Multicast RSVP [CH00]	MRSVP [TBA01]	HMRSVP [TLL01]	HO-RSVP [LMD06]	MARSP [Ble+07]	Fast RSVP [Sun+11]	NSIS-Mobility
Support for existing Mobility Management Protocol	Yes	Yes	No	Yes	Yes	Yes	Yes	Yes
Decentralized Session Management	Yes	Yes	Yes	Yes	Yes	No	Yes	Yes
Avoiding over-reservations in adjacent subnets	Yes	No	No	Yes	Yes	Yes	Yes	Yes
Support for anticipated handovers	No	Yes	Yes	Yes	Yes	Yes	Yes	Yes
Independence of QoS model	No	No	No	No	No	Yes	No	Yes
Support for sender- and receiver-initiated reservations	No	No	No	No	No	Yes	No	Yes

Table 4.1: *Functional comparison of different proposals toward mobility-aware QoS signaling solutions*

When using a mobility management protocol the applications always refer to a "logical" address information which remains constant even if the MN moves to a different location. A QoS signaling protocol must, however, adapt a resource reservation based on the "actual" address information of the MN's current location. Furthermore, a QoS signaling instance must also be mobility-aware in the sense that it needs to be informed about mobility events and mobility-related data path characteristics.

This challenge can be addressed by creating a node-local binding between the mobility management protocol instance and the QoS signaling instance. The QoS signaling instance can then be informed about mobility events and access mobility-related address information of the mobility management protocol instance. This solution does neither require the mobility management protocol nor the QoS signaling protocol to be adapted. Section 4.4 provides an analysis and design for a Mobile IPv6-based solution.

Another challenge is related to role of the participating signaling entities in a mobile environment. While a MN's QoS signaling instance may be aware of mobility events and mobility-related address information,[2] a CN may not be aware of a MN's movement. For instance, simply because only the MN uses a mobility management protocol, but not the CN.

This becomes problematic whenever a signaling session is "controlled" by the CN. In these cases, the signaling protocol must provide means to allow the MN to inform the CN in order to trigger an adaptation of the already established resource reservation.

4.3.1 Mobility Scenarios for QoS Signaling

Due to the different roles of the participating entities in a mobile environment, it is important to differentiate which signaling entity actually "controls" a signaling session. Furthermore, it must be considered whether a QoS signaling protocol allows for sender- and receiver-initiated reservations. Since the signaling protocol's operation differs in each of these cases, the following four combinations are considered throughout this chapter:

- M1 – MN is data flow sender and signaling initiator

- M2 – MN is data flow sender and signaling responder

- M3 – MN is data flow receiver and signaling initiator

- M4 – MN is data flow receiver and signaling responder

Whenever the MN acts as sender of the data flow (scenarios M1 and M2) it "controls" the signaling operation. In terms of QoS NSLP signaling the MN would have to emit a QoS NSLP QUERY or QoS NSLP RESERVE message in order to reflect changes of the underlying's data path. Mobility events at the MN can therefore be used as a local "handover trigger" (HO trigger) for subsequent QoS NSLP actions in order to adapt existing reservations.

This is exemplified for QoS NSLP signaling procedures in the following. In scenario M1 the MN can initiate a new RESERVE message for the new data flow f_n directly after it has changed its point of attachment and got a new source IP address, as illustrated in Figure 4.2a.

In scenario M2, where a receiver-initiated reservation is used, the MN simply emits a new QoS NSLP QUERY message in downstream direction, as depicted in

---

[2]e.g., due to a node-local binding between the mobility management protocol instance and the QoS signaling instance

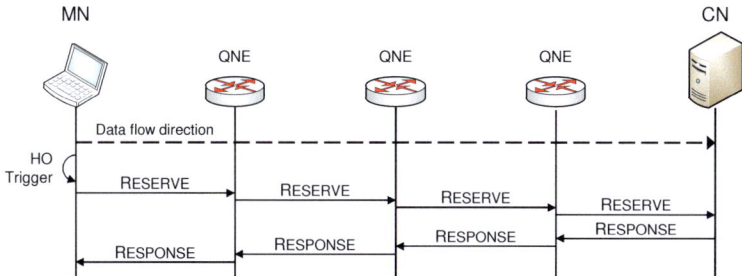

(a) Scenario M1 – establishment of a sender-initiated reservation where the MN establishes a new signaling flow by sending a RESERVE message toward the CN along the new data path in downstream direction

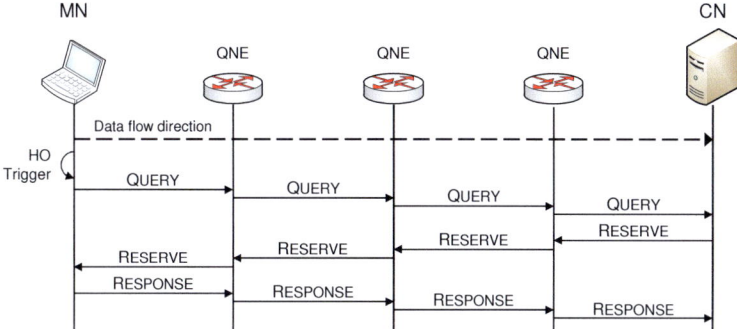

(b) Scenario M2 – establishment of a receiver-initiated reservation where the MN establishes a new signaling flow by sending a QUERY message toward the CN along the new data path in downstream direction

Figure 4.2: *Scenarios where the MN acts as the sender of the data flow*

Figure 4.2b. Whenever the MN acts as receiver of the data flow (scenarios M3 and M4), QoS NSLP actions must be triggered at the CN, as conceptually illustrated in Figure 4.3. In this example, a HO trigger is used to emit QoS NSLP messages upon which a new signaling flow can be established.

The scenarios where the MN acts as data flow receiver are, however, more difficult to handle. In both cases the CN "controls" the signaling session in its downstream direction. The following challenge arises when the MN acts as the receiver of the data flow:

The information that the MN moved to a different location must be propagated toward the CN (denoted "HO Trigger" in Figures 4.3a and 4.3b). If the CN also uses a mobility management protocol, it can use a node-local binding between the mobility management protocol instance and the QoS signaling instance. In case

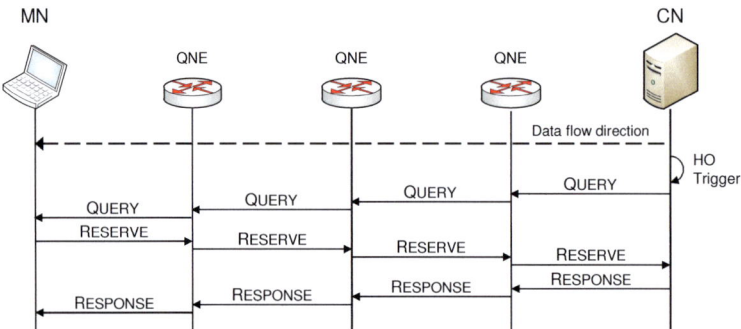

(a) Scenario M3 – establishment of a new signaling flow for a receiver-initiated reservation in response to an HO trigger which results in the emission of a QUERY message at the CN

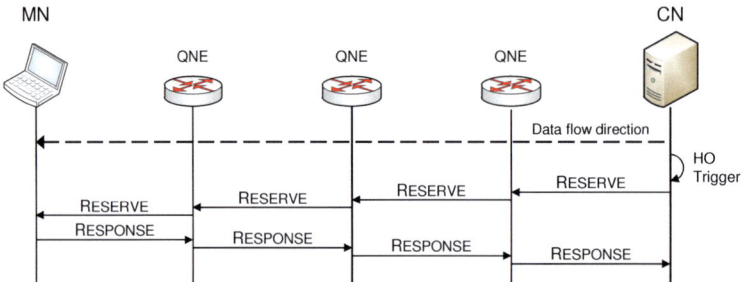

(b) Scenario M4 – establishment of a new signaling flow for a sender-initiated reservation in response to an HO trigger which results in the emission of a RESERVE message at the CN

Figure 4.3: *Scenarios where the MN acts as receiver of the data flow*

the CN is not mobility-aware in a sense that it does not use a mobility management protocol, the QoS signaling protocol must provide means to allow for the realization of a "HO trigger" that is issued by the MN.

4.4 Quality-of-Service Signaling with Mobile IPv6

A mobility management solution for IP-based networks is provided by Mobile IP. However, Mobile IP itself is only concerned with the correct routing of data packets toward the mobile endpoint and does not cover QoS mechanisms. In order to establish resource reservations by means of a signaling protocol in mobile environments, the signaling protocol must be aware of an end system's mobility and provide mechanisms that allow to react upon a mobility event accordingly.

This section shows how QoS signaling for mobile users can be accomplished in conjunction with Mobile IPv6 as mobility management protocol. The design is based on the NSIS protocol suite and its QoS NSLP signaling application. The concepts and implementation details were first outlined in [BR09a] and [Lai08]. Some of the findings were also incorporated into RFC 5980 which discusses the applicability of the NSIS protocols in mobile environments [RFC5980].

4.4.1 Analysis of QoS NSLP Signaling in Mobile IPv6-based Domains

Mobile IP allows users to be mobile and keep the mobility aspect transparent from its applications. This abstraction does, however, impose challenges on the use of QoS signaling protocols. While Mobile IP manages the adaptation of the data path, the QoS signaling protocol manages the corresponding reservation for this data path. Hence, as soon as a MN moves to a different location the data flow's address information changes upon which the resource reservation must be adapted accordingly. However, if the QoS signaling protocol is not aware of a MN's movement, it can not adapt an already established reservation.

Therefore, it is necessary that the QoS signaling instance is mobility-aware in a sense that it stays informed by the Mobile IP instance whenever a mobility event occurs and that it is aware of the actually used addresses. Furthermore, a mobility event must lead to the emission of a new QoS signaling message at the signaling entity which controls the signaling session.

Within a Mobile IP scenario an MN can be located either in its home network or away from home in a foreign network. Whenever it is located in its home network, it acts like a static node within this network and operates independently of any home agent. Hence, in this case the QoS signaling protocol can be used without any further considerations.

Whenever the MN is located in a foreign network, Mobile IPv6 provides two modes of operation: a *tunnel mode* and a *route optimized mode*. In both of these modes, the MN is assigned a HoA and a CoA. While the HoA is transparently used by applications to address the MN, the CoA refers to the *actual location* of the MN and is hidden from the applications. A signaling protocol instance must, however, be aware of the actual location and hence, of the MN's current CoA. Furthermore, the tunnel mode and the route optimized mode introduce the notion of different flows that must be considered (cf. Figure 2.4 on page 16). For a QoS signaling protocol, it is important to differentiate between these flows, their corresponding paths in the network, and the addresses that are used by these flows. Since both modes are used in Mobile IP scenarios, a QoS NSLP signaling instance must be aware of and provide support for both modes.

4.4.1.1 Requirements for a Mobility-Aware QoS Signaling Instance

In order to fully support Mobile IPv6 in tunnel mode and route optimization mode, a mobility-aware NSIS signaling instance must fulfill the following requirements:

Awareness of Mobile IP bindings By using Mobile IP the "logical flow"—as referred to by the applications—differs in Mobile IP from the "actual flow" taken by the data packets. That is, the mobility aspect is kept transparent from the applications. However, a QoS signaling instance must be aware of the current Mobile IP bindings in order to choose the right addresses for a corresponding resource reservation. Furthermore, it must be aware whether Mobile IP's tunnel mode is used or not.

Reaction on mobility events Applications on the CN only refer to the MN's HoA and are not aware of a MN's movement. However, in case the CN "controls" a QoS signaling session it needs to be aware of a MN's movement such that an existing resource reservation can be immediately adapted. Therefore, in order to issue or trigger new reservation requests upon a change of the MN's location, the signaling instance must be able to react on mobility events.

Crossover node processing Each signaling entity must be able to serve as potential CRN and therefore distinguish between different signaling flows that belong to the same signaling session and take appropriate action on the new and the old signaling flows.

Overhead awareness The overhead incurred by Mobile IP due to tunnel encapsulation or IPv6 extension headers should be considered by the resource reservation requests issued by the signaling entities.

It is important to note, that the MN, the HA, and—in case route optimization should be used—the CN are the only signaling entities which must provide explicit support for Mobile IPv6-aware QoS signaling. Neither a potential CRN must be made mobility-aware nor the access routers or any other signaling entity involved in the QoS signaling session.

4.4.1.2 QoS NSLP Signaling in Tunnel Mode

Tunnel mode is always used within Mobile IP initially and whenever the CN does not support Mobile IP itself. When tunnel mode is used, the HA acts as proxy for the MN's HoA and establishes a tunnel toward the MN's current CoA. The applications on the CN and on the MN always refer to the *logical flow* between the CN's IP address and the MN's HoA.

In tunnel mode it is important to differentiate between the *tunneled flow* and the *tunnel flow* as depicted in Figure 2.4 on page 16. In terms of QoS NSLP the tunneled flow refers to the end-to-end QoS reservation between the MN and the CN across the HA. The tunneled path between the HA and the MN appears to both nodes as one single hop and since the tunneled end-to-end reservation is encapsulated in outer tunnel packets, its packets will not be intercepted by any intermediate signaling entities on the path. Hence, the tunneled flow cannot be used to establish resource reservations on the path between the MN and the HA.

In order to allow for resource reservations from end-to-end it is therefore important to establish resource reservations for the actual tunnel flow. RFC 5979 [RFC5979] specifies how QoS NSLP signaling should be conceptually used in tunnel mode operation and can therefore be applied to the Mobile IPv6 tunnel mode case.

Figure 4.4 illustrates how a sender-initiated QoS signaling session from the CN toward the MN must be processed in Mobile IPv6's tunnel mode—this corresponds to mobility scenario M4. In this case the HA acts as the *Tunnel Entry Point* and the MN acts as the *Tunnel Exit Point*. At first, a RESERVE message destined toward the MN's HoA reaches the HA which acts as proxy for this address. The HA is now responsible to establish a dedicated QoS reservation for the tunnel flow toward the MN's CoA which corresponds to the original reservation request, such that this request can be intercepted and processed by all intermediate signaling entities. The original reservation request from the CN must then be forwarded toward the MN within the existing tunnel.

Since both reservations—for the tunnel flow and for the tunneled flow—belong conceptually to the same signaling session, it is the HA's and the MN's responsibility to logically bind both reservation requests together. Only if both reservation requests could be established successfully, the signaling session can be used from end-to-end. QoS NSLP already provides required mechanisms to realize this dependency. In the sender-initiated case the tunnel entry point (HA in the example provided above) includes a randomly generated 128-bit MSG-ID for the reservation of the outer tunnel flow. After that the tunnel entry point includes a BOUND-MSG-ID

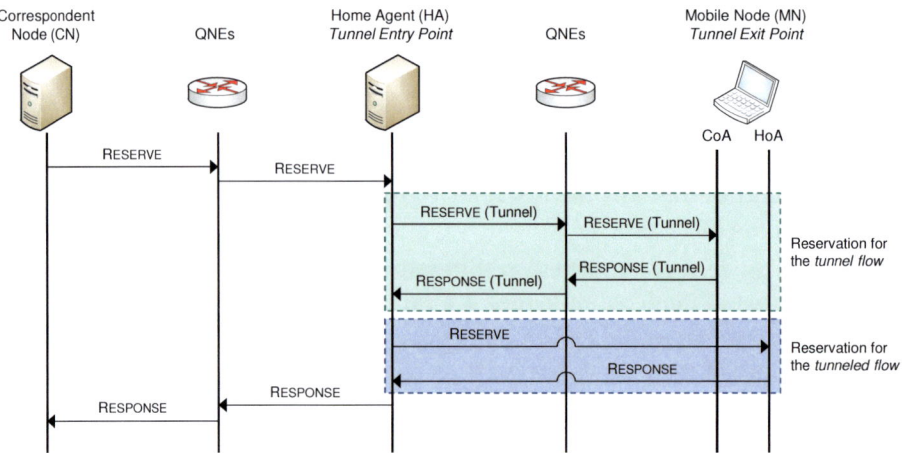

Figure 4.4: *Message sequence diagram in Mobile IPv6's tunnel mode for mobility scenario M4 – MN acts as receiver of the data flow and signaling responder*

and a BOUND-SESSION-ID to the inner tunneled flow. The BOUND-MSG-ID contains the same MSG-ID as the tunnel flow and the BOUND-SESSION-ID contains the same SESSION-ID as the tunnel flow. These tuples allow the tunnel exit point (MN in the example provided above) to establish an association between these two reservations. In case the MN acts as the flow sender and therefore triggers or initiates a reservation request for the logical flow, it also has to assure that reservations are triggered or initiated for both flows.

The conceptual operation of a receiver-initiated reservation in tunnel mode is slightly more complicated but also discussed in RFC 5979. A Mobile IPv6-aware QoS NSLP implementation must therefore provide support for tunnel mode operation for sender- and receiver-initiated reservations. Note, however, that this affects only the HA and the MN which act as tunnel entry and tunnel exit points.

Figure 4.4 also clearly shows that the two reservation requests from the HA for the tunneled and for the tunnel flow are addressed toward different destination addresses at the MN. While the reservation request for the tunneled flow is still addressed toward the MN's HoA, the reservation request for the tunnel flow must be addressed toward the MN's actual CoA in order to allow for a path-coupled signaling operation.

The requirement to transmit the original reservation request through the tunnel toward the HoA leads, however, to a specific challenge for NSIS signaling with Mobile IPv6. Since the Mobile IPv6 instance on the HA has an active binding with the MN's HoA, the initial GIST QUERY message won't be sent through the tunnel but instead sent "route-optimized" toward the MN's current CoA. That is, the destination address of the GIST QUERY's IP header would be set to the MN's CoA, while the GIST QUERY's message routing information carries the MN's HoA. This would lead to the situation that the GIST QUERY gets intercepted and interpreted by the first signaling entity on the data path instead of being tunneled directly toward the MN.

This issue can be solved by introducing a second alternative HA address which is used by the NSIS signaling instance on the HA whenever tunnel mode is used. It is important to note, that this issue only affects the direction from the CN to the MN. In case the MN acts as the initiator of the reservation request, the initial GIST QUERY message is addressed toward the CN. Since tunnel mode is used, the Mobile IPv6 instance will then automatically tunnel this signaling message toward the HA. The MN must only ensure to establish a reservation for the tunnel itself between the MN's CoA and the HA. Furthermore, this issue only affects the initial GIST QUERY sent from the HA since this QUERY is responsible to establish message routing state and is therefore sent using query-mode encapsulation in order to be intercepted by signaling entities residing on the data path. All subsequently sent signaling messages are exchanged between and addressed toward directly adjacent signaling entities.

4.4.1.3 QoS NSLP Signaling in Route Optimization Mode

In route optimization mode, the MN and the CN, are both Mobile IPv6-aware. In this case the MN can inform the CN about its new CoA by means of the return routability procedure and binding update process (cf. Figure 2.6 on page 18). From a QoS NSLP signaling perspective the MN or the CN must be able to react upon a changed MN's CoA in order to adjust the reservation for the new actual data path.

Since QoS NSLP supports sender- as well as receiver-initiated reservations and the MN can be either the data flow sender or data flow receiver, four different scenarios may occur. Note, that in case bi-directional resource reservations are requested, two of these four potential scenarios must be used. Hence, in the following, the signaling operation for all four mobility scenarios in route optimization mode are described in detail.

Figure 4.5 illustrates mobility scenario M1 where the MN is the sender of the data flow and acts as the initiator of the QoS NSLP signaling session. Before it moves to a different location it is connected to the old access router AR_O and communicates from a corresponding old CoA toward a CN. The reservation for the old signaling flow is established as usual.

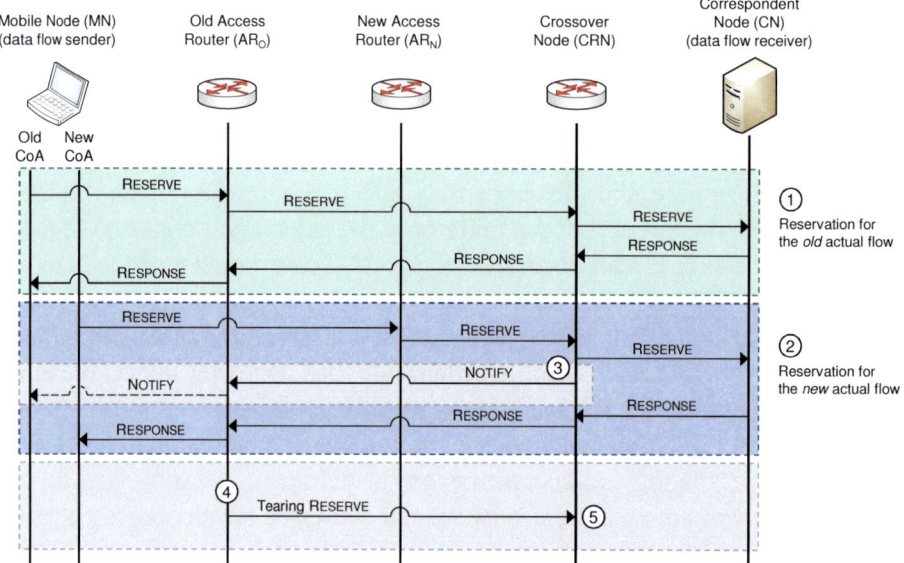

Figure 4.5: *Message sequence diagram in Mobile IPv6's route optimization mode for scenario M1 – MN acts as sender of the data flow and signaling initiator*

Once the MN moves to a new access router AR_N it is assigned a new CoA. After it updated its Mobile IP bindings with the CN (not depicted in Figure 4.5) it would then be necessary to update its reservation for the new actual flow in a second step. This is challenging since it requires an interaction between the Mobile IP instance and the QoS signaling instance on the MN.

In case the MN's QoS signaling instance retrieves the required information from the Mobile IP instance, it must issue a new QoS NSLP RESERVE with a new flow identifier in form of a new MRI toward the CN. Once the CRN on the path receives the new reservation request with the new MRI but with the same Session ID, it forwards this new RESERVE toward the CN but is now also responsible to trigger a tear down of the old reservation along the old path. In this scenario, the CRN is located in upstream direction of the reservation request. Hence, it cannot issue a "tearing RESERVE" itself. Instead, it must issue a NOTIFY message of type "route changed" toward the MN's old CoA in a third step. This NOTIFY eventually reaches AR_O which tries to forward the message toward the MN's old CoA in case it is not aware of the MN's movement.[3]

In a fourth step AR_O finally detects that it cannot reach the MN at its old CoA anymore and that it is the last hop of this signaling flow. In case AR_O is not actively informed that the MN is not reachable anymore, QoS NSLP's retransmission timer will eventually detect the MN's unreachability. In either case AR_O can now issue a "tearing RESERVE" for the obsolete path. This tear down message eventually reaches the CRN in a fifth step which is now responsible to prevent this tearing RESERVE from being propagated further along the path.

Figure 4.6 illustrates the scenario where the MN is still the sender of the data flow, but now acts as responder of the reservation. At first the resource reservation is triggered from the MN's old CoA by means of a QoS NSLP QUERY message upon which the CN issues a RESERVE for the old actual flow.

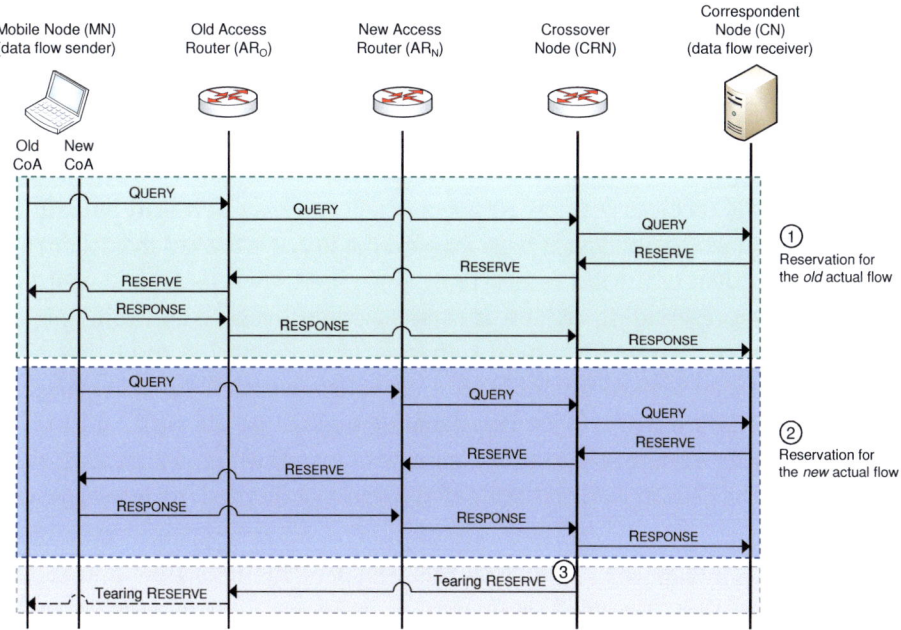

Figure 4.6: *Message sequence diagram in Mobile IPv6's route optimization mode for scenario M2 – MN acts as sender of the data flow and signaling responder*

---

[3]It could be aware, for instance, by relying on a *neighbor unreachability detection*

Once the MN changes its location and is assigned a new CoA from its new access router AR_N, it issues a new QoS NSLP QUERY toward the CN. The reservation for the new actual flow carries the new MRI but still the same Session ID and can be established as usual. Upon receiving the final QoS NSLP RESPONSE from the new reservation request, the CRN forwards the RESPONSE but is also responsible to tear down the reservation for the obsolete path. Since the CRN is now located in downstream direction of the reservation request, it can issue the corresponding tearing RESERVE along the old path itself in a third step. Once the tearing RESERVE reaches AR_O it tries to forward the message toward the MN's old CoA if it is not aware of the MN's absence, otherwise the tear down procedure is finished at AR_O.

Figure 4.7 illustrates scenario M3 where the CN is the sender of the data flow and receiver-initiated reservations are used. At first the CN triggers a receiver-initiated resource reservation by issuing a QoS NSLP QUERY toward the MN's old CoA upon which the QoS NSLP RESERVE and RESPONSE messages are exchanged subsequently along the old path.

Once the MN changes its location toward a new access router AR_N it receives a new CoA and updates existing Mobile IP bindings with its CN. As soon as the binding at the CN is updated it can then establish a reservation request for the new actual data path in a second step. This is again triggered by a QoS NSLP QUERY toward the MN's new CoA upon which the MN can issue a corresponding RESERVE from its new CoA.

Once the CRN receives the new RESERVE which carries a new MRI but still the same Session ID as the old flow, it must forward the RESERVE toward the CN but also trigger a tear down of the old reservation. Since the CRN is located in upstream direction of the reservation request it cannot issue a RESERVE by itself. Instead, it sends a NOTIFY message in a third step indicating a detected route change in upstream direction toward the MN's old CoA which eventually reaches AR_O. As soon as AR_O is aware that it is the last signaling hop on the old path,[4] it can then issue a tearing RESERVE in a fourth step in order to tear down the reservation along the old path. The CRN must then ensure that it does not forward the tearing reserve toward the CN.

Scenario M4, where the CN acts as the sender of the data flow and sender-initiated reservations are used, is illustrated in Figure 4.8. In a first step the reservation for the old actual flow is established. In this case the QoS NSLP RESERVE is issued from the CN, too.

---

[4]E.g., by means of a *neighbor unreachability detection* or in response to a retransmission timeout

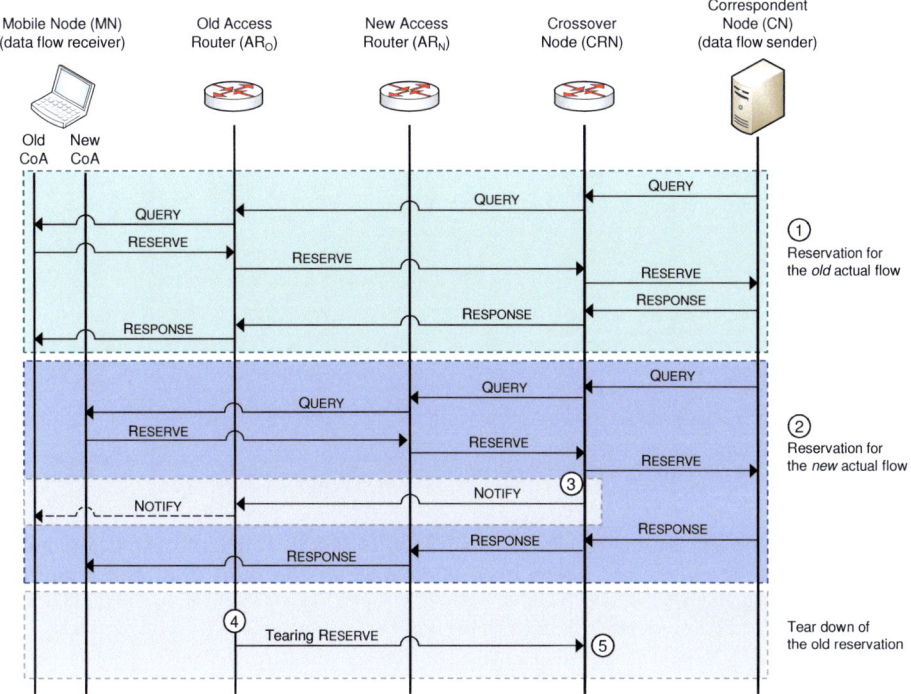

Figure 4.7: *Message sequence diagram in Mobile IPv6's route optimization mode for scenario M3 – MN acts as receiver of the data flow and signaling initiator*

In a second step, the MN moves to AR$_N$ and gets a new CoA assigned from the AR$_N$. Bindings are then updated between the MN and the CN by means of Mobile IPv6. This allows the CN to be aware of the MN's movement and its new CoA upon which it can initiate a reservation request for the new actual flow.

The CRN finally receives the QoS NSLP RESPONSE of the new reservation request and can then take appropriate actions to tear down the reservation along the old path in a third step. Since it is again located in downstream direction, it can issue the tearing RESERVE by its own toward the MN's old CoA and resources along the old path are freed.

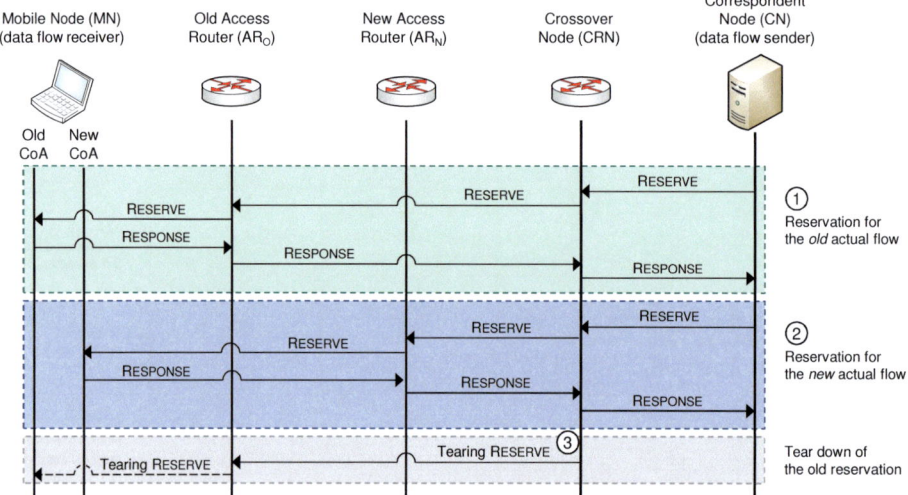

Figure 4.8: *Message sequence diagram in Mobile IPv6's route optimization mode for scenario M4 – MN acts as receiver of the data flow and signaling responder*

4.4.2 Design and Implementation of Mobile IPv6-Aware NSIS Signaling

One of the most important concepts regarding the design of a Mobile IPv6-aware NSIS signaling instance is to break the transparency of the system's mobility and its related state. The NSIS signaling instance should be able to monitor and query state of the Mobile IPv6 instance in order to use the right care-of-addresses for its signaling flows, be aware of the currently used Mobile IP mode of operation (tunnel mode or route optimization mode) and the herein involved per-packet overhead. Furthermore, the NSIS signaling instance should be notified instantaneously upon the occurrence of important mobility events, such as handovers, new care-of-addresses, or updated binding caches and binding update lists in order to react accordingly.

Keeni et al. [RFC4295] specify a Mobile IPv6 Management Information Base (MIB) which can be used to monitor and control Mobile IPv6 related state on the MN, HA, or CN. The use of a MIB by means of SNMP would introduce another level of indirection between the NSIS signaling instance and the Mobile IPv6 instance across an SNMP agent. The NSIS signaling instance would have to be extended by or interact with an SNMP client and the Mobile IPv6 instance would have to be extended by a MIB module that provides access to its managed objects. Both instances would then interact with each other on behalf of an SNMP agent.

Since there is currently no working implementation of this Mobile IPv6 MIB available for existing Mobile IPv6 implementations and an SNMP-based solution is expected to impose additional overhead due to the increased level of indirection, this dissertation provides a light-weight alternative instead. This so-called *Flow Information Service* element is proposed in order to exchange the necessary information between the NSIS signaling instance and the Mobile IPv6 instance.

4.4.2.1 The Flow Information Service Element

As already outlined above the proposed Flow Information Service element is used to allow the NSIS signaling instance to be aware of the Mobile IP related state of its current signaling flows. In order to query state and get notified upon state changes, the design of the Flow Information Service element follows a request-response mechanism. This design allows the NSIS signaling instance to react on mobility events, i.e., adapt signaling flows accordingly or emit new signaling messages.

The request-response-based design allows to query the state of one particular flow at a time and therefore prevents the NSIS signaling instance from mirroring the entire state of the Mobile IPv6 instance. A request from the NSIS signaling instance must contain the signaling flow's source and destination address of the logical flow. The response from the Mobile IPv6 instance carries the request's address pair as reference, the current mobility state of the flow, and the resulting per-packet overhead resulting from the Mobile IP usage.

The queried flow can be in one of three possible mobility states:

No Mobile IP Flow In case Mobile IP is not used for this flow, no IP address transformation occurs and hence no further action is required.

Mobile IP Flow in Tunnel Mode In this state the response reports the tunnel's source and destination addresses as well as the amount of per-packet overhead of the tunnel.

Mobile IP Flow in Route Optimization Mode In this state the response reports the source and destination addresses which are used for the route optimized flow, i.e., the CoAs. Furthermore, the response informs the signaling instance of the per-packet overhead resulting from the Mobile IPv6 extension headers.

Another important design decision is related to the actual location of the Flow Information Service element—i.e., whether it can be realized as part of the NSLP or as part of the NTLP—and its interaction with the NSIS signaling instance. While the lower layered NTLP is responsible for the routing and transport of signaling messages, the upper layered NSLP specifies the signaling flow's MRI. A transparent mapping of the addresses contained in the MRI by the NTLP would not suffice since the NSLP must also take appropriate actions on mobility events. For instance, the Mobile IP related overhead must be taken into account by the reservation request and the use of Mobile IP's tunnel mode implies the establishment of a second resource reservation for the tunnel flow which can only be triggered by the QoS NSLP.

A conceptual overview of the interaction between the Flow Information Service element and the NSIS signaling layers is illustrated in Figure 4.9. Four different internal message types were defined which can be exchanged between the NSIS signaling instance and the Mobile IPv6 instance, namely REQUEST, REPLY, NOTIFICATION, and ERROR.

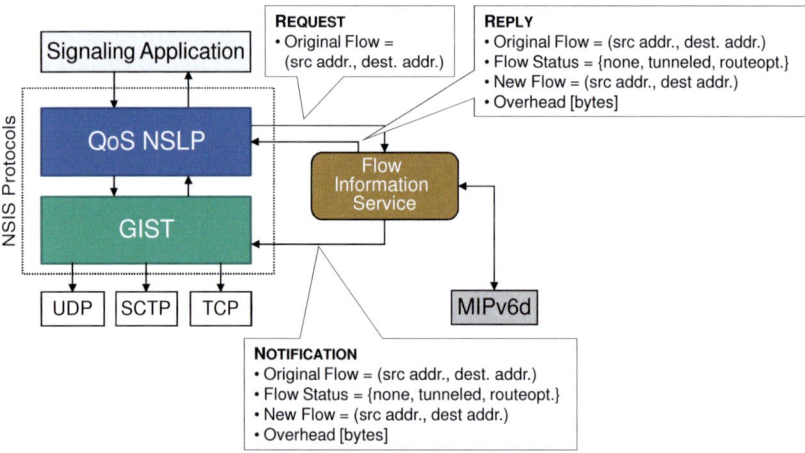

Figure 4.9: *Conceptual overview of the interaction between the Flow Information Service element and the NSIS signaling instance*

The NSIS signaling instance can issue a REQUEST toward the Flow Information Service Element with a signaling flow's (logical) source and destination IP address in order to query its current mobility state. The Flow Information Service element responds with a REPLY message which contains the REQUEST's IP address pair (denoted "Original Flow" in Figure 4.9) and the corresponding mobility related information. This contains the current mobility status of the flow, the actually used IP addresses when being transmitted by Mobile IPv6 (denoted "New Flow" in Figure 4.9), and the corresponding per-packet overhead in bytes.

The information contained in a REQUEST is also used for a NOTIFICATION message which is sent toward the NSIS signaling instance whenever a mobility event occurs. Furthermore, an ERROR message can be used to signal erroneous conditions.

The Flow Information Service element was implemented for the NSIS-ka protocol suite [Ble+12a] and the open source Mobile IPv6 implementation of the USAGI project [USA07] (more detailed information is provided by Laier [Lai08]). The Flow Information Service element is realized as a pair of modules on the NSIS signaling side and on the Mobile IPv6 side. This is necessary since the Mobile IPv6 daemon runs as an independent process and its internal state variables can only be extracted therein. The two modules communicate via a UNIX Domain Socket interface. Since both layers on the NSIS side—the QoS NSLP and the NTLP—need access to the mobility state, they are both equipped with an interface toward the Flow Information Service element. The integration and logical placement of the Flow Information Service element modules in the NSIS-ka architecture and USAGI's Mobile IPv6 daemon is illustrated in Figure 4.10.

In case a resource reservation request is issued by a signaling application, the signaling application creates a RESERVE or QUERY message which is passed toward the NSIS-ka instance in step ①. Since mobility is kept transparent from the application, the request refers to the logical flow and contains the MN's HoA as source or destination address. The QoS NSLP's StateModule implements the protocol state machine and therefore creates and maintains session context for this reservation request. The StateModule stores and operates on the request's logical flow ID (step ②).

In step ③ the QoS NSLP StateModule queries the Flow Information Service element whether the logical flow refers to a mobility flow upon which information about this flow is exchanged between the Flow Information Service element on the NSIS side and the Flow Information Service element in the Mobile IPv6 daemon (steps ④ and ⑤). The corresponding reply is then sent back to the QoS NSLP's StateModule. In case the logical flow refers to a mobility flow, the QoS NSLP StateModule must transform the MRI's addresses to refer to the actual flow. If tunnel mode is used, it must furthermore initiate new RESERVE or QUERY messages for the tunnel flow. After that, the NTLP's StateModule can start the actual reservation request by initiating a GIST three-way handshake that refers to the actually intended flow (step ⑥).

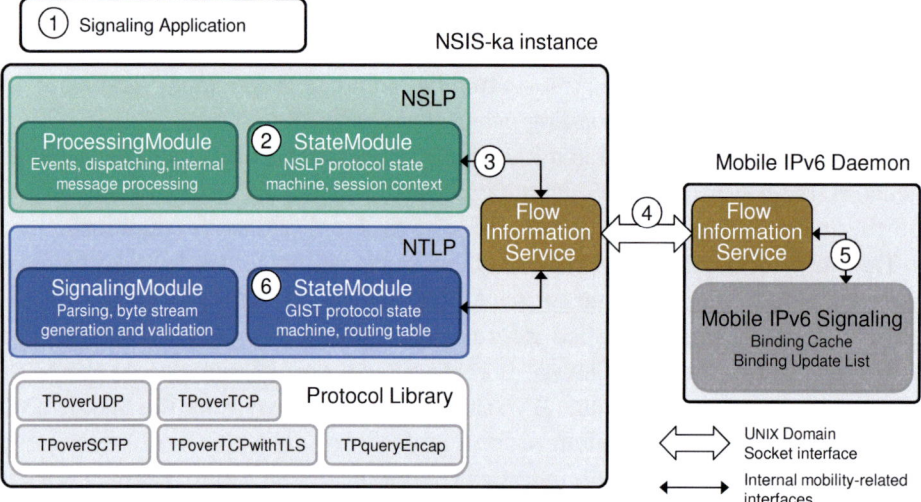

Figure 4.10: *Conceptual overview of the integration and placement of the Flow In-formation Service element modules in the NSIS-ka architecture and USAGI's Mobile IPv6 daemon*

The communication interface between the Flow Information Service element and NTLP's StateModule is used for asynchronous notifications of mobility events. A NOTIFICATION carries the same information as a REPLY which is sent upon a dedicated REQUEST, i.e., the current status of the flow, the original MRI of the logical flow, the MRI of the new actual flow, the involved per-packet overhead, and—if necessary—the MRI of the tunnel flow.

In order to inform the QoS NSLP of these mobility events, two new NetworkNo-tification GIST API calls have been defined: *Home Binding Update* and *Binding Update*. Both notifications carry only the logical flow's MRI such that the NSLP can use this information as a referral to its internal session context table. The NSLP is then responsible to request the updated information concerning the logical flow from the Flow Information Service element.

4.4.2.2 Crossover Node Processing

As outlined in Section 4.1 an important requirement for a mobility-aware QoS signaling protocol is concerned with an active release of unused resources. This affects the old path between the old access router and the CRN. In order to release the resources along the old path, the CRN must detect that it actually acts as CRN for two signaling flows of the same signaling session and must then actively tear down the signaling session along the old path accordingly.

A signaling entity must detect that it has to act as CRN. This detection does, however, not differ from a normal re-routing detection mechanism. It can be accomplished by means of the SII-Handle ("Source Identification Information") which is an API-local identifier of the next signaling peer in up- or downstream direction. The SII-Handle is reported to the NSLPs via the GIST API. In order to finally tear down a signaling session along the old path, the CRN needs to be aware of the old SII-Handle. In case the CRN does not emit the tearing RESERVE itself along the old path it must also store the old MRI until it receives a tearing RESERVE from the old access router and stop a further propagation of this tearing RESERVE along the common path.

4.4.3 Evaluation of Mobile IPv6-based QoS signaling

The evaluation aims at demonstrating that the concepts developed in this chapter allow for resource reservations in Mobile IPv6-based environments. For this purpose all four possible mobility scenarios were evaluated using Mobile IPv6's route optimized mode and tunnel mode. Furthermore, the evaluation aims at confirming that signaling can be performed reasonably fast, i.e., the necessary amount of time for processing signaling messages must be very low compared to typical propagation delays that can be experienced in the Internet.

The evaluation environment had to be designed to allow for measurements which are affected by external influences as little as possible. Therefore, each testbed router was equipped with identical hardware and software. The evaluation environment used a topology which consisted of six different signaling entities, among them were three ARs, one HA, one MN, and a stationary CN. The MN could be either connected to the HA or one of the three ARs, as illustrated in Figure 4.11. Appendix A provides detailed material about the evaluation environment.

For each mobility scenario 50 distinct measurements were performed, each consisting of an initial resource reservation between the MN and the CN and updated reservations after a MN's movement to a new AR. Finally, the average of each measurement was determined.[5] The use of active tear downs was not configured on the signaling entities and therefore not explicitly evaluated. Based on the mobility concepts outlined in this chapter it can be expected, that the reservation setup time (1) increases with every additional intermediate signaling

---

[5]Packet traces from all testbed router's interfaces of all measurements can be obtained at `http://nsis-ka.org`.

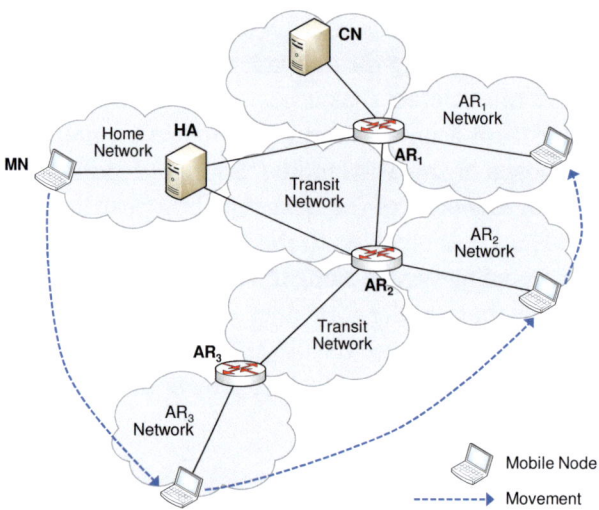

Figure 4.11: *Topology of the testbed environment for the evaluation of QoS signaling with Mobile IPv6*

entity along the signaling's path and (2) is lower for sender-initiated reservations as opposed to receiver-initiated reservations.

In Mobile IPv6's tunnel mode two resource reservations must be established, one for the "logical" flow between the MN and the CN—which refers to the MN's HoA—and one for the tunnel between the HA and the MN. Due to this reason the initial reservation setup reflects the time necessary until *both* reservations were successfully established. Once the MN moves to a new access router only the tunnel reservation must be updated, while the reservation for the "logical" flow remains unchanged.

Table 4.2 shows the measurement results obtained for all four mobility scenarios in Mobile IPv6's tunnel mode. First, the MN is connected to AR_1 when it establishes an initial resource reservation toward the CN. After that it changes toward AR_2 upon which the reservation for the tunnel flow is adapted automatically and then it changes toward AR_3 upon which its reservation for the tunnel flow is adapted to its new location again.

The measurement results clearly show that the initial reservation established from AR_1 requires much more time than subsequently updated reservations from AR_2. This is due to the fact, that the initial reservation is only established once both, the reservation for the "logical" flow and the reservation for the tunnel flow were successfully established. Whenever the MN acts as data flow sender (scenarios M1

Scenario	Initial reservation MN at AR_1	Updated reservation MN at AR_2	Updated reservation MN at AR_3
M1 – MN acts as data flow sender and signaling initiator	4.53 ms	3.66 ms	5.02 ms
M2 – MN acts as data flow sender and signaling responder	5.23 ms	3.16 ms	4.84 ms
M3 – MN acts as data flow receiver and signaling initiator	6.13 ms	5.32 ms	6.65 ms
M4 – MN acts as data flow receiver and signaling responder	5.84 ms	4.85 ms	5.98 ms

Table 4.2: *Average of the measurement results of reservation setup after movement between access routers AR_1, AR_2, and AR_3 for Mobile IPv6 tunneled flows*

and M2) it can trigger the establishment of both reservations nearly simultaneously. However, in case the CN acts as data flow sender (scenarios M3 and M4), the CN establishes only a *single* reservation toward the MN's HoA which reaches the HA upon which the HA is responsible for establishing a tunnel reservation toward the MN's actual CoA. This leads to an additional delay in the total reservation setup time.

From the measurement results it can also be obtained that the updated reservation times increase whenever the MN moves from AR_2 to AR_3. This is due to the fact, that an additional intermediate signaling entity (AR_3) participates in this signaling session, such that a reservation being issued from AR_3 crosses four signaling hops as opposed to three signaling hops when being issued from AR_2.

While the round trip time between any two signaling entities only amounts for approximately 0.27 ms in this testbed, the absolute values for the reservation setup times are still in a single-digit range. This means that the time required for processing these signaling messages is very small compared to typical propagation delays that can be found in the Internet.

In case Mobile IPv6 can be used in route optimized mode no additional tunnel reservations are required. However, in this case the MN and the CN must be Mobile IPv6 aware. For these evaluations, the MN is initially located in its home network and an initial resource reservation between MN and CN is established. The evaluations measure the time required in order to adapt this resource reservation once the MN moves to its access routers AR_1, AR_2, and AR_3.

Table 4.3 contains the evaluation results for all four mobility scenarios when Mobile IPv6's route optimized mode is used. The measurement results again clearly demonstrate that the reservation setup times increase with each additional signaling hop. For instance, if the MN is located in AR_1's network, signaling is performed across two signaling hops, while at AR_2's network it is performed across three signaling hops, and while at AR_3's network signaling is performed across four signaling hops. Furthermore, the measurement results confirm, that sender-initiated reservations (scenarios M1 and M4) consume less time compared to receiver-initiated reservations (scenarios M2 and M3).

Scenario	Updated reservation MN at AR_1	Updated reservation MN at AR_2	Updated reservation MN at AR_3
M1 – MN acts as data flow sender and signaling initiator	2.01 ms	3.37 ms	4.52 ms
M2 – MN acts as data flow sender and signaling responder	2.99 ms	4.45 ms	5.66 ms
M3 – MN acts as data flow receiver and signaling initiator	3.55 ms	5.00 ms	6.00 ms
M4 – MN acts as data flow receiver and signaling responder	3.27 ms	4.45 ms	5.62 ms

Table 4.3: *Average of the measurement results of reservation setup after movement for Mobile IPv6 route optimized flows*

However, note that the values obtained for the same form of reservations, i.e., scenarios M1 and M4 (for sender-initiated reservations), as well as M2 and M3 (for receiver-initiated reservations) differ, although these scenarios operate conceptually identical. Despite the fact that all testbed routers were equipped with identical hardware and software, detailed measurement analysis revealed, that the processing times of single signaling messages varies between different testbed routers. While these processing times are quite stable on each testbed router with a very low standard deviation over all measurements, their difference has a significant impact on the plain overall setup time in these testbed-based measurements.

Nevertheless, the total reservation setup time is still very low compared to typical propagation delays that can be found in the Internet. Depending on the actual number of signaling hops and the propagation delays between any two signaling entities, it therefore provides a good estimate that the signaling operation can be performed "reasonably" fast. Section A.8 on page 268 provides the detailed evaluation results for all 50 measurements of all mobility scenarios.

4.5 Anticipated Handover Support for Quality-of-Service Signaling

Whenever an MN moves, it will be forced to change its point of attachment eventually, in order to keep its network connectivity alive. However, switching to a new access point results in a (partial) new path for the data flow. In case a resource reservation has been established along an old path, the previously assured QoS parameters cannot necessarily be assumed to be met on the new path. If this resource reservation is only re-established *after* the access point was changed, a certain amount of time elapses until a new reservation is established or until the re-reservation request is assumed to have failed.

Section 4.4 showed how QoS signaling can be performed in mobile environments in conjunction with Mobile IPv6 as mobility management protocol. This approach is, however, based on a *hard handover* technique, i.e., a reservation is only adapted once the MN already switched to its new AR. This, in turn, leads to periods of time during which no QoS guarantees are provided until a new resource reservation has been finally established from the new point of attachment, if resources permit.

Instead, it is desirable for a user to switch to a new access point at which his resource reservation was already established beforehand an is thus ready to be used instantaneously. In order to accomplish this goal, a resource reservation must be signaled along the anticipated data path by the MN *in advance*, before it actually changes its point of attachment. This so-called *anticipated handover* technique provides seamless QoS support for MNs, because the reservation is made before the connectivity breaks (make-before-break). This section develops a concept for anticipated handovers in combination with resource reservations. The concept is developed exemplary around the NSIS protocol suite since NSIS provides feature-rich and still extensible signaling protocols for IP-based networks. With respect to mobility support, the distinction between signaling sessions and signaling flows as being present in NSIS proves to be very useful, while its complexity and huge amount of protocol mechanisms and functionalities lead to substantial changes.

4.5.1 Analysis of QoS Signaling for an Anticipated Handover

In order to allow end-to-end resource reservations to be used seamlessly by MNs, an anticipated handover needs to be signaled in advance. This can be exemplified with the scenario depicted in Figure 4.1 on page 99. At first, the MN establishes a resource reservation from end-to-end along the data path from its old access router AR_O toward the CN. The MN may then move into the coverage area of a new access router AR_N upon which the MN anticipates to change its point of attachment toward AR_N. However, since the data path from AR_N to the CN differs from the old data path, a resource reservation request must be initiated for the new data path from AR_N in advance.

This dissertation assumes that the signaling instance is triggered by the network whenever a handover is anticipated to take place and therefore abstracts from specific mechanisms implemented by the physical or the link layer. However, in order to initiate an anticipated handover and to establish a reservation along the new path, the MN needs to know at least the Layer-2-ID (*L2-ID*) of the anticipated new access point.[6] The CARD protocol [RFC4066] can then be used to obtain the IP address of the corresponding access router.

The following set of requirements must be fulfilled by a distributed QoS signaling protocol in order to allow for seamless QoS guarantees in mobile environments:

Trigger new reservations independent of a mobility management protocol The signaling procedure to establish new reservations should conceptually operate independently of a specific mobility management protocol. This provides the necessary flexibility to allow for anticipated handovers no matter which mobility management protocol is actually used underneath. How the anticipated handover is triggered on the MN itself and how the MN resolves the IP address of the new access router is not part of the QoS signaling protocol and must be provided by external mechanisms.

Allow for path-decoupled signaling Since the new access router AR_N is actively involved into the anticipated resource reservation, the QoS signaling protocol must provide means to deliver signaling messages directly toward this signaling entity.

Initiate signaling to or from the anticipated access router Once the anticipated access router AR_N was notified by the MN about its resource reservation request, the AR_N must act as proxy for the MN in order to initiate a resource reservation along the data path between AR_N and the CN. This adapted reservation request cannot be initiated by the MN, since the MN is at this point in time still attached to AR_O and therefore not aware of the anticipated data path between AR_N and CN.

---

[6]E.g., by means of a link layer scan when coming into the range of a new access point.

Allow for tear down of old reservations after handover Once a new resource reservation is established in response to an anticipated handover, the old reservation should be torn down as soon as the handover was successfully performed. This is an important requirement in order to prevent resources from being reserved unnecessarily long by old reservations even if these reservations can no longer be actively used anymore.

Provide means for a hard handover as fallback solution A resource reservation request triggered by an anticipated handover may fail like any other reservation request or simply because the MN decided to move eventually to a different access router. Hence, it should be possible to provide a hard handover as fallback solution, i.e., initiate the reservation request automatically after the MN already switched to its new access router AR_N.

In general the CN must be assumed to be unaware of the MN's mobility. Hence, the QoS signaling protocol itself must provide mechanisms to trigger anticipated reservations that are initiated to or from the anticipated access router AR_N. For instance, consider the scenario depicted in Figure 4.12 where a receiver-initiated reservation is established between the CN and the MN. Since the CN acts as data flow sender in this scenario, it "controls" the signaling session and sends a QUERY message toward the MN.

However, even though the MN itself receives an anticipated handover trigger ("AHO trigger"), the CN is not aware of the MN's anticipated movement since the QoS signaling protocol does not provide any mechanisms for the MN to inform the CN of its anticipated new location and no mobility management protocol, such as Mobile IP, is used. Hence, the necessary signaling procedure to adapt the reservation along the new data path (highlighted in Figure 4.12) is not initiated. Once the MN eventually changes its point of attachment (and receives a local "HO trigger"), there is no reservation established along the new data path.

In order to allow for an anticipated handover the signaling procedure can be conceptually separated into three distinct phases as illustrated in Figure 4.13. Note, that this concept is independent of the actually used QoS signaling protocol. At first, the MN is connected to its old access router AR_O. Once the MN receives an AHO trigger it initiates an anticipated handover by sending a Reservation Change Request toward its new access router AR_N (phase ①). At that time the MN is still connected to its access router AR_O.

After that (phase ② in Figure 4.13) AR_N acts as proxy for the MN and establishes a new reservation between AR_N and CN. This reservation is called a *preliminary reservation*. As soon as this preliminary reservation request is completed, AR_N

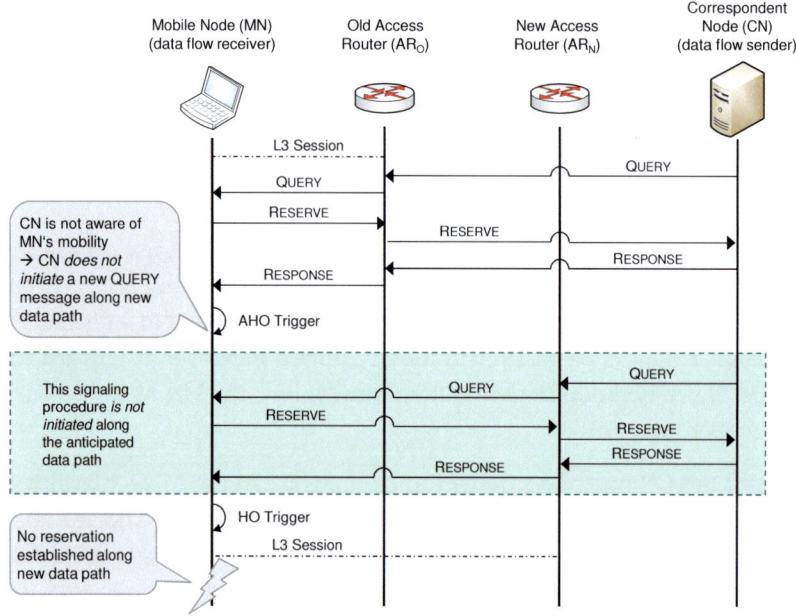

Figure 4.12: *In case a MN's movement cannot be signaled toward the CN a reservation won't be adapted*

triggers a Reservation Change Response toward the MN in order to confirm whether the reservation request was successful. The AHO trigger should come early enough to allow for completion of the reservation signaling, i.e., before the MN's connection to AR$_O$ actually breaks. Otherwise, the preliminary reservation cannot be activated, i.e., the anticipated handover procedure cannot be completed, upon which reservation state for the preliminary reservation times out and a hard handover reservation mechanism must be used as fallback solution.

In case the reservation was successful and the MN's QoS signaling instance receives a local handover trigger ("HO trigger")—which indicates the actual change to AR$_N$'s network—the already established preliminary reservation must finally be activated in phase ③ by sending a Reservation Change Complete confirmation toward AR$_N$. This establishes a reservation between the MN and AR$_N$ and allows access router AR$_N$ to finally activate the preliminary reservation between AR$_N$ and the CN.

The currently specified NSIS protocols do, however, not provide all of the necessary functionality to allow for anticipated handover signaling. As already mentioned above this dissertation assumes the MN to be aware of the new access router's IP

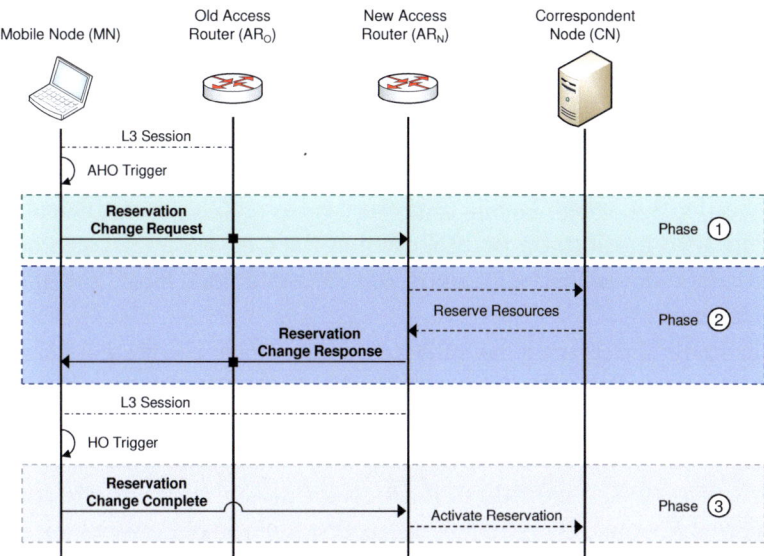

Figure 4.13: *Conceptual message exchange procedure for an anticipated handover*

address while still being connected toward its old access router AR_O. The reservation request for the anticipated reservation ("Reservation Change Request" in phase ①) must therefore be signaled directly toward AR_N without installing state on any intermediate signaling entities. This *path-decoupled* signaling is currently not provided by GIST's specified message routing methods.

Furthermore, this Reservation Change Request must also be supported on a QoS NSLP level, i.e., a corresponding QoS NSLP mechanism must allow the MN to trigger the adaptation of a reservation which is initiated by AR_N on behalf of the MN. Once the Reservation Change Request was signaled toward AR_N and a new reservation was initiated along the new data path, the MN must then also be informed about the result of this signaling procedure. Therefore, a Reservation Change Response must also be supported on QoS NSLP level and has to be signaled path-decoupled toward the MN.

QoS NSLP does currently not provide the necessary mechanisms to trigger the initiation of adapted reservations in response to a changed location of the MN. In case the MN acts as data flow sender, a reservation can be adapted by means of a RESERVE (for sender-initiated reservations) or a QUERY (for receiver-initiated reservations) which are issued by AR_N on behalf of the MN. However, in case the MN acts as data flow receiver, the CN "controls" the signaling session and is responsible for sending new QUERY or RESERVE messages toward the MN at its new location. Since the CN is not aware of the MN's changing location, these messages are not emitted and the reservation is not adapted to the new data path. Therefore, QoS NSLP needs additional mechanisms that allow the MN to trigger reservations to be adapted even if it is located in upstream direction of the reservation's data path. In Section 4.4, where Mobile IPv6 was used as mobility management protocol, the Mobile IPv6 instance on the CN notified the QoS NSLP instance on the CN about the MN's movement by means of the proposed node local flow information service element.

The challenge of triggering the initiation of an adapted reservation does not only concern the MN and the CN. It also affects the CRN which is supposed to actively tear down a reservation along the old data path. While the CRN is already able to initiate a tear down toward AR_O on its own if AR_O is located in downstream direction of the CRN, it can't do so if AR_O is located in upstream direction of the CRN. In order for the CRN to trigger a tear down of the old reservation on behalf of AR_O, the CRN must be able to inform the old access router about the MN's movement by means of dedicated QoS signaling mechanisms.

4.5.2 Design of QoS NSLP Signaling for an Anticipated Handover

Based on the conceptual anticipated handover procedure provided above (cf. Figure 4.13), this section shows how anticipated handovers for resource reservations can be realized for QoS NSLP. Since the role of the two communicating entities (MN and CN) and the direction of the data flow has an impact on the concrete signaling procedure for anticipated handovers, this section provides the design for each of the four resulting signaling scenarios (cf. Section 4.3.1 on page 104).

4.5.2.1 M1 – Mobile Node is Data Flow Sender and Reservation Initiator

First of all, the MN can act as data flow sender and initiator of a corresponding reservation. Figure 4.14 illustrates the signaling procedure for this scenario. At the beginning a reservation is established between the MN and the CN while the MN is still attached toward AR_O (denoted "Original reservation" in Figure 4.14). After that, the MN receives an AHO trigger upon which an anticipated handover reservation can be established.

According to the conceptual signaling procedure outlined in Section 4.5.1, the MN sends a Reservation Change Request toward AR_N in phase ①. Since the NSIS protocols do currently not provide means to send such a request path-decoupled

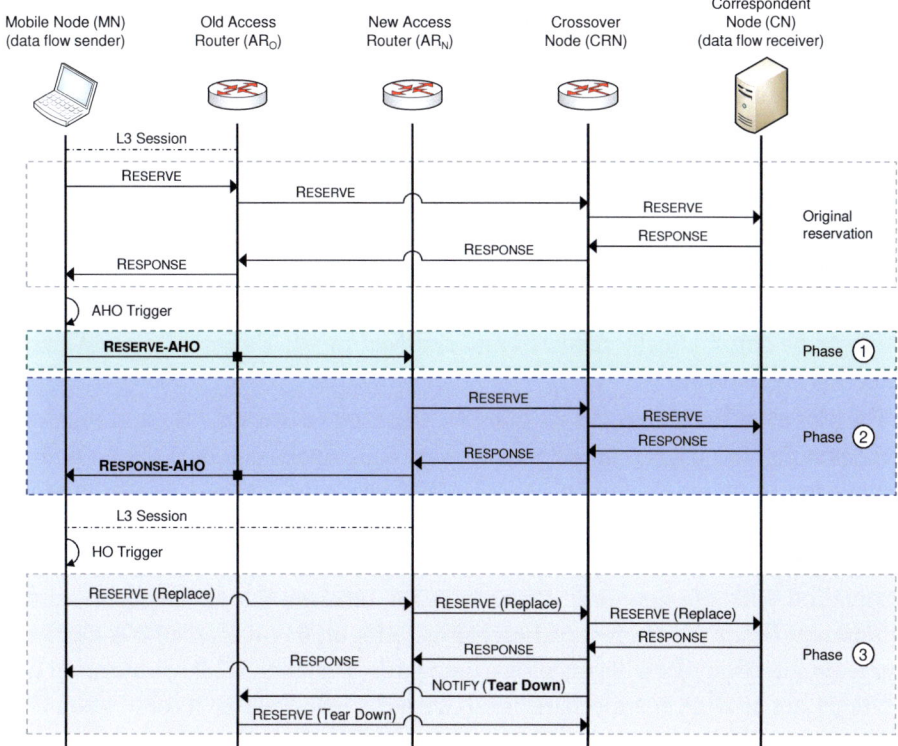

Figure 4.14: *Anticipated handover signaling procedure for scenario M1 – MN acts as data flow sender and signaling initiator*

toward AR_N, a new signaling message denoted "RESERVE-AHO" must be introduced. In order to be sent path-decoupled an already proposed *Explicit Signaling Target Message Routing Method* (EST-MRM) [Ble10] for GIST can be used. This EST-MRM carries the necessary addressing information for the signaling message transport from the MN toward AR_N and contains information about the new signaling flow between the MN's anticipated IP address and the CN's IP address. The signaling message has the proxy flag set in order to inform AR_N that it should act as proxy for a new reservation request.

AR_N uses the addressing information of the new flow in order to establish a reservation toward the CN in phase ②. This reservation is established for the new signaling flow (i.e., the RESERVE carries the new MRI) but is still identified by the same Session ID of the old signaling flow. Once AR_N receives the RESPONSE message, a new "RESPONSE-AHO" message is used in order to signal a Reservation Change

Response toward the MN. This signaling message is also sent path-decoupled by means of the EST-MRM.

Note, that this reservation request is established for an *anticipated* handover and it is still possible, that the handover to AR_N never happens. Therefore, the preliminary reservation established during phase ② should not replace the existing original reservation until the anticipated handover finally succeeded and the MN sent its Reservation Change Complete confirmation. This results in two reservations being established in parallel during a short period of time. Furthermore, route changes may occur along the new signaling path between phase ② and phase ③. This will, however, be automatically detected and resolved by GIST's periodic route change detection mechanism.

The MN eventually changes its point of attachment toward AR_N and receives a corresponding HO trigger. In order to activate (i.e., finally commit) the preliminary reservation in phase ③, the MN sends a path-coupled RESERVE message with a Replace flag set (denoted "RESERVE (Replace)" in Figure 4.14) toward the CN. This replacing RESERVE instructs all intermediate signaling entities to replace the old reservation with the new one. Once the CRN receives this replacing RESERVE it cannot tear down the old reservation toward AR_O on its own, since it is located in upstream direction of the reservation's data path. The QoS NSLP specification does currently not provide any mechanisms to trigger a tear down of a reservation if the triggering signaling entity is located in upstream direction. Hence, it is necessary to introduce a new NOTIFY signaling message of type "Tear down" which instructs the receiving signaling entity to initiate a tear down RESERVE (denoted "NOTIFY (Tear Down)" in Figure 4.14). Note, that the CRN must then take care to stop forwarding this tearing RESERVE further along the path to avoid releasing the currently used reservation.

4.5.2.2 M2 – Mobile Node is Data Flow Sender and Reservation Responder

The case where the MN acts as sender of the data flow and reservation responder corresponds to a *receiver-initiated reservation*. Figure 4.15 illustrates this scenario. At the beginning a receiver-initiated reservation is established between the MN and the CN. Once the MN receives an AHO trigger it must signal a Reservation Change Request toward its anticipated access router AR_N in phase ①. Since the NSIS protocols do not provide means to accomplish this task, a new QUERY-AHO signaling message is introduced that is sent directly to AR_N via the EST-MRM and instructs AR_N to establish a preliminary reservation toward the CN.

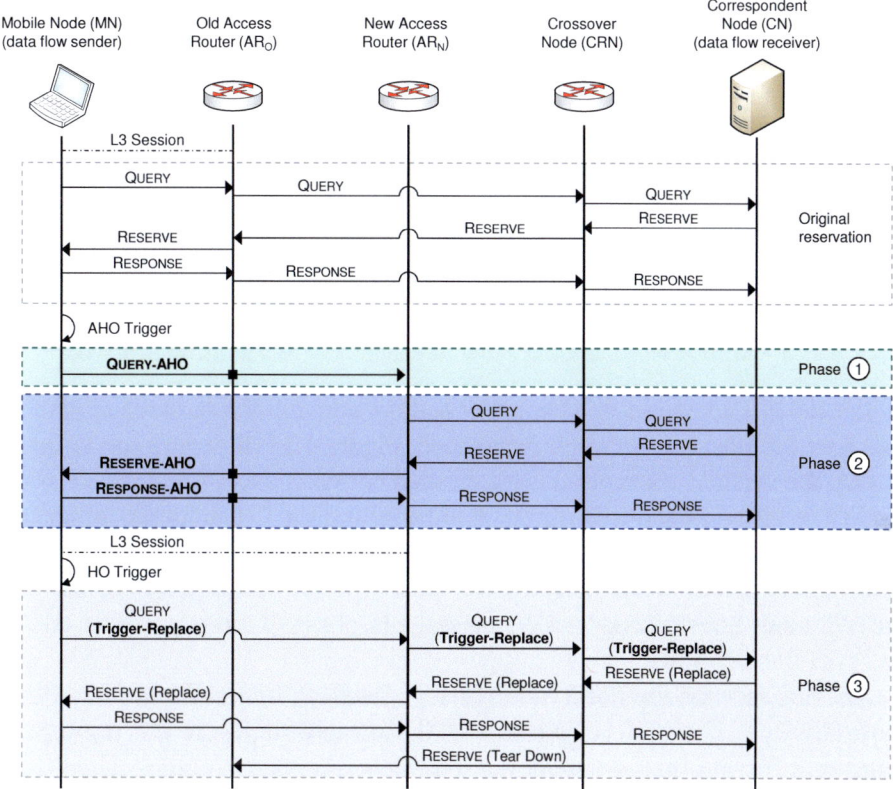

Figure 4.15: *Anticipated handover signaling procedure for scenario M2 – MN acts as data flow sender and signaling responder*

In phase ② AR$_N$ acts as proxy for the MN and establishes a receiver-initiated reservation for the new signaling flow. Once AR$_N$ receives the RESERVE message from the CN, it forwards this message via the newly introduced RESERVE-AHO message directly toward the MN by means of the EST-MRM. As soon as the MN receives the RESERVE-AHO message it knows whether the reservation along the new path could be established or not. The MN acknowledges the preliminary reservation by sending a RESPONSE-AHO message to AR$_N$. AR$_N$ finally forwards this RESPONSE toward the CN.

Once the MN actually changes its point of attachment toward AR$_N$, it receives a local HO trigger upon which the preliminary reservation for the new data path must be activated in phase ③ of the anticipated handover procedure. In order to trigger the CN to activate the newly established reservation and replace the original one, the MN would have to send a corresponding signaling message toward the CN. Since the QoS NSLP specification does currently not provide mechanisms that allow the MN to instruct the CN to send a replacing RESERVE, the QUERY message is sent with a newly introduced "Trigger-Replace" flag.

Upon receiving this QUERY message, the CN can finally activate the preliminary reservation and replace the old one by emitting a replacing RESERVE along the new data path. Once the CRN receives the corresponding RESPONSE message, it can tear down the original reservation along the old data path by issuing a tearing RESERVE.

4.5.2.3 M3 – Mobile Node is Data Flow Receiver and Reservation Initiator

In case the MN is receiver of a data flow and the initiator of a resource reservation, a *receiver-initiated reservation* is performed. Figure 4.16 illustrates this situation. At first, the original reservation is established between the MN and the CN. Once the MN receives a local AHO trigger, it must inform the CN about the anticipated handover and instruct AR_N to act as proxy for the newly established reservation. By following the conceptual anticipated handover procedure outlined in Section 4.5.1, the MN sends a new RESERVE-AHO message in phase ① directly toward AR_N by means of the EST-MRM.

Once AR_N receives this Reservation Change Request, it must determine whether the reservation's data path is directed from the MN toward the CN or in the opposite direction. The information about the data flow direction is encapsulated in the EST-MRI of the RESERVE-AHO message. Since in this case the reservation's data path is directed from the CN toward the MN, AR_N must instruct the CN to initiate the reservation along the new data path in phase ② of the anticipated handover concept. This requires the installation of reverse-path state on all intermediate signaling entities along the new data path by means of a QUERY message, before a corresponding RESERVE can be issued.

The QoS NSLP specification does currently not provide mechanisms to trigger the initiation of a QUERY message. Hence, a NOTIFY message of a newly introduced type "Init QUERY" is used to instruct the CN to send a QUERY message toward AR_N. After that, a preliminary receiver-initiated reservation is established along the new data path between CN and AR_N. Once AR_N receives the corresponding RESPONSE message, it forwards the confirmation of the reservation request toward the MN (which is still located at its old location) by means of a RESPONSE-AHO message.

Once the MN changes its point of attachment toward AR_N, it receives a local HO trigger and must then finally activate the preliminary reservation along the new data path in phase ③. Since the receiver-initiated reservation is "controlled"

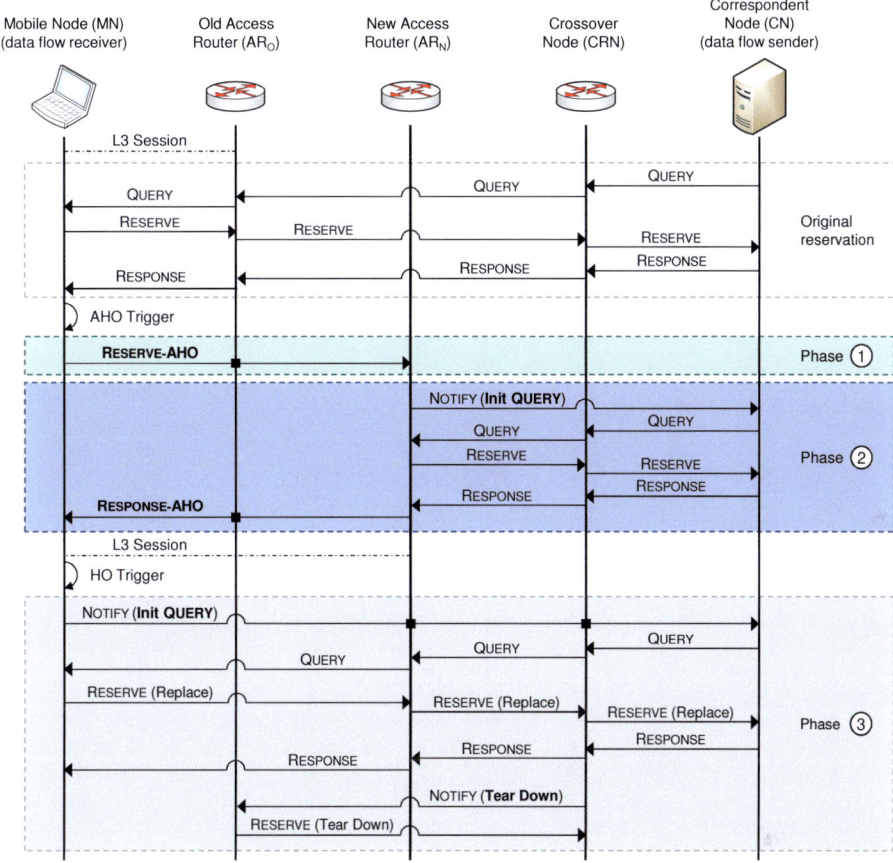

Figure 4.16: *Anticipated handover signaling procedure for scenario M3 – MN acts as data flow receiver and signaling initiator*

by the CN, the MN must instruct the CN to send a new QUERY message. This can be accomplished by means of the newly introduced NOTIFY message of type "Init QUERY" which is sent directly via the EST-MRM toward the CN. Furthermore, this NOTIFY message must also carry the newly introduced "Trigger-Replace" flag which is then used by the CN's subsequent QUERY message. Upon receiving this QUERY message, the MN sends a replacing RESERVE across AR_N toward the CN. The CRN on the path can speed up the process of tearing down the old reservation by triggering a tearing RESERVE. It does so by sending a NOTIFY message of the newly introduced type "Tear Down" toward the old access router AR_O, upon which AR_O emits the tearing RESERVE. The CRN is then responsible to stop forwarding this tearing RESERVE further along the path in order to avoid releasing the currently used reservation.

4.5.2.4 M4 – Mobile Node is Data Flow Receiver and Reservation Responder

Whenever the MN is the data flow receiver of a sender-initiated reservation, the MN acts as the reservation responder. In this case, a reservation is initiated by the CN toward the MN by means of an initial RESERVE message. Figure 4.17 illustrates how an anticipated handover can be performed within this scenario.

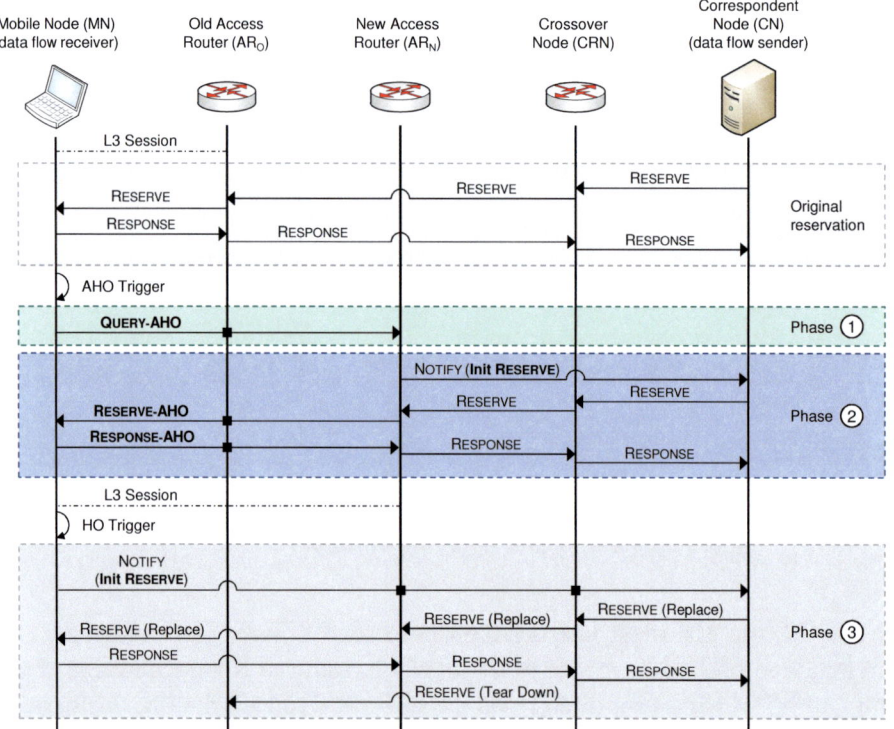

Figure 4.17: *Anticipated handover signaling procedure for scenario M4 – MN acts as data flow receiver and signaling responder*

Since the reservation is initiated by the CN, the MN must inform the new access router and the CN about its anticipated movement. In order to initiate a Reservation

Change Request and trigger the establishment of a new preliminary reservation along the new data path, the MN sends a new QUERY-AHO message directly toward AR$_N$ by means of the EST-MRM in phase ① of the anticipated handover procedure. The information contained in the EST-MRI of the MN's QUERY-AHO message must be used by the AR$_N$ in order to determine the data flow direction of the corresponding reservation request. AR$_N$ acts as proxy for the MN and since it is located in upstream direction of the reservation's data path in this case, it cannot establish a new reservation on its own (as opposed to scenario M1), but only trigger the CN to do so. Since the QoS NSLP specification does not provide appropriate mechanisms to trigger a new reservation request, AR$_N$ uses a NOTIFY message of a newly introduced type "Init RESERVE". Upon receiving this request in phase ②, the CN can then issue a new RESERVE toward AR$_N$. This RESERVE is then forwarded by AR$_N$ directly toward the MN by means of the RESERVE-AHO message. The MN sends a RESPONSE-AHO back to AR$_N$ upon which AR$_N$ forwards this RESPONSE toward the CN.

Once the MN changes its point of attachment toward AR$_N$ it receives a local HO trigger upon which it can activate the preliminary reservation in phase ③. In order to do so, the MN uses the newly introduced NOTIFY message of type "Init RESERVE" which has the newly introduced "Trigger-Replace" flag set and is sent directly toward the CN by means of the EST-MRM. The CN then issues a replacing RESERVE along the new data path which activates the new reservation and replaces the old one. Once the CRN receives the corresponding RESPONSE message, it can directly issue a tearing RESERVE toward AR$_O$ since AR$_O$ is located in the old reservation's downstream direction.

4.5.3 Design of a Hard Handover Fallback Solution

An anticipated handover may fail, for instance simply because the MN does not move to its anticipated new access router or because the reservation could not be successfully established along the new data path. However, in case the MN moves to a new access router for which a new reservation could not be established in advance, it is necessary to provide mechanisms for a hard handover as fallback solution.

A hard handover can already be initiated with the specified NSIS protocols for sender- and receiver-initiated reservations, if the MN is the sender of the data flow. In these cases, the MN establishes a new reservation simply by means of a new QUERY message (for receiver-initiated reservations) or a new RESERVE message (for sender-initiated reservations) which are sent in downstream direction toward the CN.

However, whenever the MN acts as receiver of the data flow, a new reservation cannot be triggered by the MN with the existing NSIS protocol mechanisms. Therefore, this section presents how hard handovers can be realized if the MN is the data flow receiver and no mobility management protocol (e.g., Mobile IP) can be used to inform the CN about the MN's movement.

4.5.3.1 M3 – Mobile Node is Data Flow Receiver and Reservation Initiator

The scenario for the MN acting as reservation initiator is illustrated in Figure 4.18. In this case the CN must be informed about the MN's movement and the MN must trigger a new QUERY in order to install reverse-path state along the new data path.

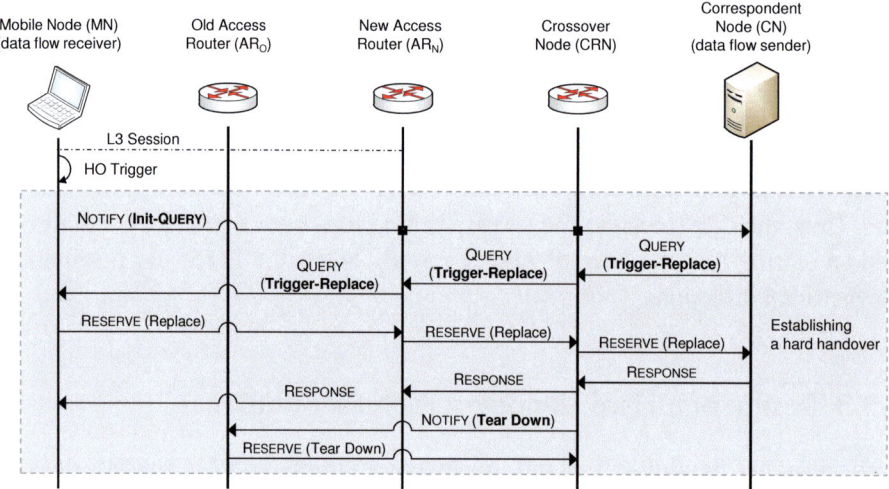

Figure 4.18: *Signaling procedure for a hard handover for scenario M3 – MN acts as data flow receiver and signaling initiator*

Since the NSIS protocols do currently not provide appropriate mechanisms to handle this scenario, the newly introduced NOTIFY message of type "Init QUERY" is sent by the MN directly toward the CN by means of the EST-MRM. Upon receiving this notification, the CN issues a QUERY message along the new data path. Since the corresponding RESERVE should replace the original reservation along the old data path, the QUERY message is sent with the newly introduced "Trigger-Replace" flag set. Once the MN receives this QUERY message it emits a replacing RESERVE toward the CN. Since AR_O is not located in downstream direction of the reservation's data path from the CRN, the CRN cannot issue a tearing RESERVE on its own. Instead, it must use the newly introduced NOTIFY message of type "Tear Down" in order to instruct AR_O to send a tearing RESERVE along the old data path. Furthermore, the CRN must take care to not forward this tearing RESERVE further along the data path toward the CN.

4.5.3.2 M4 – Mobile Node is Data Flow Receiver and Reservation Responder

In case the MN acts as reservation responder, it must inform the CN about its movement and trigger a corresponding RESERVE to be issued by the CN along the new data path. Figure 4.19 shows how this task can be accomplished.

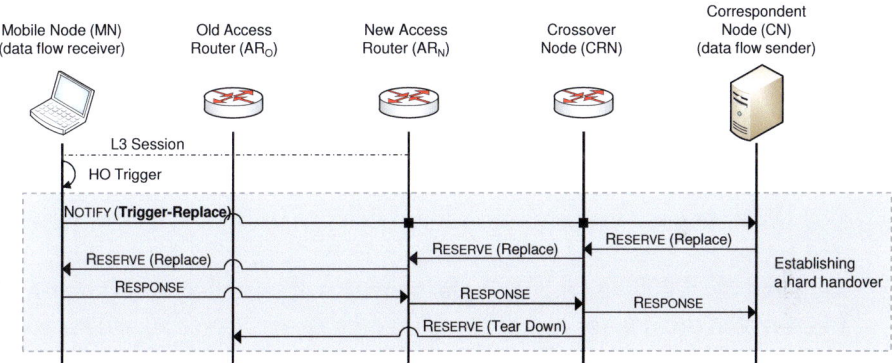

Figure 4.19: *Signaling procedure for a hard handover for scenario M4 – MN acts as data flow receiver and signaling responder*

Once the MN moved to the new access router AR_N it receives a local HO trigger upon which it must inform the CN to establish a new reservation. In order to do so it sends a NOTIFY message of the newly introduced type "Trigger-Replace" directly toward the CN via the EST-MRM. Upon receiving this NOTIFY message, the CN can then send a replacing RESERVE along the new data path toward the MN. Once the corresponding RESPONSE message reaches the CRN, the remaining original reservation along the old path can be torn down by means of a tearing RESERVE sent by the CRN.

4.5.4 Necessary Protocol Extensions

Although the NSIS protocols already provide some of the basic protocol functionality in order to realize anticipated handovers or hard handovers, several mechanisms are still not provided by the specifications. This section summarizes the necessary protocol extensions.

First of all, path-decoupled signaling as required in all cases to explicitly address AR_N from the MN is not specified by the current GIST specification [RFC5971]. Therefore, the MN and the new access router AR_N must both support the *Explicit Signaling Target Message Routing Method* (EST-MRM) [Ble10].

Reservations in QoS NSLP are always controlled by the data flow sender, either in form of a RESERVE message or in form of a QUERY message. In case the MN acts as receiver of a data flow—regardless of being the initiator or responder of the reservation—the situation becomes more complicated, since the initial RESERVE or QUERY message that must be sent by the CN has to be triggered by the MN. Therefore, besides supporting path-decoupled signaling the following protocol extensions are necessary for an anticipated handover:

- A new H-flag ("Anticipated Handover") in the generic flags section of the QoS NSLP common header is introduced that can be used in QUERY, RESERVE, and RESPONSE messages which needs only be supported by the MN, AR_O, AR_N, and CN (cf. Figure 4.20). In the scenarios discussed above, QUERY-AHO, RESERVE-AHO, and RESPONSE-AHO are used for QUERY, RESERVE, and RESPONSE messages that have the H-flag set.

- A new X-flag ("Trigger-Replace") for QUERY and NOTIFY messages is introduced that can be used to trigger a RESERVE message with Replace flag set and that can also be used to activate an anticipated reservation (cf. Figure 4.20)

- New NOTIFY messages of type "Init Reserve" and "Init Query" are introduced which trigger reservations to be established or QUERY messages to be sent by the data flow's receiver

- A new optional NOTIFY message of type "Tear Down" is introduced to allow resources on an old branch to be released

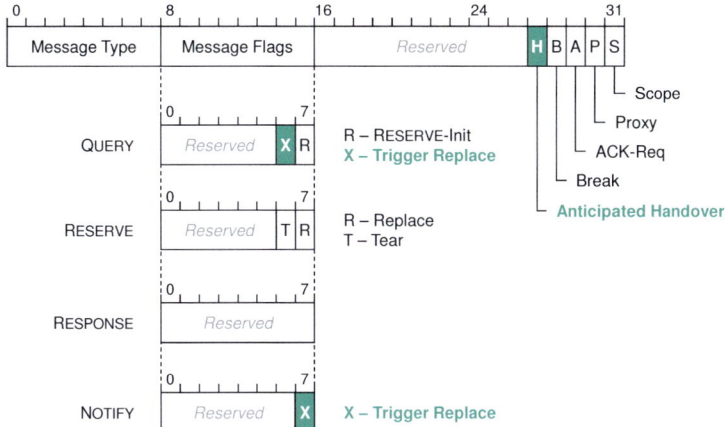

Figure 4.20: *Object format of the QoS NSLP common header with the newly introduced "Anticipated Handover" and "Trigger-Replace" flags.*

The newly introduced NOTIFY types are realized via InfoSpec objects with a class field set to Informational (0x1) and new corresponding error fields Init Query (0x07), Init Reserve (0x08), and Tear Down (0x09). Note, that no new message types are necessary in order to support anticipated reservations.

4.5.5 Evaluation of Anticipated Handover QoS Signaling

This section evaluates the signaling performance of the anticipated handover and the hard handover concepts. The evaluation aims at demonstrating that the concepts developed in this chapter allow for anticipated handover signaling and aims at confirming that signaling can be performed reasonably fast, i.e., the necessary amount of time for processing signaling messages is expected to be very low compared to typical propagation delays that can be experienced in the Internet.

The proposed protocol extensions were implemented into the NSIS-ka protocol suite [Ble+12a] in [Det10]. All four mobility scenarios analyzed in Section 4.5.1 were evaluated within the same testbed used for the Mobile IPv6 based evaluations (cf. Figure 4.11 on page 122) but without using the HA.

According to the design outlined in Section 4.5.2 the signaling procedure for all four anticipated handover scenarios is conceptually separated into three distinct phases. Within each of those phases signaling messages are exchanged across a different set of intermediate signaling entities. The time to establish and activate an anticipated handover, and the time to tear down an old reservation depends

on the number of participating intermediate signaling entities and the round trip
times between each of those signaling entities.

Figure 4.21 illustrates along which paths signaling messages are exchanged in
the anticipated handover concept. During the establishment of an anticipated
handover the Reservation Change Request in phase ① is exchanged between the
MN—which is attached to AR_O—and its anticipated access router AR_N across α
signaling hops.

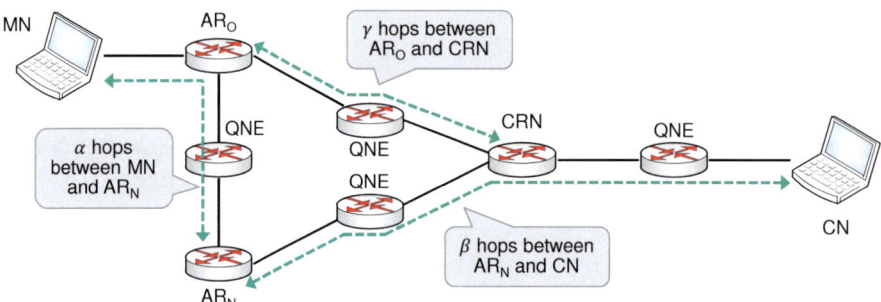

Figure 4.21: *Paths for signaling message exchange in the anticipated handover con-*
cept

The resource reservation between AR_N and the CN during phase ② of the anticipated handover concept spans β signaling hops and the signaling path between the
CRN and AR_O, which is used for an active tear down of the old reservation, spans γ
signaling hops. In the example depicted in Figure 4.21 $\alpha = 3$, $\beta = 4$, and $\gamma = 2$.
These three parameters can then be used to estimate the time needed to establish
anticipated handovers.

4.5.5.1 M1 – Mobile Node is Data Flow Sender and Reservation Initiator

Whenever the MN is data flow sender and reservation initiator, the Reservation
Change Request in phase ① is issued by the MN by means of the newly introduced
RESERVE-AHO QoS NSLP message. Figure 4.22 illustrates the different processing
times in a message sequence diagram.

In this case the MN performs a GIST three-way handshake with AR_N by means
of the EST-MRM, i.e., the signaling messages are exchanged directly between the
MN and AR_N without being interpreted (in terms of QoS signaling) by any other

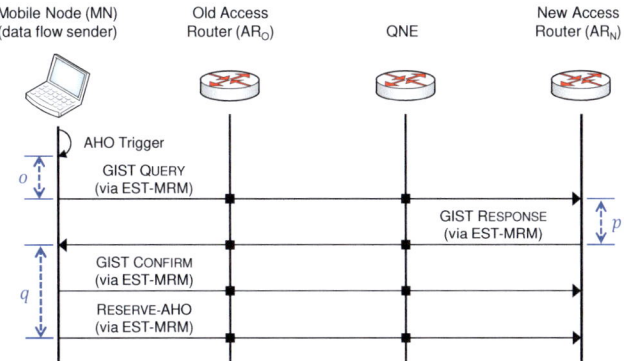

Figure 4.22: *Processing times within phase ① of the anticipated handover signaling procedure for mobility scenario M1 – MN is data flow sender and reservation initiator*

intermediate signaling entity. However, the signaling messages are still routed along a path with intermediate signaling entities (illustrated by the black squares in Figure 4.22).

In the following, the processing time needed to create an initial GIST QUERY is represented by parameter o, the time needed at the responding node to process the GIST QUERY and respond with a GIST RESPONSE is represented by parameter p, and the time needed to process the GIST RESPONSE and issue a GIST CONFIRM with a subsequent RESERVE-AHO is represented by parameter q. The propagation delay between signaling entity i and its directly adjacent signaling entity $i+1$ is assumed to be t_i and the corresponding round trip time between those two signaling entities is then assumed to be $\mathrm{RTT}_i := 2 \times t_i$. For phase ① of the anticipated handover concept there are α signaling hops between the MN and $\mathrm{AR_N}$. For the MN acting as sender of the data flow and reservation initiator (scenario M1), the time needed for phase ① of the anticipated handover concept can be expressed by

$$t_{\mathrm{AHO}}^{(1)} = o + p + q + \sum_{i=1}^{\alpha} \frac{3}{2}\mathrm{RTT}_i \qquad (4.1)$$

In phase ② of the anticipated handover concept, $\mathrm{AR_N}$ establishes a new resource reservation on behalf of the MN toward the CN. The corresponding signaling message exchange is illustrated in Figure 4.23.

The time needed at the QoS NSLP responder to process the RESERVE and send a corresponding RESPONSE can be expressed by parameter v, and the processing time

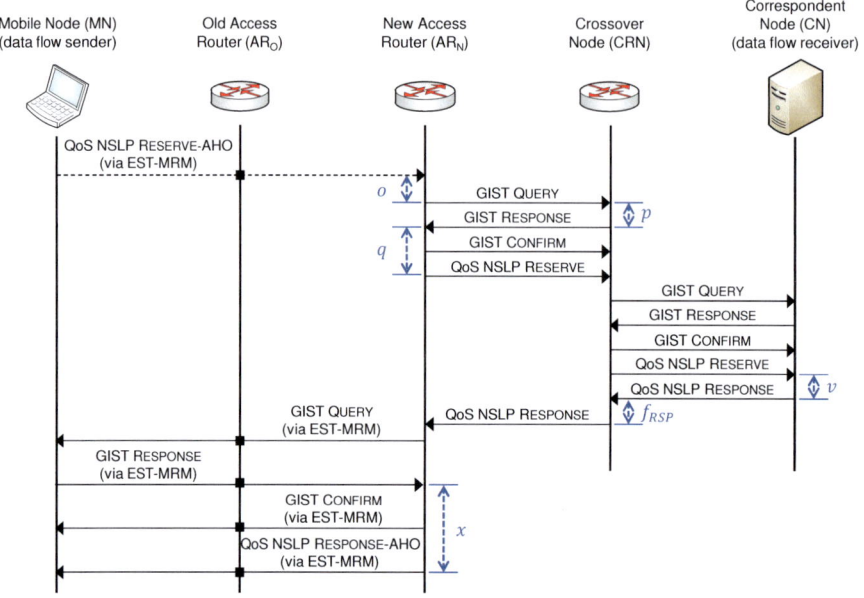

Figure 4.23: *Processing times within phase ② of the anticipated handover signaling procedure for mobility scenario M1 – MN is data flow sender and reservation initiator*

needed to forward a QoS NSLP RESPONSE message is represented by parameter f_{RSP}. In case there are β signaling hops between AR_N and the CN, the time needed for phase ② of the anticipated handover concept and this scenario can be expressed by

$$
t_{AHO}^{(2)} = \left(\sum_{i=1}^{\beta} o_i + p_i + q_i + \frac{3}{2}\text{RTT}_i \right) + v + \left(\sum_{i=1}^{\beta-1} f_{RSP_i} + \frac{1}{2}\text{RTT}_i \right)
$$
$$
+ o + p + x + \left(\sum_{i=1}^{\alpha} \frac{3}{2}\text{RTT}_i \right) \tag{4.2}
$$

Since the establishment of an anticipated reservation is based on a combination of phase ① and ②, the resulting time needed to establish an anticipated reservation in this scenario can be expressed by equation (4.3):

$$t_{AHO}^{(1+2)} = 2 \times (o + p) + v + x + \left(\sum_{i=1}^{\alpha} \frac{3}{2}RTT_i \right)$$

$$+ \left(\sum_{i=1}^{\beta-1} f_{RSP_i} + \frac{1}{2}RTT_i \right) + \left(\sum_{i=1}^{\beta} o_i + p_i + q_i + \frac{3}{2}RTT_i \right) \quad (4.3)$$

If the round trip times are assumed to be significantly bigger than the single processing times, the dependency on the round trip times can be expressed as follows:

$$t_{AHO}^{(1+2)} \approx RTT \times \left(\frac{3}{2}\alpha + \frac{1}{2}(\beta - 1) + \frac{3}{2}\beta \right)$$

$$\approx RTT \times \left(\frac{3}{2}\alpha + 2\beta - \frac{1}{2} \right) \quad (4.4)$$

Phase ③ of the anticipated handover concept basically consists of the time needed to activate the anticipated reservation once the MN changed its point of attachment and the time needed to tear down the reservation along the old path (cf. Figure 4.24).

The time needed to activate the anticipated reservation in phase ③ can then be expressed by

$$t_{AHO}^{(3)} = o + p + q + v + 2 \times RTT + \left(\sum_{i=1}^{\beta} f_{RSV_i} + f_{RSP_i} + RTT_i \right) \quad (4.5)$$

In case the time needed to process and forward a NOTIFY message is denoted z_{NOTIFY}, the time needed to tear down the old reservation can be expressed by

$$t_{AHO}^{(3)'} = z_{NOTIFY} + \left(\sum_{j=1}^{\gamma-1} f_{NOTIFY_j} \right) + \left(\sum_{j=1}^{\gamma} \frac{RTT_j}{2} \right) + y + \left(\sum_{j=1}^{\gamma-1} f'_{RSV_j} \right) + \left(\sum_{j=1}^{\gamma} \frac{RTT_j}{2} \right)$$

$$= z_{NOTIFY} + y + \left(\sum_{j=1}^{\gamma-1} f_{NOTIFY_j} + f'_{RSV_j} \right) + \sum_{j=1}^{\gamma} RTT_j \quad (4.6)$$

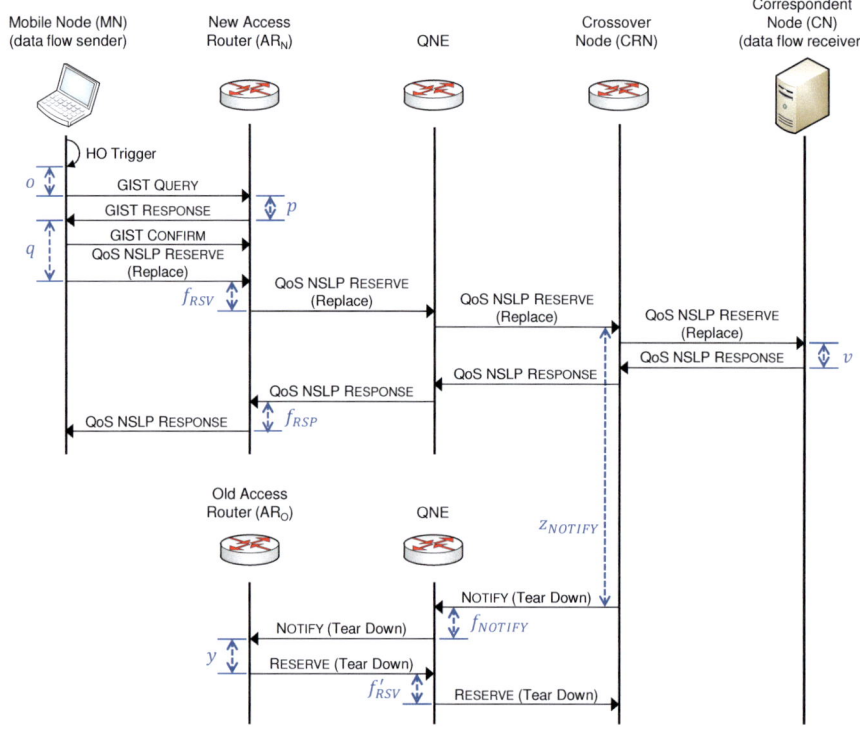

Figure 4.24: *Processing times within phase ③ of the anticipated handover signaling procedure for mobility scenario M1 – MN is data flow sender and reservation initiator*

4.5.5.2 M2 – Mobile Node is Data Flow Sender and Reservation Responder

The case in which the MN acts as data flow sender and reservation responder, reflects a receiver-initiated reservation and corresponds to the scenario depicted in Figure 4.15. The message sequence diagrams with the detailed processing components and the derivation of the evaluation formulae are presented in Appendix B.1.

In this case the time needed to establish an anticipated reservation in phases ① and ② of the anticipated handover concept can be expressed by

$$t_{\text{AHO}}^{(1+2)} = o + p + r + u + v + \left(\sum_{i=1}^{\alpha} \frac{5}{2} \text{RTT}_i \right) + \left(\sum_{i=1}^{\beta-1} f_{RSV_i} + \frac{1}{2} \text{RTT}_i \right)$$
$$+ \left(\sum_{i=1}^{\beta} o_i + p_i + r_i + f_{RSP_i} + 2 \times \text{RTT}_i \right) \tag{B.3}$$

Therefore, if the round trip times are assumed to be significantly bigger than the single processing times, the dependency on the round trip times can be expressed as follows:

$$t_{\text{AHO}}^{(1+2)} \approx \text{RTT} \times \left(\frac{5}{2}\alpha + \frac{1}{2}(\beta - 1) + 2\beta \right)$$
$$\approx \text{RTT} \times \left(\frac{5}{2}\alpha + \frac{5}{2}\beta - \frac{1}{2} \right) \tag{4.7}$$

The time needed to activate an anticipated reservation after the MN performed a handover to its anticipated access router can be expressed by

$$t_{\text{AHO}}^{(3)} = o + p + r + \frac{5}{2}\text{RTT} + \left(\sum_{i=1}^{\beta} f_{QUERY_i} + f_{RSV_i} + f_{RSP_i} + \frac{3}{2}\text{RTT}_i \right) + u + v \tag{B.4}$$

The time needed to tear down the old reservation can be expressed by

$$t_{\text{AHO}}^{(3)'} = z_{RSV} + \sum_{j=1}^{\gamma-1} f'_{RSV_j} + \sum_{j=1}^{\gamma} \frac{\text{RTT}}{2} \tag{B.5}$$

4.5.5.3 M3 – Mobile Node is Data Flow Receiver and Reservation Initiator

The case in which the MN acts as data flow receiver and reservation initiator reflects a receiver-initiated reservation and corresponds to the scenario depicted in Figure 4.16. The detailed message sequence diagrams with the corresponding processing components and the derivation of the evaluation formulae for this scenario are presented in Appendix B.2. The time needed to establish an anticipated reservation in phases ① and ② of the anticipated handover concept can be expressed by

$$t_{AHO}^{(1+2)} = 3 \times (o+p) + q + s + u + v + x + \left(\sum_{i=1}^{\alpha} \frac{3}{2} \text{RTT}_i \right)$$

$$+ \left(\sum_{i=1}^{\beta-1} f_{RSV_i} + f_{RSP_i} \right) + \left(\sum_{i=1}^{\beta} o_i + p_i + r_i + 4 \times \text{RTT}_i \right) \tag{B.8}$$

Therefore, if the round trip times are assumed to be significantly bigger than the single processing times, the dependency on the round trip times can be expressed as follows:

$$t_{AHO}^{(1+2)} \approx \text{RTT} \times (3\alpha + 4\beta) \tag{4.8}$$

The time needed to activate an anticipated reservation in phase ③, after the MN changed its point of attachment, can be expressed by

$$t_{AHO}^{(3)} = 2(o+p) + r + s + u + v + w + \left(\sum_{i=1}^{\beta} f_{QUERY_i} + f_{RSV_i} + f_{RSP_i} + 3\text{RTT}_i \right) + \frac{7}{2}\text{RTT}$$

$$\tag{B.9}$$

The time needed to tear down the old reservation can be expressed by

$$t_{AHO}^{(3)'} = z_{NOTIFY} + \left(\sum_{j=1}^{\gamma-1} f_{NOTIFY_j} + f'_{RSV_j} \right) + y + \sum_{j=1}^{\gamma} \text{RTT}_j \tag{B.10}$$

4.5.5.4 M4 – Mobile Node is Data Flow Receiver and Reservation Responder

The case where the MN acts as data flow receiver and reservation responder reflects a sender-initiated reservation and corresponds to the scenario depicted in Figure 4.17. Detailed message sequence diagrams and derivations of the formulae for the time needed to establish and activate an anticipated handover reservation in this scenario are presented in Appendix B.3. The time required to establish an anticipated reservation in phases ① and ② can be expressed by

$$t_{\text{AHO}}^{(1+2)} = 3 \times (o + p) + q + r + s + v + \left(\sum_{i=1}^{\alpha} \frac{7}{2}\text{RTT}_i \right)$$

$$+ \left(\sum_{i=1}^{\beta} o_i + p_i + q_i + f_{RSP_i} + \frac{7}{2}\text{RTT}_i \right) \tag{B.13}$$

Therefore, if the round trip times are assumed to be significantly bigger than the single processing times, the dependency on the round trip times can be expressed as follows:

$$t_{\text{AHO}}^{(1+2)} \approx \text{RTT} \times \left(\frac{7}{2}\alpha + \frac{7}{2}\beta \right) \tag{4.9}$$

After the MN changed toward its new point of attachment, the anticipated reservation must be activated in phase ③. The time needed to activate an anticipated reservation can be expressed by

$$t_{\text{AHO}}^{(3)} = 2(o + p) + q + s + v + y + \left(\sum_{i=1}^{\beta} f_{RSV_i} + f_{RSP_i} + \frac{5}{2}\text{RTT}_i \right) + \frac{7}{2}\text{RTT} \tag{B.14}$$

The time needed to tear down the old reservation can be expressed by

$$t_{\text{AHO}}^{(3)'} = z_{RSV} + \sum_{j=1}^{\gamma-1} f'_{RSV_j} + \sum_{j=1}^{\gamma} \frac{\text{RTT}_j}{2} \tag{B.15}$$

4.5.5.5 Testbed Based Measurement Results

The testbed based measurements used the same topology and hardware that was used for the Mobile IPv6 based evaluations (cf. Section 4.4.3 on page 121). That is, the topology consisted of three access routers, one MN, and one CN. Since the anticipated handover signaling concept doesn't rely on Mobile IPv6, the HA was not used in these evaluations. The number of signaling hops between the different signaling entities was therefore $\alpha = 2$, $\beta = 2$ if the MN moves from AR_1 to AR_2, $\beta = 3$ if the MN moves from AR_2 to AR_3, and $\gamma = 1$. The chosen topology with its corresponding parameters allows to evaluate the impact of a linearly increasing number of signaling hops on the overall reservation setup time.

All four mobility scenarios were evaluated in 50 distinct measurement runs. Each measurement run consisted of an initial reservation request when the MN was located at AR_1 and two subsequent handovers to access routers AR_2 and AR_3. For each anticipated handover the time for the *establishment* of a reservation along the anticipated path (phase ① and ②) and the time for the actual *activation* (phase ③) after an L3 handover was measured. Section B.4 on page 288 provides the detailed evaluation results for all 50 measurements of all mobility scenarios.

Table 4.4 summarizes the measurement results obtained in this testbed environment. It is again important to note, that the concrete time values obtained by these measurements only exemplify how much time is needed for these signaling operations in this testbed environment. In particular the propagation delay between any two signaling entities in the testbed was very low. In Internet-like scenarios, the round trip time between adjacent signaling entities can be expected to be a magnitude higher than the processing time for the different signaling messages.

Scenario	Initially MN at AR_1	Phase ① and ② MN at AR_2	Phase ③ MN at AR_2	Phase ① and ② MN at AR_3	Phase ③ MN at AR_3
M1 – MN acts as data flow sender and signaling initiator	2.71	4.27	2.21	5.51	2.63
M2 – MN acts as data flow sender and signaling responder	3.50	5.08	3.05	6.37	3.48
M3 – MN acts as data flow receiver and signaling initiator	3.92	5.74	4.69	7.16	5.48
M4 – MN acts as data flow receiver and signaling responder	3.52	5.52	3.65	6.63	4.05

Table 4.4: *Average of the measurement results of reservation setup for anticipated handovers* [ms]

It can be observed that the reservation setup time increases with every additional intermediate signaling entity and that sender-initiated reservations (scenarios

M1 and M4) can be established faster than the corresponding receiver-initiated reservations (scenarios M2 and M3).

The measurement results can be interpreted as follows: since an anticipated reservation is established in phase ① and ②, a MN acting as data flow sender and signaling initiator would have to initiate an anticipated handover in this testbed setup at least 4.27 ms before it leaves access router AR_1 toward access router AR_2. Once it completed the L3 handover toward AR_2, the newly established reservation can instantaneously be used but must be activated in order to not time out eventually. This activation from AR_2 is part of phase ③ of the anticipated handover concept and can be accomplished in 2.21 ms in this testbed setup.

The numbers obtained give only a rough estimate about the time needed to perform the required signaling operation in this specific testbed. However, the absolute numbers are again fairly small. In Internet-like scenarios the propagation delay between any two signaling entities can be expected to dominate. If the number of signaling entities along a signaling path and the propagation delays are known in advance, the time needed to perform an anticipated handover can be estimated by the given formulae.

4.5.5.6 Hard Handover

Since an anticipated handover may fail or an anticipated handover could not be successfully completed before the MN actually performed its L3 handover, this chapter introduced a hard handover fallback solution. Note, that a hard handover has the disadvantage, that there has no resource reservation been established in advance. Therefore, the MN must establish a new resource reservation after its L3 handover. This section provides measurement results for hard handover signaling in the same testbed environment used for Mobile IPv6 and anticipated handover signaling evaluations.

As already outlined in Section 4.5.3 a hard handover can already be established by the existing NSIS protocols whenever the MN acts as data flow sender. That is, the signaling procedure required after an handover does not differ from the signaling procedure required to setup an initial resource reservation whenever the MN acts as data flow sender. Therefore, this section concentrates on evaluation formulae for the two cases in which the MN acts as receiver of the data flow. In these cases, a hard handover can only be performed by means of the proposed protocol extensions in Section 4.5.4.

In case the MN is data flow receiver and reservation initiator (scenario M3), the MN must send a Notify message directly toward the CN in order to trigger a QoS NSLP QUERY which is used to install reverse-path state in downstream direction and triggers a replacing RESERVE to be sent by the MN subsequently. This corresponds to the scenario depicted in Figure 4.18 on page 138. The detailed message sequence diagram and the derivation of the evaluation formulae for this scenario are presented in Appendix C.1.

The time needed to establish a new reservation by means of a hard handover in this scenario can then be expressed by

$$
t_{\text{HHO}} = o + p + s + u + v + \text{RTT} + \left(\sum_{i=1}^{\beta} f_{RSV_i} + f_{RSP_i} + \text{RTT}_i \right)
$$
$$
+ \left(\sum_{i=1}^{\beta+1} o_i + p_i + r_i + 3 \times \text{RTT}_i \right) \tag{C.1}
$$

The time needed to tear down the old reservation along the old path can be expressed by

$$
t'_{\text{HHO}} = z_{NOTIFY} + y + \left(\sum_{j=1}^{\gamma-1} f_{NOTIFY_j} + f'_{RSV_j} \right) + \left(\sum_{j=1}^{\gamma} \text{RTT}_i \right) \tag{C.2}
$$

In case the MN is data flow receiver and signaling responder (scenario M4), the MN must send a NOTIFY message directly toward the CN in order to trigger a replacing RESERVE to be sent by the CN. This scenario corresponds to the one depicted in Figure 4.19 on page 139. The detailed message sequence diagram for this scenario and the derivation of the evaluation formulae are presented in Appendix C.2.

The time needed to establish a new reservation by means of a hard handover in this scenario can then be expressed by

$$
t_{\text{HHO}} = o + p + s + v + \frac{\text{RTT}}{2} + \left(\sum_{i=1}^{\beta} f_{RSP_i} + \frac{\text{RTT}_i}{2} \right)
$$
$$
+ \left(\sum_{i=1}^{\beta+1} o_i + p_i + q_i + 3 \times \text{RTT}_i \right) \tag{C.3}
$$

The time needed to tear down the old reservation along the old path can be expressed by

$$t'_{\text{HHO}} = z_{RSV} + \left(\sum_{j=1}^{\gamma-1} f_{RSV_j} \right) + \left(\sum_{j=1}^{\gamma} \frac{\text{RTT}_i}{2} \right) \tag{C.4}$$

Table 4.5 summarizes the results obtained in the testbed for hard handovers. Again, it can be observed that sender-initiated reservations can be established faster than the corresponding receiver-initiated reservations and that the reservation setup time increases with each additional signaling entity along the path.

Scenario	MN at AR$_1$	MN at AR$_2$	MN at AR$_3$
M1 – MN acts as data flow sender and signaling initiator	2.77	3.50	4.47
M2 – MN acts as data flow sender and signaling responder	3.52	4.36	5.40
M3 – MN acts as data flow receiver and signaling initiator	3.91	5.61	6.60
M4 – MN acts as data flow receiver and signaling responder	3.55	5.31	6.31

Table 4.5: *Average of the measurement results of reservation setup for hard handovers* [ms]

The results can be interpreted as follows: In case the MN acts as data flow sender and signaling initiator (scenario M1), the MN establishes an initial resource reservation from AR$_1$ in this testbed in 2.77 ms on average. Once the MN moves to AR$_2$, it can update the existing resource reservation within 3.50 ms.

It can also be observed that the two hard handovers where the MN acts as data flow receiver (scenarios M3 and M4) consume slightly more time, since an updated reservation must initially be triggered by the MN by means of QoS NSLP NOTIFY messages for which a separate GIST three-way handshake must be performed in advance.

4.6 Conclusion

This chapter presented the analysis and design of Quality-of-Service signaling for mobile users. The solution presented allows to establish resource reservations in conjunction with Mobile IPv6. The solution relies on a node-local binding between the Mobile IPv6 instance and the QoS signaling instance. Therefore, it only requires the Mobile IPv6 and the QoS signaling protocol implementations to be adapted, but does neither require Mobile IPv6 itself to be adapted, nor the QoS signaling protocol to be changed. In order to be used in all mobility scenarios, only the MN, the CN, and the HA must support this node-local solution.

Furthermore, this chapter presented the design of anticipated handovers which allows for pre-established resource reservations along an anticipated data path. The QoS signaling solution can be used independently of a mobility management protocol. The design is robust by providing a hard handover fallback mechanism which can be used whenever an anticipated reservation could not be successfully completed.

The design supports sender- as well as receiver-initiated reservations to be adapted to new data paths, works fully decentralized and also across different administrative domains. The newly introduced NSIS protocol extensions can be easily added to the current protocol specifications without breaking existing protocol semantics for signaling entities that are not mobility-aware.

Chapter 5

Advanced Quality-of-Service Signaling for IP Multicast

A multitude of upcoming interactive multimedia applications imposes a high demand on the network's underlying resources. 3D tele-immersion environments or multi-player gaming spaces combine high definition cameras and displays with very high resolutions [Nah+11]. While resulting data streams of these applications impose a high bandwidth demand, they do also require real-time interactivity with strict end-to-end delay constraints.

These applications have, however, also in common, that they typically follow a group communication paradigm. While IP multicast [RFC1112; DC90] is often used in today's networks in order to deliver data flows across a group of receivers, supporting high bandwidth streams across larger networks, e.g., for live multimedia events, requires corresponding QoS guarantees for these IP multicast flows.

This chapter provides concepts for advanced QoS signaling in IP multicast environments. In Section 5.1 the problem statement and necessary requirements for IP multicast-aware QoS signaling are outlined. The challenges that must be solved by an IP unicast QoS signaling protocol if it is adapted to be used in IP multicast environments are discussed in Section 5.2. Although RSVP was already designed as a QoS signaling protocol for multicast flows, it lacks support for more advanced signaling capabilities, such as support for mobile end-users, support for sender-initiated reservations, or independence of the underlying QoS architecture. While the NSIS protocol suite already provides support for these advanced signaling capabilities it was not designed to be used in IP multicast-based environments. Therefore, Section 5.3 outlines how IP multicast support can be provided for the

NSIS protocol suite and its QoS signaling protocol QoS NSLP. The proposed concepts of advanced QoS signaling for IP multicast were published in [BR11] and a prototypical implementation for the NSIS protocols was integrated into the NSIS-ka suite [Ble+12a].

5.1 Problem Statement and Requirements

Group communication, e.g., in form of IP multicast, provides a well-investigated communication model in the data plane where data can be efficiently replicated toward a group of receivers. While resource reservations build a necessary requirement to achieve QoS guarantees for particular data flows, reservations being managed in the control plane must fit to the actual data flow delivery, i.e., the QoS signaling protocol must be able to establish reservations for IP multicast flows.

If only unicast reservations can be established for a group communication application, the high amount of single reservations leads to scalability problems in the control plane, since each single reservation requires state to be installed for a corresponding data flow. Consider the scenario depicted in Figure 5.1 where a resource reservation for a corresponding data flow should be established from the data flow sender toward a high number of data flow receivers, e.g., for a high-definition video stream of a live event.

In order to establish resource reservations for all n receivers, the data flow sender would have to maintain n signaling sessions and the intermediate signaling entities would also have to maintain as many separate signaling sessions as there are receivers in downstream direction. However, by using IP multicast, the data flow sender would only have to send a single reservation request toward the group of receivers and each intermediate signaling entity would only have to maintain as many signaling sessions as there are outgoing links for the corresponding multicast tree.

In order to allow advanced QoS signaling to be used in IP multicast environments, the following set of requirements must be fulfilled:

- *Support for Sender- and Receiver-initiated Reservations*

    Resource reservations can be either initiated by the sender or by the receiver of a data flow. While RSVP only provides support for receiver-initiated reservations, a multicast-capable QoS signaling protocol should not be limited to a particular reservation style but instead provide support for both reservation types. In particular, support for sender-initiated reservations should be pro-

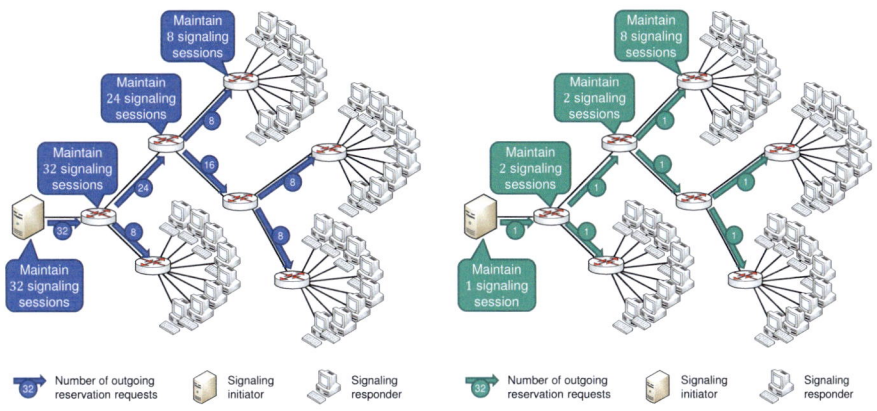

(a) By relying on IP unicast the signaling ini- (b) By using IP multicast the signaling initiator
    tiator has to maintain as many signaling   must only establish one single signaling
    sessions as there are data flow receivers in   session toward a group of receivers
    downstream direction

Figure 5.1: *Scenario for the establishment of signaling sessions for resource reserva-*
tions from one signaling initiator toward a group of signaling responders

vided since data senders (i.e., sources where data traffic originates, such as
video servers) are more likely to be charged by network providers as opposed
to consuming data receivers.

- *Allow for Group Membership Dynamics*

  Since members of a multicast group can leave and join groups at any given
  moment in time, the signaling protocol should provide means to adjust a QoS
  signaling session accordingly. Joining members of a multicast group should
  be added to an already established signaling session and signaling flows along
  a branch with no more actively participating members should be actively torn
  down.

- *Merge Reservations from Different Branches*

  In case receiver-initiated reservations are initiated by signaling entities at
  different branches of a multicast tree, the branching node should merge
  the different reservation requests into one single reservation in upstream
  direction.

5.2 Challenges in Adapting an IP Unicast-based QoS Signaling Protocol to IP Multicast

This section provides an overview of challenges that must be solved when IP unicast-based QoS signaling protocols are adapted to be used in IP multicast environments.

5.2.1 Manage Signaling Routing State for Multicast Peers

In order to establish resource reservations across a set of signaling entities, a QoS signaling protocol must establish signaling routing state on these signaling entities. That is, each signaling entity must have a notion of its directly adjacent signaling peer in downstream direction. However, in case of IP multicast, the exact number of downstream peers that are reached by a signaling message that is sent via IP multicast cannot be known a priori. Furthermore, this number can not be assumed to be fixed due to dynamically joining or leaving peers in a multicast group.

Therefore, in case of IP multicast, a signaling entity must cope with more than one directly adjacent signaling peer per signaling session and maintain state for each of those peers. However, the fact that the exact number of signaling peers is not known, imposes some challenges. For instance, it is difficult for a signaling entity to determine at which point in time signaling routing state for a signaling peer can be removed from the list of signaling neighbors due to the lack of responses. These challenges affect a signaling protocol's internal state machine, signaling routing state maintenance, and timer management.

5.2.2 Replication and Forwarding of Signaling Messages

In an IP multicast environment data packets destined to an IP multicast address are simply replicated at IP multicast routers without being modified. However, in case signaling messages are exchanged between directly adjacent signaling entities, these signaling messages must contain address information about the particular signaling entities. Otherwise, the receiver of a signaling message cannot determine the sender of this signaling message, upon which signaling parameters could not be negotiated and signaling session state information could not be exchanged between both signaling entities. Therefore, the exchange of signaling messages in IP multicast environments requires an adaptation of the address information contained in a signaling message.

A simple replication of signaling messages in IP multicast-based environments may also be problematic in case a signaling protocol relies on the use of connection-oriented transport protocols like TCP or SCTP to transmit signaling messages, since most of these transport protocols do not support IP multicast.

Furthermore, signaling messages that are sent in an IP multicast environment may only be relevant for directly adjacent signaling peers. With respect to scalability considerations, a signaling entity located near the multicast tree's root should not necessarily be affected by signaling operations performed near the multicast tree's leaves. It is therefore a challenging task to mitigate the scope of signaling message propagation in IP multicast environments.

5.2.3 Potential Sender Implosion

IP multicast is used for efficient data delivery in downstream direction. However, if signaling entities are used to negotiate signaling sessions, directly adjacent signaling entities must exchange signaling messages with each other, i.e., exchange data in downstream and in upstream direction. If a signaling request is disseminated to an entire group of receivers by IP multicast, the receiving signaling entities need to respond to this request. If these responses reach the requesting signaling entity in a very short fraction of time, it may get overwhelmed by the potentially huge amount of responses. This is a typical challenge in IP multicast environments and is commonly referred to as *sender implosion*. IP multicast-capable signaling protocols should mitigate the probability of sender implosions by delaying responses by a randomly chosen additional delay value.

5.2.4 Identification of the Last Signaling Hop

A QoS signaling session is always established along a path between two signaling entities acting as signaling initiator and signaling responder. The signaling responder is the signaling entity where the signaling session terminates and where signaling messages are not propagated any further. While in IP unicast environments the IP unicast address can be used to determine a signaling session's last signaling hop, an IP multicast address does not belong to a single system and hence, cannot be used to determine the last signaling hop. This requires that a signaling entity's signaling instance can determine whether it serves as signaling responder of a particular multicast signaling session or not.

5.2.5 Group Membership Dynamics

In IP multicast environments peers may join or leave a multicast group at any given moment in time. A QoS signaling protocol is challenged by this group membership dynamics. While signaling routing state must already be maintained for an entire group of directly adjacent signaling entities per multicast signaling session, it is challenging for a signaling entity to determine if a signaling peer left the group or if route changes happened. The signaling entity must also be able to add newly joining peers to an already established multicast signaling session. This does not only challenge the signaling routing state but must also be addressed in terms of QoS application logic, since a newly joining peer must be provided with the signaling session's QoS parameters. Furthermore, if reservations are to be initiated for the same multicast signaling session from signaling entities located at the multicast tree's leaves, the reservation requests belonging to different branches must be eventually merged. This is a challenging task for a QoS signaling entity since these requests are not synchronized and may potentially contain heterogeneous reservation requirements.

5.3 Advanced QoS Signaling for IP Multicast with NSIS

The NSIS protocol suite already provides support for a number of important signaling capabilities but was only designed to be used in IP unicast environments. Based on the requirements and challenges identified above, this section provides concepts for an adaptation of the NSIS protocol suite to be used in IP multicast environments. Since the NSIS protocol suite follows a two-layered approach where the routing and transport of signaling messages is conceptually decoupled from the signaling application's logic, the required adaptations affect both layers, i.e., the GIST protocol and the QoS NSLP protocol.

5.3.1 Design of Multicast Extensions for GIST

Each NSIS signaling session starts with an initial GIST handshake where not only connection related parameters are negotiated, but also routing of signaling messages is performed by determining the next GIST signaling entity in downstream direction that participates in this signaling session. The scope of an analysis of how GIST must be extended to support IP multicast is therefore limited to the segment between two adjacent GIST signaling entities.

IP multicast routing protocols (e.g., PIM-SM, PIM-DM) establish a distribution tree along the data path in order to efficiently convey messages to a group of receivers. GIST's default signaling message transport was designed to use path-coupled signaling where signaling messages strictly follow the data path. This is accomplished by sending a GIST QUERY message with an RAO and an IP destination address of the user data flow. For multicast data flows, the destination address of the QUERY is thus the multicast address. The RAO is required since the next GIST signaling entity along the data path should intercept and process the signaling message instead of forwarding it as regular data packet further toward the destination.

By using IP multicast, GIST QUERY messages from a QN can reach multiple RNs basically in different ways. A multicast packet can be replicated within the network itself, either on link layer (consider several RNs attached to the same subnet) or at the IP layer via intermediate GIST-unaware multicast routers. GIST-aware multicast routers, however, have to actively replicate GIST QUERY packets toward multicast destination addresses for all attached outgoing interfaces, because the *Network Layer Information* (NLI) in the QUERY message must reflect the actual related outgoing interface address.

Applying IP multicast to GIST QUERY messages therefore implies that a GIST signaling entity may discover n different signaling entities in downstream direction for one single signaling session. Note, however, that even in case of IP multicast, there will still be only one single signaling entity in upstream direction per signaling session. Figure 5.2 illustrates what happens in case a GIST QN sends a GIST QUERY message toward a multicast destination.

Since the resource reservation should be established for a multicast flow, the QN's QUERY message Q_1 does not only contain the multicast address in its IP destination field, but must also carry the multicast address in the signaling flow's MRI destination field. In this case an IP multicast router on the path simply replicates QUERY message Q_1 and forwards this message unmodified compared to the regular unicast case along the multicast tree (step ① in Figure 5.2).

Two GIST RNs RN_1 and RN_2 eventually intercept this QUERY message and participate in this signaling session. Hence, both RNs send a corresponding RESPONSE message back. While the initial QUERY is addressed toward the signaling endpoint's multicast address, the subsequently sent RESPONSE messages R_1 and R_2 are directly addressed toward the QN's unicast address.

However, since both RESPONSE messages reach the QN subsequently and both messages correspond to the same initial QUERY message, a QN would normally interpret the second RESPONSE as a re-routing event (cf. step ② in Figure 5.2). This

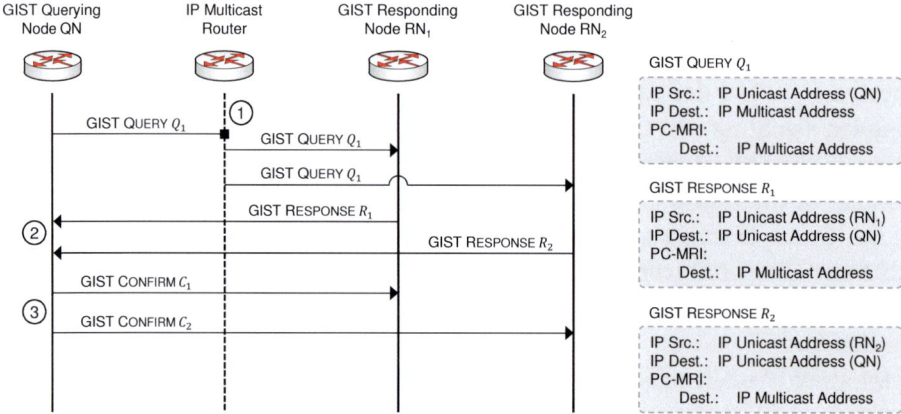

Figure 5.2: *Conceptual message exchange for an initial GIST handshake between a QN and two RNs in case the* QUERY *is addressed to a multicast destination*

is due to the fact, that signaling routing state is basically identified by GIST's NLI object. The NLI contains, amongst other information, an opaque signaling entity's peer-identity and an interface address. The NLI stays constant during a signaling entity's lifetime and GIST's periodic probing allows directly adjacent signaling entities to detect a route change in the underlying IP network. Consequently, a *multicast-aware* GIST signaling entity must be able to handle signaling messages and states for several downstream peers in relation to a single (multicast) data flow and confirm each RESPONSE by a dedicated CONFIRM if requested (cf. step ③ in Figure 5.2).

Furthermore, a GIST signaling entity must also actively replicate DATA messages (e.g., QoS NSLP RESERVE messages) per downstream peer, since GIST addresses peers directly via their unicast interface address (taken from the NLI) and may also use different *Messaging Associations* (e.g., TCP or SCTP connections) for different peers. Therefore, an IP multicast-based replication can only be applied to GIST QUERY messages.

Moreover, IP multicast group memberships are dynamic, i.e., new peers can join or leave the group anytime. Thus, a multicast-aware GIST must cope with dynamic group memberships and has to provide means for detecting new peers as well as for removing state for peers that left the multicast group.[1]

---

[1]The exact detection mechanism depends on the actually used multicast routing protocol. For instance, PIM-DM and PIM-SM use Join or Prune messages which can be used to detect joining or leaving multicast peers.

Another issue occurs at the QN since all RNs receive the Query at nearly the same time due to multicast replication, so they will respond nearly simultaneously. If the number of RNs is large, intermediate systems and the QN may be overwhelmed by the number of Response messages.

5.3.1.1 Replication of GIST Query Messages

A GIST Query message carries an RAO in its IP header for packet interception. Hence, whenever a GIST Query message reaches a branching GIST signaling entity in a multicast distribution tree, the Query is intercepted due to the RAO and cannot simply be forwarded in downstream direction according to the multicast routing table.

Furthermore, an outgoing Query's NLI must reflect the particular outgoing interface address. In case of multicast replication at a branching GIST signaling entity, each of the replicated Query messages therefore needs to carry an individual NLI. Hence, since no simple packet replication is possible, it builds an important requirement that a branching GIST signaling entity *actively replicates* Query messages according to the IP multicast routing table.

According to the GIST specification a route change can be detected by different means, e.g., by monitoring the link-state topology database or simply by periodic GIST probing. Once a detected route change affects signaling routing state, a new Query message should be generated in order to update the signaling routing state. Similar to this IP unicast operation, a newly joining receiver or entire branch leads to a new multicast routing entry in IP multicast environments. It is important for a GIST signaling instance to react accordingly and generate a corresponding Query message as soon as it gets notified about a newly joining receiver.

A branching GIST signaling entity should generate new Query messages which carry the NLI of the corresponding outgoing interface. The outgoing interface can be determined by means of the IP multicast routing table's entries.

5.3.1.2 Manage Signaling Routing State for Multicast-Peers

Once a GIST Query message is replicated by means of IP multicast, it is also intercepted by a number of different signaling entities upon which each received Query leads to an individually sent GIST Response message. A multicast-aware NSIS signaling entity requires that each Response message must be processed individually and signaling routing state must be established and maintained for each corresponding RN.

The main challenge is, however, that in case of IP multicast, the exact number of RNs reached via a single QUERY message cannot be determined a priori by a QN. This implies that after having received the first RESPONSE, the QN must accept further RESPONSE messages from different RNs. In particular, once signaling routing state has been established for a multicast session with a set of RNs, newly joining peers should be added to the list of RNs and peers that left the multicast group should also be removed from the list of RNs.

However, the QN does not know how many RNs are located in downstream direction, i.e., it cannot determine at which point in time it received the RESPONSE messages from all RNs. The design of a multicast-aware GIST protocol must provide mechanisms to choose an appropriate timeout value for the reception of RESPONSE messages. Furthermore, GIST's state machine must be adapted to reflect these necessary protocol extensions.

Since GIST was designed for IP unicast environments, timeout values were chosen to be used for the maintenance of signaling routing state with one single RN per signaling session. In GIST, the RN determines the time during which signaling routing state between a QN and a RN can be considered valid. This *routing-state-validity* time is encapsulated in the NLI of a GIST RESPONSE message, is configurable at the specific signaling entity, and has a recommended default value of 30 seconds. According to the GIST specification [RFC5971] signaling routing state is refreshed by means of a refreshing GIST QUERY which should be sent as soon as 1/2 to 3/4 of the validity time has elapsed.

However, since unreliably sent refreshing QUERY messages may get lost or be corrupted in the network, a retransmission timer allows a QN to retransmit QUERY messages that did not receive a RESPONSE. Figure 5.3 illustrates the relation between the *routing-state-validity* time and the retransmission timer.

In case a refreshing QUERY is sent, the retransmission timer is started. It's value is configurable by each signaling entity and has a recommended default value of $T_1 = 500$ ms. Retransmissions use a binary exponential backoff process where the timeout value increases up to a default value of $T_2 = 64 \times T_1$.

In case of IP multicast, GIST RESPONSE messages carry each an individual *routing-state-validity* timer value, as illustrated in Figure 5.4. In this example, RN_1 chose the smallest *routing-state-validity* time out of the three RNs and upon expiration of this timer, a refreshing QUERY must be sent by the QN. Since this QUERY is sent by means of IP multicast, each of the RNs is expected to receive this message.

Hence, all *routing-state-validity* timers at the QN belonging to this multicast signaling session are reset and started again. Since only the smallest timer value

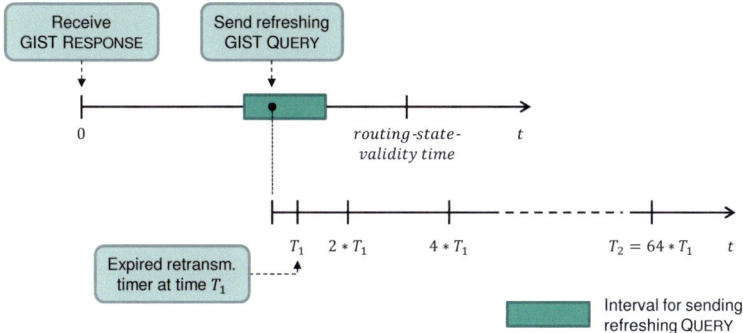

Figure 5.3: *Conceptual relation between the routing state validity timer and the retransmission timer for regular unicast operation*

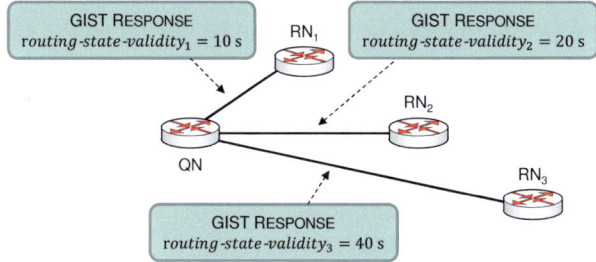

Figure 5.4: *Different routing-state-validity times are used by multicast signaling*

is of interest for refreshing signaling routing state of a multicast signaling session and maintaining timers is expensive in terms of processing costs, it is important to maintain only one single *routing-state-validity* timer per multicast signaling session.

The QN starts a signaling session's retransmission timer once the corresponding GIST QUERY was sent. In case of a multicast signaling session, there is only one retransmission timer started. Maintaining separate retransmission timers per RN would not be appropriate, since each QUERY message is sent toward the entire group of multicast receivers, anyway. Furthermore, each expired retransmission timer would ultimately result in the emission of a QUERY for the entire group (if sent via IP multicast) and therefore lead to an unnecessary high amount of signaling message traffic, especially if the expired retransmission timer belongs to a peer that left the multicast group. Therefore, one retransmission timer per multicast session is sufficient and in case no RESPONSE is received from any peer upon the transmission of a multicast QUERY, the retransmission timer is used as in the IP unicast case.

However, the QN's list of RNs belonging to a multicast signaling session can at no point in time expected to be fixed. Instead, group memberships in IP multicast environments are dynamic and peers may join or leave the group at any time. A missing RESPONSE of one of the RNs does, however, not necessarily indicate, that this RN has actually left the multicast group since QUERY or RESPONSE messages may get lost.[2]

Therefore, each RN belonging to a multicast signaling session should get a certain number of opportunities to respond to a QUERY message before it is removed from the list of peers. A so-called missed_responses counter is maintained per RN and is increased with every QUERY message that has been sent toward this multicast destination address. In case a RESPONSE is received from an RN, its missed_responses counter is reset to zero. Once an RN's missed_responses counter reached the number of l unsuccessful attempts, the RN is expected to have left the multicast group and is removed from the set of multicast peers for this signaling session.

The number of necessary attempts, in order to successfully deliver a GIST QUERY, depends on the concrete loss probability of the corresponding connection. In case a specific connection's loss probability is known in advance, the QN is able to approximate the number of refreshing QUERY messages that should be sent before routing state finally expired at the RN.

This can be modeled by a sequence of Bernoulli trials with a geometric distribution $G(p)$ where delivery of a QUERY message *succeeds* with probability p. Then the probability for l necessary attempts, i.e., $(l-1)$ failed attempts precede one successful attempt, can be expressed by

$$\Pr(X = l) = (1 - p)^{l-1} p$$

The expected value $E(X)$ of this geometrically distributed random variable X is $\frac{1}{p}$ such that an assumed loss probability of one percent leads to an expected value of $E(X) = \frac{1}{0.99} \approx 1.01$. Since $l > 1$ one additional QUERY message should be sufficient in this case. Nevertheless, in a more conservative approach a QN may choose to increase this value by a fixed amount or simply double the estimated value.

In order to maintain signaling routing states for an entire set of RNs that belong to one multicast signaling session, the QN's routing table must be extended and the corresponding QN's GIST state machine must be slightly adapted. GIST's state machine, as being specified in RFC 5971 is depicted in Figure 5.5 with multicast adaptations being highlighted in blue.

---

[2]See discussion about the retransmission timer on page 165

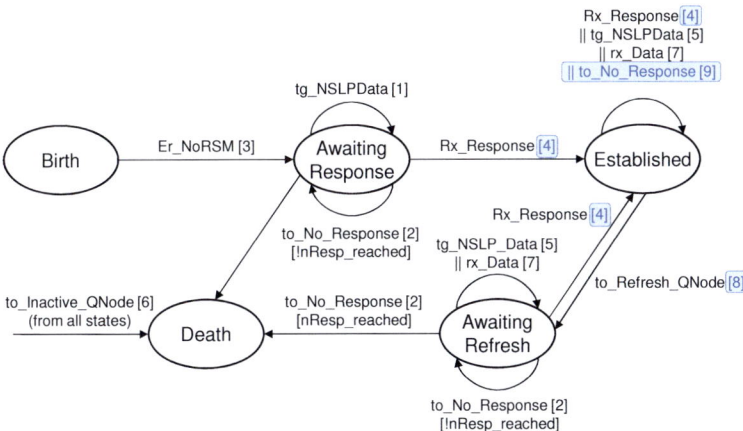

Figure 5.5: *Illustration of a GIST QN's state machine, according to RFC 5971. Multicast adaptations are highlighted in blue.*

The following listing shows the original GIST specification's state machine's processing rules, with added multicast adaptations highlighted in blue. Note, that a single RN's RESPONSE suffices to establish signaling routing state.

Rule 1:
>Store the message for later transmission

Rule 2:
if number of Queries sent has reached the threshold
>// nQuery_isMax is true
>indicate No Response error to NSLP
>destroy self

else
>send Query
>start No_Response timer with new value

Rule 3:
// Assume the Confirm was lost in transit or the peer has reset;
// restart the handshake
send Query
(re)start No_Response timer

Rule 4:
if a new messaging association state machine is needed create one
if the R-flag was set send a Confirm
send any stored Data messages
if multicast session
>if RN already in list of multicast peers

            reset RN's `missed_responses` counter
     else
         add corresponding RN to list with `missed_responses` = 0
else
   stop No_Response timer
start Refresh_QNode timer
start Inactive_QNode timer if it was not running
if there was piggybacked NSLP-Data
     pass it to the NSLP
     restart Inactive_QNode timer

Rule 5:
send Data message
restart Inactive_QNode timer

Rule 6:
   Terminate

Rule 7:
pass any data to the NSLP
restart Inactive_QNode timer

Rule 8:
send Query
increment each RN's `missed_responses` counter
start No_Response timer
stop Refresh_QNode timer

Rule 9:
remove RNs with too many missing RESPONSE messages

The multicast adaptations affect two existing processing rules and require one additional processing rule. The first adaptation affects transition rule no. 4, where the QN is either in state Awaiting Response, i.e., a QUERY message was sent and the QN waits for the corresponding RESPONSE message, or it is in state Established, i.e., the first RESPONSE message was already received.

In case an incoming RESPONSE message (i.e., transition rule rx_Response) belongs to a multicast signaling session, the corresponding RN must be added to the list of RNs. This ensures to keep track of more than one RN per signaling session in downstream direction and add newly joined multicast peers to the list of RNs. In case one of the RNs is already in the list of multicast peers, its missed_responses counter is reset to zero. This helps to maintain the set of active peers.

The next adaptation affects processing rule no. 8 where the to_Refresh_QNode timeout indicates that a refreshing QUERY message must be sent before routing state to an RN expired. Since a refreshing QUERY is emitted upon expiration of this timer, each RN's `missed_responses` counter must be incremented by one in case of an IP multicast signaling session.

Finally, according to the concepts outlined in this section, each RN that belongs to a multicast signaling session should only have a fixed amount of opportunities to send a RESPONSE upon the reception of a QUERY message. Once an RN exceeds this number of opportunities, the RN can be considered no longer part of this multicast group and hence, should be removed from the list of active peers. Therefore, whenever the QN is in state Established, it must check each RN's `missed_responses` counter and remove RNs with too many missing RESPONSE messages. This is accomplished by adding a new processing rule no. 9 of type `to_No_Response` to the QN's Established state.

The routing table must be extended accordingly in order to store state for each single RN of a multicast signaling session. A routing key is identified by the triple of Message Routing Information (MRI), Session-ID, and NSLP-ID. To maintain signaling routing state for a set of peers, a routing key entry must then point to a nested table for the corresponding multicast peers. This can be achieved, for instance, by defining a hash table for all RNs belonging to this multicast signaling session. Since an RN's NLI serves as an RN's unique identifier it can be used as the hash table's key. In case an RN's NLI is yet unknown, the RN is added to the list of multicast peers, otherwise an existing RN's entry is updated according to the processing rules stated above.

5.3.1.3 Replication of DATA Messages

Once a GIST handshake has been successfully established between a QN and an RN, GIST manages the transfer of signaling application data, e.g., QoS NSLP RESERVE messages, which are transmitted by means of GIST DATA messages. By employing GIST in IP multicast environments, GIST DATA messages can, however, not simply be forwarded toward a group of receivers by using the IP multicast address as IP destination address. According to the GIST specification, a DATA message's IP destination address must be set to the IP address of the particular adjacent GIST peer. This address is based on the RN's NLI and therefore an IP unicast address.

Furthermore, the IP multicast address can hardly be used to transfer GIST DATA messages whenever dedicated Messaging Associations (MA) are established between two adjacent signaling entities. An MA may consist of a TCP, SCTP, or a TLS-protected connection between a QN and an RN. Most of these transport protocols do not support IP multicast. Hence, IP multicast cannot be employed for transmission of GIST DATA messages. Instead, GIST is responsible to replicate and transmit GIST DATA messages toward each RN separately.

In IP unicast environments, once transmitted toward a RN, a GIST DATA message can be removed from the NSLP data send queue. This is different for IP multicast environments, since GIST DATA messages must be distributed among the set of RNs that belong to the particular multicast group. Therefore, the corresponding queue for GIST DATA messages must not be emptied until all multicast peers in downstream direction received this DATA message and the QN should keep track of the DATA messages that were sent toward each RN.

Due to the dynamics of IP multicast, new peers may be discovered while DATA messages are transmitted. New neighbors should then be added to the list of multicast peers and receive a dedicated copy of all currently queued DATA messages that have been passed from the signaling application toward GIST.

5.3.1.4 Avoid Sender Implosion

Most multicast adaptations are related to QNs only, since—different from IP unicast—a QN ends up with n different peers in downstream direction, whereas a RN has still only one single peer in upstream direction—even in case of IP multicast. However, since all RNs send a dedicated GIST RESPONSE message upon the reception of a single multicast GIST QUERY, the RN's GIST protocol behavior must also slightly be adapted in order to operate in IP multicast environments.

A typical challenge in multicast environments occurs, whenever a multitude of receivers "flood" the sender within a very short fraction of time, also known as *sender implosion*. The sender may get overwhelmed by the number of return messages and the processing overhead imposed by each returned message may result in resource exhaustion at the sender. Since a GIST RESPONSE message is usually emitted by a RN as soon as possible, the number of RESPONSE messages may also overwhelm the receiving QN.

This effect can be mitigated by artificially stretching the interval during which RESPONSE messages are sent toward the QN. Therefore, each RN should add an artificial delay in case of an IP multicast signaling session, before a GIST RESPONSE message is sent toward the QN. In order to avoid synchronization effects between RNs (cf. [FJ93]) the concrete delay δ should be chosen from a uniformly distributed interval that ranges from 0 to a predefined *MaxMulticastResponseDelay* value.[3]

---

[3]This value is a system-specific parameter which can be configured and also adapted by the network operator, e.g., depending on the expected or observed loss probability or signaling traffic in the network.

This value should, however, not exceed the initial retransmission timeout of a GIST QUERY, i.e., time T_1 (with a default value of 500 ms). Indeed, it should be even smaller than T_1 in order to take the propagation delay between both signaling entities into account. The artificial response delay δ should then be chosen from an interval as follows:

$$\delta = rand(0, \alpha \cdot T_1) \quad 0 < \alpha < 1$$

The parameter α is used to ensure that only a fraction of T_1 is actually used and can be adjusted by each RN individually. For instance, for a maximum response delay that should not exceed 80% of the actual retransmission timeout T_1, the parameter α equals 0.8.

5.3.2 Design of Multicast Extensions for QoS NSLP

This section describes the design of multicast extensions for QoS NSLP. According to the challenges identified in Section 5.2, the QoS signaling protocol must be able to identify the last signaling hop within a multicast signaling session and must cope with group membership dynamics. Furthermore, it is important to mitigate the scope of signaling message propagation in multicast environments in order to allow for scalable reservations. In this section the underlying GIST instance is assumed to be already multicast-aware.

5.3.2.1 Identification of the Last Signaling Hop

Signaling is always performed between a signaling initiator and a signaling respon- der. While intermediate signaling entities forward signaling messages between the initiator and the responder, forwarding of these signaling messages is terminated at the signaling responder. In IP unicast environments an IP address is used to identify a host's interface. Therefore, this IP address can be used by a signaling entity to determine whether it is supposed to serve as endpoint of the signaling session or not.

However, within IP multicast a destination's IP address corresponds to a group's multicast address and does not identify a single host's interface, but rather belongs to an entire group of receivers. Hence, an IP multicast address cannot be used by a signaling entity to determine if it acts as last hop of a signaling session. This affects all receivers of a multicast session, that is all leaf nodes in a multicast distribution tree.

In order to resolve this problem a signaling protocol instance could either follow a *pull model* or a *push model*. By using a pull model the signaling protocol instance must pull the required information from its own multicast routing table, if present. If this table doesn't contain any entries for this particular multicast address, the signaling entity does not forward the signaling messages and can assume to serve as the signaling session's endpoint. This pull model requires a system-specific interface between the signaling protocol instance and the system's multicast routing table.

Alternatively, a push model can be applied where the application which uses the multicast group communication service must notify the signaling protocol instance about its use of a particular multicast address. That is, the signaling protocol instance obtains a list of multicast addresses from its applications. This model requires applications to be aware of the signaling protocol instance and also requires a corresponding interface definition between the application and the signaling protocol to exchange this information.

5.3.2.2 Rerouting in Case of Multicast

The detection of rerouting events plays an important role for network signaling protocols in IP-based networks which follow a path-coupled message routing approach, in order to adapt the paths of signaling flows to the corresponding data flows. In IP unicast environments rerouting can usually be detected by periodically probing whether the next signaling peer in downstream direction changed. In case a new signaling peer is detected in response to a probe message, rerouting can be assumed to have happened.

Rerouting is not only a matter of adapting a signaling flow's path. In case a new signaling peer is detected, this affects also the signaling application's logic, i.e., in case of QoS signaling this new signaling peer must be provided with the current QoS parameters (e.g., in form of a RESERVE message). Furthermore, a reservation along the obsolete path can be torn down in order to free no longer used resources.

However, in IP multicast environments a newly reported signaling peer in downstream direction does not necessarily correspond to a rerouting event. Instead, this new signaling peer can be part of a multicast group. Hence, in this case the new signaling peer should be equipped with the required reservation information and also join the reservation's signaling session. Furthermore, it must be ensured that in case a new signaling peer is reported for a multicast signaling session, the existing reservation to another signaling peer of the same multicast signaling session is not torn down. Otherwise, only one signaling peer in downstream direction could actually be part of this signaling session and establish a reservation.

In order to resolve this issue a QoS signaling instance must maintain an entire list of adjacent signaling peers for multicast signaling sessions. This list can then be used to determine whether a new reservation needs to be established toward a signaling peer or whether a reservation already exists. The NSIS protocols use so-called implementation-specific "SII-handles" in order to refer to adjacent signaling entities. A QoS NSLP signaling instance would therefore be required to maintain a list of SII-handles for a multicast signaling session.

5.3.2.3 Send Complete Reservation Information to Newly Joining Signaling Peers

Newly joining peers in a multicast signaling session must be equipped with the necessary reservation information. Although soft-state signaling protocols send refreshing signaling messages periodically along their signaling path, these signaling messages do not provide appropriate means to equip a new signaling peer with the required reservation information. This is due to the fact that these refreshes are only sent within a fixed time interval.[4] This would lead to unnecessary delays until a new peer would actually receive the reservation information. Furthermore, since refreshing signaling messages are only used to reset a soft-state timer for an already established reservation, these signaling messages do not necessarily contain the complete reservation information.

Therefore, a QoS signaling instance should rather send the complete reservation information instantaneously upon being reported about a new signaling peer. In terms of NSIS a signaling entity's QoS NSLP instance can issue a new QUERY or RESERVE message upon receiving a new SII-handle from its GIST instance.

Furthermore, in multicast signaling sessions an entire branch of signaling entities can be located behind a new signaling peer. It must therefore be ensured that the new signaling peer forwards the signaling information in this case. With respect to NSIS-based signaling this can be accomplished by means of the RII object. Since this object requires a response to be sent by the last signaling hop, intermediate signaling entities are required to forward this signaling message further along the path.

5.3.2.4 Forwarding of Signaling Messages

For an end-to-end resource reservation a QoS signaling session must be established between a signaling initiator and a signaling responder along an entire path of

---

[4]The QoS NSLP specification [RFC5974] recommends a default value of 30 s for the so-called refresh period

intermediate signaling entities. In order to negotiate parameters of a signaling session—either during its establishment or during runtime—signaling messages must be exchanged from end to end.

In an IP multicast environment this may impose severe scalability issues. If each multicast receiver's response to a single sender's reservation request is forwarded toward the sender, the intermediate signaling entities and the multicast sender could easily be overwhelmed by the potentially huge number of incoming responses. Furthermore, the information contained in each of those responses does not necessarily contain relevant information for the sender.

Hence, in order to allow for scalable end-to-end reservations in IP multicast environments it must be ensured that only those signaling messages are forwarded in the multicast distribution tree's upstream direction (i.e., toward the tree's root node), which are actually of interest for the next signaling peer in upstream direction. That is, a response should only be forwarded in upstream direction if the upstream peer did not yet receive a response or if the response contains new information.[5]

Consider the following scenario: A signaling entity initiates the establishment of a resource reservation in an IP multicast environment. Therefore, this signaling entity acts as sender of the data flow and as signaling initiator. The reservation request (e.g., a QoS NSLP RESERVE message) is forwarded by each intermediate signaling entity in the multicast tree's downstream direction until it reaches the multicast tree's leaf nodes. These signaling entities act as data flow receiver and signaling responder in this scenario. Each of those signaling responders replies with a corresponding response (e.g., a QoS NSLP RESPONSE message) upon which a branching node in the multicast tree receives multiple responses from its downstream peers. Instead of forwarding all responses, this signaling entity only forwards the first received response in upstream direction toward the signaling initiator. This ensures that each signaling entity along the multicast distribution tree and the signaling initiator only receive as many responses as they have *directly adjacent* signaling peers in downstream direction.

5.3.2.5 Merging of Reservations Belonging to Different Branches

When receiver-initiated reservations are used in an IP multicast environment, the reservation requests refer to the same multicast signaling session but are issued by different signaling initiators. That is, these reservation requests cannot necessarily be assumed to contain identical reservation information. They may

---

[5]E.g., due to changed reservation conditions.

request a different amount of resources and request different validity times for their reservation state.

Signaling entities at branching nodes of a multicast tree will eventually receive reservation requests from different signaling initiators in downstream direction. It is therefore necessary that these branching nodes maintain individual reservation state per directly adjacent signaling peer in downstream direction. That is, with respect to QoS NSLP, these signaling entities are required to maintain individual RSNs and reservation validity timers per directly adjacent signaling peer in downstream direction.

Since these signaling entities act as a branching nodes within the multicast tree they are also responsible for merging multiple reservation requests into one single reservation request that is then forwarded in upstream direction. However, the handling of reservation requests and the allocation of resources is the responsibility of the *Resource Management Function* (RMF). Therefore, no signaling protocol changes are required for this to be applied. In case a reservation must be changed in response to an RMF trigger, an updated reservation request can simply be issued by the branching node in upstream direction.

5.4 Analysis of Multicast Efficiency for QoS Signaling

Multicast communication provides a big advantage for distributed applications by efficiently replicating data streams along a distribution tree and hence reducing the overall bandwidth demand in the network. This section analyzes the efficiency of using multicast communication for QoS signaling with NSIS. Regarding signaling protocols, the efficiency is usually characterized in terms of state that must be hold for a number of signaling sessions.

In a multicast distribution tree, intermediate multicast-aware signaling entities replicate signaling messages that are sent from a sender to a group of receivers. Each signaling entity may have a different number of successors in the tree, called *fanout*. The total number of signaling entities in a multicast distribution tree with depth d and an average fanout F is then given by

$$N = \sum_{v=0}^{d} F^v$$

Correspondingly, for each signaling entity e_j^i of level i in the tree a subtree $s(e_j^i)$ contains a total number of N_i signaling entities which can be expressed by

$$N_i = \sum_{v=0}^{d-i} F^v$$

As illustrated in Figure 5.6 the number of receivers (i.e., leaf nodes) in a subtree $s(e_j^i)$ is given by

$$n_i = F^{d-i}$$

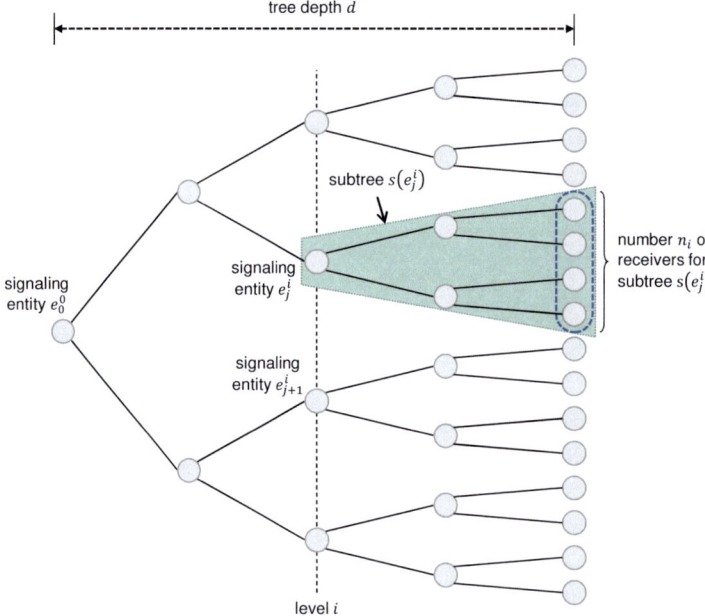

Figure 5.6: *A fully balanced multicast distribution tree with a constant fanout of $F = 2$ and a tree depth of $d = 4$.*

Figure 5.6 illustrates a fully balanced multicast distribution tree with a fanout of $F = 2$ and a tree depth of $d = 4$. Note, that the actual tree's depth and the fanout can vary.

The difference of how much state is stored for signaling sessions between unicast communication and multicast communication therefore solely depends on the signaling entity's level in the tree and hence, the number of receivers in the corresponding subtree. In case unicast communication is used, an intermediate signaling entity e_j^i must establish $n_i = F^{d-i}$ separate signaling sessions toward its receivers.

As depicted on the left hand side of Figure 5.7 (i.e., in case of IP unicast) signaling entity e_j^i has two successor nodes and a total of n_i receivers in its subtree. Hence, signaling entity e_j^i must establish n_i separate signaling sessions which expands to n_i different GIST handshakes (with its directly adjacent signaling entities e_j^{i+1} and e_{j+1}^{i+1}) and n_i subsequent resource reservation requests.

In case of unicast reservations, the amount of signaling session state that needs to be maintained on signaling entity e_j^i has a complexity of $O(n)$ where n corresponds to the number of receivers. Since the total number of receivers in a subtree is significantly higher at the subtree's root (i.e., at the sender's side) than near the subtree's leaf nodes (i.e., near the receivers), the number of signaling sessions that must be maintained is much higher near the sender. Note, that this situation applies to sender- as well as to receiver-initiated reservations since signaling sessions are always initiated from the data flow sender.

In case multicast communication can be employed by a signaling protocol, only one signaling session must be established per multicast group, regardless of the number of receivers in the subtree. This session must be, however, actively replicated toward the signaling entity's successors in the tree which equals to the fanout F. This situation is depicted on the right hand side of Figure 5.7 where signaling entity e_j^i only establishes one signaling session toward its two successors e_j^{i+1} and e_{j+1}^{i+1}, regardless of the number of leaf nodes in the tree. This results in an overall complexity of $O(1)$ regarding the state that must be stored within node e_j^i for signaling sessions.

Furthermore, once multicast communication is used, a signaling session for the multicast group is only replicated F times, regardless of the signaling entity's level in the multicast distribution tree. Hence, in case the sender has $F = 3$ successors in the multicast distribution tree and the multicast group has 10 000 receivers, the sender must establish only *one* signaling session that is replicated three times when using multicast, as opposed to 10 000 sessions that must be established when using unicast.

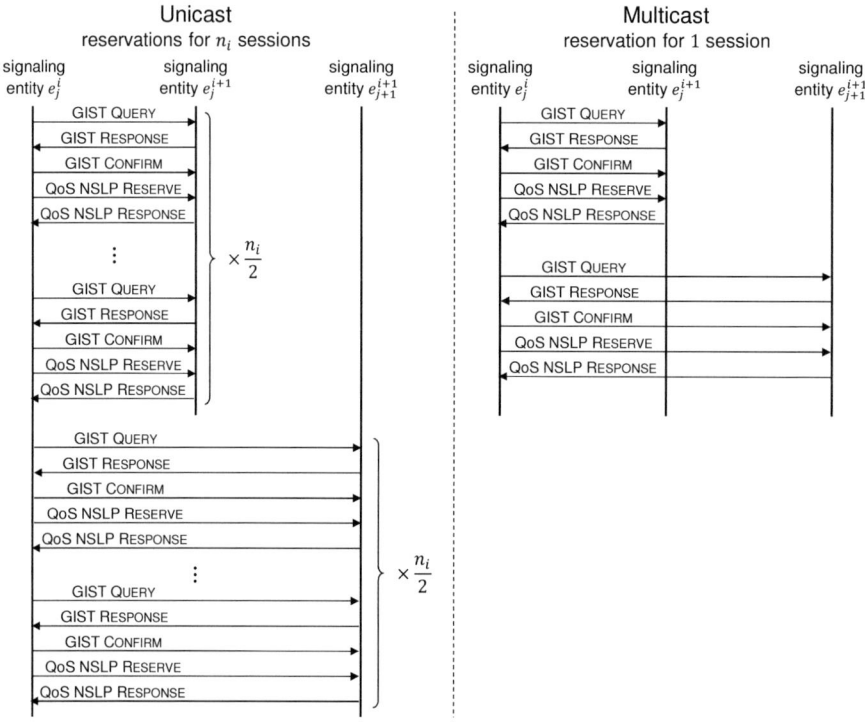

Figure 5.7: *Analysis of sender-initiated reservations using unicast communication (left hand side) where signaling entity e_j^i must establish n_i signaling sessions and multicast communication (right hand side) where signaling entity e_j^i must establish only one multicast signaling session*

5.5 Implementation and Evaluation

The multicast extensions were prototypically implemented by Lenk [Len10] for the NSIS-ka protocol suite [Ble+12a]. This section discusses some important implementation details and evaluates the signaling performance of the proposed design. Since the NSIS-ka implementation is based on Linux, the multicast routing tables, the multicast routing daemon, or the corresponding multicast APIs were also based on Linux. The protocol mechanisms outlined in Section 5.3.1 and Section 5.3.2 are, however, not affected by these implementation-specific design decisions. Note, that this section does not evaluate any QoS-related metrics of user data flow packets such as latency or jitter, since the NSIS protocols act only as plain signaling protocols.

One of the most important design decisions related to the existing GIST implementation is the extension of its internally used routing table. The routing table is structured as a hash table for unicast communication only, i.e., a routing key (which is a tuple of MRI, Session ID, and NSLP ID) serves as an index for a routing entry of one specific GIST peer. However, in case of multicast communication, the same key should be related to a group of multicast peers. The routing table's routing entry was therefore extended by a `multicast_peers` hash table where information about all multicast peers is stored. Figure 5.8 illustrates the extended routing table.

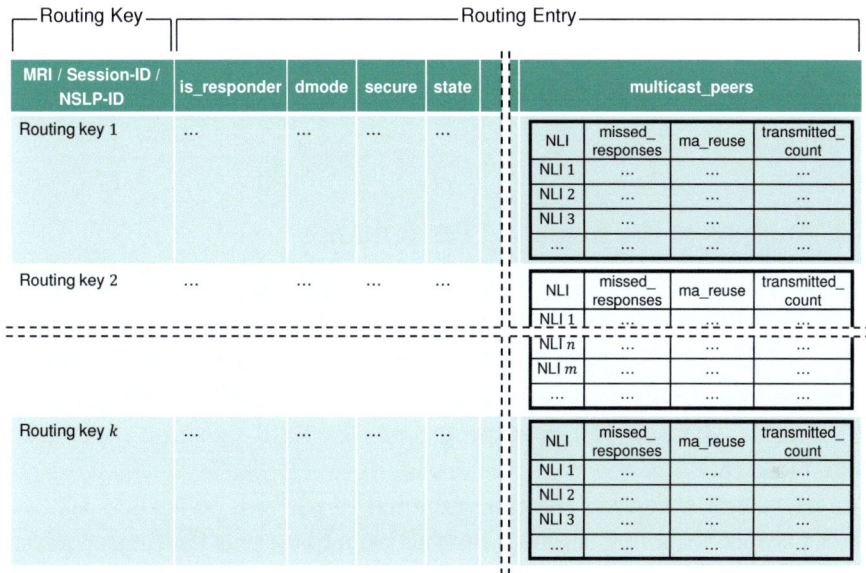

Figure 5.8: *Extended routing table where the new field multicast_peers stores relevant information about each multicast peer*

Within the newly introduced `multicast_peers` hash table, each peer's NLI object is used as the hash table's key so that the following attributes can easily be maintained and quickly accessed:

- A counter specifies the number of QUERY messages that a peer did not respond to in a row, called `missed_responses`

- A boolean value, called `ma_reuse`, indicates whether a peer requested to reuse an existing MA

- A field `transmitted_count` keeps track about the DATA messages (e.g., QoS NSLP RESERVE) that were already delivered to this multicast group

Furthermore, the GIST routing table was extended by entries for the following fields (not illustrated in Figure 5.8):

- A boolean flag, called `is_multicast_querier` that is set to true in case an incoming QUERY used an IP multicast address

- A dedicated slot for the `NoResponse` timer

- A value that keeps track of the minimum of all routing state validity timers of all peers

5.5.1 Analysis of the Signaling Performance

The time required to setup a signaling session depends on processing times for different signaling messages, the number d of signaling entities along a signaling session's path, the propagation delay t between two directly adjacent signaling entities, and the randomly chosen delay δ for GIST RESPONSE messages (cf. Section 5.3.1.4). The different processing times for NSIS signaling messages are depicted in Figure 5.9.

The parameter o denotes the time required to perform policy and admission control upon an incoming resource reservation request plus the time required to generate and transmit a subsequent GIST QUERY message. The parameter q is used for the time between an incoming GIST RESPONSE message and an outgoing QoS NSLP RESERVE message. The time needed to forward a QoS NSLP RESPONSE message is denoted f_{RSP}. At the signaling responder, the time required to perform policy and admission control for a resource reservation request and generate a corresponding QoS NSLP RESPONSE message is denoted v.

A signaling session is established, once the sender receives the QoS NSLP RESPONSE message. Regarding multicast signaling sessions, this depends on the path with the lowest delays in terms of the propagation delay t and the artificially added delay δ for GIST RESPONSE messages. Depending on whether sender- or receiver-initiated reservations are used, the propagation delay must be accounted σ times. For sender-initiated reservations, $\sigma = 4$ (for GIST QUERY, GIST RESPONSE, QoS

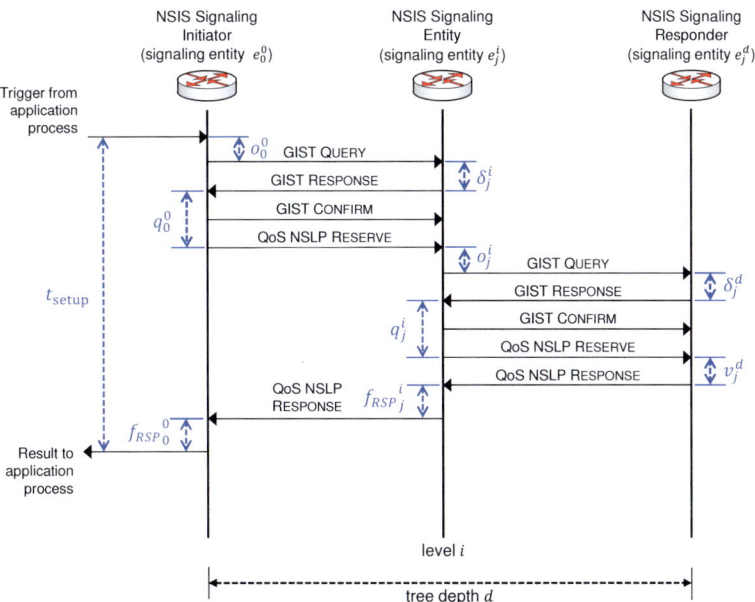

Figure 5.9: *Message sequence diagram for the evaluation of the signaling performance for sender-initiated reservations*

NSLP RESERVE, and QoS NSLP RESPONSE messages), for receiver-initiated reservations $\sigma = 5$ (for the additional QoS NSLP QUERY). Hence, the lowest accumulated delay between signaling entity e_j^{i-1} and all its directly adjacent successor nodes at level i of the tree can be estimated by

$$\Delta_i = \min_j(\delta_j^i + \sigma \times t_j^i)$$

Assuming that the signaling path extends from the multicast distribution tree's root (e.g., the signaling initiator) toward a leaf (e.g., the signaling responder) it spans d signaling entities, according to the tree's depth.

The total setup time t_{setup} for a signaling session of a sender-initiated reservation can then be estimated by

$$t_{\text{setup}} = \sum_{i=0}^{d}(o_j^i + q_j^i + f_{RSPj}^i + \Delta_i) + v_j^d$$

Regarding receiver-initiated reservations the reservation is initiated by the data flow receivers (i.e., the leaves of the multicast tree) in upstream direction. Hence, first of all reverse-path state must be installed in downstream direction on all intermediate signaling entities by means of a QoS NSLP QUERY message upon which the data flow receivers can send a RESERVE message in upstream direction. Figure 5.10 illustrates the resulting processing times for receiver-initiated reservations.

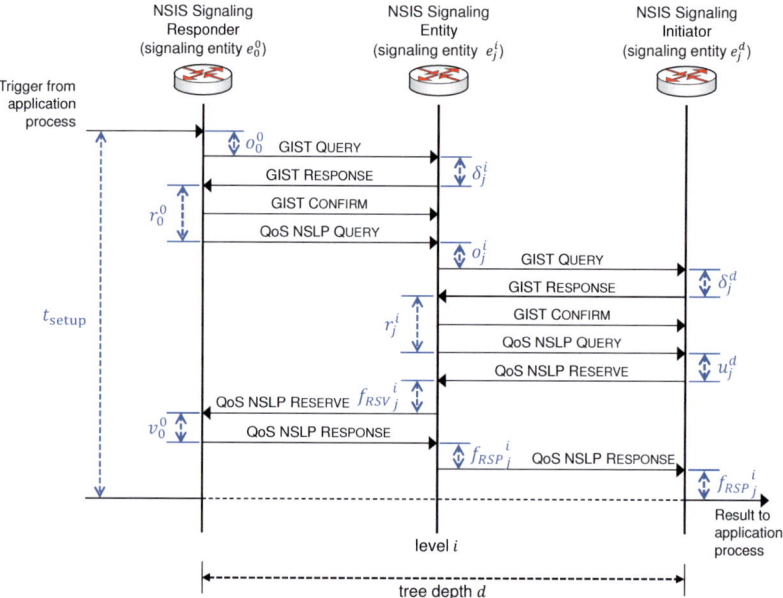

Figure 5.10: *Message sequence diagram for the evaluation of the signaling performance for receiver-initiated reservations*

The parameters δ, v, and f_{RSP} reflect the same processing times as in the sender-initiated case. The parameter o denotes the time required to install reverse-path state and emit a GIST QUERY message in downstream direction. The time required for completing the GIST handshake until a QoS NSLP QUERY message is sent is denoted r. The parameter u only occurs once at a leaf node (i.e., the signaling initiator) and reflects the time to perform policy and admission control and generate a corresponding QoS NSLP RESERVE message. The parameter f_{RSV} also reflects the time on an intermediate signaling entity to perform policy and admission control and "forward" a QoS NSLP RESERVE message.

The total setup time t_{setup} for a signaling session of a receiver-initiated reservation can then be estimated by

$$t_{\text{setup}} = \sum_{i=0}^{d}(o_j^i + r_j^i + f_{RSPj}^i + \Delta_i) + \sum_{i=0}^{d-1} f_{RSVj}^i + v_j^d + u_j^i$$

Based on the assumption that the processing times for single signaling messages are low, compared to the propagation delay, it can be obtained that the total setup time heavily depends on the artificially added GIST RESPONSE delay and the corresponding propagation delay between any two signaling entities. Since only the parameter δ for the GIST RESPONSE delay can actually be influenced by a signaling entity (i.e., its system administrator), its exact value must be chosen based on the expected network's topology and the expected signaling usage.

5.5.2 Signaling Performance Measurements

Signaling performance measurements were performed in order to demonstrate that the concepts developed in this chapter allow for QoS signaling in IP multicast environments and in order to evaluate the processing overhead that is imposed by IP multicast-based QoS signaling. The proposed multicast extensions were evaluated in a testbed environment following the setup depicted in Figure 5.11. Each node was equipped with Intel Xeon X3430 quadcore CPUs running at 2.40 GHz, 4 GB RAM, and four Intel 82580 Gigabit Ethernet network interfaces, interconnected by a Cisco Catalyst Switch 6500 running CatOS. All nodes used an Ubuntu 10.10 server installation with a 2.6.35 Linux kernel. The latency between the endpoints was small (approximately 1.235 ms on average between tb6 and the multicast destinations tb14 – tb21, measured by 100 ping tests) in order to concentrate measurements on the pure protocol and processing overhead.

Fine-grained measurements for the artificial delays for GIST RESPONSE messages were performed by putting measurement points into specific places within the code. Once such a reference point is hit, the value of the calculated delay is stored in memory. After the entire experiment is finished, the recorded values are written into a file. This prevents the measurements from being unnecessarily affected by file I/O operations. While the implementation supports IPv4 and IPv6 multicast it can be expected that the choice of one of these two IP version doesn't affect the signaling performance significantly. Hence, this section concentrates on evaluations for IPv4 multicast only.

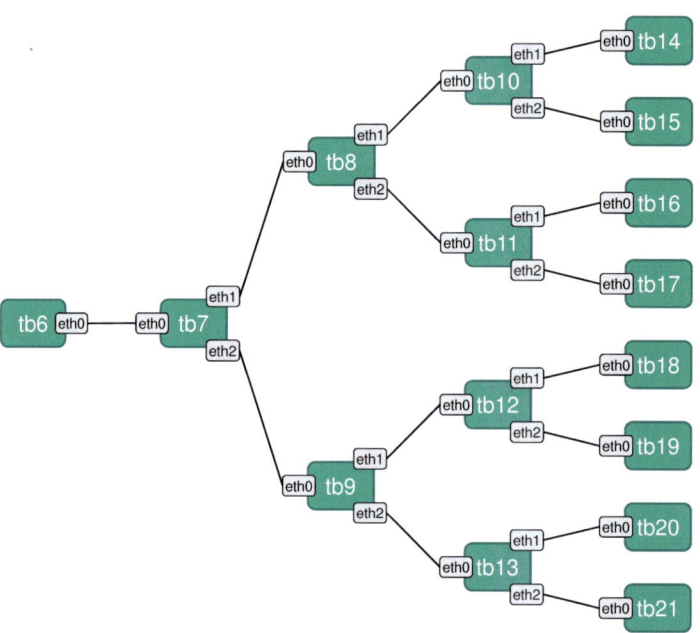

Figure 5.11: *Network topology used for evaluation tests. Testbed routers tb14 to tb21 were configured to act as multicast destinations.*

Measurements were generally performed with tb6 acting as the data flow sender, testbed routers tb14 to tb21 acting as multicast receivers, and all intermediate testbed routers acting as NSIS capable IP multicast routers. Therefore, all nodes actively participated in the NSIS multicast evaluations.

5.5.3 Sender-initiated Multicast Reservations

In order to evaluate the signaling performance of the proposed multicast extensions and compare the results to IP unicast-based scenarios, 50 different measurement runs were performed in total for sender-initiated multicast reservations. The 50 runs consist of 10 series of measurements, each containing 5 single sender-initiated reservations that were subsequently torn down within an interval of 5 and 2 seconds, respectively. The GIST multicast response delay for each node was configured to be in a range of $[0, 50]$ ms. Furthermore, each signaling entity's GIST state lifetime parameter was configured to not interfere the measurements with refreshing QUERY messages.

Figure 5.12 shows the results for the sender-initiated multicast reservations. The total duration of sender-initiated reservations, originating from a GIST QUERY until the QoS NSLP RESPONSE is received by tb6, is illustrated by the red bullet points. The rather alternating behavior stems from the artificial randomly chosen GIST response delay that is added by each intermediate signaling entity. These artificial delays were traced by the aforementioned fine-grained measurements. This allowed to calculate the resulting delay of the path with the lowest cumulative GIST delays (not shown in the figure). The difference between the total signaling time and the cumulative artificial delay is the actual plain signaling overhead, shown by the blue line at the bottom.

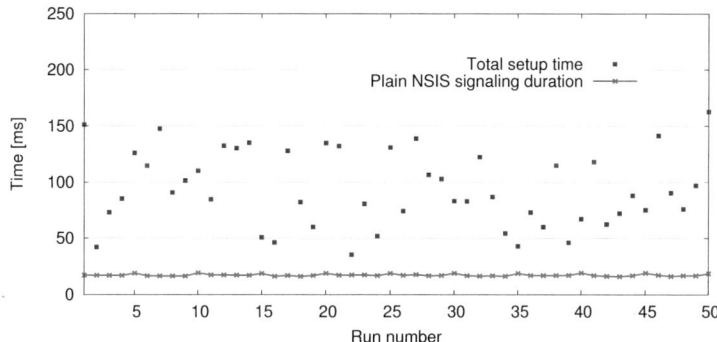

Figure 5.12: *Duration of sender-initiated reservations and the calculated artificial delay for GIST* RESPONSE *messages*

The plain NSIS signaling duration to setup a sender-initiated multicast reservation averages to 17.5 ms. Figure 5.13 shows the setup time (dashed blue line) in a higher resolution together with the time required to tear down a sender-initiated multicast reservation (red line). The small peaks of the setup time result from the aforementioned 10 separate measurement series where the first run takes a bit longer due to the instantiation of states and caches.

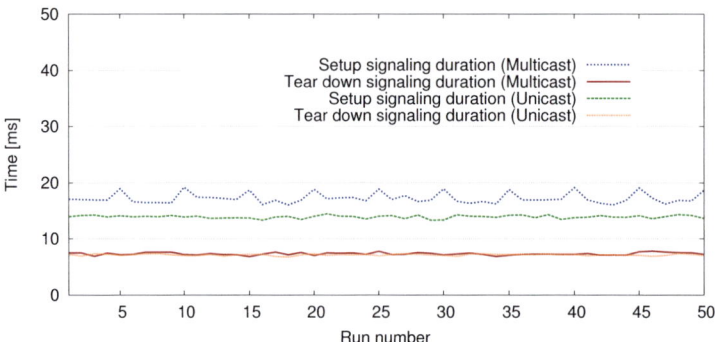

Figure 5.13: *Plain signaling overhead of sender-initiated reservations and tear down overhead*

Measurements were also performed for sender-initiated *unicast* reservations from tb6 to tb14 for comparison. The results for the setup time and the tear down time are also depicted in Figure 5.13. The time required to tear down a sender-initiated multicast reservation (7.31 ms on average) is almost identical to the one for a sender-initiated unicast reservation (7.11 ms on average), whereas a unicast reservation is slightly faster instantiated (13.97 ms on average).

From these results can be obtained, that the artificially added GIST RESPONSE delay has a great impact on the total setup time. Furthermore, it can be obtained from the plain signaling overhead measurements that multicast-based reservations require more time until a reservation has been established than unicast-based reservations (across a path of only four signaling hops in these scenarios). This can be mainly attributed to an increased complexity on the required signaling state maintenance. Since the additional overhead accumulates along a multicast tree, the overhead obtained corresponds to the multicast tree's depth, i.e., the number of signaling hops from the root to a leaf node.

However, it can be expected that the number of signaling hops will not be significantly higher in Internet-like scenarios, whereas the tree's fanout will be significantly higher toward the tree's leaf nodes. A high number at the tree's leaf nodes does, however, not affect the time required to establish a reservation from end to end, since this time always depends on the time at which a signaling entity receives its first response (independent of the number of subsequently arriving responses).

5.5.4 Receiver-initiated Multicast Reservations

Since NSIS supports both, sender- and receiver-initiated reservations, evaluations were also performed for receiver-initiated reservations. The results for 50 consecutive runs are depicted in Figure 5.14. This time, tb6 initiates a QoS NSLP QUERY toward the multicast destination upon which all multicast receivers initiate a RESERVE. The top red bullet points again correspond to the entire signaling duration as seen by tb6 ranging from the initial GIST QUERY until a QoS NSLP RESPONSE is emitted. By subtracting the artificially added GIST multicast response delays of the path with the lowest cumulative delays (not shown in this figure), the plain NSIS signaling overhead for receiver-initiated multicast reservations was retrieved. The time to setup such reservations takes about 26.5 ms on average.

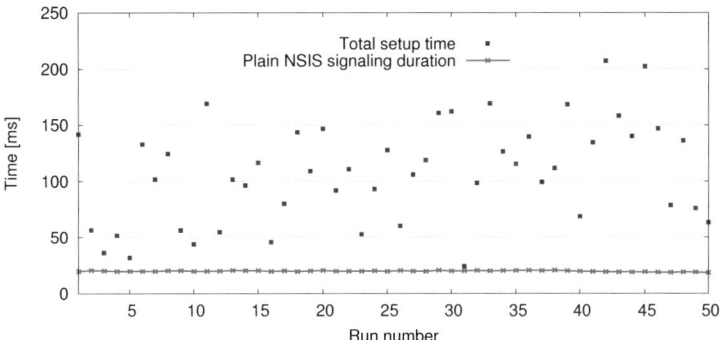

Figure 5.14: *Duration of receiver-initiated reservations and the calculated artificial delay for GIST* RESPONSE *messages*

From these numbers it can also be obtained that the artificially added GIST RESPONSE delay has a great impact on the actual signaling setup time. As can be expected, receiver-initiated reservations take longer to be established than sender-initiated reservations, since receiver-initiated reservations require an additional end-to-end signaling message exchange. However, the results do also show that the plain signaling overhead is still in a range where the propagation delays that can be expected in Internet-like scenarios dominate.

5.6 Conclusion

This chapter showed how Unicast-based QoS signaling protocols can be adapted
to be used in IP multicast environments. This opens up new opportunities for
signaling applications. One benefit of the herein described QoS signaling protocols
and their multicast extensions is the possibility to supply *scalable sender-initiated
reservations*. While sender-initiated reservations are the natural choice for offering
on-demand services, e.g., for video-on-demand services, resource reservations in
IP multicast environments could so far only be provided by relying on receiver-
initiated reservations.

   While proposed concepts can be mainly applied to QoS signaling protocols in
general they were exemplified on the NSIS protocols GIST and QoS NSLP. This
chapter showed that the NSIS protocols can be extended to support IP multicast
without the need to change the protocol's behavior regarding its unicast capabilities
or the introduction of any new protocol data units.

   Furthermore, it is now possible to use a "reliable" signaling messaging transport
for multicast flows, since multicast transmission is only used to detect directly
adjacent signaling peers upon which a multicast session is managed by single
unicast associations between directly adjacent signaling peers. Since a reliable
transport is only provided in a hop-by-hop manner, a really reliable end-to-end
mechanism has to be implemented within the signaling application. However, it is
possible to transfer large signaling messages reliably between adjacent signaling
entities.

   The evaluation results demonstrate that the concepts developed in this dissertation allow for multicast-based QoS signaling. The overhead imposed by the
additional functionality is low compared to expected delays stemming from propagation delays that can be encountered in the Internet.

   A further advantage of the proposed approach is that the NSIS protocols provide
support for mobile users (cf. Chapter 4). Thus, the integration of mobile multicast
users would be a next step for further investigations. Moreover, the multicast
extension of GIST could also be used for other signaling applications, e.g., for
signaling the setup of virtual nodes in network virtualization architectures.

Chapter 6

Dynamic Inter-Domain Aggregation of Resource Reservations

Providing on-demand QoS guarantees requires signaling of the resource demand, admission control, and resource reservation within the control plane upon which differential treatment and policing can be used in the data plane. End-to-end resource reservations are usually established on a per-flow basis along a set of intermediate signaling entities by means of dedicated signaling protocols. However, per-flow reservation state that needs to be maintained by each intermediate signaling entity leads eventually to scalability issues in the control plane, especially in the core domains of the Internet.

In the data plane the Differentiated Services (DiffServ) architecture provides an example for an approach that employs *aggregation* to achieve the necessary scalability with respect to the number of data flows. Similarly, scalability in the control plane could be achieved by aggregating resource reservations along shared segments of the data path.

The conceptual idea of aggregating resource reservations is to replace a number of resource reservations which are established along a common path segment and are of similar type, by a single aggregate reservation. By following this approach, intermediate signaling entities along this path segment must only maintain state for one (aggregate) resource reservation instead of for all single resource reservations.

An exemplified scenario is illustrated in Figure 6.1. This scenario consists of a hierarchy of provider domains and Internet routers (cf. Figure 2.2 on page 11). A large number of end systems is usually connected toward a single edge router and a number of edge routers is connected toward a domain's gateway router. Different provider domains are connected to each other via core routers.

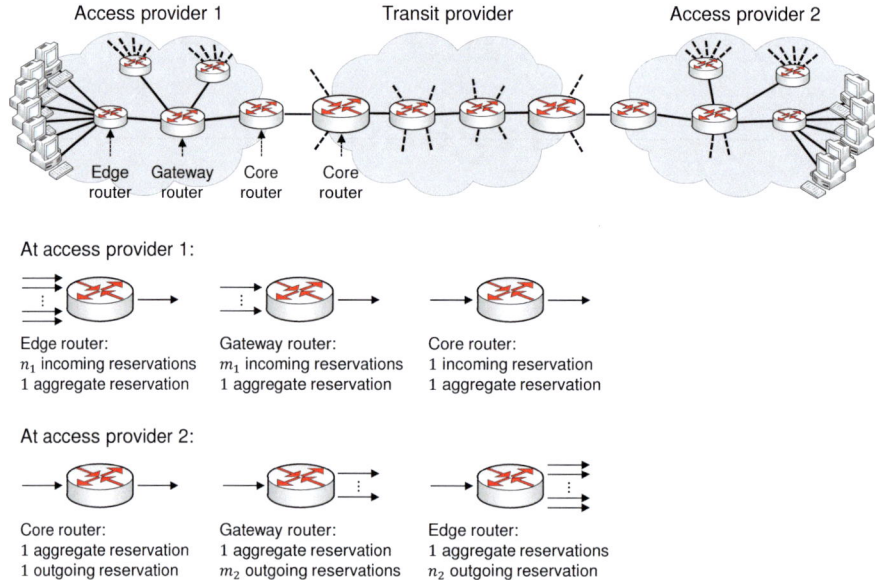

Figure 6.1: *Scenario of aggregating and deaggregating resource reservations amongst a set of signaling entities*

In case a number of end systems located at access provider 1 establish resource reservations, e.g., for VoIP internet telephony, toward end systems located at access provider 2, each edge router located at access provider 1 could aggregate its n_1 incoming reservation requests into one aggregate reservation that ends at an edge router at access provider 2. The gateway router could as well aggregate the m_1 reservation requests coming from its edge routers toward its next core router. Especially the core routers would benefit from an aggregation approach, since they are the most heavily loaded entities with respect to signaling along the path. By relying on aggregation, each core router along the path must then ideally only maintain signaling state for one aggregate reservation request in this scenario.[1] At access provider 2 the gateway and edge routers would have to act as

---
[1]Note, however, that a core router is usually connected to more than just one access provider

deaggregators and split aggregate reservations into single reservations again. This chapter analyzes how resource reservations can be aggregated and presents the design of shared-segment-based inter-domain aggregation mechanisms.

6.1 Problem Statement and Requirements

In order to set up the services described by a resource reservation request, an actively participating intermediate signaling entity must install and maintain reservation state in the control plane. Since reservation state is stored in memory and corresponding protocol messages must be processed by the CPU, each signaling session imposes costs in terms of signaling message processing and maintenance of reservation state.

Whenever resource reservations are established from end-to-end across a set of intermediate service providers, the number of accumulated single resource reservations can impose scalability problems especially in the core domains of the Internet. Therefore, this dissertation aims at providing a scalable solution by establishing inter-domain wide aggregates for resource reservations. In order to "bundle" a set of single resource reservations into an aggregate reservation, this section specifies the necessary requirements.

6.1.1 Establishing Aggregate Reservations

In order to aggregate a number of single resource reservations, it is necessary to identify the set of resource reservations which (1) *share a common data path segment* and are (2) *mapped to the same service class* along this data path segment. Only if these two conditions are met, it makes sense to establish an aggregate reservation which replaces this set of single reservations. Hence, the QoS signaling protocol must be able to collect the necessary information about each single reservation along the reservation's path. As soon as a pre-defined threshold of k single resource reservations fulfills these two conditions, the establishment of an aggregate reservation can be initiated.

6.1.2 Determination of Aggregator and Deaggregator

Whenever aggregation is used within a *single* administrative domain, the determination of an aggregator and a corresponding deaggregator is less challenging. Usually, boundary routers of the domain can be chosen to act as aggregator and deaggregator for a set of resource reservation requests. However, in case inter-domain aggregates should be established, the determination of aggregator and deaggregator becomes less obvious.

Once the number of aggregatable resource reservations reached the threshold of k reservations, a signaling entity may decide to act as the aggregator of a new aggregate reservation. After that, a corresponding deaggregator must be determined subsequently. Each signaling entity should, however, be able to decide autonomously whether it is willing to serve as (de-)aggregator for a set of resource reservations. In order to determine the deaggregator of a potential aggregate, the information, whether a signaling entity along the path is willing to serve as deaggregator should already be collected in advance.

6.1.3 Signaling between Aggregate Endpoints

Signaling messages related to an aggregate are only meaningful to the aggregator and deaggregator of this particular aggregate. This may affect, for instance, the adaptation of an existing aggregate's capacity. Furthermore, due to the signaling protocol's soft-state approach, the single reservations contained in an aggregate still need to be refreshed periodically. State for these reservations has been removed on each of the aggregate's intermediate signaling entities, i.e., with respect to the aggregate only the aggregator and the deaggregator have a notion of the single reservations. It must therefore be ensured that aggregation-related signaling messages between the aggregator and the deaggregator are transparently bypassed by all intermediate signaling entities along the aggregate.

6.1.4 Route Change Detection of Aggregated Flows

Resource reservations are only meaningful if they refer to the actually used data path. In IP-based networks, the data path may change over time, e.g., due to link failures or traffic engineering policies. Whenever the control plane is only loosely coupled with the data plane, reservations must be dynamically adapted to reflect route changes.

Even in case single reservations have been aggregated, route changes may still affect each single reservation contained in an aggregate over time. Therefore, a QoS signaling protocol must provide means to periodically probe whether each single reservation's data path matches with the aggregate's one. This should, however, not require state to be installed for each single reservation on each intermediate signaling entity, since this would contradict the aggregate's goal of reducing the number of signaling state that is to be maintained on those systems.

6.1.5 Maintaining Aggregates

Whenever aggregates are in place it is necessary that new reservation requests can be properly *inserted* into existing aggregates. It may, however, be the case that a signaling entity acts as aggregator of more than one established aggregate. In this case the aggregator must decide which of the existing aggregates is appropriate for the new reservation request. A shared data path segment and the use of the same service class mappings are essential preconditions for an integration of the new reservation request. Furthermore, a longer aggregate should be preferred over a shorter one, since longer aggregates save more state on intermediate signaling entities.

In case of hierarchical aggregates the signaling protocol must ensure that a higher-level aggregate's capacity is increased before the new reservation request is integrated into a lower-level aggregate. Depending on the level of hierarchies used on this shared data path segment, it may be required to perform this operation recursively.

Once reservations are no longer used, the reserved capacities should also be *removed* from the corresponding aggregate in order to free allocated resources. It may, however, be reasonable to delay the decrease of an aggregate's capacity, since new reservation requests may reach the aggregator shortly after the adaptation and hence, lead to another increase of the aggregate's capacity again. In case there is no more reservation active for a given aggregate, the aggregate should, however, be torn down.

6.2 Challenges for Reservation Aggregations

While establishing aggregate reservations provides a useful way to significantly reduce the number of states for resource reservations on intermediate signaling entities, establishing aggregates imposes a number of challenges that must be resolved.

6.2.1 Determination of a Reservation's Data Path

In IP-based networks the data path of an application's data flow is controlled by IP routing (which may still be influenced by a provider's traffic engineering policies). A resource reservation must therefore be established for this particular data path. Hence, in order to establish aggregate reservations for single reservation flows, the corresponding data path segments must traverse the same set of signaling entities.[2]

The determination of a reservation's data path is, however, a challenging task, since in IP-based networks a reservation's data path cannot be known a priori. While a central domain manager may be aware of a reservation's data path in its domain, a decentralized operating signaling entity cannot be assumed to have "global knowledge" about all routing tables, especially not in inter-domain wide scenarios. Therefore, the information about a reservation's data path must be collected while the reservation is established.

6.2.2 Determination of Service Class Mappings

Aggregating resource reservations is only meaningful if the reservations are mapped to the same service classes along the potential aggregate's data path segment, because all flows within the same aggregate must be allocated from the same resource pool. While reservation requests are usually mapped consistently to the same service classes within one administrative domain, it cannot be assumed that the same service class mappings are used in an inter-domain wide scenario where the data path segment spans more than one administrative domain. Even the use of the same QoS model, such as a DiffServ architecture, cannot be assumed in general. Furthermore, network operators do usually not want to expose their service class mappings, e.g., in form of DiffServ code points.

It is therefore a challenging task to identify which single reservations are mapped to the same service classes along a shared data path segment and still retain information about the actually used service class mappings of a network operator. This challenge can be addressed by collecting the information about a reservation's service class mapping during the reservation establishment phase. Furthermore, the actually used service class for a reservation request (e.g., its DiffServ code point) need not be exposed by a signaling entity. Instead, the signaling entity can use a "local" service class identifier, to which a reservation's service class is translated consistently and which is only meaningful on this particular signaling entity.

---

[2]Note, that these signaling entities need not necessarily belong to the same administrative domain.

6.2.3 Avoidance of Aggregation Conflicts

In case aggregate reservations are established it must be ensured that an anticipated aggregate reservation does not cause any conflicts with existing aggregate reservations. Aggregation conflicts were first analyzed by Bless [Ble02] and can even occur in a centralized aggregation approach.

Figure 6.2 illustrates a conflict between two potential aggregates. In this case aggregate A_1 has already been established by signaling entity ② to signaling entity ④ when signaling entity ① tries to establish an aggregate A_2 toward signaling entity ③. This does not cause any problems as long as both aggregates do not share the same set of single reservation flows. However, as soon as the new aggregate A_2 contains one reservation that has already been aggregated by A_1 the new aggregate cannot be established, since the aggregator and the deaggregator nodes must be aware of any single reservation flow contained in the corresponding aggregate.

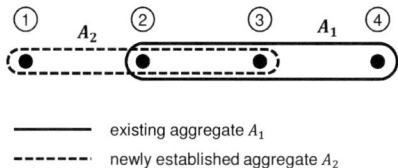

Figure 6.2: *Potential aggregation conflict between aggregates A_1 and A_2 (see also [Ble02])*

Another potential aggregation conflict may occur whenever two or more aggregating nodes try to establish conflicting aggregates at nearly the same time, resulting in a *race condition*. Figure 6.3 illustrates how race conditions can occur. In this case, reservations R_1 and R_2 are already established and share only a common data path segment between signaling entities ② and ③. Since this data path segment spans only one hop, an aggregate would not result in reduced state and hence is not established. Once reservation R_3 is initiated, two aggregates can conceptually be established—either between signaling entity ② and signaling entity ④ (cf. option 1 in Figure 6.3) or between signaling entity ① and signaling entity ③ (cf. option 2 in Figure 6.3). However, only one of them can actually be used at a time. Hence, it is important that an aggregation concept for resource reservations is able to detect and resolve potential aggregation conflicts. This becomes especially challenging for decentralized aggregation concepts, since there is no centralized coordinator available that may resolve occurring conflicts.

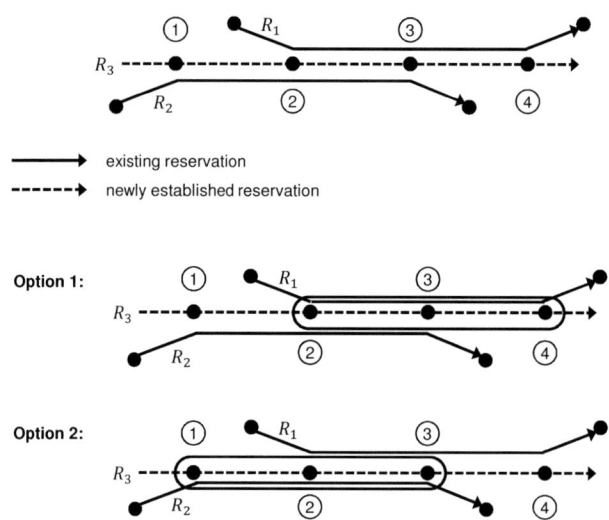

Figure 6.3: *Potential race condition during establishment of reservation aggregates*

As already shown by Bless [Ble02] a longer aggregate can be established as long as the shorter aggregate is always entirely covered by the longer one. This situation is illustrated in Figure 6.4. In these cases reservation state for the reservations contained in aggregate A_1 is not removed at signaling entities ② and ④ once aggregate A_2 is established.

6.3 Related Work

This section provides an overview of related work on existing protocols and mechanisms which rely on aggregation of resource reservations in order to achieve scalable QoS services. While aggregation as a concept was also adapted by QoS routing approaches [PS07b], this dissertation does not further examine QoS routing concepts. This is due to the fact that QoS routing basically adapts existing routing paths in order to meet QoS constraints. It can, however, neither establish aggregates on-demand, nor reserve resources for a particular user.

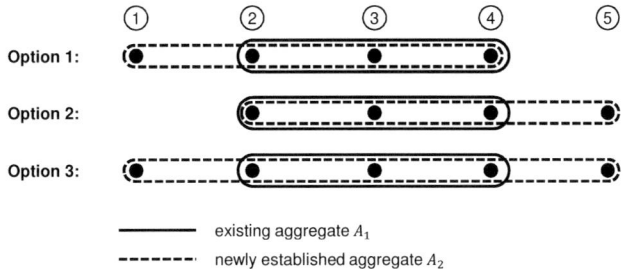

Figure 6.4: *Establishment of longer aggregates that do not cause any aggregation conflicts with existing shorter ones (cf. [Ble02])*

This section focuses therefore on QoS signaling protocols that specifically target at providing scalability by aggregating resource reservations. It compares and reviews the functionalities of the different approaches. The following criteria are used for a functional comparison:

- *Decentralized operation* — A decentralized operation of a QoS signaling protocol allows signaling to be performed independent of central domain managers and therefore to be more robust against failures of a central entity. Furthermore, scalability of signaling services can be achieved much more efficient in a decentralized environment.

- *Support of different QoS models* — Since different QoS models, such as IntServ or DiffServ, are used by different network operators, the QoS signaling's QoS model support should not be limited to a single model.

- *Dynamic establishment of aggregates* — Aggregates should be established and removed dynamically and on-demand, since statically configured aggregates impose a significant management overhead.

- *Inter-domain wide operation* — Aggregates should be established across different administrative domains, rather than being limited to an intra-domain scenario only. Otherwise, border routers of the Internet's core could not benefit from an aggregation, since they will have to manage all single reservations.

6.3.1 RSVP Aggregation

The QoS signaling protocol RSVP is able to establish receiver-initiated resource reservations from end-to-end across different administrative domains. It was, however, not designed to address scalability concerns from the beginning. Hence, aggregation of resource reservations being controlled by RSVP was introduced by Baker et al. [RFC3175]. By following this approach, signaling messages for single reservations are not processed by signaling entities that belong to an aggregation region. This is accomplished by changing the signaling message's IP protocol number at the aggregate's ingress to reflect the value RSVP_E2E_IGNORE (134) and revert this value at the aggregate's egress to the original value RSVP (46).

This approach does, however, impose a number of problems. Border routers serve as aggregators and deaggregators are thus determined statically and a priori, instead of allowing the protocol to determine these two aggregator roles dynamically and on-demand. Furthermore, RSVP aggregation is limited to DiffServ domains only and therefore does not provide independence of the underlying QoS architecture. While this approach can technically be used across different administrative domains,[3] it requires the aggregate's egress to be aware of the DiffServ codepoints used across *all* these domains in order to map single reservations to an aggregate. However, since network operators do usually want to be flexible and appoint their DiffServ mappings independently of other network operators, this inter-domain wide aggregations can hardly be realized by this approach.

6.3.2 Border Gateway Reservation Protocol

In order to aggregate resource reservations across domain boundaries, Pan et al. [PHS99; PHS00b] propose a newly defined Border Gateway Reservation Protocol (BGRP). BGRP assumes DiffServ to be used in the data path and aims at achieving scalability with respect to the number of reservations. BGRP is based on the Internet routing hierarchy and the signaling protocol only operates between border routers of different administrative domains. Resource reservations are then aggregated toward the same destination border router in form of sink trees.

BGRP establishes reservations in two phases as depicted in Figure 6.5. Reservation sources (e.g., router ① in Figure 6.5) send PROBE messages in downstream direction toward a destination. These messages contain information about the QoS demand, the destination address, and a route record object, where information about all intermediate border routers is stored. Upon receiving a PROBE message, reservation sinks (e.g., router ⑧ in Figure 6.5) actually establish reservations by returning a GRAFT message. By relying on the information contained in the route record object, the GRAFT message traverses the request's path in reverse direction. A

---

[3]given that an RSVP's RAO is preserved during transit

reservation request either results in a newly established sink tree or the reservation is attached to an already existing sink tree. This allows intermediate routers to maintain only one single reservation state per sink tree.

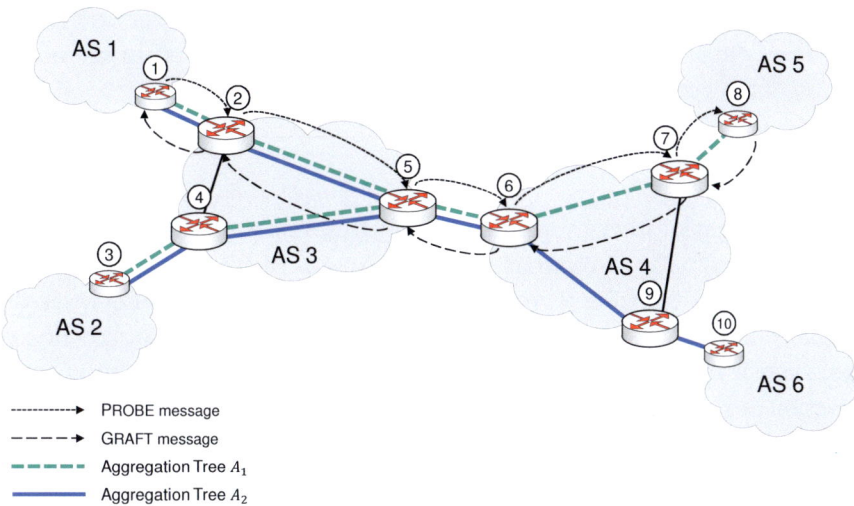

Figure 6.5: *Example of BGRP aggregation reservations with two sink trees A_1 and A_2*

BGRP follows a soft-state approach, i.e., REFRESH messages are periodically exchanged between signaling entities to maintain signaling state. BGRP optionally allows to establish reservations with some spare capacity in order to reduce the number of necessary signaling messages. Since BGRP is only designed to operate between border routers, it doesn't support end-to-end reservations. While BGRP already allows to significantly reduce the number of signaling states on intermediate routers, the sink tree-based approach can also result in an unnecessarily high number of aggregates. This can happen whenever resource reservations are initiated from the same source but toward different destinations. For instance, consider the situation depicted in Figure 6.5 where the two sink trees A_1 and A_2 are used by routers ① and ②. Even though these reservations share a set of intermediate routers (i.e., the same segment of their data paths toward their destinations, e.g., between routers ① to ⑥), these reservations cannot be further aggregated by BGRP.

BGRP is currently limited to a pure bandwidth reservation approach and therefore abstracts from actually used—and potentially heterogeneous—QoS models that are used in the different domains. A sink tree-based approach may also be of limited use due to its uni-directional mode of reservation operation.[4] Furthermore, in a sink tree-based approach resources are reserved for the data path in downstream direction from a tree's leaf toward a sink. This proves to be disadvantageous since network load usually rarely aggregates at the destination (i.e., the sink), such as at a popular video-on-demand server. Instead, data traffic is rather sent from the server (i.e., the sink) toward the clients (i.e., the tree's leaves) in the opposite direction of the actual reservation.

6.3.3 SICAP

The Shared-Segment Inter-Domain Control Aggregation Protocol (SICAP) [SGV03; Sof03] was designed to overcome the limitations of BGRP by employing shared-segment aggregations of resource reservations. This allows building reservation aggregates of single reservations that share segments of their corresponding data paths, even if the destination domains differ. SICAP uses the same two-phase reservation mechanism and signaling messages as BGRP and therefore also employs a receiver-initiated reservation approach. Aggregates are built between so-called *Intermediate Deaggregation Locations (IDLs)*. SICAP uses heuristic algorithms in order to determine these IDLs, e.g., aggregates are only established upon covering a minimum number of intermediate signaling entities or by choosing IDLs that have a high number of AS neighbors.

SICAP's shared segment approach and the use of IDLs is exemplified in Figure 6.6. In this scenario three aggregates are established: aggregate A_1 builds a sink tree where router ⑥ serves as IDL_1 and root of the tree. It interconnects aggregate A_1 with two other aggregates, namely A_2 and A_3. By following this shared segment approach, routers along the path need only to store per-IDL reservation state.

However, SICAP's employed heuristics may lead to non-optimal choices of deag-gregators and be a potentially complex and cost-intensive operation. For instance, the algorithm may choose a core router to serve as deaggregator simply because of its high number of interconnections toward different domains. Relying on core routers as (de-)aggregators can be considered disadvantageous, since core routers were then required to process and keep state about each single reservation request. Aggregating resource reservations should instead lower the load on core routers. Furthermore, SICAP does not consider hierarchical aggregates where a "longer" ag-gregate is nested in another "shorter" one—instead aggregates can only be stitched together.

---

[4]Which can be considered a receiver-initiated reservation approach

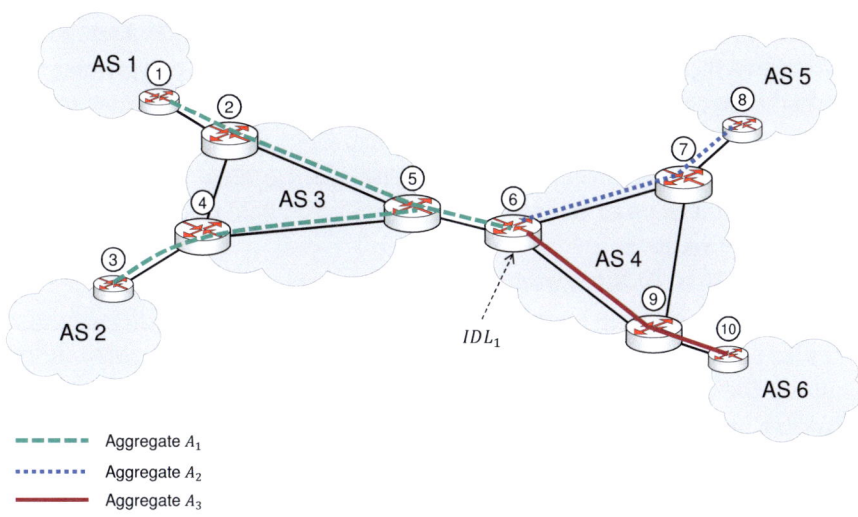

Figure 6.6: *Example of SICAP reservations with three aggregates A_1, A_2, and A_3*

Since SICAP considers only the inter-domain signaling part between border routers of different domains, it would also require an inter-working with different end-to-end signaling protocols. Furthermore, it does not discuss the applicability of the chosen approach in case resource reservations are mapped to different service classes.

6.3.4 DARIS

The Dynamic Aggregation of Reservations for Internet Services (DARIS) [Ble02; Ble04] architecture was designed as a management architecture for DiffServ domains that also allows for aggregations of resource reservations. DARIS follows a bandwidth broker approach where resource reservations and aggregates are controlled by a central resource manager, called Differentiated Services Domain Manager (DSDM). Signaling between DSDMs belonging to different domains and between end systems and DSDMs is achieved by using a dedicated Domain Manager Signaling Protocol (DMSP). Each DSDM is assumed to have knowledge about the inter-domain routing table upon which AS graph representations can be created in order to manage aggregate reservations. While DARIS supports sender- and receiver-initiated reservations, it was designed to be used within DiffServ domains only and assumes interacting domains to agree on a common service definition.

DARIS also follows a shared-segment approach in order to build aggregates but also introduces more sophisticated aggregation mechanisms. An aggregate can be established between two network nodes whenever they span more than two hops and the aggregate covers at least k reservations. Once an aggregate is created or must be increased dynamically, DARIS increases the aggregate's capacity with an additional amount in order to avoid updating the aggregate reservation with every new reservation request.

As one of the first, DARIS introduces the notion of hierarchical aggregates where longer (and more efficient) aggregates can be nested within shorter aggregates. DARIS also considers a recursive adaptation of hierarchical aggregates. In order to improve the performance of these recursive adaptations, the corresponding requests can be parallelized. DARIS introduces *waiting conditions* that allow for a synchronization of these requests. Furthermore, and different from BGRP and SICAP, DARIS resolves potential *aggregation conflicts* and *re-routing* of single reservations.

While DARIS already allows to dynamically create, update, or remove aggregate reservations it heavily relies on a centralized domain manager and is only designed to be used within DiffServ domains.

6.3.5 Inter-Domain Reservation Aggregation for QoS NSLP

The idea of extending the NSIS signaling protocol suite to allow for inter-domain wide reservation aggregations was proposed by Bless and Doll [BD07]. The concept follows a shared-segment based approach and takes some important aggregation aspects into consideration. For instance, the authors propose to establish aggregates with a slightly larger capacity than required in order to prevent aggregators from having to adapt an aggregate's capacity with every joining or leaving reservation. The presented approach also considers the use of a direct signaling association between the aggregator and the deaggregator.

Furthermore, the authors identify important challenges that must be solved by a QoS signaling solution and also propose ideas for a potential realization. The challenges comprise the determination of aggregator and deaggregator in inter-domain wide scenarios, the establishment of a direct signaling association between the aggregator and the deaggregator, and an priori determination of a reservation's path, and the issue of route change detection for aggregated flows.

While most of the concepts proposed in [BD07] have not been finalized, the design proposed in this dissertation is based in parts on some of these concepts. For instance, the QoS NSLP aggregation concept introduces data structures to obtain information about a single reservation's path (so-called `Route Record` object) and a data structure that contains information about all reservations that are managed by an aggregate (so-called SESSION_ID_LIST). Furthermore, a special-purpose message routing method is introduced (called AF-MRM) which allows to exchange signaling messages directly between the aggregator and the deaggregator, add reservations to an established aggregate, and to detect route changes of aggregated reservations.

However, the concepts outlined in [BD07] provide only a starting point of how QoS NSLP-based signaling can be extended to support aggregate reservations. In particular, the concept proposed does not take into consideration that single reservations must also be mapped to the same service classes along the corresponding data path segment in order to be aggregated. Furthermore, the proposal does not provide information about the detection and resolution of potentially occurring aggregation conflicts, e.g., due to race conditions.

6.3.6 Summary and Discussion

QoS signaling protocols build an essential component in order to allow for on-demand resource reservations in the Internet. While scalability of resource reservations can already be achieved in the data plane by the DiffServ architecture, corresponding mechanisms in the control plane for QoS signaling protocols are still missing.

Each of the research proposals outlined above explicitly focuses on the scalability of resource reservations. Table 6.1 provides a functional comparison and evaluation of the proposed approaches. RSVP aggregation was only designed to support statically established aggregates and considers DiffServ domains only. BGRP relies on the establishment of sink trees and does not provide an end-to-end signaling solution. SICAP's shared segment approach overcomes some of BGRP's weaknesses but relies on heuristics to choose its deaggregator and can afterwards only build a chain of subsequent aggregates. DARIS also provides a shared segment approach but already considers aggregate conflicts and allows the establishment of hierarchical aggregates. It is, however, strictly based on a centralized domain manager which may be a single source of failure or become a bottleneck in case a very large number of reservations within a domain needs to be maintained. Furthermore, while most proposals simply assumed a consistent use of DiffServ in the data plane, none of them considered the use of different QoS models along a reservation's path, or even that resource reservations can be mapped to different service classes within different domains.

Criterion	RSVP Aggr. [RFC3175]	BGRP [PHS00b]	SICAP [SGV03]	DARIS [Ble04]
Decentralized operation	+	+	+	−
Support of different QoS models	−	−	−	−
Dynamic establishment of aggregates	−	+	+	+
Inter-domain wide aggregates	−	+	+	+

Table 6.1: *Comparison and evaluation of different QoS signaling protocols*

Therefore, a scalable and decentralized QoS signaling approach is still missing which takes the Internet's heterogeneity into account. Support for sender- and receiver-initiated reservations would be beneficial in order to provide the most generic form of resource reservations. From the research proposals can be conducted, that aggregations should be established following a shared-segment based approach. This allows signaling entities on a heavily loaded path to decide on their own whether an aggregate should be established or not. In a sink tree-based approach only the tree's root node establishes aggregate reservations. Furthermore, regarding the domain-specific mappings of reservation requests to service classes a sink tree-based approach would require that each signaling entity along the path from the tree's root toward its leaves selects the same service class. A shared segment based approach therefore provides much greater flexibility. Finally, hierarchical aggregations—as being introduced by the DARIS architecture—and the consideration and avoidance of aggregation conflicts build important requirements for the establishment of reservation aggregations.

6.4 Design of Inter-Domain Reservation Aggregations

This section provides the design for inter-domain reservation aggregation mechanisms that fulfill the requirements outlined in Section 6.1 and directly address the challenges presented in Section 6.2. The design aims at providing generic QoS signaling solutions. In order to demonstrate the use of the proposed concepts, the NSIS protocol suite serves as prototypical example for a decentralized QoS signaling protocol. Therefore, some NSIS specific details are considered where necessary.

6.4.1 Identification of Aggregatable Resource Reservations

Before aggregates are actually established, aggregatable resource reservations must be properly identified. According to the requirements for reservation aggregations, the single resource reservations must share a common data path segment and they must be mapped to the same service classes along this data path segment. Since this information is not available at a potential aggregator a priori, it is necessary to allow a QoS signaling protocol to collect this information accordingly.

The specific information needed to identify aggregatable resource reservations should consist of the following parts. First, the signaling entities along a reservation's path must be tracked, since aggregates can only be established along a common data path segment. Second, the reservation's service class mapping on each intermediate signaling entity must be tracked, since only reservations being mapped to the same service classes can be aggregated. Third, each of the intermediate signaling entities must determine whether it would like to serve as aggregator of resource reservations or not.

In order to collect the required information about a reservation's data path an appropriate data structure must be used. According to the proposal in [BD07] a ROUTE RECORD object is introduced for this purpose. This object can be either inserted into a reservation request by the reservation initiator or by any other intermediate signaling entity along the reservation's path. Once a reservation request contains a ROUTE RECORD object, each intermediate signaling entity being aware of this object enters its information about its identity and its service class mapping for this reservation into the object.

It is important, that a signaling entity can be uniquely identified. Even though the IP addresses of routers could already be used as unique identifiers, it is not clear which of a router's configured IP address should be chosen and also whether IPv4 or IPv6 addresses should be used. Therefore, a unique ROUTER ID should be used instead, which is composed of the following: the 32 bit AS number of the router's location and a 128 bit number which can be chosen by the network operator.[5] Furthermore, it is important to enter an IP address into the ROUTE RECORD object under which the signaling entity is reachable, e.g., since it may serve as (de-) aggregator and the ROUTER ID does not necessarily contain an IP address.

Each intermediate signaling entity adds a symbolic *service class identifier* to the object which identifies to which service class a reservation request is mapped on

---

[5]e.g., by simply using the lowest configured IP address on that router. Note, that this rather long number allows network operators to choose a number with a very high probability of uniqueness.

this particular signaling entity. However, instead of using the exact (potentially confidential) actual service class of a specific reservation request—e.g., the concrete DiffServ code point—, the meaning behind a specific service class identifier has only node-local significance. This adds a new level of abstraction which allows to use a consistent data type for the representation of service class mappings for reservation requests across different administrative domains and which can be applied independently of the underlying QoS model being used. For aggregation purposes, an aggregator does not need to know which service class is actually used on a signaling entity for a reservation request. Instead, the aggregator must only ensure that the set of aggregatable resource reservations is mapped to the same service classes along a shared data path segment.

Note, that it doesn't constitute a mandatory precondition that all intermediate signaling entities enter their information into the ROUTE RECORD object in order to allow for an aggregate reservation. It is, however, the only way to determine to which service class a specific reservation is mapped by these signaling entities. Since not all signaling entities are capable or willing to serve as potential aggregators, an *aggregator flag* must be set by those signaling entities that would like to serve as aggregators of resource reservations.

6.4.2 Determination of Potential Aggregates

An aggregate should only be established once a pre-defined threshold $k > 2$ of aggregatable reservations is reached at an aggregator node. This threshold can be independently chosen by each signaling entity, e.g., by means of a system-specific configuration variable. Furthermore, the longer the aggregate (in terms of intermediate participating signaling entities) the more state can be saved in total. Therefore, an aggregator should aim at building the longest possible aggregate which still contains at least k reservations.

From an aggregator's point of view, potential aggregates for all outgoing resource reservations can be regarded as a tree which branches either in case reservations leave the path segment or once the service class mapping changes between different sets of reservations. Therefore, a new system internal data structure called *flow aggregation tree* is introduced. This data structure takes each reservation's intermediate signaling entities and its corresponding service class mappings into account. The term local service class is used to refer to a single reservation's service class mapping on a particular signaling entity. The term reservation specification refers to a single reservation's list of participating signaling entities (i.e., each signaling entity's ROUTER ID) and the corresponding local service classes.

The idea how the longest aggregatable path for a set of resource reservations can be retrieved from the flow aggregation tree follows the approach of a longest prefix match function used by IP routing. The reservation specification entries serve as key within the flow aggregation tree, i.e., whenever the reservation specification entries of two single reservations differ between each other at a given index position (either because of diverging paths or because of different service class mappings), the flow aggregation tree branches. At each level of the flow aggregation tree, all aggregatable reservations are inserted into a *flow bucket* data structure. The number of entries contained in each of these flow buckets allows to determine whether an aggregate should be established and which reservations are to be inserted into this anticipated aggregate.

Figure 6.7 depicts a scenario for the use of the flow aggregation tree. In this scenario three different resource reservation requests were initiated by signaling entity S_1. Two reservations, namely R_1 and R_2 are established toward signaling entity S_2, whereas reservation R_3 is established toward signaling entity S_3. While all three reservations are mapped to the same local service class in AS1, the reservations R_1 and R_2 are inserted into different local service classes within AS2. Therefore, R_1 and R_2 can only be aggregated up to signaling entity ③, even though they share the same path up to signaling entity S_2.

The corresponding flow aggregation tree is illustrated in Figure 6.8. The three reservation specifications for the three different reservations R_1, R_2, and R_3 (as seen by signaling entity S_1) are composed of tuples for the ROUTER ID and the reservation's local service class. For instance, reservation R_3 traverses signaling entity ①, ②, ③, ④, and ⑥ with local service class 1, and finally signaling entities ⑨ and ⑩ with local service class 6. Hence reservation R_3 can be represented by

$$R_3 := ((①,1),(②,1),(③,1),(④,1),(⑥,1),(⑨,6),(⑩,6))$$

In Figure 6.8 the three reservation specifications differ the first time at index 2. Hence, the Next index variable is set to 2 at the tree's root node. At index 2 the reservations R_1 and R_3 are in the same reservation specification and are therefore inserted into the same new flow bucket, whereas R_2 is inserted into another flow bucket. The two remaining reservations R_1 and R_3 differ again at index 4—this time due to a diverging path. Therefore, the flow aggregation tree branches again, such that reservations R_1 and R_3 are inserted into different flow buckets.

The longest possible path for an aggregate reservation (above threshold k) can then simply be determined as follows: a newly established reservation terminates at any given leaf of the flow aggregation tree. The aggregator checks whether

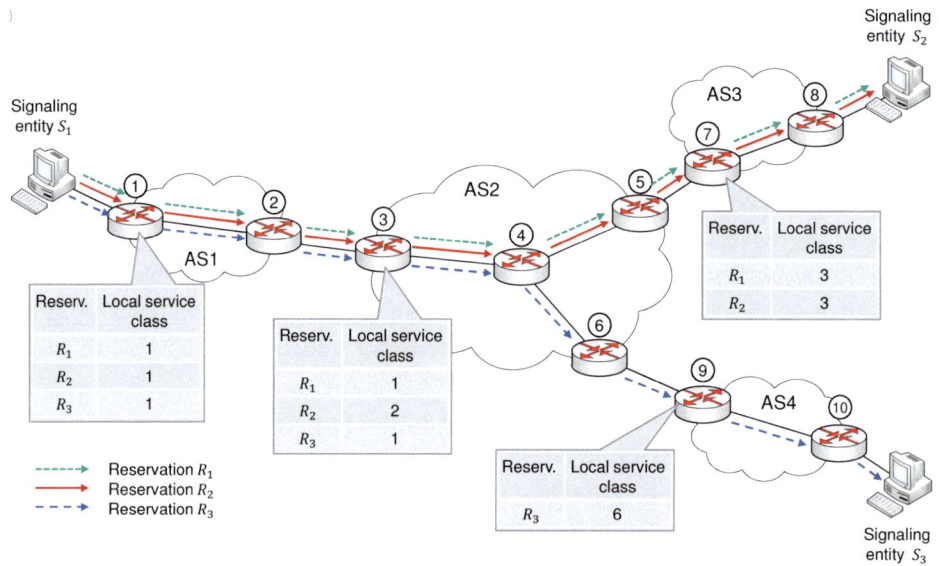

Figure 6.7: *Scenario for the determination of potential aggregates*

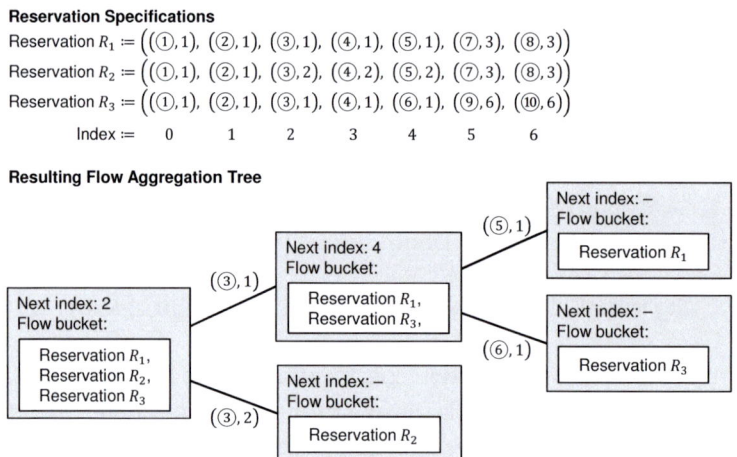

Figure 6.8: *Flow aggregation tree as being created on signaling entity S_1*

threshold k is reached by the number of reservations contained in the leaf's flow bucket. If this is the case, the longest possible aggregate for this new reservation is already found and can be established. Otherwise, the aggregator goes one level up toward the root in the flow aggregation tree and repeats the procedure until an appropriate path is found or it determines that not enough reservations are established to create a new aggregate.

Note, that the flow aggregation tree must only be created on signaling entities that would like to serve as aggregators (according to their system configuration). That is, for sender-initiated reservations the flow aggregation tree is created on aggregators, whereas for receiver-initiated reservations it is created on deaggregators as discussed in Section 6.4.4.1.

6.4.2.1 Construction and Maintenance of a Flow Aggregation Tree

Once a new reservation request reaches a signaling entity, it is inserted into the signaling entity's flow aggregation tree. The reservation must be inserted into each intermediate node of the flow aggregation tree along a path from the tree's root node up to a leaf node. The insert() method therefore begins to insert the reservation at the tree's root node and iterates through all nodes along a path as illustrated in Listing 6.1.

```
1   while true do
2       // Check whether flow bucket of current node is empty
3       if currentNode.flowBucket = ∅ then
4           currentNode.flowBucket.insert(newReservation)
5           break
6       end
7       // Check whether all reservations in this bucket
8       // share the same reservation specification with
9       // the new reservation
10      if (allRsvSpecsEqual(newReservation, currentNode.flowBucket)
            ) then
11          currentNode.flowBucket.insert(newReservation)
12          break
13      end
14      // A new branch must be created
15      else
16          determine branchIndex
17          // The current node is a leaf node
18          if currentNode.nextNodes = ∅ then
19              // Create two new successor nodes of current node
20              create newNode1
21              copyFlowBucket(currentNode, newNode1, branchIndex)
22              create newNode2
23              newNode2.flowBucket.insert(newReservation)
```

```
24              currentNode.nextIndex ← branchIndex
25              currentNode.nextNodes ← newNode1
26              currentNode.nextNodes ← newNode2
27              break
28          end
29          // The current node is a branching node in
30          // the middle of the tree
31          else
32              // It must be branched earlier than before, i.e.,
33              // a new intermediate node and a new leaf node
34              // for the new reservation must be created
35              if branchIndex < currentNode.nextIndex then
36                  // Create two new successor nodes of current
                        node
37                  create newNode1
38                  copyFlowBucket(currentNode, newNode1,
                        branchIndex)
39                  create newNode2
40                  newNode2.flowBucket.insert(newReservation)
41                  newNode1.nextIndex ← currentNode.nextIndex
42                  currentNode.nextIndex ← branchIndex
43                  newNode1.nextNodes ← currentNode.nextNodes
44                  currentNode.nextNodes ← newNode1
45                  currentNode.nextNodes ← newNode2
46                  break
47              end
48              // It is branched at the same index
49              // Check if a new branch must be created
50              // or if an existing branch can be followed
51              if branchIndex = currentNode.nextIndex then
52                  // Follow an existing branch
53                  if needed branch already exists then
54                      currentNode.flowBucket.insert(newReservation
                            )
55                      move to next node in tree
56                  end
57                  // Create new branch for the new reservation
58                  else
59                      create newNode1
60                      newNode1.flowBucket.insert(newReservation)
```

```
61                          currentNode.flowBucket.insert(newReservation
                              )
62                          currentNode.nextNodes ← newNode1
63                          move to next node in tree
64                  end
65              end
66          end
67      end
68 end
```

Listing 6.1: *Inserting reservations into the flow aggregation tree*

First of all, the new reservation can be inserted into the current node's flow bucket if the node's flow bucket is empty (cf. lines 3 – 6) or if all reservations contained in the node's flow bucket share the same reservation specification with the new reservation (cf. lines 10 – 13).

Whenever these two conditions are not met, a new branch in the flow aggregation tree must be created and the current node's branch index must be determined. If the current node is a leaf node, the new reservation must be inserted into the current node and two new successor nodes must be created—one containing all reservations of the current node and one containing the new reservations (cf. lines 18 – 28). This situation is illustrated in Figure 6.9 where the newly arriving reservation R_4 is inserted into a flow aggregation tree. Since reservation R_4 does not share the same reservation specifications with the leaf node's reservations R_1, R_2, and R_3, a new branch must be created accordingly.

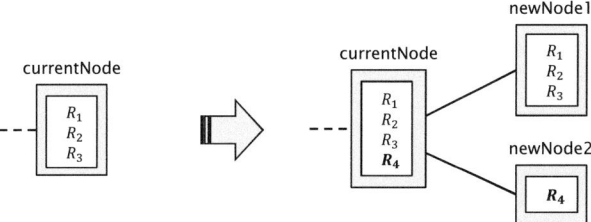

Figure 6.9: *Insertion of reservation R_4 if the current node is a leaf node in the flow aggregation tree*

However, the reservation specification of the newly arriving reservation can also differ from other reservation specifications before a leaf node is reached. In this case, the new reservation requires the creation of a new branch in the middle of the tree. In this case it must be further distinguished, whether the current node's branch index is smaller than the current node's next index variable or not. If the determined branch index is smaller, the branch must be established in front of the current node. Then, two new nodes must be created—one that contains the current node's reservations and which is a successor node of the current node, and one for the new reservation which is also a successor node of the current node (cf. lines 35 – 47).

This situation is illustrated in Figure 6.10 where the newly arriving reservation R_4 is inserted into the flow aggregation tree. Since the branch index for the new reservation is smaller than the next index variable contained in the current node, a new branch must be created in front of the current node.

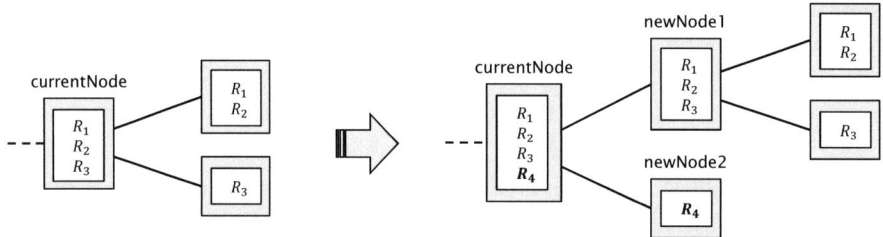

Figure 6.10: *Insertion of reservation R_4 if the current node is a branching node in the flow aggregation tree and the branch index is smaller than the current node's next index*

If the determined branch index equals the next index of the current node but the current node is no leaf node, it must be determined whether an existing branch can be followed (cf. lines 53 – 56) or if a new branch must be created (cf. lines 58 – 64). If an existing branch can be followed (illustrated at the bottom right of Figure 6.11), the new reservation is simply inserted into the current node and it is moved to the next node along the path in the tree. If a new branch must be created, a new node must be created for the new reservation as successor of the current node as illustrated at the top right of Figure 6.11.

As soon as a new reservation has been inserted into the flow aggregation tree, it is checked whether the new reservation can be used within an aggregate by means of the checkAggregationTrigger() method. This method is initially called from

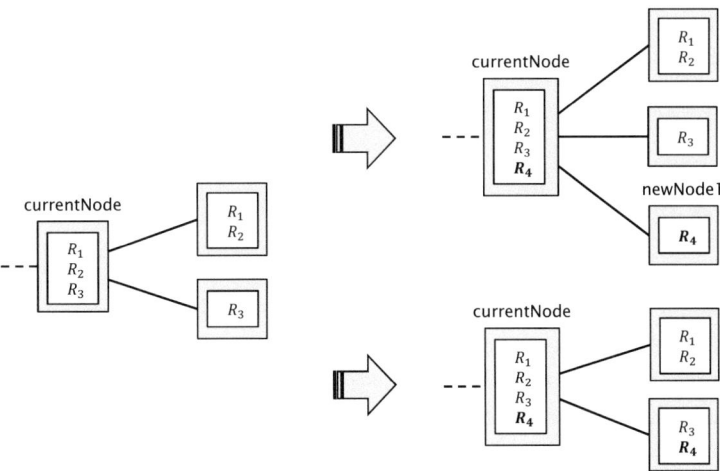

Figure 6.11: *Insertion of reservation R_4 if the current node is a branching node in the flow aggregation tree and the branch index equals the current node's next index*

the leaf node where the newly added reservation is stored. It checks whether the reservation can be inserted into an already established aggregate or whether a new aggregate can be established. In the latter case, the aggregation threshold must be met at any time and the minimum and maximum index for a potential aggregate is determined. After that it is verified whether the node located at the determined index position is willing to serve as aggregator, i.e., this method searches for the longest possible aggregate. If an aggregation node is found, a temporary vector with aggregatable reservations is created. Only those reservations, which are not already contained in an aggregate or which are part of an already existing shorter aggregate are inserted into this vector. If the aggregation threshold is met, the method tries to establish an aggregate with the identified single reservations contained in the vector. If no aggregation node is found at the determined index, the method takes one step backwards recursively toward the root of the tree and checks again for a shorter aggregate or tries to add the reservation to an existing aggregate.

Note, that this method searches for the longest possible aggregate which is not necessarily the "best" possible aggregate in terms of the number of state that can be saved by building an aggregate. However, since resource reservations are expected to be highly dynamic and the calculation of the "best" possible aggregate can be computationally very expensive, this dissertation only provides a way to search for the longest possible aggregate.

6.4.3 Signaling between Aggregate Endpoints

Once aggregates have been established, it is necessary to exchange reservation state information about the aggregated (single flow) reservations between the aggregator and the deaggregator, e.g., to refresh, change, or even tear down a reservation. This information must be exchanged directly between both aggregate endpoints, since intermediate signaling entities have not installed any state anymore for the single reservations contained in an aggregate.

The term *signaling state* comprises the state required for the reservation request and signaling routing state between adjacent signaling entities. In terms of NSIS signaling, the former belongs to QoS NSLP and the latter to GIST. Usually single reservation requests along a path of three signaling entities establish state in QoS NSLP's and GIST's signaling instances as depicted in Figure 6.12. In this case each signaling entity must maintain an incoming and an outgoing signaling routing state at GIST level for each of the single reservation requests, as well as reservation state at QoS NSLP level for each single reservation request.

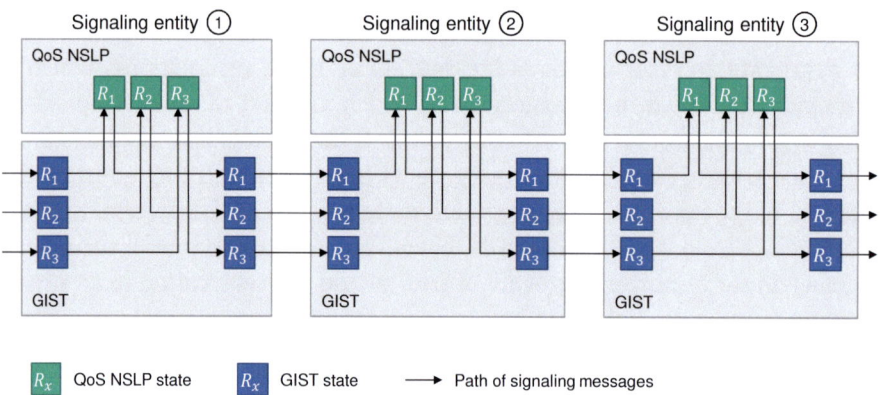

Figure 6.12: *Signaling state for single reservation requests along three signaling entities if no aggregation is used*

In order to reduce state at signaling entity ② and still allow single reservations $R_1, \ldots, R_3$ to be refreshed between signaling entities ① and ③, it is necessary that an aggregator and its deaggregator become direct signaling routing peers for the single reservations (here $R_1, \ldots, R_3$) at GIST level. This allows periodic refreshes for the single reservation requests to be exchanged between the aggregator and the deaggregator, while signaling entities along the aggregate are not required to maintain signaling routing state for single reservations. The conceptual design is illustrated in Figure 6.13.

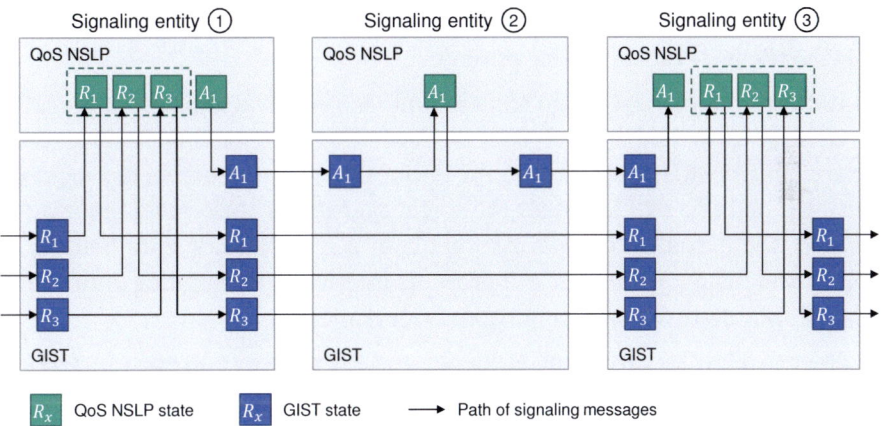

Figure 6.13: *Situation with a reduced number of signaling state for single reservation requests and one aggregate reservation along three signaling entities by bypassing single reservation refreshes at GIST level*

The way how signaling messages can be exchanged directly between two signaling entities and therefore bypass intermediate signaling entities was already considered by the GIST specification [RFC5971]. The specification proposes to make use of an individually defined RAO value or an individually defined NSLP ID that is only meaningful to the aggregator and deaggregator. However, similar to RSVP's approach where the IP protocol number is changed to RSVP_E2E_IGNORE, the number of RAOs and NSLP IDs is limited to 16 bit only, allowing for 65 536 different pairs of aggregators and deaggregators. This is clearly insufficient to be used in inter-domain scenarios where ASes themselves are already identified by a 32 bit number. In chapter 4 the *Explicit Signaling Target Message Routing Method*

(EST-MRM) was proposed to be used to address signaling messages directly toward a signaling entity. The EST-MRM does, however, not allow to detect route changes of single reservations contained in an aggregate reservation (cf. Section 6.4.5) since it was designed to carry only a single Session ID.

Therefore, a new message routing method must be introduced that serves the purpose of exchanging signaling messages directly between an aggregator and a deaggregator by still allowing to detect route changes of aggregated flows without installing state on intermediate signaling entities. Rather than identifying an aggregate by a fixed single value, such as an RAO, the *Aggregate Message Routing Method* (A-MRM)—as introduced in [BD07]—uses the unique identification of the aggregation flow, i.e., the path-coupled message routing information (PC-MRI) of the aggregate reservation for this purpose.

In order to directly exchange signaling messages for aggregated reservations between aggregator and deaggregator, the A-MRM's corresponding message routing information (A-MRI) contains two PC-MRIs: One, that identifies the aggregate reservation and one that identifies the single aggregated reservation request. This allows for the exchange of information about a reservation's state between aggregator and deaggregator but still prevents intermediate signaling entities from re-establishing state for these aggregated reservations.

In order to allow for this stateless operation, GIST's QUERY processing needs to be adjusted for the A-MRM. The modification aims at periodically sending refreshing GIST QUERY messages for each aggregated reservation. Signaling entities along the path should, however, only install signaling routing state if they serve as aggregator or deaggregator for this particular reservation.

Figure 6.14 illustrates the signaling operation between an aggregator and a deaggregator for sender- and receiver-initiated reservations when the A-MRM is used. The initial GIST QUERY message is still intercepted by all intermediate signaling entities, but instead of establishing signaling routing state, each signaling entity must verify whether it serves as receiver of the aggregate reservation by inspecting the A-MRI entries. If this is not the case, no signaling routing state is established and the GIST QUERY message is forwarded further along the path. This stateless interception builds an important requirement for the detection of route changes (cf. Section 6.4.5). Once the GIST QUERY message reached the designated destination, the corresponding GIST RESPONSE and GIST CONFIRM messages can be exchanged directly between the aggregator and deaggregator without being intercepted by any intermediate signaling entity, upon which QoS NSLP messages can also be exchanged directly between the aggregator and the deaggregator.

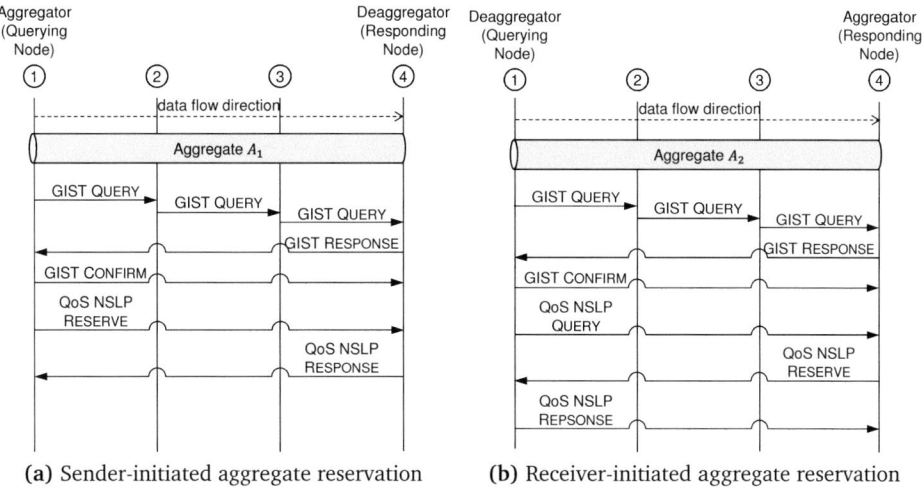

(a) Sender-initiated aggregate reservation   (b) Receiver-initiated aggregate reservation

Figure 6.14: *Signaling operation for aggregate reservations in case the A-MRM is used*

6.4.4 Establishing Aggregate Reservations

Whenever a new aggregatable reservation request reaches an aggregator, the aggregator must decide whether this single reservation is inserted into an existing aggregate reservation or whether a new aggregate must be created. Figure 6.15 illustrates a scenario where aggregate A_1 was established by signaling entity ② toward signaling entity ④ in order to aggregate reservations R_1 and R_2. Once a new reservation request R_3 reaches signaling entity ②, it must decide whether this reservation can be integrated into the existing aggregate A_1 or if a new aggregate must be established. Based on the assumption, that reservations R_1, R_2, and R_3 are consistently mapped to the same local service classes along their paths, four possible scenarios must be examined.

The new reservation request R_3 can reach signaling entity ② from a new signaling entity ⑧ and leave the common path segment at signaling entity ④ as illustrated in Figure 6.16. Based on the information contained in R_3's ROUTE RECORD object, signaling entity ② can determine that the reservation request does not share another common predecessor with the reservations contained in aggregate A_1 and that it also does not share a common successor with the reservations contained in aggregate A_1. Therefore, signaling entity ② can integrate reservation R_3 into the

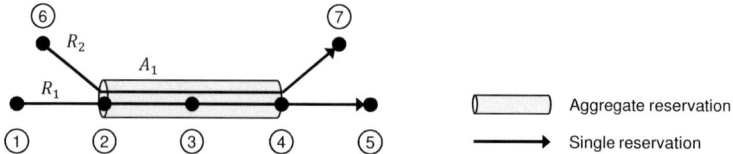

Figure 6.15: *Initial situation for an aggregate reservation between signaling entity ②
and signaling entity ④ for two reservations R_1 and R_2*

existing aggregate A_1 under the precondition that the aggregate's capacity already
fulfills the resource demands or can be increased along the path.

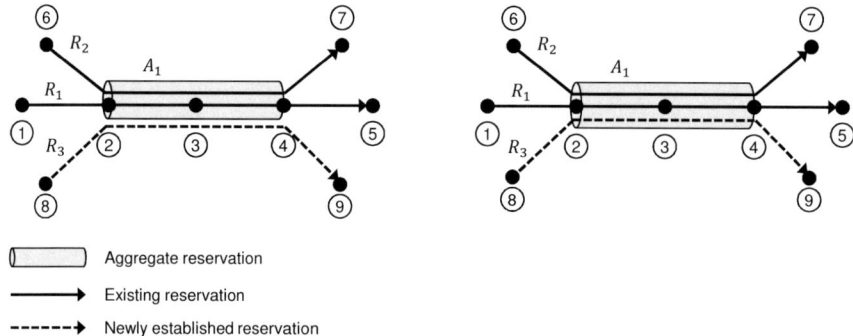

Figure 6.16: *Scenario 1—integration of a new reservation R_3 into an existing aggregate A_1*

Figure 6.17 illustrates another scenario where the new reservation request R_3
still reaches signaling entity ② from signaling entity ⑧. However, in this case R_3
shares a common data path segment up to signaling entity ⑤. Now the reservations
R_1 and R_3 could be aggregated into a longer aggregate between signaling entities ②
and ⑤. This makes sense, since a longer aggregate saves more state than a shorter
one. Therefore, this new aggregate A_2 would have to be integrated into the already
existing aggregate A_1, building a hierarchy of aggregates. According to option 2 of
Figure 6.4 this is a conflict-free combination for aggregate reservations. The final
solution is illustrated on the right hand side of Figure 6.17.

A further scenario is illustrated in Figure 6.18 where the newly arriving reservation request R_3 originates from signaling entity ① and is directed toward signaling

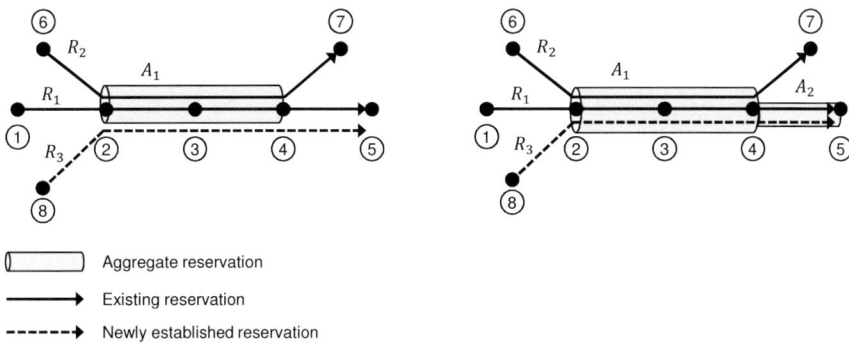

Aggregate reservation

Existing reservation

Newly established reservation

Figure 6.17: *Scenario 2—establishment of a new aggregation A_2 that is integrated into the existing aggregate A_1.*

entity ⑤. Hence R_3 shares the entire data path segment with reservation R_1. Signaling entity ②—which serves as aggregator of aggregate A_1—could now establish a new aggregate that covers the reservations R_1 and R_3 between signaling entities ② and ⑤. This would, however, prevent signaling entity ① from building an even more efficient aggregate A_2 between signaling entities ① and ⑤ that is integrated into aggregate A_1 as illustrated on the right hand side of Figure 6.18.

In order to allow for the more efficient solution, signaling entity ② must verify whether the reservations R_1 and R_3 share a common predecessor.[6] In case there is such a signaling entity that also signaled to serve as aggregator, signaling entity ② should not establish a new aggregate reservation. In case signaling entity ① actually establishes aggregate A_2, state for the reservations R_1 and R_3 would be removed from signaling entity ② and be replaced by aggregate reservation A_2 (see Section 6.4.7).

A fourth scenario is illustrated in Figure 6.19. In this case the reservation request R_3 originates again from signaling entity ① but leaves the common data path segment at signaling entity ④. Therefore, signaling entity ② realizes that a more efficient aggregate A_2 can be established by its predecessor ① which eventually results in the situation illustrated on the right hand side of Figure 6.19.

6.4.4.1 Signaling Operation for the Establishment of Aggregate Reservations

This section examines the signaling operation which is necessary in order to establish aggregate reservations. Once the number k of aggregatable reservations is reached, an aggregator can initiate an aggregate reservation request. An aggregate

---

[6]This can be accomplished by means of the information contained in the ROUTE RECORD objects

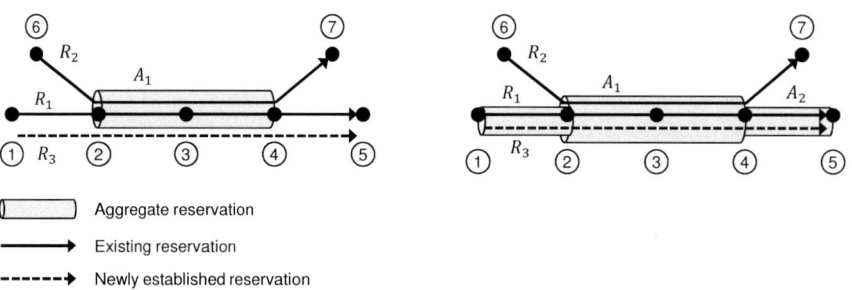

Figure 6.18: *Scenario 3—establishment of a more efficient aggregate A_3 between signaling entities ① and ⑤*

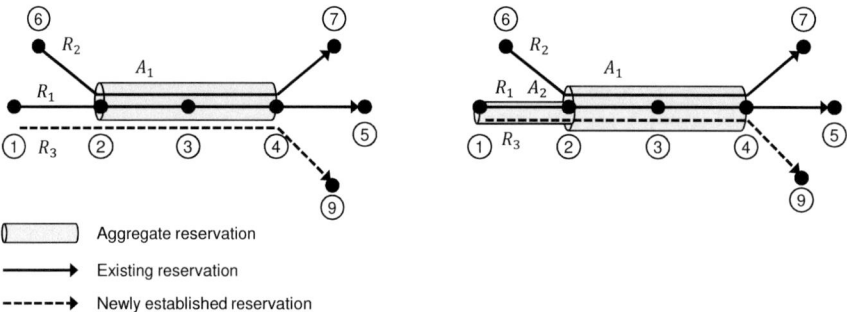

Figure 6.19: *Scenario 4—establishment of aggregate A_2 that is "tunneled" through aggregate A_1*

reservation aims at establishing reservation state along the entire path between an aggregator and a corresponding deaggregator and thereby replacing state for the single reservations contained in the aggregate on each of the aggregate's intermediate signaling entities. In order to allow all intermediate signaling entities to actively participate in the aggregate reservation, the corresponding aggregate reservation request should conceptually operate like a normal reservation request. In terms of NSIS signaling, an aggregate reservation request should be sent via the PC-MRM in order to allow all intermediate signaling entities along the anticipated aggregate's path to participate in the signaling session. Note, that if this reservation request was sent via the newly introduced A-MRM instead, none of the intermediate signaling entities would participate in this signaling session and hence, none of them would install state for this aggregate reservation.

The aggregate reservation request must be distinguishable from a reservation request that is used for a normal single reservation. Furthermore, since its purpose is to establish an aggregate reservation that replaces a number of single reservations, it should contain a list of reservations that should be replaced by this aggregate. Regarding the QoS NSLP signaling protocol, a reservation request is issued by means of a RESERVE message which is sent along the corresponding data flow's path toward a reservation responder. A newly introduced *Establish-flag* (E-flag) identifies a request for an aggregate reservation. In order to carry a list of reservations that should be aggregated, a newly introduced FLOW LIST object can be used. Within this object, each single reservation is uniquely identified by its Session ID *and* its MRI.

Furthermore, an aggregate reservation request refers to a reservation to which the sum of resources for all aggregated single reservations is assigned. The QoS NSLP protocol uses the QSPEC object in order to encapsulate the information about the required resources of a reservation request. An aggregate reservation should therefore contain a QSPEC object where the amount of requested resources corresponds to the sum of requested resources by all single reservations. It is, however, out of scope of this dissertation to determine how an aggregate's QSPEC is actually built. Instead, the aggregation mechanisn provided in this dissertation focuses only on the accumulation of the resource "bandwidth".

In order to allow newly established aggregate reservations to be integrated into already existing aggregates, the aggregate reservation request should contain a ROUTE RECORD object and a REQUEST IDENTIFICATION INFORMATION (RII) object. While the former is used to record the route and service class mapping of the reservation request, the latter instructs the deaggregator to reply to the RESERVE message with a corresponding RESPONSE, which is otherwise optional. The RESPONSE also carries the completed ROUTE RECORD object in order to finally allow aggregators on the path to build a flow aggregation tree and potentially insert this new aggregate into existing aggregates.

Figure 6.20 illustrates how a signaling entity establishes an aggregate reservation for sender-initiated reservations. In this case, aggregate A_1 was already established between signaling entities ③ and ⑤. The reservations R_1 and R_2 share a data path segment between signaling entities ② and ⑥ upon which signaling entity ② decides to establish aggregate reservation A_2.

The initial RESERVE message for the anticipated aggregate A_2 is sent by the aggregator ② toward the anticipated deaggregator ⑥. The RESERVE message contains a PC-MRI object which describes the signaling flow of the anticipated aggregate between signaling entity ② and signaling entity ⑥. Furthermore, the RESERVE has the E-flag set, contains a FLOW LIST object with all single reservations that are to be aggregated, a ROUTE RECORD object in order to record information about

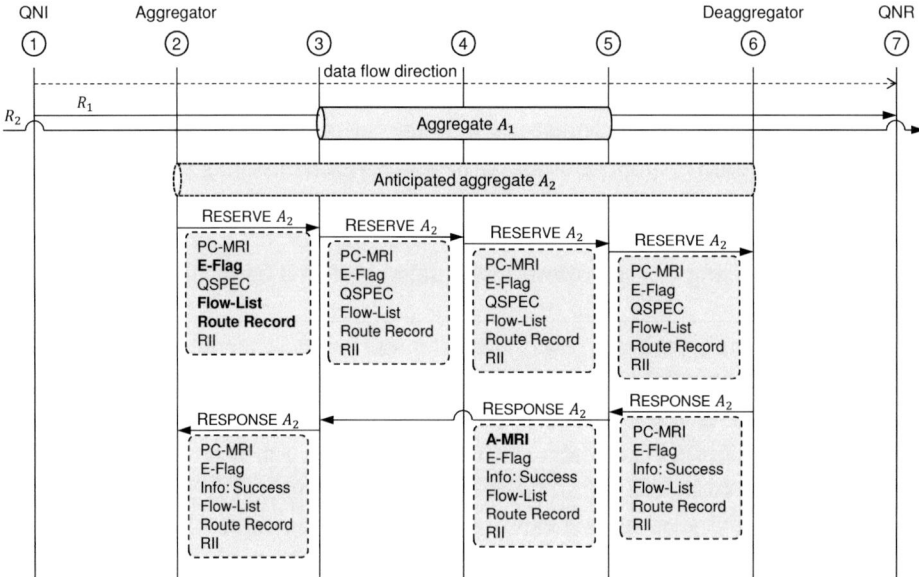

Figure 6.20: *Establishing a sender-initiated aggregate A_2 between signaling entities ② and ⑥. Newly introduced message flags and objects are emphasized.*

the reservation's path, a QSPEC object which describes the QoS characteristics of aggregate A_2's reservation request, and the RII object in order to request a RESPONSE from the deaggregator. The ROUTE RECORD object must be used even in case of establishing an aggregate reservation in order to allow for the detection and resolution of potential race conditions (cf. Section 6.4.6).

Since aggregation requests can fail due to aggregation conflicts or simply because the information contained in a signaling entity's local flow aggregation tree is outdated, it is a necessary requirement that each signaling entity that participated in the aggregation process verifies that all requirements for aggregate reservations are still satisfied. First, a signaling entity must ensure that all reservations contained in a potential aggregate follow the same data path. Therefore, upon receiving an aggregate RESERVE message a signaling entity verifies whether it has state established for all reservations contained in the FLOW LIST object.

According to the aggregation requirements, all reservation requests must be mapped to the same local service classes along the data path segment. This can be verified by each signaling entity in the same way as for the reservation's route. Note, that signaling entity ④, which is already part of aggregate A_1, has no more state installed for the single reservations and hence, cannot validate the mappings of the reservations' local service classes.

Finally, the third aggregation requirement must be fulfilled by the aggregation reservation request, i.e., it must be ensured that establishing aggregate A_2 does not cause conflicts with existing aggregates. How race conditions can be detected and resolved is discussed in Section 6.4.6. In order to avoid conflicts resulting from potentially overlapping reservations (cf. Figure 6.2 on page 195) deaggregator node ⑥ must simply verify that it has state installed for all reservations contained in the FLOW LIST object.

Whenever an aggregation reservation request fails, a corresponding RESPONSE message of type "Aggregation Failure" must be returned (not shown in Figure 6.20). In case of a successful aggregation reservation, the RESPONSE message carries the FLOW LIST object which enables signaling entities on the path to remove state for the herein contained reservations. Before a signaling entity forwards such a RESPONSE message it must check whether the reservations contained in the new aggregate are already mapped into an existing aggregate. This happens to signaling entity ⑤ in Figure 6.20 which does not forward the RESPONSE message toward signaling entity ④ but instead to signaling entity ③ by means of the newly introduced A-MRM (cf. Section 6.4.3), since the reservations R_1 and R_2 are already contained in aggregate A_1. The temporary state for aggregate A_2 on signaling entity ④ is not acknowledged by a RESPONSE message and hence, times out eventually due to soft state timers.

Since the new aggregate A_2 is conceptually embedded into the existing aggregate A_1, signaling entity ③ must check whether the surrounding aggregate A_1 already provides enough capacity or if A_1's capacity must be increased before the RESPONSE message is forwarded to signaling entity ②. Consequently, it may be necessary to increase an entire hierarchy of aggregates (cf. Section 6.4.8.1).

Establishing reservation aggregates for receiver-initiated reservations works basically as follows. First, there must be enough (receiver-initiated) reservations that share the same data path segment and are mapped to the same local service classes. The QUERY message of each single reservation request carries the RESERVE-INIT-Flag (R-Flag) in order to trigger a corresponding RESERVE. The subsequently sent RESERVE must then carry the ROUTE RECORD object and the RII object in order to trigger a RESPONSE message.

Figure 6.21 finally shows how an aggregate reservation is established in case receiver-initiated reservations are used. In order to trigger the establishment of an aggregate reservation, signaling entity ② sends a QUERY message in downstream direction toward its anticipated aggregation partner. Since this QUERY message belongs to an aggregate reservation, it has the E-Flag set and carries a FLOW LIST object which contains the list of single reservations that should be aggregated. Once the QUERY message reached the destination for this aggregate (signaling entity ⑥ in this example) the corresponding RESERVE and RESPONSE message exchange follows the one for sender-initiated reservations.

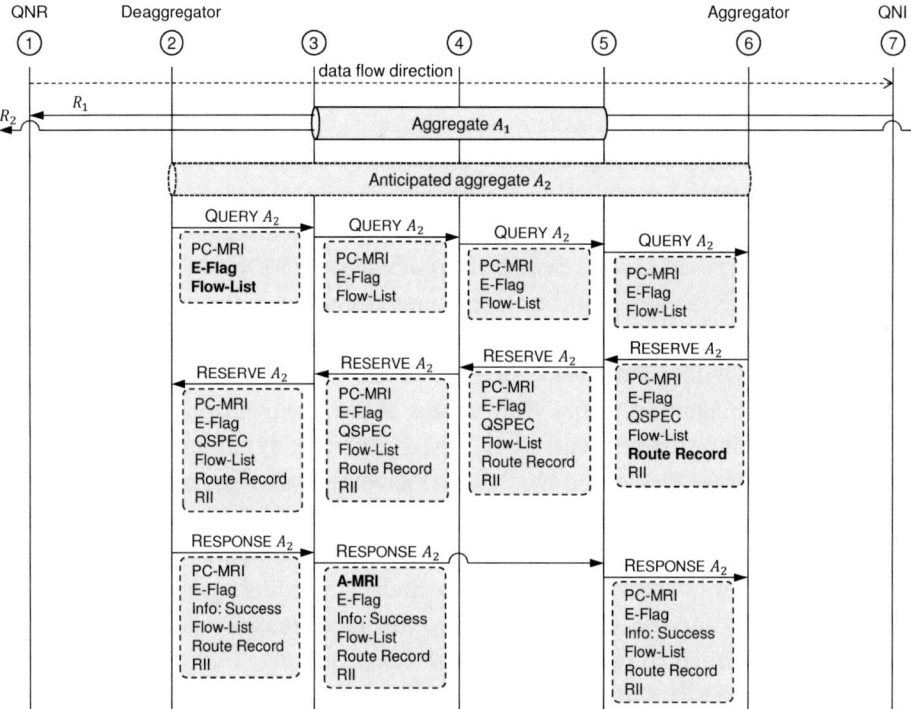

Figure 6.21: *Establishing a receiver-initiated aggregate A_2 between signaling entities ② and ⑥. Newly introduced message flags and objects are emphasized.*

The most significant difference compared to the sender-initiated case is how the aggregators and deaggregators are determined. In the sender-initiated case, the flow aggregation tree on signaling entity ② is built in order to determine the anticipated *deaggregator*, whereas in the receiver-initiated case the flow aggregation tree being built on signaling entity ② tries to determine the *aggregator* of the anticipated aggregate reservation. Hence, the aggregator is always the entity emitting the RESERVE message. Therefore, in order to serve as aggregator or deaggregator for receiver-initiated reservations and for sender-initiated reservations, two separate flow aggregation trees must be maintained on a corresponding signaling entity.

6.4.5 Route Change Detection of Aggregated Flows

According to the requirements outlined in Section 6.1 aggregates must be established along common data path segments. However, routes of aggregated data flows may change during an aggregate's lifetime, due to route changes in the network or due to mobile users (cf. Chapter 4). Once the route of an aggregated single reservation changes, this reservation must be removed from the aggregate and the aggregator needs to re-initiate the reservation request for this single reservation.

It is therefore essential to detect route changes of aggregated reservations without installing signaling routing state for the aggregated reservations on intermediate signaling entities and—in case a route change was detected—react accordingly. In order to detect route changes, an NSIS signaling entity uses periodic GIST probing for each of its single reservations. This can, however, not be used in case of aggregate reservations, since intermediate signaling entities have no signaling routing state installed for the aggregated reservations anymore.

As already outlined in Section 6.4.3, signaling for aggregated reservations is performed by means of the newly introduced A-MRM. The A-MRM uses a slightly adapted GIST three-way-handshake, where an aggregator or deaggregator sends a GIST QUERY message toward its aggregation partner for every aggregated reservation. Each intermediate signaling entity intercepts this GIST QUERY message and checks whether it is the designated receiver. If not, it simply forwards the message further along the path without installing signaling routing state.

Since the A-MRM was designed to be used for direct signaling message exchange between an aggregator and a deaggregator, it was not important whether the signaling messages where sent in downstream or in upstream direction of the corresponding data flow's path. However, since each reservation request is triggered by the data flow sender and therefore always refers to a data flow's path in downstream direction—no matter whether sender- or receiver-initiated reservations are used—it is also necessary to probe in downstream direction in order to detect route changes. For sender-initiated reservations the *aggregator* must act as GIST Querying Node (QN) and for receiver-initiated reservations the *deaggregator* must act as QN for route change detections (cf. Figure 6.14).

Each signaling entity that receives a signaling message being sent via the A-MRM must perform a stateless IP routing table lookup in order to determine whether it serves as receiver of this signaling message. It can do so by comparing the signaling message's destination address with all locally configured IP addresses. Signaling entities belonging to an aggregate simply forward the signaling message.

Since the A-MRI contains not only the aggregate's destination address but also the IP address of an aggregated reservation, a signaling entity belonging to an aggregate could then simply perform another stateless IP routing table lookup for this aggregated reservation. By comparing the "next hop" entries of these two lookups the signaling entity can determine whether the path of the aggregate reservation differs from the path of the single aggregated reservation.

Once a signaling entity noticed a diverging path, it must then inform the aggregator about the detected route change. Furthermore, the aggregator must take appropriate action upon such an event. In order to inform the aggregator about the route change, a newly introduced GIST ERROR message of type "Route Divergence" can be used.

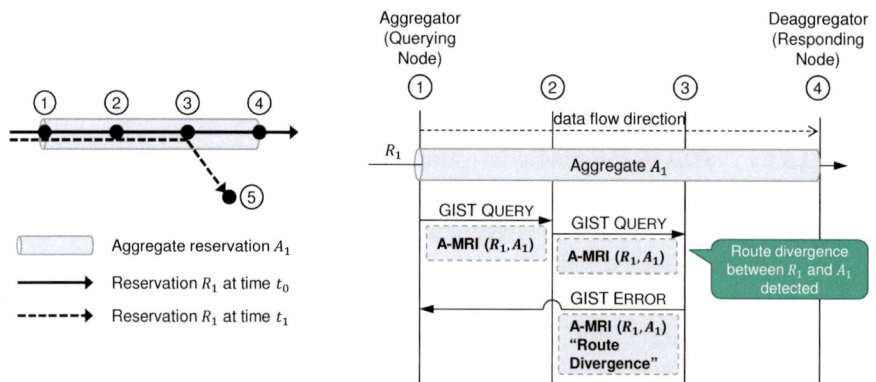

Figure 6.22: *GIST error notification once the route change was detected for an aggregated reservation*

Figure 6.22 illustrates how this error message can be used. In this scenario reservation R_1 was inserted into aggregate A_1 at time t_0. At time t_1 reservation R_1's path changes at signaling entity ③ and leaves the aggregate. Therefore, signaling entity ③ detects a route divergence between reservation R_1 and aggregate A_1 upon which it sends the GIST error message toward the source address contained in the A-MRI object, i.e., the (de-)aggregator which served as GIST QN for this probing message (signaling entity ① in Figure 6.22). Once the aggregator receives this GIST error message, its GIST instance must inform the QoS NSLP instance about this route change by means of a network notification event. The QoS NSLP instance must then remove the corresponding reservation from the aggregate's set and re-initiate the single reservation by means of a new RESERVE message (for sender-initiated reservation) or a new QoS NSLP QUERY message (for receiver-initiated reservations).

Due to its soft-state approach, NSIS requires signaling state to be periodically refreshed. For sender-initiated reservations these refreshing RESERVE messages are sent by the aggregator. For receiver-initiated reservations the refreshing QoS NSLP QUERY messages are sent by the deaggregator. Both, these RESERVE and QUERY messages are always sent in downstream direction and rely on the use of the A-MRM upon which routing state is also periodically probed for the aggregated reservations.

However, a special case is concerned with the establishment of sender-initiated aggregates, where the first signaling message being sent by means of the A-MRM is a QoS NSLP RESPONSE message that is sent in upstream direction (cf. Figure 6.20). In this case, there has no routing state been installed yet for the aggregate reservation in downstream direction. Even though the EST-MRM (cf. Chapter 4) allows to send a signaling message directly toward a destination, it was designed to carry one Session ID only. This is not sufficient for the aggregate reservation which carries information about the aggregate itself and the aggregated reservation. Therefore, the A-MRM had to be extended by means of an ADD-TO-AGGREGATE mode which is used to allow signaling messages for an aggregate to be sent in upstream direction. This mode can, however, not be used to detect route changes.

Note, that route changes of aggregated reservations can only be detected and processed by GIST-aware routers along the reservation's path. That is, in case a reservation's path segment changes along routers that do not actively participate in this signaling session, this route change cannot be detected by the proposed approach. This is, however, an uncritical constraint, since resources cannot be reserved on routers that do not actively participate in a signaling session, anyway.

6.4.6 Resolving Race Conditions

The aggregation concept proposed by this dissertation follows a decentralized approach. Therefore, establishing aggregate reservations is not controlled or synchronized by a central domain manager. Instead, each signaling entity decides on its own whether an aggregate should be established or not. This can eventually lead to race conditions between two aggregate reservation requests and end up in aggregation conflicts.

Figure 6.23 illustrates the message sequence diagram of a scenario where a race condition between two aggregate reservation requests occurs. In this case two single sender-initiated reservations R_1 and R_2 are already established and the aggregation threshold is assumed to be $k = 2$. While reservation R_1 is established between signaling entity ③ and ⑧, reservation R_2 is established between signaling entity ① and ⑥. Even though both reservations share a common data path segment between signaling entities ④ and ⑤, there has no aggregate been established yet, since this path segment is only one hop long.

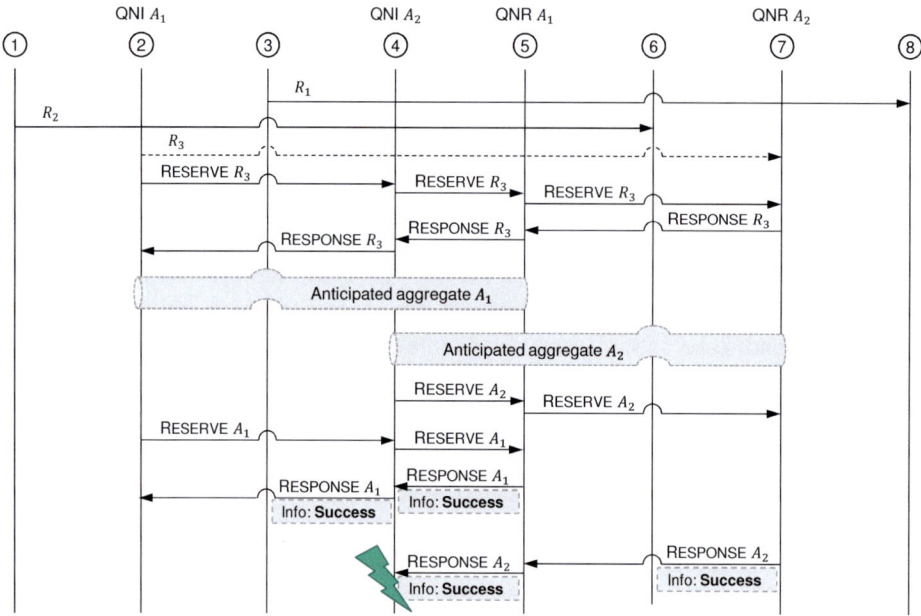

Figure 6.23: *Potentially occurring race condition between two aggregate reservations*

The situation changes once reservation R_3 is going to be established between signaling entities ② and ⑦. The ROUTE RECORD object contained in R_3's RESPONSE message allows potential aggregators on the path to update their internal flow aggregation trees in order to establish aggregate reservations. In this case reservation R_3 shares a common data path segment with reservation R_1 (between signaling entities ② and ⑤) upon which signaling entity ② establishes an aggregate reservation A_1 toward signaling entity ⑤. However, reservation R_3 also shares a common data path segment with reservation R_2 (between signaling entities ④ and ⑦) upon which signaling entity ④ decides to establish aggregate A_2 toward signaling entity ⑦.

Without loss of generality it is assumed that the reservation request for aggregate A_2 is initiated prior to the reservation request for aggregate A_1, since signaling entity ④ receives R_3's RESPONSE ahead of signaling entity ②. Once signaling entities ⑤ and ⑦ receive these aggregate reservation requests they verify whether the aggregation requirements are fulfilled. In this case signaling entity ⑤ has state installed for all single reservations since aggregate A_2 has not yet been established. Hence, signaling entity ⑤ sends the RESPONSE message A_1 back to signaling entity ② upon which aggregate A_1 gets established and state for the corresponding reservations is removed on the intermediate signaling entities. Once signaling entity ⑦ sends its RESPONSE message A_2 back to signaling entity ④, an aggregation conflict occurs on signaling entity ④ since this signaling entity just removed its state for the reservations R_1 to R_3.

In order to avoid such race conditions, each single reservation that is to be inserted into an aggregate must be marked locally by the corresponding signaling entity. A subsequent attempt to insert the same reservation into another aggregate can then be rejected. Figure 6.24 illustrates how the race condition from Figure 6.23 can be prevented. Signaling entity ④ again initiates the aggregate reservation request for aggregate A_2 first. However, in this case signaling entity ④ marks the reservations R_1 and R_3 locally, since they are to be inserted into aggregate A_2.

Once signaling entity ④ receives aggregate reservation request A_1, it recognizes that reservation R_3 has already been marked locally and therefore prevents RESERVE message A_1 from being forwarded further along the path. However, signaling entity ④ does not reject request A_1 by means of a negative RESPONSE message. This allows signaling entity ② to repeat the request after the expiration of its retransmission timer. In the meantime, aggregate A_2 can be successfully established. Once the retransmitted request for aggregate A_1 reaches signaling entity ④, the signaling entity notices that reservation R_3—which is part of the anticipated aggregate A_1—has already been aggregated within aggregate A_2 upon which the aggregate reservation request for A_1 is finally rejected by means of an "Aggregation-Failure" RESPONSE message. The reason not to reject A_1's request immediately stems from the fact that the establishment of the conflicting aggregate A_2 may still fail, since it has not yet been acknowledged and a later attempt to establish aggregate A_1 may then succeed.

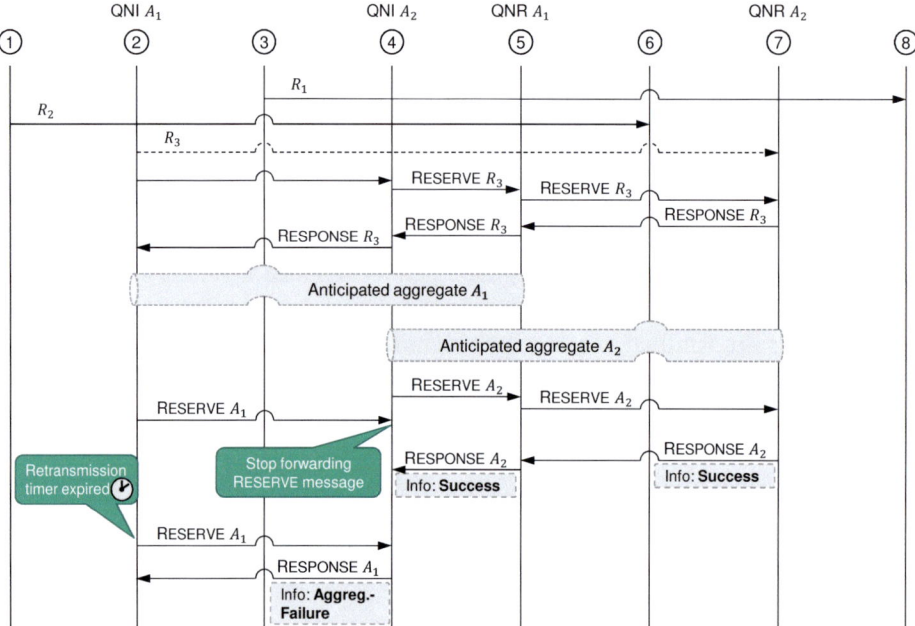

Figure 6.24: *Resolving race condition between two potential aggregate reservations*

Note, that the mechanism to detect and resolve race conditions does not differ for sender- to receiver-initiated reservations. This is due to the fact, that this mechanism is only effective for receiver-initiated reservations, after the QUERY message was sent. After that, both reservation types operate conceptually identical for aggregate reservations. Furthermore, note that this approach on resolving race conditions does not necessarily result in the best possible solution with respect to the choice of the aggregate which saves the maximum number of reservation state. However, this solution does not require global knowledge and is simple to realize.

6.4.7 Integrating and Removing Reservations from Aggregates

Once reservation aggregates have been established, new reservation requests should be integrated into existing aggregates. Figure 6.25 exemplifies such a scenario. In this case aggregates A_1 (between signaling entities ③ and ⑥) and A_2 (between signaling entities ② and ⑥) were already established. Signaling entity ① acts as QNI for its reservation request R_1. The corresponding RESERVE message is sent via the PC-MRM in downstream direction toward signaling entity ⑦ and carries a

ROUTE RECORD object in order to keep track of the intermediate signaling entities and service class mappings.

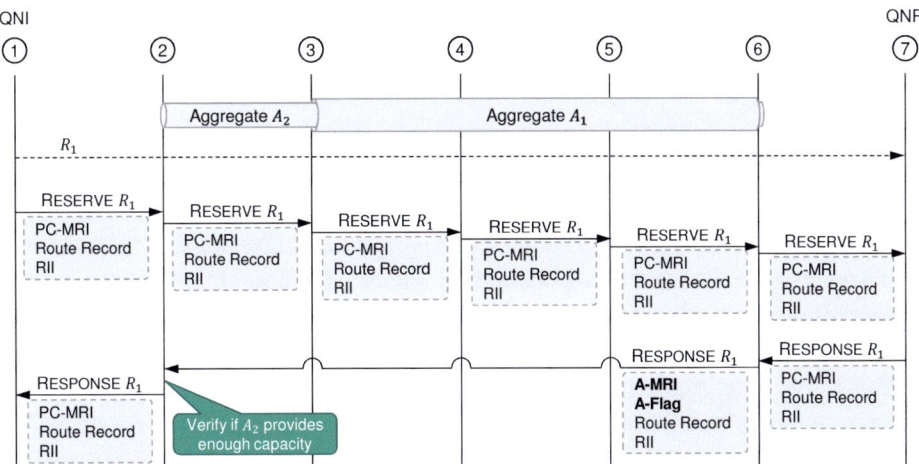

Figure 6.25: *Integrating a single sender-initiated reservation into an existing aggregate*

Signaling entity ⑦ acts as QNR of the reservation request R_1 and hence, replies with a RESPONSE message which carries the ROUTE RECORD object back toward signaling entity ①. Once the RESPONSE message hits the deaggregator of any given aggregate along the data path—cf. node ⑥ in Figure 6.25—the deaggregator checks whether the reservation can be integrated into an existing aggregate. It therefore verifies whether the data path segment and the corresponding service class mappings match an aggregate's path and service class mappings. Since it acts as deaggregator of an aggregate reservation, it must compare reservation R_1's path and service class mappings in reverse order with the path and service class mappings of each of its aggregates. In the example provided above, signaling entity ⑥ decides to integrate reservation R_1 into aggregate A_2 since aggregate A_2 spans more intermediate signaling entities than aggregate A_1.

In order to integrate reservation R_1 into aggregate A_2, signaling entity ⑥ must then send a signaling message directly toward signaling entity ② by means of the newly introduced A-MRM. Furthermore, a new ADD-TO-AGGREGATE flag (A-Flag) is inserted into the RESPONSE message in order to advise receiving signaling entity

② to add the corresponding reservation R_1 into aggregate A_2. Since the RESPONSE message is sent via the A-MRM, it is not intercepted by the intermediate signaling entities ③, ④, and ⑤, upon which the temporary established state for reservation R_1 times out eventually on these signaling entities.

Once the RESPONSE message reaches signaling entity ② it verifies whether aggregate A_2 provides enough capacity to integrate reservation R_1. If this is not the case, signaling entity ② does not forward the RESPONSE message until the capacity of aggregate A_2 (and potentially even recursively of its surrounding aggregates, cf. Section 6.4.8) was successfully increased.

In order to tear down a single reservation, the reservation's QNI initiates a tearing RESERVE message toward its QNR. Once an aggregator receives this tearing RESERVE message it must forward this information toward its deaggregator and it must potentially reduce the aggregate's capacity accordingly. In order to forward this tearing RESERVE and remove the corresponding reservation from the aggregate at the same time, the aggregator sends a tearing RESERVE directly toward its deaggregator by means of the A-MRM. The corresponding A-MRI contains the PC-MRI of the reservation that is to be torn down and allows the deaggregator to remove the reservation and forward a tearing RESERVE message toward the single reservation's QNR.

6.4.8 Controlling an Aggregate's Capacity

Whenever single reservations are torn down, these reservations must be removed from an aggregate's set of reservations. Furthermore, the aggregate's capacity should be adapted to reflect its current utilization in order to avoid resources from being reserved while actually not being used. An aggregate's utilization U is characterized by the ratio of currently used resources ("used capacity") versus the reserved amount of resources for the aggregate ("reserved capacity"):

$$U = \frac{\text{used capacity}}{\text{reserved capacity}} \tag{6.1}$$

An aggregate's capacity should initially be established with an additional amount of reserved resources to the sum of all aggregated reservation's resources. This factor $\alpha \geq 1$ is used to prevent an aggregate's capacity from being adapted with every new incoming reservation request. Hence, at the beginning of an aggregate's lifetime, an aggregate's utilization U_0 can be expressed by $U_0 = \frac{1}{\alpha}$.

Whenever an aggregate's utilization U changes, due to newly inserted or removed aggregated reservations (i.e., due to a changed "used capacity"), its "reserved capacity" could also be adapted in order to retain the same utilization factor. However, not every event stemming from changed aggregated reservations should lead to an instantaneous adaptation of the corresponding aggregate since this would impose a significant signaling and processing overhead.

Therefore, it is necessary to obtain an estimated value $\bar{U}$ for the aggregate's utilization, which behaves less sensitive to slight fluctuations and takes the utilization's history into account. This can be accomplished, for instance, by periodically calculating the utilization's exponential weighted moving average as follows:

$$\bar{U}_t = \beta * U + (1 - \beta) * \bar{U}_{t-1} \tag{6.2}$$

$\bar{U}_t$ is the estimated utilization for time t, U the current aggregate's utilization, $\bar{U}_{t-1}$ the most recently estimated utilization, and $0 \leq \beta \leq 1$ serves as a smoothing factor to control the impact of the most recently estimated utilization on the new value. A greater value for β allows to react more quickly on changes than a smaller value. Once an aggregate is established, $\bar{U}$ is periodically updated in Δt intervals.

Whenever $\bar{U}$ falls below a predefined threshold γ, the aggregate's capacity can be reduced and should be adapted to $\alpha \times$ [used capacity]. That is, initially γ should be chosen to be $\gamma < \frac{1}{\alpha}$. In case there is no more aggregated reservation present, the aggregate can then also be torn down. The variables α, β, γ, and Δt can be configurable system-specific parameters.

6.4.8.1 Signaling Procedure to Increase an Aggregate's Capacity

Once a number of single reservations has been integrated into an existing aggregate, it is necessary to increase the aggregate's capacity eventually. According to Section 6.4.4 aggregates can also be nested into higher-level aggregates. In this case it may even be necessary to increase an entire hierarchy of aggregates recursively.

In order to increase an aggregate's capacity, the aggregator needs to signal an updated reservation request toward its deaggregator. This updated reservation request must be interpreted by all intermediate signaling entities belonging to the aggregate reservation, since each of the intermediate signaling entities actively participates in the corresponding aggregate's signaling session. In terms of NSIS signaling, the updated reservation request must therefore be sent by means of the PC-MRM and must carry an updated QSPEC object. Furthermore, the reservation request must carry an incremented *Reservation Sequence Number* (RSN) in order to inform its receivers that the reservation request changed and an RII object in order to request the deaggregator to reply with a subsequent RESPONSE message. The RESPONSE message finally informs the aggregator whether the aggregate's capacity could be increased or not.

As already outlined above, the aggregate may itself also be part of a (higher-level) aggregate, upon which it is necessary to increase the surrounding aggregate. In this case, the signaling operation works conceptually as follows. Once an aggregator of a surrounding aggregate receives an updated reservation request for an "inner" aggregate, it must not forward this request until the surrounding aggregate has been increased to the needed capacity, too. Therefore, the aggregator of the surrounding aggregate must perform two distinct operations. First, it must increase the capacity of the surrounding aggregate which can be accomplished identically to the procedure outlined above. Once the aggregator received a positive acknowledgment for the increase of the surrounding aggregate, it can forward the updated reservation request for the "inner" aggregate in a second step. It therefore signals this reservation request directly toward the deaggregator of the surrounding aggregate. In terms of NSIS signaling this can be accomplished by means of the newly introduced A-MRM.

Following this approach leads, however, to the situation that RESERVE messages belonging to lower level aggregates cannot be forwarded until higher level aggregates have been successfully increased. Since increasing an aggregate requires one entire round trip time, the RESERVE message belonging to the lowest level aggregate would have to wait for one round trip time per aggregation hierarchy, depending on the number of hierarchies that must be recursively increased.

In order to parallelize and speed up this process so-called *waiting conditions* were already introduced by the DARIS architecture [Ble02]. The idea behind waiting conditions is to express a dependency between a pair of messages in order to suspend processing of one message until the other one has been received. This allows the aggregator to forward the RESERVE message for the "inner" aggregate at the same time as it initiates a new RESERVE message for the surrounding aggregate. In case the deaggregator receives the RESERVE message for the "inner" aggregate first, processing of this message is delayed until the corresponding RESERVE message for the surrounding aggregate arrived.

Since the QoS NSLP protocol already allows to express dependencies between two different signaling messages by means of the MSG-ID and BOUND-MSG-ID objects, the concept of waiting conditions can be realized by QoS NSLP as well.

Figure 6.26 shows a recursive increase of aggregate capacities by means of these waiting conditions.

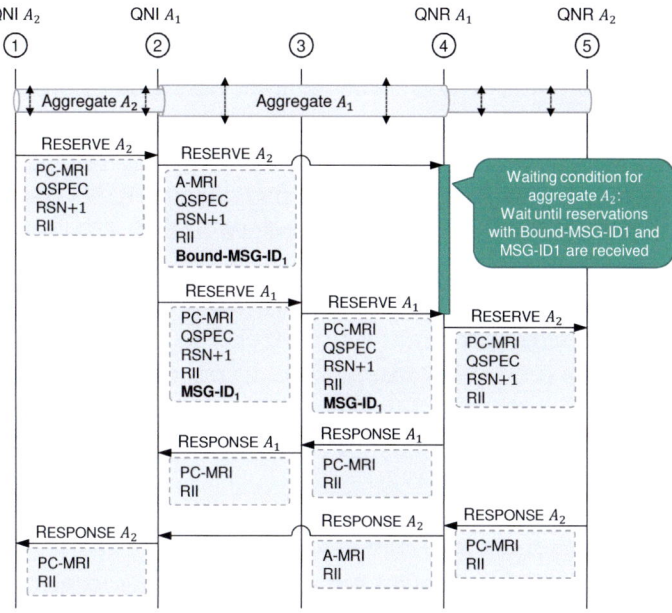

Figure 6.26: *Parallelized recursive increase of A_1's and A_2's capacity by means of waiting conditions*

In this example, aggregate A_2 is encapsulated into a surrounding aggregate A_1. In order to increase A_2's capacity, aggregator ① sends a RESERVE message toward its corresponding deaggregator ⑤. This RESERVE message is intercepted by signaling entity ②, since it serves as aggregator for aggregate A_1 and this surrounding aggregate A_1 must be increased, too. Therefore, signaling entity ② performs two signaling operations. It forwards the RESERVE message A_2 for the "inner" aggregate toward its deaggregator ④ by means of the A-MRM. In order to synchronize the signaling exchanges for A_1 and A_2, signaling entity ② adds a BOUND-MSG-ID object to A_1's RESERVE message which expresses a dependency toward a message with a corresponding MSG-ID. This allows signaling entity ② to send its RESERVE message A_1, which carries the corresponding MSG-ID, at the same time in order to increase the capacity of its aggregate A_1.

Once signaling entity ④ receives RESERVE message A_1, the waiting condition is met and it can forward RESERVE A_2 toward signaling entity ⑤. The subsequently sent RESPONSE messages finally confirm the increase of A_1's and A_2's capacity.

6.4.8.2 Signaling Procedure to Decrease an Aggregate's Capacity

In case the aggregate's capacity must be reduced, the signaling procedure follows conceptually the one used in order to increase an aggregate's capacity. That is, the aggregator sends a RESERVE message via the PC-MRM toward its deaggregator which carries an adapted QSPEC object, an incremented RSN object in order to signal that this is not a simple refreshing RESERVE, and an RII object, in order to request a corresponding RESPONSE message.

Note, that these operations must be performed recursively for higher-level aggregates and that each aggregator must verify whether its currently used aggregate's utilization requires a subsequent adaptation of its reserved resources.

6.5 Implementation

This section provides some information about the implementation of the aggregation concepts outlined in Section 6.4 and presents the format of the newly introduced NSIS protocol objects. All presented aggregation concepts were prototypically implemented for the NSIS-ka suite by Dettling [Det12]. Since the evaluation was performed by means of the OMNeT++ simulation framework [Var+12], this section provides also some details about the integration of the existing NSIS-ka implementation into the OMNeT++ simulator.

6.5.1 Integration of the NSIS-ka Implementation into OMNeT++

While the NSIS-ka framework already provides standards compliant implementations of GIST [RFC5971], QoS NSLP [RFC5974], and QSPEC [RFC5975], these implementations were primarily designed to be used on real hardware. An evaluation of the proposed aggregation concepts would, however, require the instantiation of a large number of end systems, which can hardly be accomplished and even managed by relying on hardware-based testbeds. In order to allow for an evaluation of network protocols in large-scale scenarios, simulation frameworks are usually employed. However, instead of creating a dedicated implementation of the NSIS protocols from scratch for an existing simulation framework, the existing

NSIS-ka implementation was ported to the OMNeT++ simulator. This provides the significant advantage of using the same code basis which ensures that the implementation used in the simulator has already been extensively tested and is not only a simplified protocol implementation which abstracts from any protocol specific details.

OMNeT++ [VH08] is a discrete event-based simulation framework which can be used to evaluate network protocols. While the GIST implementation and the Protlib library were already ported to OMNeT++ [Har09; BR10b], the necessary adaptations for an integration of the QoS NSLP protocol were realized by Dettling [Det12].

Both, the OMNeT++ simulator and the NSIS-ka implementation are based on C++ and are highly modularized. In order to preserve this logical separation, the NSIS-ka modules were modeled via OMNeT++'s cSimpleModules as illustrated in Figure 6.27. The QoS NSLP and GIST layer, as well as the Protlib library were logically encapsulated into distinct OMNeT++ CompoundModules.

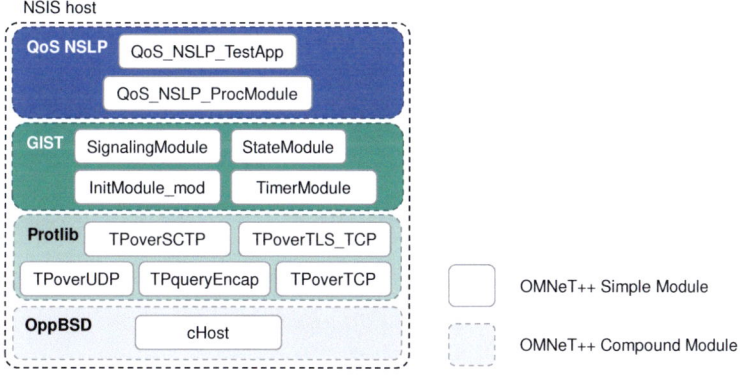

Figure 6.27: *OMNeT++ modules that are used to model a single NSIS system*

As already outlined above, the NSIS-ka implementation was originally designed to be used on real hardware. Therefore, it also uses Sockets to actually transmit and receive signaling messages over the network. However, since OMNeT++ does not provide a Socket interface, the OppBSD model [BD04; Ble+12b] had to be used instead. OppBSD provides a simulation model of the FreeBSD kernel's TCP/IP stack for the OMNeT++ simulator. This provides the additional advantage of using a "real-world" TCP/IP stack underneath the NSIS implementation instead of a simplified underlay.

6.5.2 Object Format of NSIS Protocol Extensions

In order to differentiate signaling messages being used for aggregate reservations from signaling messages being used for single reservations, some new QoS NSLP specific message flags were introduced in Section 6.4. The adapted QoS NSLP message and object format is illustrated in Figure 6.28. In order to allow for the establishment of aggregate reservations, a new ESTABLISH flag (E-flag) can be used by QUERY messages (for receiver-initiated aggregate reservations, cf. Figure 6.21) and by RESERVE messages (for sender-initiated aggregate reservations, cf. Figure 6.20). Furthermore, a RESPONSE message carrying an E-flag belongs to a corresponding aggregate reservation request. In order to add a single reservation to an existing aggregate, a RESPONSE message can have the ADD-TO-AGGREGATE flag (A-flag) set (cf. Figure 6.25).

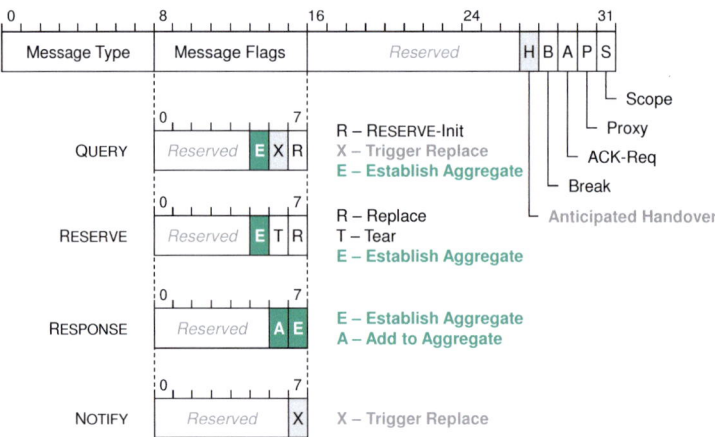

Figure 6.28: *Newly introduced message flags in QoS NSLP's common header in order to allow for resource reservation aggregation*

Figure 6.29 exemplifies the format of a ROUTE RECORD object. An object consists of one or more *route record entries*, each of which contains the information about one signaling entity along the data path.

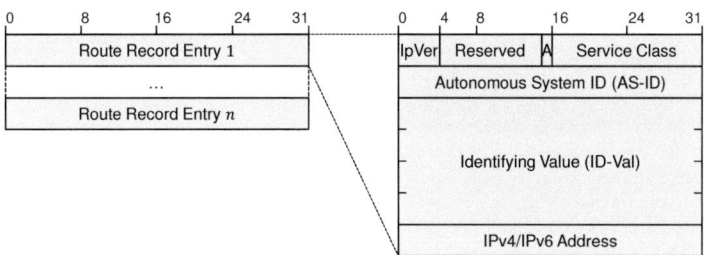

Figure 6.29: *Format of a* ROUTE RECORD *object and its enclosed route record entries*

The first entry in a route record entry contains the IP version of the IP address which should be used to address this signaling entity in case an aggregate reservation is to be established. This IP address is stored at the end of a route record entry. Since each signaling entity is free to decide whether it wants to actively participate in an aggregate signaling session, the A flag of a route record entry allows each signaling entity to express its willingness. The reservation's service class mapping is stored in a 16 bit Service Class field. In order to uniquely identify a signaling entity within a QoS NSLP signaling session, the route record entry contains a 32 bit wide Autonomous System ID which directly reflects the signaling entity's AS number and a 128 bit wide Identifying Value. This value must be unique within an AS, i.e., it must be chosen by the AS provider and may reflect one of the system's configured IPv6 addresses, for instance.

In order to inform participating signaling entities about the single reservations that are bundled into an aggregate reservation, the FLOW LIST object was introduced in Section 6.4.4.1. Its protocol object format is depicted in Figure 6.30. The FLOW LIST object contains a list of *flow list entries*. Since a single reservation cannot only be uniquely identified by its Session ID (cf. mobility scenarios as discussed in Chapter 4), each flow list entry contains the single reservation's Session ID and the flow's unique PC-MRI.

In Section 6.4.3 the Aggregate Message Routing Method (A-MRM) was introduced in order to allow for a direct signaling message exchange between aggregator and deaggregator, as well as to detect route changes of aggregated reservations. The information required for this A-MRM is encapsulated in a corresponding Aggregate Method Routing Information (A-MRI) object. The A-MRI's protocol object format is depicted in Figure 6.31 and follows GIST's standard MRI format (cf. [RFC5971] Section A.3.1).

The A-MRI contains the MRM's type (MRM-ID $= 126$) and an N flag which signals whether contained address information must be processed by a NAT gateway or not.

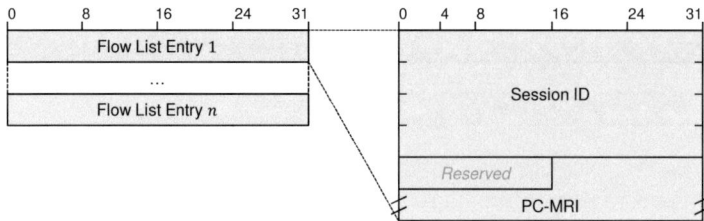

Figure 6.30: *Format of a* FLOW LIST *object and its enclosed flow list entries*

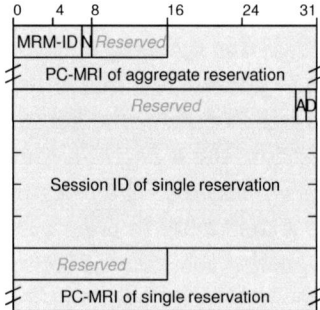

Figure 6.31: *Format of an A-MRI object*

After that, the method-specific addressing information follows with the aggregate's PC-MRI, a 32 bit wide flag field—where currently only the SEND DIRECT (D) flag and the ADD TO AGGREGATE (A) flags are defined—and a description of the single reservation via its Session ID and PC-MRI.

The D flag is used for two distinct purposes. First, it allows to exchange signaling messages directly between an aggregator and a deaggregator, i.e., intermediate signaling entities do not participate in the signaling message exchange. Second, it is used to detect route changes of aggregated single reservations. This requires both, the aggregator and the deaggregator, to establish GIST routing state for each single reservation contained in an aggregate between each other.

The A flag is used to add new sender-initiated reservations (or lower-level aggregates) into an existing (higher-level) aggregate. This requires the installation of a separate GIST routing state on both aggregate endpoints.

6.6 Evaluation

This section provides an evaluation of the proposed design for inter-domain aggregation of resource reservations. The aggregation concept aims at achieving scalability at the core of the Internet by significantly reducing the load of resource reservations in terms of signaling state from Internet core routers. Therefore, the evaluation focuses primarily on the number of states that a router must maintain for resource reservations if aggregation of resource reservations is used, compared to the case if no aggregation is used.

In order to make a statement about a protocol's behavior in an Internet-like scenario, a simulation model should model the Internet's structure as close to reality as possible. The *Realistic Simulation Environments for OMNeT++* (ReaSE) framework [GS08] provides a tool set which can be used to generate topologies for OMNeT++-based simulations. ReaSE takes the Internet's hierarchical structure into account by building AS-level topologies as well as topologies on router-level within each AS.

The connectivity between different ASes can be modeled as a graph consisting of ASes being represented by nodes and interconnections between two ASes being represented by edges. Following the research community's approach the node degree usually follows a power law distribution [Sig+03; Lab+10], where most nodes have a low node degree whereas few have a high node degree. Each AS is then classified into stub AS (for access providers) or transit AS (for transit providers), respectively.

Regarding the router-level topology being used inside an AS (cf. Figure 2.2 on page 11), ReaSE uses a heuristically optimal topology (HOT) based approach [Li+04]. HOT-based topologies do not only follow a power law distribution, but take also market demands, link costs, and hardware constraints into consideration.

The AS-level topology used to evaluate the proposed aggregation concepts was generated by ReaSE and is depicted in Figure 6.32. Four stub ASes sas0, sas2, sas3, and sas4 are connected to each other across one transit AS tas1. In this scenario, end systems are only present at stub ASes and not at the transit AS.

Each stub AS is equipped with one core router (e.g., sas0.core0) that builds the transit point toward the transit AS and one gateway router (e.g., sas0.gw2) that interconnects the different edge routers within one stub AS. End systems are only connected toward an edge router of their stub AS. Figure 6.33 exemplifies the topology generated for stub AS sas0 which consists of one core and one gateway router, four edge routers, and 20 end systems.[7]

---

[7]Appendix E shows the router-level topologies used at stub ASes sas2, sas3, and sas4

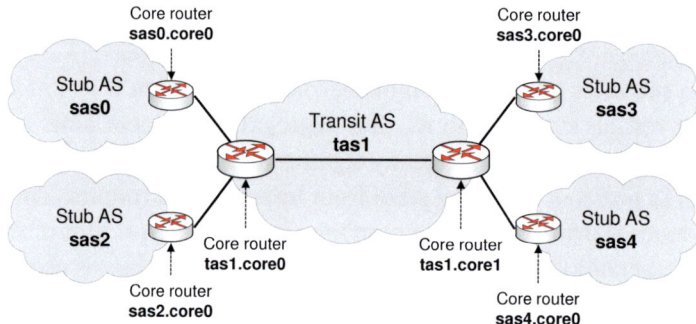

Figure 6.32: *Structure of the evaluation scenario with one transit AS and two stub ASes*

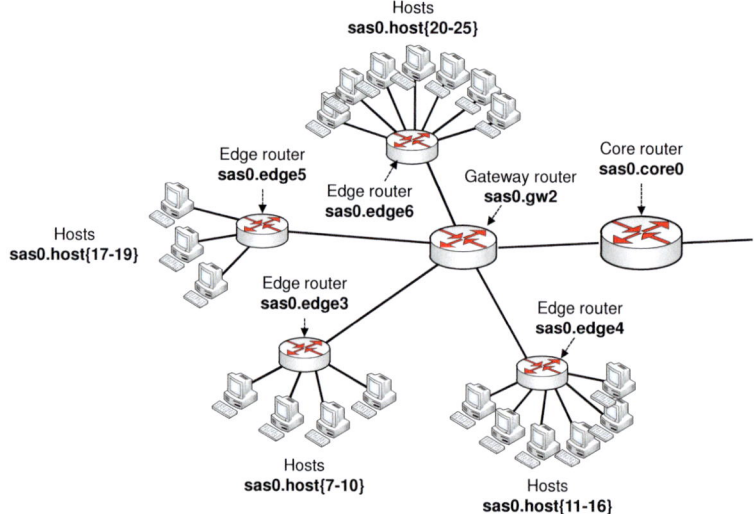

Figure 6.33: *Topology used within stub AS sas0 for evaluation scenario*

While every router and end system is an NSIS-aware signaling entity and actively participates in the resource reservation's signaling session, only the edge, gateway, and core routers were configured to be used as potential aggregators. Not choosing end systems as potential aggregators is due to the fact, that an end system may have limited resources (e.g., consider smartphones), is usually located only at a network's edge which doesn't serve as good aggregation point, and usually establishes only a limited number of simultaneous resource reservations.

The evaluation scenario therefore consists of six core routers, four gateway routers, 14 edge routers, and 69 end systems. Each end system within stub AS sas0 initiates resource reservations toward one of the remaining end systems of all stub ASes. A reservation's destination is determined based on a uniform distribution which is the worst case for reservation aggregations.

Based on findings by Floyd and Paxson [FP01] traffic patterns in the Internet show characteristics of self-similarity, i.e., they show the same patterns at different time-scales, e.g., within one second, one minute, or one hour. While the time between any two reservation requests which are initiated by an end system can be modeled by an exponential distribution $\text{Exp}(\lambda)$ with expectation $\frac{1}{\lambda}$, the duration of each reservation is commonly modeled by a random variable X with a Pareto distribution $\text{Par}(x_{\min}, j)$ (cf. [FP01]), given a minimum possible value $x_{\min}$ of X and a shape parameter j.

The probability density function of a pareto distribution is given by equation 6.3:

$$f(x) = \begin{cases} \dfrac{j}{x_{\min}} \left(\dfrac{x_{\min}}{x} \right)^{j+1} & x \geq x_{\min} \\ 0 & x < x_{\min} \end{cases} \tag{6.3}$$

By following this distribution, a reservation is established for at least $x_{\min}$ seconds. The Pareto distribution has an infinite variance for $j \leq 2$ and an expected value of

$$E[X] = x_{\min} \frac{j}{j-1} \tag{6.4}$$

for $j > 1$. Therefore, by choosing $1 < j \leq 2$, a reservation has an expected duration of $x_{\min} \frac{j}{j-1}$ seconds.

The goal is to create a set of reservations that follow the Pareto distribution. According to equation 6.4 the shape parameter j can be calculated by

$$j = \frac{E[X]}{E[X] - x_{\min}} \tag{6.5}$$

Hence, by choosing the parameters $E[X]$ for an expected reservation duration and $x_{\min}$ for the minimum reservation duration, the shape parameter j can then simply be calculated, and a set of reservations can be generated that follows the Pareto distribution.

In the simulation an end system of stub AS sas0 initiates approximately every five seconds ($E(Y) = 5$ s) a new reservation request. Each reservation is established for at least 15 seconds ($X \geq 15$ s) with an expected duration of one minute ($E(X) = 60$ s). The aggregation threshold is set to $k = 3$. The simulation establishes 439 sender-initiated reservations, each of which requesting a bandwidth of 1.0 Mbit/s. Note, that this experiment uses homogeneous reservation requests in order to focus on the potential of reducing state on signaling entities if homogeneous resource reservations were aggregated.

The experiment was performed in two different modes—in the first mode all signaling entities were configured to establish reservations without using aggregate reservations and in the second mode the core, gateway, and edge routers were configured to establish aggregates if possible. Table 6.2 contains the parameters and their values used in the simulations.

Notation	Value	Comments
k	3	aggregation threshold
α	1.5	factor for an additional amount of reserved resources
β	0.7	smoothing factor for the estimated utilization
γ	0.5	threshold for a lower-bound factor upon which an aggregate should be reduced
Δt	5 s	interval size upon which an aggregate's utilization is re-calculated
X	≥ 15 s	random variable for a reservation's duration ($X \geq x_{min} = 15$ s)
$E[X]$	60 s	expected duration of a single resource reservation
$E[Y]$	5 s	expected interval between two subsequent reservation requests initiated by a signaling entity

Table 6.2: *Parameters used for the evaluation of the aggregation concepts*

The aggregation concept basically aims at significantly reducing signaling load in terms of signaling state at core routers. Therefore, the evaluation focuses on the number of reservation state that each signaling entity maintains during the lifetime of the signaling sessions. The evaluations show the results for a single simulation run, since the number of actually used signaling states is only meaningful to be examined in the time-based context of a single run and not on an average over many runs.

Figure 6.34 illustrates the results obtained for end system sas0.host7 and its edge router sas0.edge3. Since the end systems were configured not to serve as aggregators of resource reservations, the number of reservation states on the end systems is the same, no matter whether aggregation is used or not. Therefore, the blue curve (reservation states when aggregation is used) covers the red curve (reservation states when no aggregation is used).

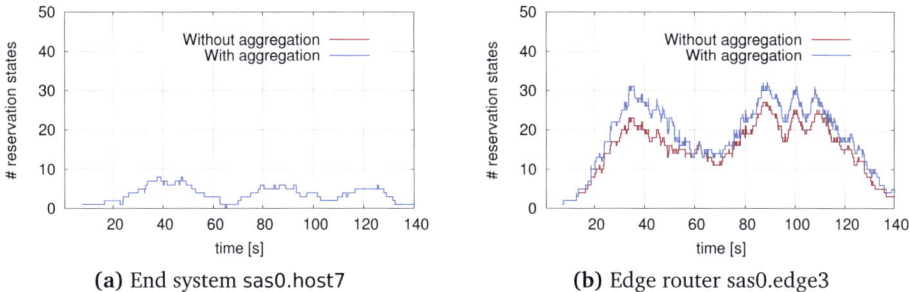

(a) End system sas0.host7   (b) Edge router sas0.edge3

Figure 6.34: *Number of reservation state hold by an end system and an edge router*

The edge routers build the lowest level of potential aggregators. Therefore, edge routers (as exemplified by edge router sas0.edge3) do still have to maintain reservation state for each single reservation belonging to one of their connected end systems but they also have to maintain one additional state per established aggregate. Hence, by aggregating resource reservations, edge routers have to maintain more reservation state compared to the case in which no aggregation is used. This additional overhead depends on the diversity of the single reservation requests regarding their destinations and service class mappings, and the threshold k of equal reservation requests upon which an aggregate can be established. The additional overhead whenever aggregation is used at an edge router can therefore not exceed $\frac{1}{k+1}$, i.e., 25% for $k = 3$—for three single reservations one additional aggregation state may become necessary.

The situation changes for routers that are located at higher levels of the network's topology. With every additional level in the topology's hierarchy, each of those routers benefits from aggregates being established by routers at a lower level. Nevertheless, such routers can also establish additional aggregates from which their higher level routers then benefit.

Figure 6.35a shows how much reservation state is maintained at gateway router sas0.gw2. The gateway router already benefits from the aggregate reservations initiated by its edge routers. On the other hand, it establishes aggregate reservations on its own which require one additional signaling state per aggregate. Furthermore, each router must temporarily establish state for each single reservation request before this request can be finally inserted into an aggregate. This temporary reservation state must be established on each intermediate signaling entity in order to record a reservation's path and its service class mappings along this path. Since this information is not known a priori, a single reservation cannot be inserted into an existing aggregate instantaneously. Each router decides autonomously on how long a temporary reservation is maintained before it is removed due to the absence of an acknowledging RESPONSE message. This timeout value should be chosen to be greater than a signaling message's expected round trip time. In this experiment temporary reservations were maintained for 2.0 s which should be sufficient enough.

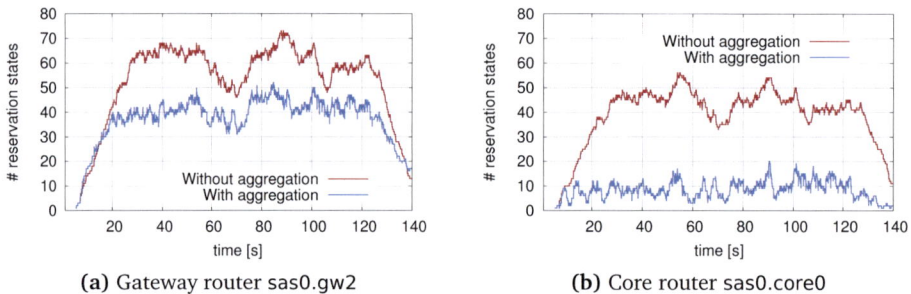

(a) Gateway router sas0.gw2   (b) Core router sas0.core0

Figure 6.35: *Number of reservation state hold by a gateway router and a core router*

Figure 6.35b shows the number of maintained reservation state at core router sas0.core0. The core router benefits significantly from the aggregation concept. In this experiment the core router never exceeds the number of 20 states that it must maintain simultaneously while it exceeds the number of 50 reservation states twice in case no aggregation is used.

It is interesting to note, that gateway router sas0.gw2 has to maintain more reservation state in case aggregation is used at the beginning of the signaling sessions (up to $t = 16.54$ s). This is due to the fact, that this gateway router also serves as aggregator for higher-level aggregates and these new aggregates are established as soon as the aggregation requirements are fulfilled. Once these new aggregates have been established, newly arriving reservation requests do only shortly cause a temporary reservation state to be established before they can be integrated into existing aggregates.

The difference in terms of reservation state between the gateway and the core router in case no aggregation is used (red curves) stems from the fact that some reservations initiated by the end systems at sas0 are directed toward end systems within the same stub AS sas0 and therefore do not even cross the core router at all. Therefore, gateway router sas0.gw2 must maintain more single reservation state than core router sas0.core0.

Note, that the reservation's destinations in this scenario were uniformly distributed amongst the set of all 69 end systems. A uniform distribution can, however, be considered the worst case scenario for the aggregation of resource reservations. The achieved results still demonstrate the effectiveness of the aggregation concept even for a uniformly distributed set of reservation destinations.

As already observed by Sofia, Guérin, and Veiga [SGV03] a high intensity of reservation requests leads to a high number of temporary reservation states. This effect could only be mitigated by inserting newly arriving reservation requests directly into existing aggregates without installing temporary reservation state. This would, however, require a "good guess" a priori about the actual path of a reservation and its service class mappings. While a reservation's path could be successfully approximated by the BGP routing information, the service class mappings could not. Hence, a speculative integration of resource reservations into aggregates would hardly be beneficial as long as there is no further information available for an aggregator a priori.

6.7 Summary and Conclusion

This chapter presented concepts for the aggregation of resource reservations along shared data path segments in order to achieve scalability in the control plane especially with respect to the heavily loaded core of the Internet. The proposed mechanisms were designed to be used by signaling protocols in a fully decentralized manner and inter-domain wide.

Highlights of the aggregation mechanisms proposed in this chapter are:

- a decentralized detection and resolution of aggregate conflicts

- a stateless route change detection of aggregated reservations

- the use of multi-hierarchical aggregates

- the consideration of a provider's individual service class mappings

Different from related proposals the aggregation concepts outlined in this chapter were designed to be independent of a particular QoS model and do not rely on complex algorithms. Evaluation results demonstrate the aggregation concept's huge potential to significantly reduce signaling routing state at the Internet's core.

## Chapter 7

Conclusion

Signaling has always been a key component in communication networks. It is used in telephone networks or the Internet in order to install and control states for network services. This allows for an on-demand management of network resources or the establishment and maintenance of multimedia sessions. Due to their capabilities to enable a wide variety of different and advanced network services, the design of signaling protocols constitutes a significant research field.

QoS signaling is used in the Internet in order to provide admission control and establish resource reservations for data flows. Designing signaling protocols for IP-based networks is a challenging task, since not only *mobile users* must be supported, but it must also be guaranteed that signaling can be performed in a *scalable* manner. Furthermore, *security* plays an important role, since services controlled by signaling protocols must be properly protected from unauthorized use. This imposes a number of additional challenges on the signaling protocol design.

7.1 Summary of Contributions

This dissertation aimed at designing advanced signaling concepts for IP-based networks. It identified three fundamental requirements which must be addressed by these signaling concepts: it should provide mechanisms that allow for secure signaling, provide support for mobile end systems, and offer very good scalability characteristics.

Since security represents a fundamental aspect in untrusted communication networks, this dissertation proposed a design for secure and authentic signaling.

The design is subject to a number of constraints which must be addressed in order to allow for authentic signaling in IP-based networks. First, signaling entities along a data path must still be able to interpret protected signaling messages; second, while pre-defined parts of a signaling message must be integrity-protected from end-to-end, remaining parts of a signaling message must still remain modifiable by intermediate signaling entities; third, in order to allow for proper authentication and authorization purposes, a signaling message's protection must refer to a user or signaling session; and fourth, in order to prevent authorization information from being used by an unauthorized entity, the authorization information must be tightly coupled with the corresponding signaling message.

Existing signaling protocols for IP-based networks either do not consider security at all or only partly address the constraints identified. The signaling concepts presented in this dissertation fulfill these constraints by providing *fine-grained* and *user-based* authentication mechanisms where authorization information can be coupled with authorized signaling messages.

Furthermore, security concepts for existing signaling protocols often propose the use of heavy-weight protection mechanisms, e.g., by relying on asymmetric cryptography and digital certificates. This imposes a considerable additional overhead and scales poorly with the number of signaling messages that must be processed by a signaling entity. Therefore, this dissertation presents a *light-weight* integrity protection of signaling messages by relying on an HMAC-based protection. The developed design uses cryptographic keys on the granularity of signaling users, rather than on single signaling sessions which results in good *scalability* characteristics. Finally, the security concepts outlined allow for *cryptographic agility*, such that cryptographic algorithms can be dynamically exchanged during a signaling session's lifetime.

Since Internet services are accessed by an increasing number of mobile devices nowadays, the second major requirement was concerned with providing QoS signaling support for mobile users. In order for established resource reservation to be adapted to a mobile user's new location, the QoS signaling protocol must always be aware of the mobile user's current location. If QoS signaling protocols are used in mobile environments they face a number of different challenges. A mobility management protocol tries to hide a device's mobility from its applications. This is problematic for a network signaling protocol, since signaling must be performed for the actual data flow and not for a logical data flow. It is a challenging task to create a linkage between the signaling protocol's control path and the data path under the constraint that an existing mobility management protocol's operation should remain unmodified. In order to resolve this challenge, this dissertation developed a node-local module which can be used to exchange mobility related information between the mobility management protocol instance and the signaling protocol instance.

However, in case a mobile user's stationary communication partner does not use a mobility management protocol but controls the resource reservation, it cannot be aware of the mobile user's changed location upon which a resource reservation would not be adapted, accordingly. Therefore, this dissertation developed QoS signaling concepts that allow a stationary signaling entity to be informed by a mobile user about the mobile user's current location in order to allow for an adaptation of an existing resource reservation.

In order to prevent resource reservations from being interrupted after a mobile node's movement until a reservation has been adapted to the mobile node's new location, this dissertation developed an *anticipated handover* concept for QoS signaling sessions. The proposed signaling mechanisms allow a mobile node to trigger the establishment of a new signaling flow toward an anticipated access router, even if the correspondent node controls the signaling session. Unlike most of the related research proposals, the design developed allows signaling flows belonging to the same QoS signaling session to be merged automatically at crossover nodes, which avoids an over-reservation along the shared path segment.

A major factor regarding the deployability of signaling protocols in large-scale IP-based networks is concerned with the signaling protocol's scalability characteristics. This dissertation developed methods that allow for scalable QoS signaling, either by the realization of QoS based group communication mechanisms, or through aggregation of resource reservations.

Group communication services play an important role whenever data is to be delivered toward an entire group of receivers. While different research proposals in the area of QoS signaling protocols have already considered integrated multicast support, they mostly rely solely on the provisioning of receiver-initiated reservations or follow a centralized approach. This dissertation is one of the first that allows for scalable sender-initiated reservations in IP multicast environments, since newly joining or leaving peers at the multicast tree's leaves do not affect the tree's root. Furthermore, signaling operates also independently of the underlying's multicast routing protocol.

In order to reduce the amount of reservation state that must be maintained at signaling entities this dissertations developed aggregation mechanisms for resource reservations. It systematically identified challenges in building aggregates for resource reservations and designed an aggregation concept for resource reservations which share a common data path segment. The aggregation concept allows signaling entities belonging to an aggregate reservation, to only maintain one aggregate reservation state instead of for a large number of single reservations. Furthermore, these signaling entities do not actively participate in signaling operations for these aggregated reservations.

While related research proposals already designed different concepts for the aggregation of resource reservations, this dissertation is one of the first that also explicitly takes the actual QoS mapping of each reservation into account. This builds a fundamental requirement in order to aggregate "similar" reservations.

Most of the related research proposals focused either on an intra-domain aggregation concept or were only designed to be used between border routers of different domains. The design outlined in this dissertation allows for an aggregation of resource reservations in an intra- and inter-domain wide fashion. Resource reservations can still be controlled by end systems and aggregates are established on demand between potential aggregators and deaggregators. Multi-hierarchical aggregates can be used to achieve a higher flexibility with respect to the establishment and maintenance of potential aggregates. Furthermore, route changes of aggregated reservations are automatically detected and resolved.

Unlike related work, the aggregation concept developed in this dissertation dynamically establishes, maintains, and tear downs aggregate reservations in a fully decentralized manner. That is, it does not rely on the provisioning of central domain managers. In order to allow for a decentralized operation, the establishment of aggregates must be coordinated between different aggregators. The developed design automatically detects and resolves potential aggregation conflicts between competing aggregators.

The applicability of the proposed aggregation concept was analyzed for an Internet-like topology. Simulative evaluations showed that reservation state can be drastically reduced at the Internet's core. Even under a highly increasing number of single reservation requests, the number of aggregate reservations at Internet core routers remains at a mostly constant low level. This demonstrates that the aggregation concept achieves its goal of narrowing down the amount of reservation states at signaling entities in high demand and constitutes a significant contribution to current research in this area.

All of the concepts outlined in this dissertation have been integrated into the open source NSIS-ka implementation, which provides a standard compliance implementation of the GIST and QoS NSLP protocols. Furthermore, all concepts have been evaluated within a hardware-based testbed or within the OMNeT++ simulator. The source code of all proposed concepts can be retrieved at `http://nsis-ka.org`.

7.2 Future Work

The signaling concepts developed in this dissertation could be extended to provide support for multipath and multihoming environments. For instance, by providing signaling capabilities for multipath TCP [Rai+12], resources could be reserved for more than a single data path at a time. The separation between signaling flows and signaling sessions may prove to be useful for such scenarios. However, maintaining signaling state for several "subflows" is a challenging task since a logical coherence must be provided between those flows and each subflow may be equipped with different capabilities, e.g., by using subflows for Wifi and 3G connections.

More recently, many research projects have been devoted to the design of a *future Internet* architecture. Some research in this area was also devoted to network virtualization, e.g., within the 4WARD project of the EU 7th Framework Programme or the G-Lab project. The use of NSIS-based signaling for the instantiation and maintenance of virtual links was already proposed by Bless et al. [BRW12]. It would be interesting to investigate how entire virtual networks could be managed by the signaling concepts outlined in this dissertation. For instance, the multicast signaling capabilities developed in this dissertation and the possibilities to transfer large signaling messages could allow virtual machines to be deployed within an existing network in order to create a customized virtual network on demand.

It would also be interesting to investigate the potential of using NSIS signaling for the instantiation and maintenance of the *Netlet-based Node Architecture* being proposed by Martin et al. [MVZ11]. Some researchers argue that the current Internet architecture is "ossified" and advocate a "clean-slate" approach which may even encompass a radical shift away from IP and a layered architecture. It would be interesting to examine the applicability of the signaling concepts developed in this dissertation within a network which is built that operates independently of IP.

QoS Signaling Evaluations with Mobile IPv6

The evaluations were performed on six testbed PCs, acting as Mobile Node (MN), Correspondent Node (CN), Home Agent (HA), Access Router 1 (AR1), Access Router 2 (AR2), and Access Router 3 (AR3). Each PC was equipped with an Intel Xeon X3430 quadcore CPU (2.40 GHz), 4 GB RAM, and four Intel 82580 Gigabit Ethernet network interfaces. All network interfaces were interconnected by a Cisco Catalyst Switch 6500 running CatOS, which allows to setup arbitrary network topologies by putting network interfaces into dedicated VLANs. The detailed configuration of the network topology is illustrated in Figure A.1.

A.1 IP Address Configuration and Routing

In order to allow for IPv6 based experiments in a local testbed, *Unique Local Addresses* (ULAs) were used from the randomly generated prefix `fdad:50b1:100::/48`. Since only the MN will receive dynamically configured addresses from router advertisements, all stationary nodes in the network must be equipped with IPv6 addresses and routing information manually. Listing A.1 shows the configuration file `/etc/network/interfaces` of AR1. Note, that all testbed PCs used interface `eth4` for external communication, such that `eth0` to `eth3` were used for experiments.

Listing A.1: *Configuration of AR1's `/etc/network/interfaces`*

```
# This file describes the network interfaces available on your system
# and how to activate them. For more information, see interfaces(5).
```

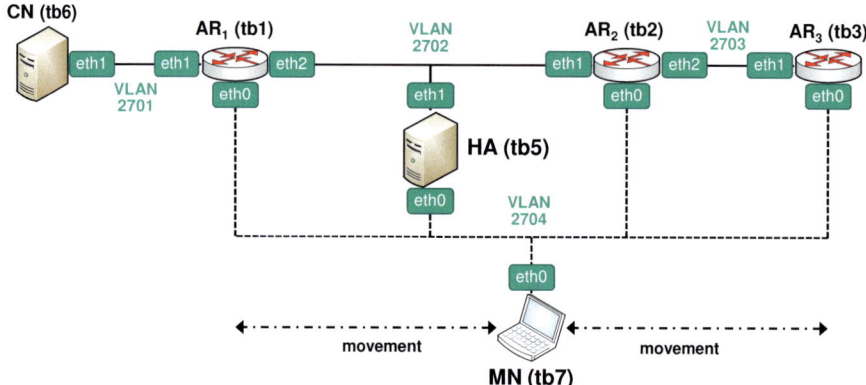

Based on user-defined network from Unique Local Address fdad:50b1:100:/48

System	Interface	Address
HA	eth0	fdad:50b1:100:**5001::1**
	eth1	fdad:50b1:100:**125::5**
CN	eth1	fdad:50b1:100:**16::6**
AR1	eth0	fdad:50b1:100:**1001::1**
	eth1	fdad:50b1:100:**16::1**
	eth2	fdad:50b1:100:**125::1**

System	Interface	Address
AR2	eth0	fdad:50b1:100:**2001::1**
	eth1	fdad:50b1:100:**125::2**
	eth2	fdad:50b1:100:**23::2**
AR3	eth0	fdad:50b1:100:**3001::1**
	eth1	fdad:50b1:100:**23::3**
MN	eth0	:5001::/64 :1001::/64 :2001::/64 :3001::/64

Figure A.1: *Detailed configuration of the network topology and each host's interfaces*

```
# The loopback network interface
auto lo
iface lo inet loopback

# The primary network interface
auto eth4
iface eth4 inet dhcp

# generated ULA fdad:50b1:100::/48

### NSIS Mobile IPv6 Experiements
### Node AR1
# eth0 into the mobile node's AR1Net
auto eth0
iface eth0 inet6 static
address fdad:50b1:100:1001::1
netmask 64

# eth1 into the CN's :16::/64 network
auto eth1
iface eth1 inet6 static
address fdad:50b1:100:16::1
netmask 64
```

```
# eth2 toward HA and AR2 :125::/64
auto eth2
iface eth2 inet6 static
address fdad:50b1:100:125::1
netmask 64
```

Furthermore, it was necessary to set some kernel parameters and set up some statically configured routes in the network (cf. Listing A.2).

Listing A.2: *Configuration of AR1's* `/etc/network/if-up.d/mobile-settings`

```
#!/bin/sh

echo 1 > /proc/sys/net/ipv6/conf/all/forwarding
echo 0 > /proc/sys/net/ipv6/conf/all/autoconf
echo 0 > /proc/sys/net/ipv6/conf/all/accept_ra
echo 0 > /proc/sys/net/ipv6/conf/all/accept_redirects

echo 1 > /proc/sys/net/ipv6/conf/eth0/forwarding
echo 0 > /proc/sys/net/ipv6/conf/eth0/autoconf
echo 0 > /proc/sys/net/ipv6/conf/eth0/accept_ra
echo 0 > /proc/sys/net/ipv6/conf/eth0/accept_redirects

echo 1 > /proc/sys/net/ipv6/conf/eth1/forwarding
echo 0 > /proc/sys/net/ipv6/conf/eth1/autoconf
echo 0 > /proc/sys/net/ipv6/conf/eth1/accept_ra
echo 0 > /proc/sys/net/ipv6/conf/eth1/accept_redirects

echo 1 > /proc/sys/net/ipv6/conf/eth2/forwarding
echo 0 > /proc/sys/net/ipv6/conf/eth2/autoconf
echo 0 > /proc/sys/net/ipv6/conf/eth2/accept_ra
echo 0 > /proc/sys/net/ipv6/conf/eth2/accept_redirects

ip -6 route add fdad:50b1:100:23::/64 via fdad:50b1:100:125::2
ip -6 route add fdad:50b1:100:2001::/64 via fdad:50b1:100:125::2
ip -6 route add fdad:50b1:100:3001::/64 via fdad:50b1:100:125::2
ip -6 route add fdad:50b1:100:5001::/64 via fdad:50b1:100:125::5
```

The configuration files for the other network nodes follow this structure but are omitted from this appendix due to space constraints.

A.2 Mobile IPv6 Capable Linux Kernel

In order to use Mobile IPv6 on the MN, the HA, and the CN, these hosts must run a Mobile IPv6 capable Linux kernel. This required the installation of a dedicated kernel which has the following kernel parameters enabled:

Listing A.3: *Linux kernel parameters for Mobile IPv6 capability*

```
CONFIG_XFRM_USER=y
CONFIG_XFRM_SUB_POLICY=y
```

```
CONFIG_XFRM_MIGRATE=y
CONFIG_XFRM_STATISTICS=y

CONFIG_NET_KEY=y
CONFIG_NET_KEY_MIGRATE=y

CONFIG_ARPD=y

CONFIG_INET_XFRM_MODE_TRANSPORT=y
CONFIG_INET_XFRM_MODE_TUNNEL=y
CONFIG_INET_XFRM_MODE_BEET=y

CONFIG_INET6_ESP=y

CONFIG_IPV6_MIP6=y

CONFIG_INET6_TUNNEL=y
CONFIG_INET6_XFRM_MODE_TRANSPORT=y
CONFIG_INET6_XFRM_MODE_TUNNEL=y
CONFIG_INET6_XFRM_MODE_BEET=y
CONFIG_INET6_XFRM_MODE_ROUTEOPTIMIZATION=y

CONFIG_IPV6_TUNNEL=y
CONFIG_IPV6_SUBTREES=y
```

Under Debian/Ubuntu the following commands may be used to compile and install a corresponding kernel

Listing A.4: *Building Linux kernel under Debian/Ubuntu*

```
$ sudo apt-get build-dep --no-install-recommends linux-image-$(uname -r)
$ sudo apt-get install fakeroot
$ apt-get source linux-image-$(uname -r)
$ cd linux-2.6.35/
$ cp debian.master/abi/2.6.35-28.49/amd64/generic
debian.master/abi/2.6.35-28.49/amd64/mip6
$ cp debian.master/abi/2.6.35-28.49/amd64/generic.modules
debian.master/abi/2.6.35-28.49/amd64/mip6.modules
$ cp debian.master/control.d/vars.generic debian.master/control.d/vars.mip6
$ sed -i "/getall amd64/s/$/ variante/" debian.master/etc/getabis
$ sed -i "/flavours/s/$/ variante/" debian.master/rules.d/amd64.mk
$ cp ~/config-2.6.35-mipv6 debian.master/config/amd64/config.flavour.mip6
$ vi debian.master/config/amd64/config.flavour.mip6
$ chmod +x debian/scripts/*
$ chmod +x debian/scripts/misc/*
$ fakeroot debian/rules clean
$ debian/rules updateconfigs
$ DEB_BUILD_OPTIONS=parallel=4 AUTOBUILD=1 NOEXTRAS=1 skipabi=true
skipmodule=true fakeroot debian/rules binary-mip6
$ cd ..
$ sudo dpkg -i linux-headers-2.6.35-28-mip6_2.6.35-28.50_amd64.deb
linux-image-2.6.35-28-mip6_2.6.35-28.50_amd64.deb
```

After that the GRUB boot manager can be updated by entering the following line

```
GRUB_DEFAULT="Ubuntu, with Linux 2.6.35-28-mip6"
```

into the /etc/default/grub file and updating GRUB via

```
$ sudo update-grub
```

A.3 Build USAGI mip6d

In order to interact with the NSIS-ka signaling instance, a patched version of USAGI's mip6d must be used.[1] Furthermore, the following software must be installed in order to build `mip6d`:

```
$ sudo apt-get install automake autoconf autotools-dev m4 indent bison
```

Once everything is prepared, the `mip6d` can be built via

```
$ tar xjfv mipv6-daemon.tbz
$ cd mipv6-daemon
$ aclocal; autoheader; automake --add-missing; autoconf
$ ./configure --enable-vt --enable-uds --disable-debug --prefix=/usr/local
$ make
$ sudo make install
```

A.4 MIP6d Configuration

The following configuration files were used on the MN, the CN, and the HA whenever route optimized mode had to be used:

Listing A.5: *Configuration file* `/etc/mip6d.conf` *on the MN*

```
NodeConfig MN;

## If set to > 0, will not detach from tty
DebugLevel 0;

## Use route optimization with CNs
DoRouteOptimizationMN enabled;

## Support route optimization with other MNs
DoRouteOptimizationCN enabled;

## Indicates if the Acknowledge bit should be set in Binding Updates
## sent to Corresponent Nodes.
UseCnBuAck enabled;

## Toggles if the Mobile Node should discard ICMPv6 Parameter Problem
## messages from its Home Agent.
MnDiscardHaParamProb enabled;

## Specifies an interface and options associated with it.
```

---

[1]This version can be retrieved from `https://svn.tm.kit.edu/trac/NSIS/attachment/wiki/MobilitySupport/mipv6-daemon.tbz`

```
Interface "eth0";

## Indicates how many times the MN should send Neighbor Unreachability
## Detection (NUD) probes to its old router after receiving a Router
## Advertisement (RA) from a new one. If the option is set to zero or
## the new router advertises a strictly higher default preference
## value than the old one (as defined in RFC 4191), the MN will move
## to the new router straight away.
MnRouterProbes 1;

## When a Mobile Node sends a Binding Update to the Home Agent, no
## Route Optimized or reverse tunneled traffic is sent until a Binding
## Acknowledgement is received. When enabled, this option allows the
## Mobile Node to assume that the binding was successful right after
## the BU has been sent, and does not wait for a positive
## acknowledgement before using RO or reverse tunneling.
OptimisticHandoff  disabled; # was enabled;

MnHomeLink "eth0" {
        ## Address is the IPv6 address of the Mobile Node's Home
        ## Agent. DHAAD is used if it is the unspecified address ::.
        HomeAgentAddress fdad:50b1:100:5001::1;
        HomeAddress fdad:50b1:100:5001:21b:21ff:fe8b:8390/64;
}

##
## IPsec configuration
##

UseMnHaIPsec disabled;
```

Listing A.6: *Configuration file /etc/mip6d.conf on the HA*

```
NodeConfig HA;

## If set to > 0, will not detach from tty
#DebugLevel 10;

## List of interfaces where we serve as Home Agent
Interface "eth0";

##
## IPsec configuration
##

## Indicates if the MN-HA MIPv6 signalling should be protected with
## IPsec.
UseMnHaIPsec disabled;

## Key Management Mobility Capability
KeyMngMobCapability disabled;
```

Listing A.7: *Configuration file /etc/mip6d.conf on the CN*

```
NodeConfig CN;

## If set to > 0, will not detach from tty
```

```
DebugLevel 0;

## Support route optimization with MNs
DoRouteOptimizationCN enabled;
```

The Mobile IPv6 daemon `mip6d` can then be started on the MN, the HA, and the CN via[2]

```
sudo mip6d -d 10 -c /etc/mip6d.conf
```

In case *tunnel mode* had to be used, the following parameters had to be set in the `/etc/mip6d.conf` files:

Listing A.8: *Configuration file /etc/mip6d.conf on the CN if tunnel mode should be used*

```
DoRouteOptimizationCN    disabled;
```

Listing A.9: *Configuration file /etc/mip6d.conf on the MN if tunnel mode should be used*

```
OptimisticHandoff        disabled;
DoRouteOptimizationMN    enabled; ### even for tunnel mode!
DoRouteOptimizationCN    enabled; ### even for tunnel mode!
```

A.5 Configuration of Router Advertisements

Whenever the MN moves to a new access router's network (or it is located in its home network), it must retrieve the necessary information in order to automatically configure its addresses and default router. Therefore, the `radvd` daemon must be configured on the HA, AR1, AR2, and AR3. Listing A.10 shows AR1's radvd.conf.

Listing A.10: *Configuration of AR1's router advertisement daemon*

```
interface eth0
{
        AdvSendAdvert on;

#
# Recommended smaller router advertisement interval
# when using Mobile IPv6
#
        MinRtrAdvInterval 0.03;
        MaxRtrAdvInterval 0.07;
        MinDelayBetweenRAs 0.03;
        AdvIntervalOpt on;

#
```

---

[2]Use of the debug-level statement `-d 10` is recommended since the `mip6d` crashed otherwise

```
# Prefix
#
        prefix fdad:50b1:100:1001::1/64
        {
                AdvOnLink on;
                AdvAutonomous on;
                AdvRouterAddr on;

                AdvValidLifetime 40;
                AdvPreferredLifetime 40;

        };
};
```

The advertised values for lifetime validity and preferred lifetime were decreased to 40 s for the mobility evaluations. On AR2 and AR3, only the prefix must be changed to prefix fdad:50b1:100:2001::1/64 and prefix fdad:50b1:100:3001::1/64 respectively.

The home agent's radvd.conf file needs some home agent specific configuration parameters as depicted in Listing A.11.

Listing A.11: *Configuration of AR1's router advertisement daemon*

```
interface eth0
{
        AdvSendAdvert on;

#
# Recommended smaller router advertisement interval
# when using Mobile IPv6
#
        MinRtrAdvInterval 0.03;
        MaxRtrAdvInterval 0.07;
        MinDelayBetweenRAs 0.03;
        AdvIntervalOpt on;

#
# Mobile IPv6 support
#
        AdvHomeAgentFlag on;
        AdvHomeAgentInfo on;
        HomeAgentLifetime 1800;
        HomeAgentPreference 10;

#
# Prefix
#
        prefix fdad:50b1:100:5001::1/64
        {
                AdvOnLink on;
                AdvAutonomous on;
                AdvRouterAddr on;
        };
};
```

On Debian/Ubuntu based distributions the `radvd` can be installed from the
package repositories and the configuration file is located under `/etc/radvd.conf`.
The `radvd` must then be started on the HA, AR1, AR2, and AR3 via

```
$ sudo radvd -C /etc/radvd.conf
```

A.6 Firewall Rules for Movement

In order to "simulate" a MN's movement between different access networks in this
testbed, firewall rules simply block traffic (and therefore router advertisements)
from all other access routers. A layer-2 MAC filter which is based on `ip6tables`
was used for this purpose.[3]

At first, the MN starts at the HA and firewall rules are loaded according to
Listing A.12.

Listing A.12: *Script start-mobility.sh*

```
#!/bin/bash

 ha="00:1b:21:8b:84:c4" # tb5:eth0
ar1="00:1b:21:8b:86:b4" # tb1:eth0
ar2="00:1b:21:8b:85:4c" # tb2:eth0
ar3="00:1b:21:8b:81:1c" # tb3:eth0

# Check for root privileges
if [[ $(/usr/bin/id -u) -ne 0 ]]
then
    echo "Must run this script as root or via sudo privileges"
    exit 1
fi

ip6tables -I INPUT 1 -m mac --mac-source $ha  -j ACCEPT
ip6tables -I INPUT 2 -m mac --mac-source $ar1 -j DROP
ip6tables -I INPUT 3 -m mac --mac-source $ar2 -j DROP
ip6tables -I INPUT 4 -m mac --mac-source $ar3 -j DROP
```

In order to move to a specific access router's network, a separate script was used
which replaces (`-R`) the corresponding firewall rules. E.g., for AR2's network, the
script looks as follows:

Listing A.13: *Script move-to-ar2.sh*

```
#!/bin/bash
```

---

[3]This requires knowledge about the particular MAC addresses used on each interface. Re-
configuring VLANs dynamically on the Cisco switch didn't work sufficiently fast. Using append
(`-A`) and delete (`-D`) iptables rules also turned out to result in some small delays where router
advertisements from "wrong" access routers passed through.

```
 ha="00:1b:21:8b:84:c4" # tb5:eth0
ar1="00:1b:21:8b:86:b4" # tb1:eth0
ar2="00:1b:21:8b:85:4c" # tb2:eth0
ar3="00:1b:21:8b:81:1c" # tb3:eth0

# Check for root privileges
if [[ $(/usr/bin/id -u) -ne 0 ]]
then
    echo "Must run this script as root or via sudo privileges"
    exit 1
fi

ip6tables -R INPUT 1 -m mac --mac-source $ha  -j DROP
ip6tables -R INPUT 2 -m mac --mac-source $ar1 -j DROP
ip6tables -R INPUT 3 -m mac --mac-source $ar2 -j ACCEPT
ip6tables -R INPUT 4 -m mac --mac-source $ar3 -j DROP
```

A.7 NSIS Experiments

A.7.1 Automatically Activate Route Optimization

Whenever the MN and the CN are configured to use route optimization (RO), it is recommended to execute a ping6 ICMP echo/reply periodically in the background on either the MN or the CN. For instance, executing ping6 on the CN toward the MN's home address would look like this

```
ping6 fdad:50b1:100:5001:21b:21ff:fe8b:8390
```

When executing `ping6` on the MN there may be small periods of time during which no mobility binding has yet been established. Instead of echo replies, this results in one of the two following outputs

```
ping: sendmsg: Invalid argument
ping: sendmsg: Operation not permitted
```

If route optimization for NSIS signaling between the MN and the CN should be used, the following patch to the MN's `protlib/src/addresslist.cpp` file must be applied until the issue is fixed in the trunk:

```
Index: src/addresslist.cpp
===================================================================
--- src/addresslist.cpp (Revision 6715)
+++ src/addresslist.cpp (Arbeitskopie)
@@ -664,8 +664,8 @@
 #ifdef IPV6_ADDR_PREFERENCES
        /* XXX: IPV6_PREFER_SRC_COA does not work */
        if (prefs != NULL && (*prefs & IPV6_PREFER_SRC_COA)) {
-               res = get_first(HomeAddr_P, canonical_dest.is_ipv4());
-               if (res != NULL) {
+//               res = get_first(HomeAddr_P, canonical_dest.is_ipv4());
+//               if (res != NULL) {
```

```
                        addrlist_t *alist;
                        alist = get_addrs(LocalAddr_P);
                        if (alist != NULL) {
@@ -680,7 +680,7 @@
                                }
                                delete alist;
                        }
-                }
+//                }
        }
 #endif
        if (canonical_dest.is_ipv4()) {
```

A.7.2 Script for Automated Movements

In order to automatically move from one network to another, a small test script can be used. Listing A.14 shows a simple script which should be executed on the MN with root privileges and which calls the aforementioned movement scripts (see above).

Listing A.14: *Test script for automated movement of the MN*

```
#!/bin/bash

waiting_period=15

# Check for root privileges
if [[ $(/usr/bin/id -u) -ne 0 ]]
then
    echo "Must run this script as root or via sudo privileges"
    exit 1
fi

if [ $# -lt 1 ]; then
        echo "Usage: $0 <measurements>"
        exit 1
fi

measurements="$1"

for ((i = 1; i <= $measurements; ++i)); do
        echo "Round " $i
        ./move-to-ar1.sh > /dev/null
        echo "    at AR1"
        sleep $waiting_period
        ./move-to-ar2.sh > /dev/null
        echo "    at AR2"
        sleep $waiting_period
        ./move-to-ar3.sh > /dev/null
        echo "    at AR3"
        sleep $waiting_period
done
```

```
echo "finishing at HA"
./move-to-ha.sh > /dev/null

exit
```

A.7.3 Building the NSIS-ka Software Suite

The NSIS-ka software can be retrieved via SVN and be built according to the build
instruction in the README file. For the access routers AR1, AR2, and AR3 the
NSIS-ka instance can be built as follows:

Listing A.15: *Retrieving and building the NSIS-ka software*

```
$ svn co https://svn.tm.kit.edu/nsis/dist/nsis-ka/trunk nsis-ka-trunk
$ cd nsis-ka-trunk
$ make -f Makefile.svn
$ ./configure
$ make -j 4
```

At the MN, the HA, and the CN the *Flow Information Service* must be enabled,
which is achieved by setting the following configure option:

Listing A.16: *Flow Information Service configure option for the NSIS-ka software*

```
$ ./configure --enable-flowinfo
```

For performance measurements the logging output produced by the NSIS-ka software should be disabled. This can be achieved by setting the following (additional)
configure option on all hosts:

```
$ ./configure --disable-logging
```

A.7.4 NSIS-ka Configuration

This section provides the relevant parts of the etc/nsis-ka.conf configuration
file for the mobility experiments. For all other parameters the default values should
be sufficient.

Listing A.17: *Important parameters with the etc/nsis-ka.conf file on the MN*

```
localaddr-v6 = "fdad:50b1:100:5001:21b:21ff:fe8b:8390"

# My Home Address
home-address = "fdad:50b1:100:5001:21b:21ff:fe8b:8390"

# Which interfaces will be mobile and see Care-Of Addresses?
coa-interfaces = "eth0"
```

Listing A.18: *Important parameters with the etc/nsis-ka.conf file on the HA*

```
localaddr-v6 = "fdad:50b1:100:5001::1 fdad:50b1:100:125::5"

# Mobility Support/MobileIP related stuff (all optional)
# Prefix of Home Network
home-netprefix =fdad:50b1:100:5001::/64

# Address of Home Agent
homeagent-address = fdad:50b1:100:5001::1

# Alternative Address of Home Agent
homeagent-address-alt = fdad:50b1:100:5001::2
```

Listing A.19: *Important parameters with the etc/nsis-ka.conf file on the CN*

```
localaddr-v6 = "fdad:50b1:100:16::6"
```

A.7.5 Establish a QoS NSLP Reservation

In order to start a QoS NSLP instance on each host, the start-qosnslp script located in the qos-nslp/src directory must be started with root privileges:[4]

```
$ cd ~/nsis-ka-trunk/qos-nslp/src
$ sudo ./start-qosnslp
```

Once all hosts in the network run an instance of the NSIS-ka software, a QoS NSLP reservation request can be issued either on the CN or on the MN via the client executable in the nsis-ka-trunk/qos-nslp/src directory. For a sender-initiated reservation from the MN toward the CN, the following command must be executed on the MN:

Listing A.20: *Sender-initiated reservation from the MN to the CN*

```
$ cd ~/nsis-ka-trunk/qos-nslp/src
$ sudo ./client fdad:50b1:100:5001:21b:21ff:fe8b:8390 fdad:50b1:100:16::6
```

For a receiver-initiated reservation that is triggered by the CN, the following command must be executed on the CN (note the parameter r at the very end which indicates that a receiver-initiated reservation should be established):

Listing A.21: *Receiver-initiated reservation from the CN to the MN*

```
$ cd ~/nsis-ka-trunk/qos-nslp/src
$ sudo ./client fdad:50b1:100:16::6 fdad:50b1:100:5001:21b:21ff:fe8b:8390 r
```

---

[4]The QoS NSLP instance can always be shut down via a SIGINT signal (i.e., Ctrl-C)

A.8 Detailed Evaluation Results for Mobile IPv6-based Experiments

This section provides the detailed measurement results from the evaluations for reservation setups in Mobile IPv6-based environments.

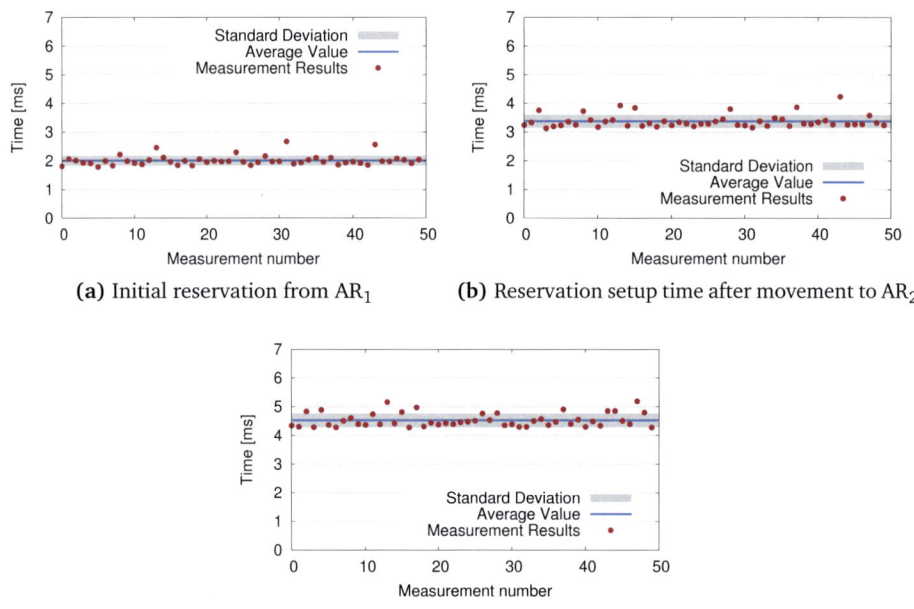

(a) Initial reservation from AR_1 (b) Reservation setup time after movement to AR_2

(c) Reservation setup time after movement to AR_3

Figure A.2: *Reservation setup time for scenario M1—MN is sender and signaling initiator—in route optimized mode*

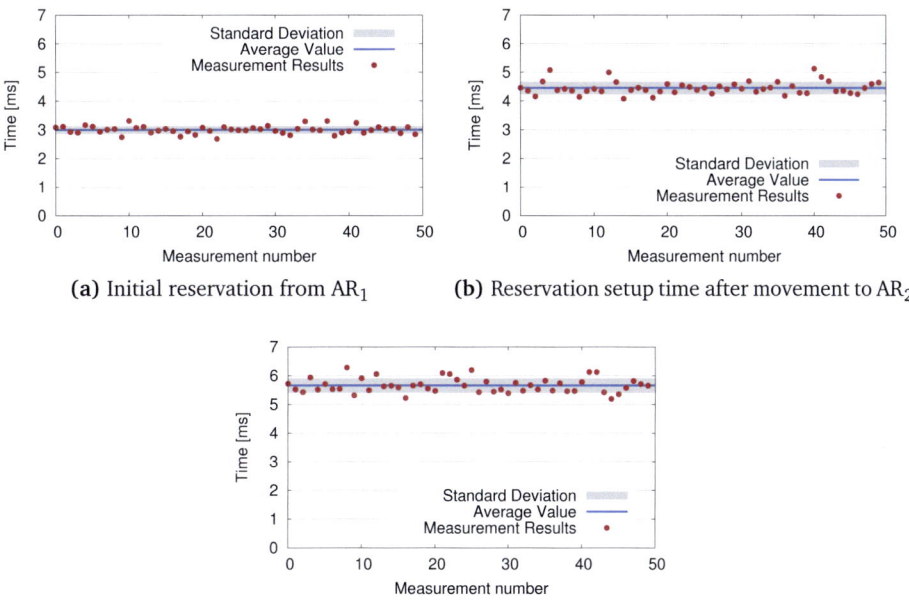

(a) Initial reservation from AR_1

(b) Reservation setup time after movement to AR_2

(c) Reservation setup time after movement to AR_3

Figure A.3: *Reservation setup time for scenario M2—MN is sender and signaling responder—in route optimized mode*

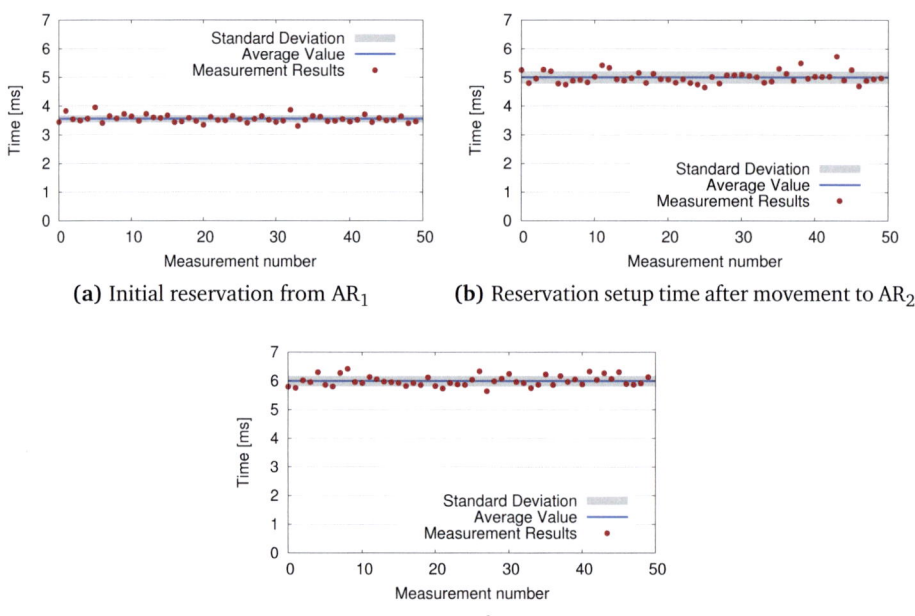

(a) Initial reservation from AR_1 (b) Reservation setup time after movement to AR_2

(c) Reservation setup time after movement to AR_3

Figure A.4: *Reservation setup time for scenario M3—MN is receiver and signaling initiator—in route optimized mode*

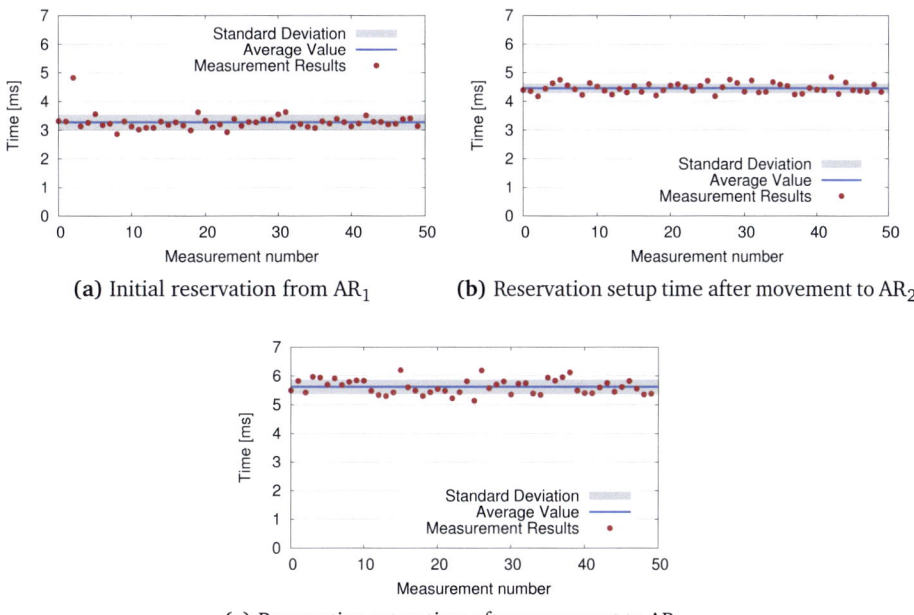

(a) Initial reservation from AR_1

(b) Reservation setup time after movement to AR_2

(c) Reservation setup time after movement to AR_3

Figure A.5: *Reservation setup time for scenario M4—MN is receiver and signaling responder—in route optimized mode*

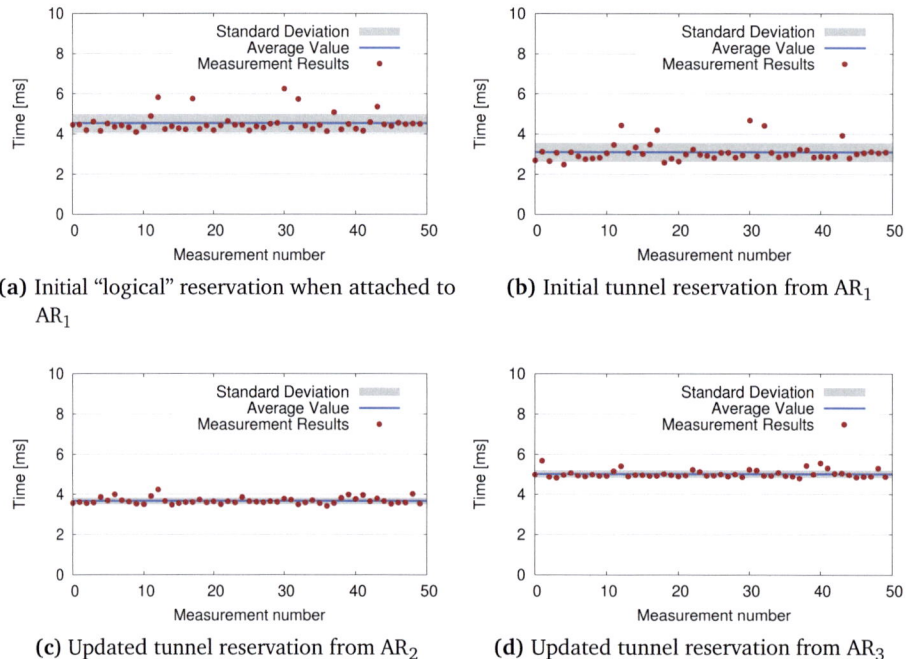

(a) Initial "logical" reservation when attached to AR$_1$

(b) Initial tunnel reservation from AR$_1$

(c) Updated tunnel reservation from AR$_2$

(d) Updated tunnel reservation from AR$_3$

Figure A.6: *Reservation setup time for scenario M1—MN is sender and signaling initiator—in tunnel mode*

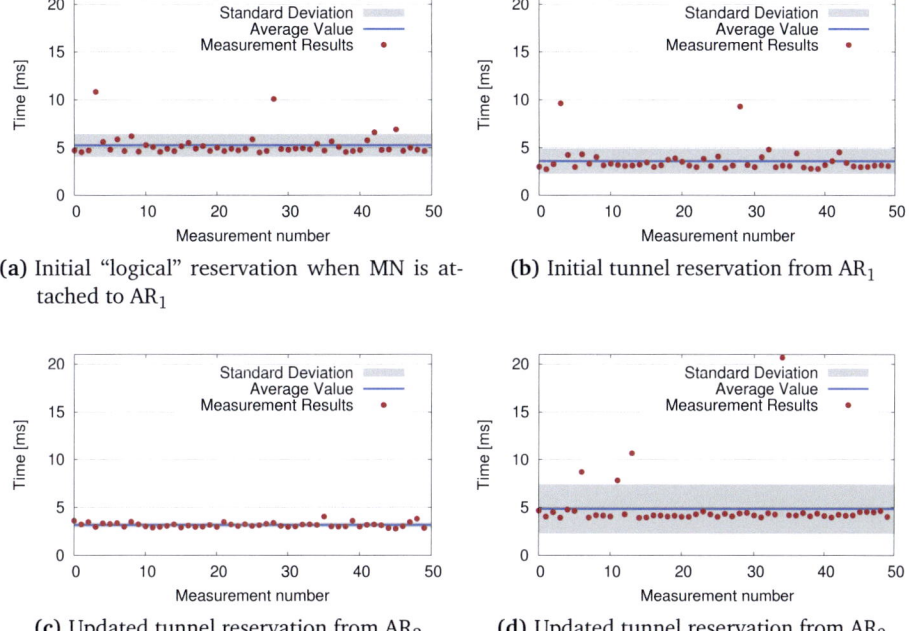

(a) Initial "logical" reservation when MN is attached to AR_1

(b) Initial tunnel reservation from AR_1

(c) Updated tunnel reservation from AR_2

(d) Updated tunnel reservation from AR_3

Figure A.7: *Reservation setup time for scenario M2—MN is sender and signaling responder—in tunnel mode*

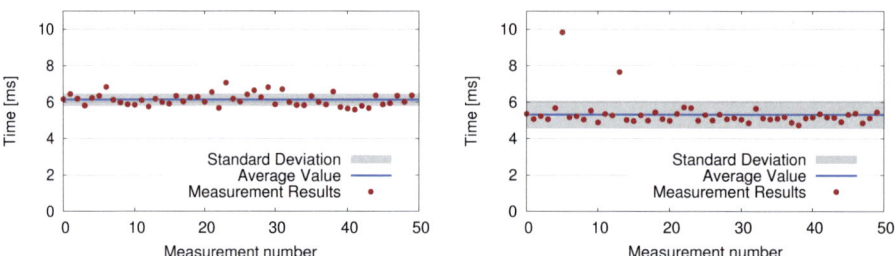

(a) Initial reservation when MN is attached to AR$_1$

(b) Updated reservation when MN is attached to AR$_2$

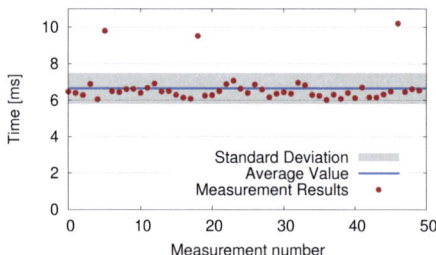

(c) Updated reservation when MN is attached to AR$_3$

Figure A.8: *Reservation setup time for scenario M3—MN is receiver and signaling initiator—in tunnel mode*

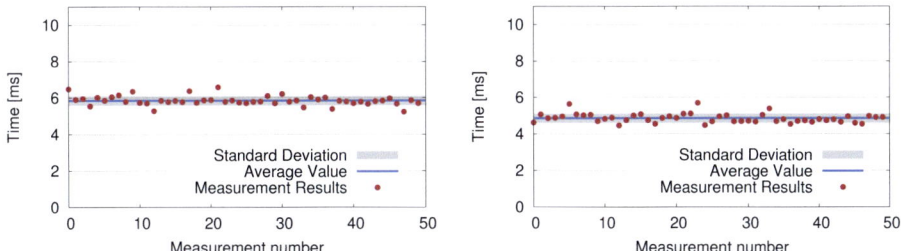

(a) Initial reservation when MN is attached to AR$_1$

(b) Updated reservation when MN is attached to AR$_2$

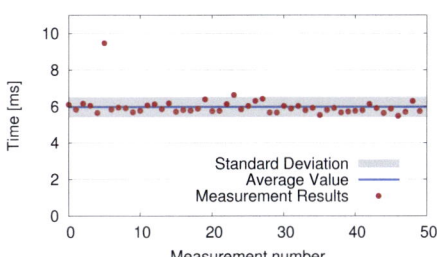

(c) Updated reservation when MN is attached to AR$_3$

Figure A.9: *Reservation setup time for scenario M4—MN is receiver and signaling responder—in tunnel mode*

Evaluation Anticipated Handover Signaling

This chapter provides more detailed analytical and measurement based evaluation results.

B.1 M2 – Mobile Node is Data Flow Sender and Reservation Responder

In case the MN is data flow sender and reservation responder, phase ① of the anticipated handover signaling consists of an initial QUERY-AHO signaling from the MN toward its anticipated access router AR_N as depicted in Figure B.1.

The time needed for phase ① can then be expressed by

$$t_{\text{AHO}}^{(1)} = o + p + r + \sum_{i=1}^{\alpha} \frac{3}{2} \text{RTT}_i \tag{B.1}$$

In phase ② of the anticipated handover concept, AR_N establishes a new resource reservation on behalf of the MN toward the CN. The corresponding signaling message exchange is depicted in Figure B.2.

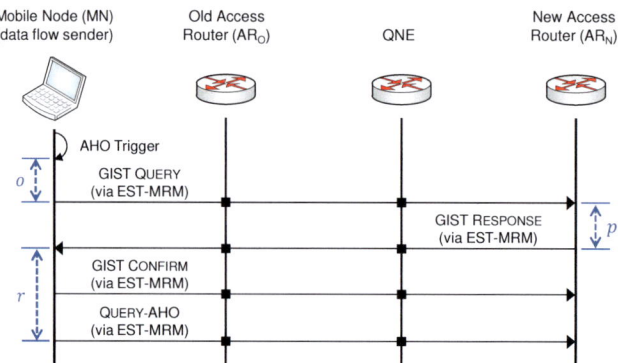

Figure B.1: *Processing times within phase ① of the anticipated handover signaling procedure for scenario M2 – MN is data flow sender and reservation responder*

The time needed to establish an anticipated reservation in phase ② can then be expressed by

$$
t_{\text{AHO}}^{(2)} = \left(\sum_{i=1}^{\beta} o_i + p_i + r_i + \frac{3}{2}\text{RTT}_i \right) + u + \left(\sum_{i=1}^{\beta-1} f_{RSV_i} + \frac{1}{2}\text{RTT}_i \right)
$$
$$
+ \left(\sum_{i=1}^{\beta} f_{RSP_i} + \frac{1}{2}\text{RTT}_i \right) + v + \left(\sum_{i=1}^{\alpha} \text{RTT}_i \right) \tag{B.2}
$$

A combination of phase ① and ② can be expressed by equation (B.3):

$$
t_{\text{AHO}}^{(1+2)} = o + p + r + u + v + \left(\sum_{i=1}^{\alpha} \frac{5}{2}\text{RTT}_i \right) + \left(\sum_{i=1}^{\beta-1} f_{RSV_i} + \frac{1}{2}\text{RTT}_i \right)
$$
$$
+ \left(\sum_{i=1}^{\beta} o_i + p_i + r_i + f_{RSP_i} + 2 \times \text{RTT}_i \right) \tag{B.3}
$$

After the MN changed toward its new point of attachment the anticipated reservation must be activated in phase ③. The corresponding signaling operation is depicted in Figure B.3.

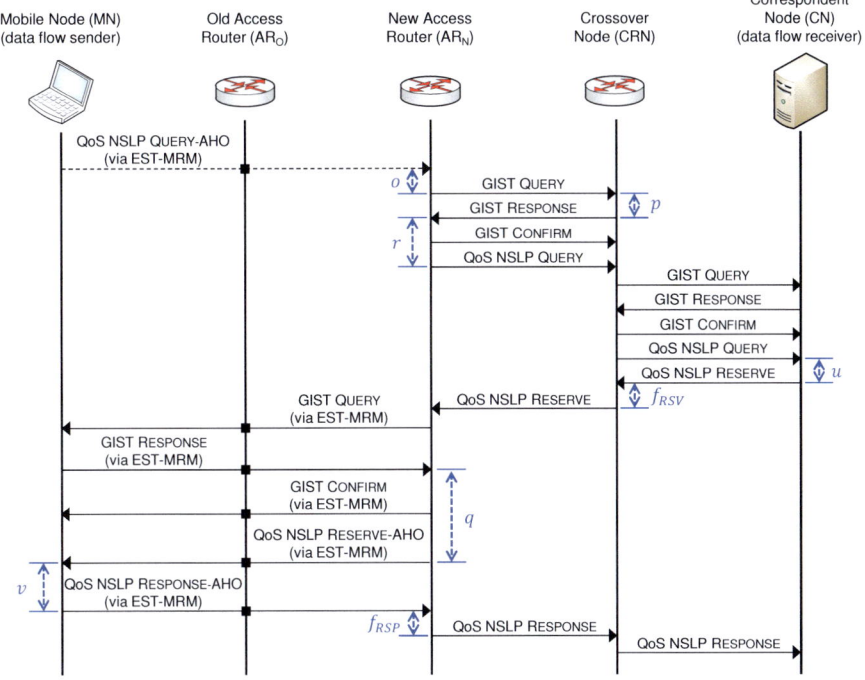

Figure B.2: *Processing times within phase ② of the anticipated handover signaling procedure for scenario M2 – MN is data flow sender and reservation responder*

The time needed to activate an anticipated reservation in phase ③ can then be expressed by

$$t_{AHO}^{(3)} = o + p + r + \frac{5}{2}\text{RTT} + \left(\sum_{i=1}^{\beta} f_{QUERY_i} + f_{RSV_i} + f_{RSP_i} + \frac{3}{2}\text{RTT}_i \right) + u + v \quad \text{(B.4)}$$

The time needed to tear down the old reservation can be expressed by

$$t_{AHO}^{(3)'} = z_{RSV} + \sum_{j=1}^{\gamma-1} f_{RSV_j}' + \sum_{j=1}^{\gamma} \frac{\text{RTT}_j}{2} \quad \text{(B.5)}$$

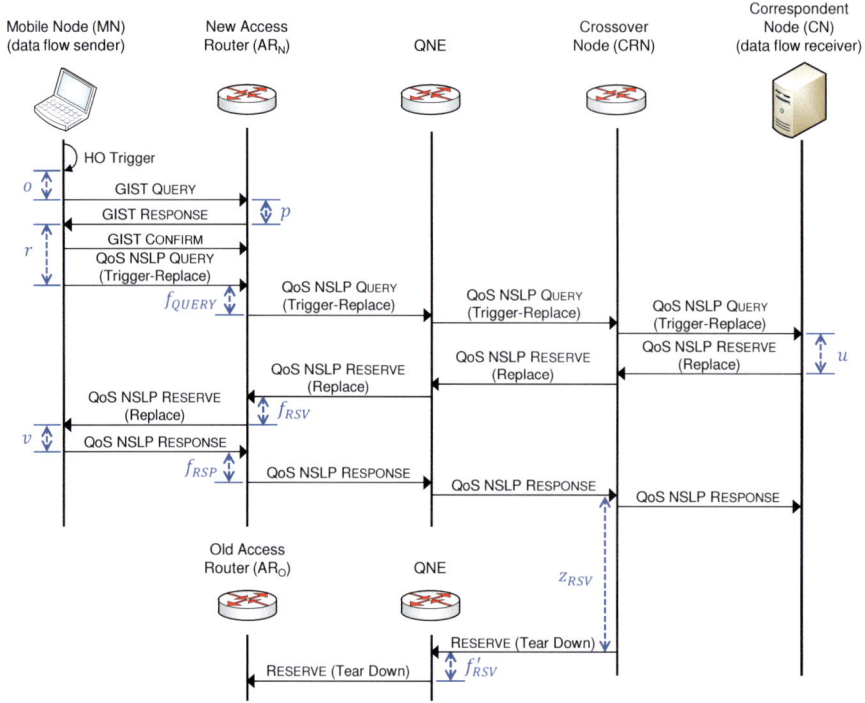

Figure B.3: *Processing times within phase ③ of the anticipated handover signaling procedure for scenario M2 – MN is data flow sender and reservation responder*

B.2 M3 – Mobile Node is Data Flow Receiver and Reservation Initiator

In case the MN is data flow receiver and reservation initiator, phase ① of the anticipated handover signaling consists of an initial RESERVE-AHO signaling from the MN toward its anticipated access router AR_N as depicted in Figure B.4.

The time needed for phase ① can then be expressed by

$$t^{(1)}_{\text{AHO}} = o + p + q + \sum_{i=1}^{\alpha} \frac{3}{2}\text{RTT}_i \tag{B.6}$$

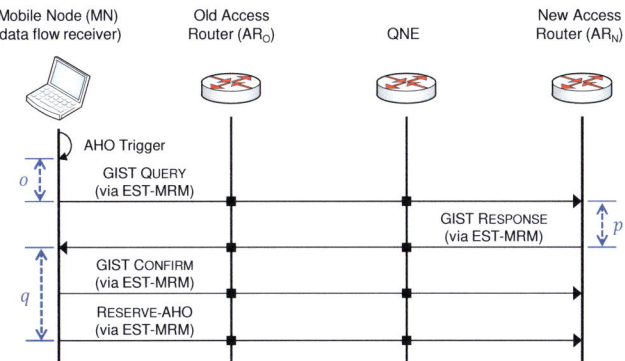

Figure B.4: *Processing times within phase ① of the anticipated handover signaling procedure for scenario M3 – MN is data flow receiver and reservation initiator*

In phase ② of the anticipated handover concept, AR_N triggers the establishment of a new resource reservation on behalf of the MN. The corresponding signaling message exchange is depicted in Figure B.5.

The time needed for phase ② can be expressed by

$$t_{AHO}^{(2)} = o + p + s + \left(\sum_{i=1}^{\beta}\frac{3}{2}RTT_i\right) + \left(\sum_{i=1}^{\beta} o_i + p_i + r_i + \frac{3}{2}RTT_i\right) + u + v$$

$$+ \left(\sum_{i=1}^{\beta} RTT_i\right) + \left(\sum_{i=1}^{\beta-1} f_{RSV_i} + f_{RSP_i}\right) + o + p + x + \left(\sum_{i=1}^{\alpha}\frac{3}{2}RTT_i\right)$$

$$= 2 \times (o + p) + s + u + v + x + \left(\sum_{i=1}^{\alpha}\frac{3}{2}RTT_i\right)$$

$$+ \left(\sum_{i=1}^{\beta-1} f_{RSV_i} + f_{RSP_i}\right) + \left(\sum_{i=1}^{\beta} o_i + p_i + r_i + 4 \times RTT_i\right) \quad (B.7)$$

A combination of phase ① and ② can be expressed by equation (B.8):

$$t_{AHO}^{(1+2)} = 3 \times (o + p) + q + s + u + v + x + \left(\sum_{i=1}^{\alpha}\frac{3}{2}RTT_i\right)$$

$$+ \left(\sum_{i=1}^{\beta-1} f_{RSV_i} + f_{RSP_i}\right) + \left(\sum_{i=1}^{\beta} o_i + p_i + r_i + 4 \times RTT_i\right) \quad (B.8)$$

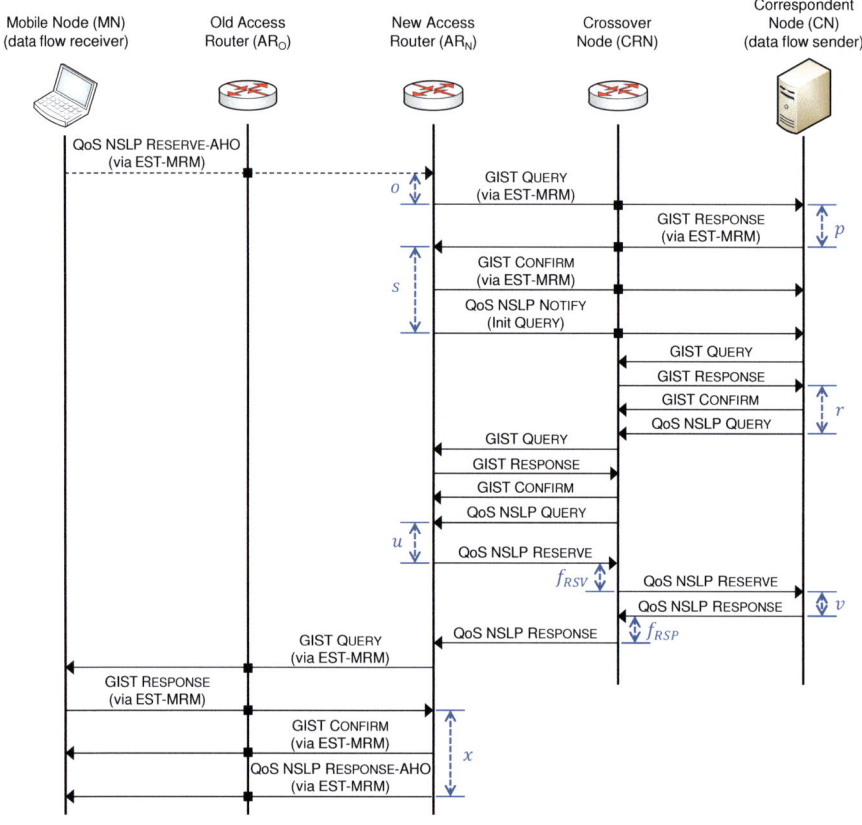

Figure B.5: *Processing times within phase ② of the anticipated handover signaling procedure for scenario M3 – MN is data flow receiver and reservation initiator*

After the MN changed toward its new point of attachment the anticipated reservation must be activated in phase ③. The corresponding signaling operation is depicted in Figure B.6.

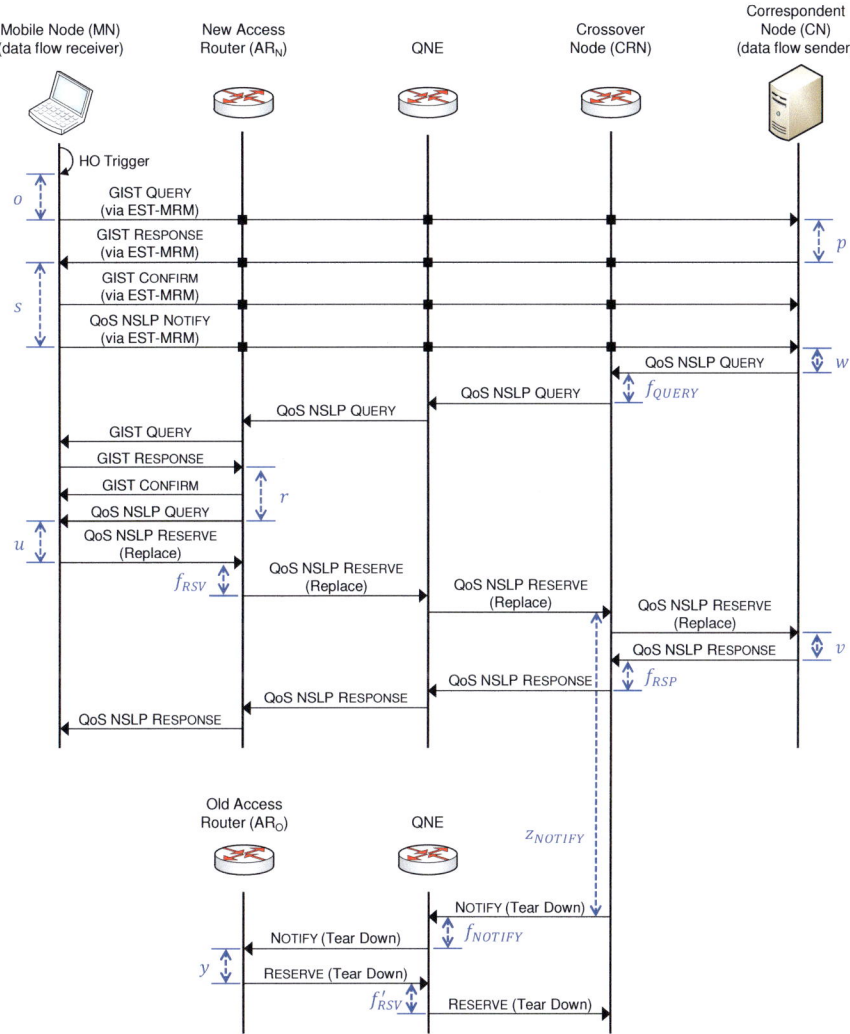

Figure B.6: *Processing times within phase ③ of the anticipated handover signaling procedure for scenario M3 – MN is data flow receiver and reservation initiator*

The time needed to activate an anticipated reservation in phase ③ can be expressed by

$$
\begin{aligned}
t_{AHO}^{(3)} &= o + p + s + \left(\sum_{i=1}^{\beta+1} \frac{3}{2} \text{RTT}_i \right) + w + \left(\sum_{i=1}^{\beta} f_{QUERY_i} + \frac{1}{2} \text{RTT}_i \right) \\
&\quad + o + p + r + u + 2 \times \text{RTT} + \left(\sum_{i=1}^{\beta} f_{RSV_i} + \frac{1}{2} \text{RTT}_i \right) + v + \left(\sum_{i=1}^{\beta} f_{RSP_i} + \frac{1}{2} \text{RTT}_i \right) \\
&= 2(o+p) + r + s + u + v + w + \left(\sum_{i=1}^{\beta} f_{QUERY_i} + f_{RSV_i} + f_{RSP_i} + 3\text{RTT}_i \right) + \frac{7}{2} \text{RTT}
\end{aligned}
$$

$$\text{(B.9)}$$

The time needed to tear down the old reservation can be expressed by

$$
t_{AHO}^{(3)'} = z_{NOTIFY} + \left(\sum_{j=1}^{\gamma-1} f_{NOTIFY_j} + f_{RSV_j}' \right) + y + \sum_{j=1}^{\gamma} \text{RTT}_j \qquad \text{(B.10)}
$$

B.3 M4 – Mobile Node is Data Flow Receiver and Reservation Responder

In case the MN is data flow receiver and reservation responder, phase ① of the anticipated handover signaling consists of an initial QUERY-AHO signaling from the MN toward its anticipated access router AR_N as depicted in Figure B.7.

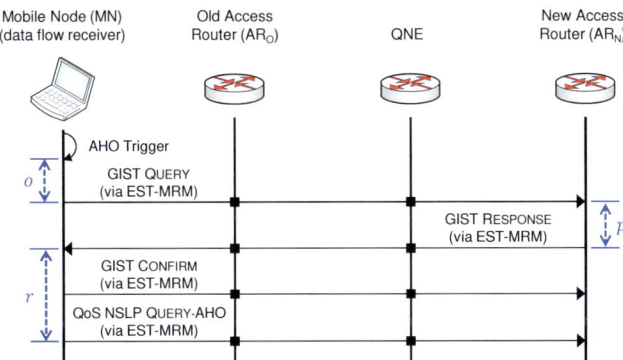

Figure B.7: *Processing times within phase ① of the anticipated handover signaling procedure for scenario M4 – MN is data flow receiver and reservation responder*

The time needed for phase ① can then be expressed by

$$t_{\text{AHO}}^{(1)} = o + p + r + \sum_{i=1}^{\alpha} \frac{3}{2}\text{RTT}_i \qquad (B.11)$$

In phase ② of the anticipated handover concept, AR_N triggers the establishment of a new resource reservation on behalf of the MN by means of a NOTIFY-AHO signaling message. The corresponding signaling message exchange is depicted in Figure B.8.

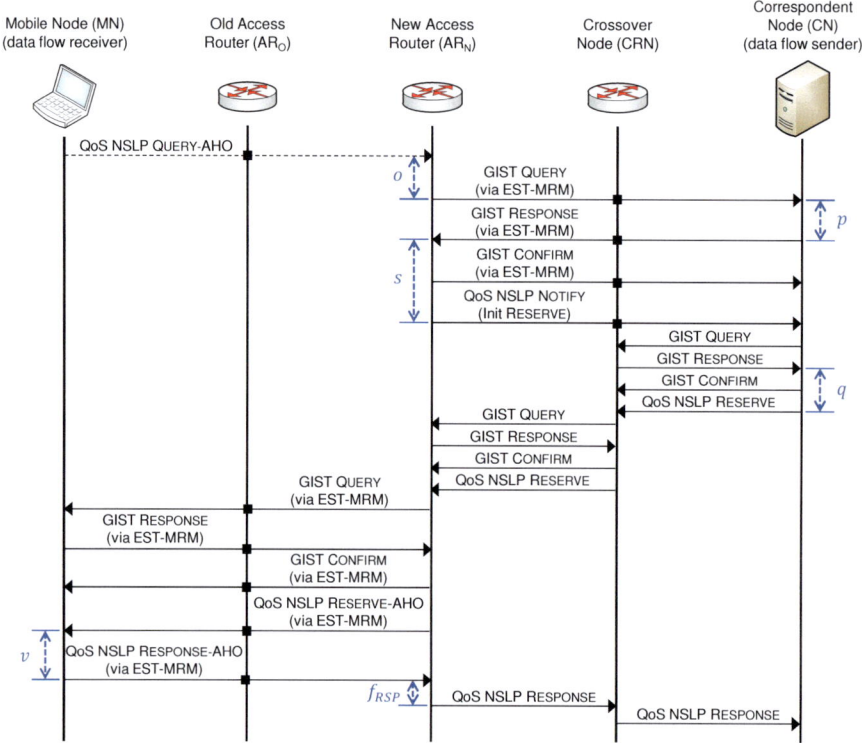

Figure B.8: *Processing times within phase ② of the anticipated handover signaling procedure for scenario M4 – MN is data flow receiver and reservation responder*

The time needed for phase ② can be expressed by

$$
\begin{aligned}
t_{\text{AHO}}^{(2)} &= o + p + s + \left(\sum_{i=1}^{\beta} \frac{3}{2} \text{RTT}_i \right) + \left(\sum_{i=1}^{\beta} o_i + p_i + q_i + \frac{3}{2} \text{RTT}_i \right) \\
&+ o + p + q + \left(\sum_{i=1}^{\alpha} \frac{3}{2} \text{RTT}_i \right) + v + \left(\sum_{i=1}^{\alpha} \frac{\text{RTT}_i}{2} \right) + \left(\sum_{i=1}^{\beta} f_{RSP_i} + \frac{\text{RTT}_i}{2} \right) \\
&= 2 \times (o + p) + q + s + v + \left(\sum_{i=1}^{\alpha} 2 \times \text{RTT}_i \right) \\
&+ \left(\sum_{i=1}^{\beta} o_i + p_i + q_i + f_{RSP_i} + \frac{7}{2} \text{RTT}_i \right)
\end{aligned}
\tag{B.12}
$$

A combination of phase ① and ② can be expressed by equation (B.13):

$$t_{AHO}^{(1+2)} = 3 \times (o + p) + q + r + s + v + \left(\sum_{i=1}^{\alpha} \frac{7}{2} \text{RTT}_i \right)$$

$$+ \left(\sum_{i=1}^{\beta} o_i + p_i + q_i + f_{RSP_i} + \frac{7}{2} \text{RTT}_i \right) \tag{B.13}$$

After the MN changed toward its new point of attachment the anticipated reservation must be activated in phase ③. The corresponding signaling operation is depicted in Figure B.9.

The time needed to activate an anticipated reservation in phase ③ can be expressed by

$$t_{AHO}^{(3)} = o + p + s + \left(\sum_{i=1}^{\beta+1} \frac{3}{2} \text{RTT}_i \right) + y + \left(\sum_{i=1}^{\beta} f_{RSV_i} + \frac{1}{2} \text{RTT}_i \right)$$

$$+ 2 \times \text{RTT} + o + p + q + v + \left(\sum_{i=1}^{\beta} f_{RSP_i} + \frac{1}{2} \text{RTT}_i \right)$$

$$= 2(o + p) + q + s + v + y + \left(\sum_{i=1}^{\beta} f_{RSV_i} + f_{RSP_i} + \frac{5}{2} \text{RTT}_i \right) + \frac{7}{2} \text{RTT} \tag{B.14}$$

The time needed to tear down the old reservation can be expressed by

$$t_{AHO}^{(3)'} = z_{RSV} + \sum_{j=1}^{\gamma-1} f'_{RSV_j} + \sum_{j=1}^{\gamma} \frac{\text{RTT}_j}{2} \tag{B.15}$$

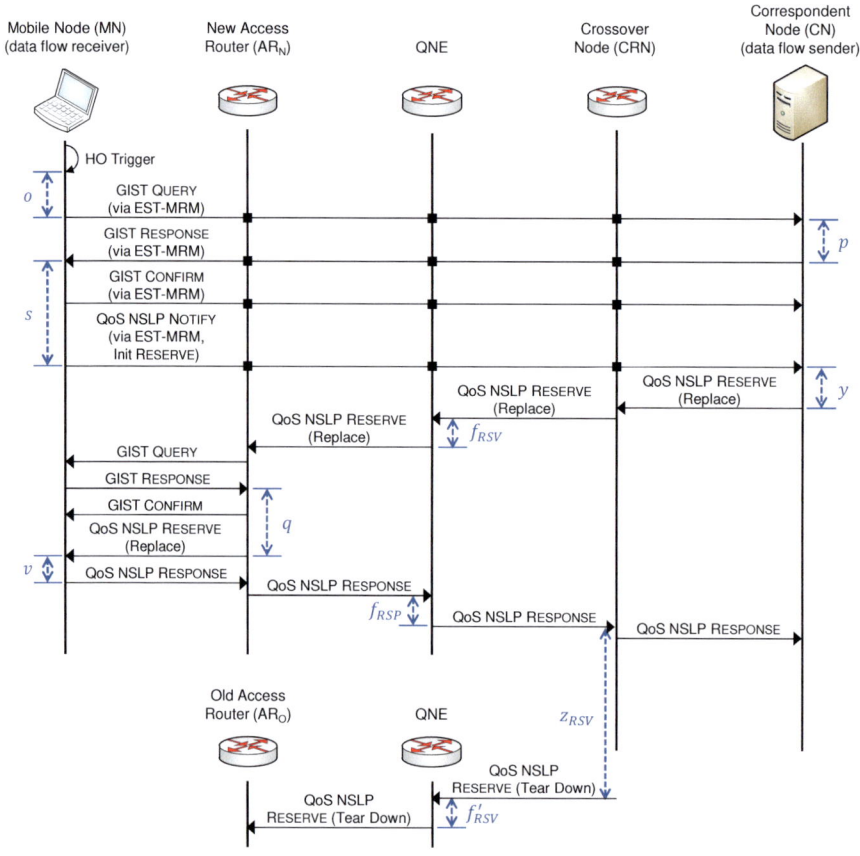

Figure B.9: *Processing times within phase ③ of the anticipated handover signaling procedure for scenario M4 – MN is data flow receiver and reservation responder*

B.4 Detailed Measurement Based Evaluation Results

This section provides the detailed measurement results from the evaluations of the anticipated handover signaling concept. In order to allow for better comparison, Figures B.10 and B.11 show detailed measurement results of the *initial* resource reservation when the MN is located at AR_1 for all four mobility scenarios.

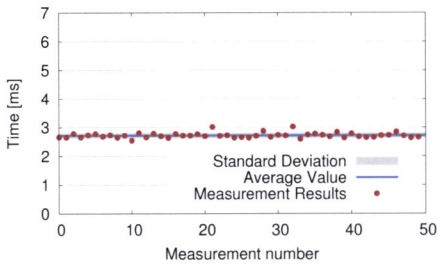 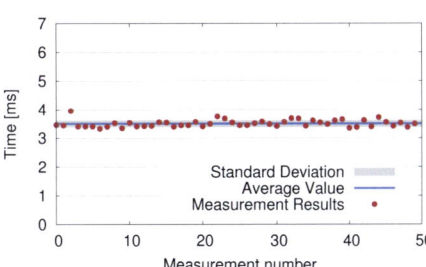

(a) M1 – MN is sender and a sender-initiated reservation is established (b) M2 – MN is sender and a receiver-initiated reservation is established

Figure B.10: *Measurement results for the initial reservation setup when MN is attached to AR_1 if MN is data flow sender*

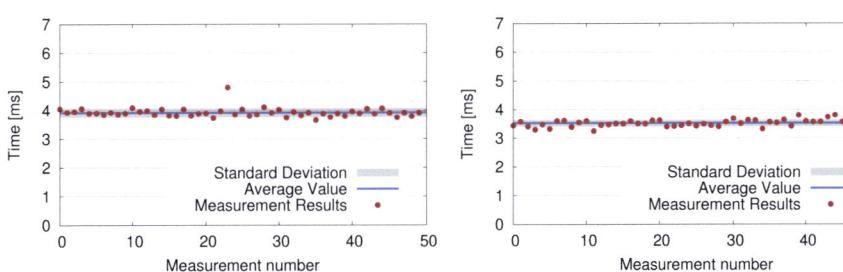

(a) M3 – MN is receiver and a receiver-initiated reservation is established (b) M4 – MN is receiver and a sender-initiated reservation is established

Figure B.11: *Measurement results for the initial reservation setup when MN is attached to AR_1 if MN is data flow receiver*

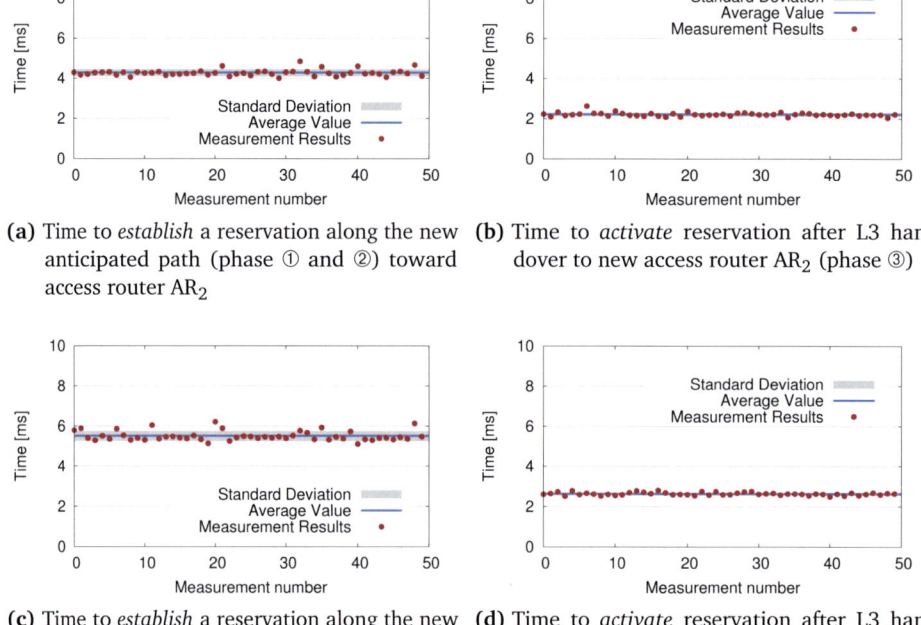

(a) Time to *establish* a reservation along the new anticipated path (phase ① and ②) toward access router AR_2

(b) Time to *activate* reservation after L3 handover to new access router AR_2 (phase ③)

(c) Time to *establish* a reservation along the new anticipated path (phase ① and ②) toward access router AR_3

(d) Time to *activate* reservation after L3 handover to new access router AR_3 (phase ③)

Figure B.12: *Measurement results for mobility scenario M1 – MN acts as data flow sender and signaling initiator*

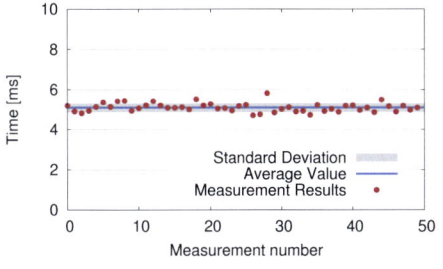

(a) Time to *establish* a reservation along the new anticipated path (phase ① and ②) toward access router AR_2

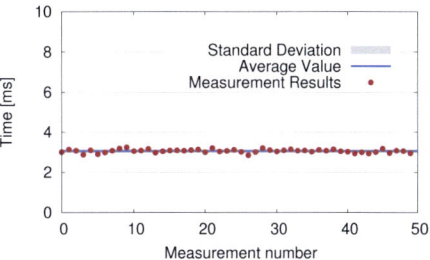

(b) Time to *activate* reservation after L3 handover to new access router AR_2 (phase ③)

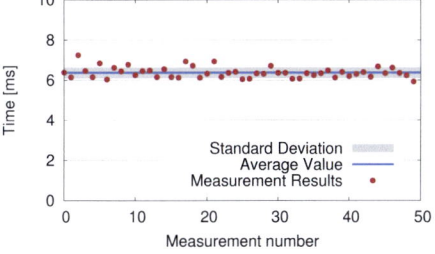

(c) Time to *establish* a reservation along the new anticipated path (phase ① and ②) toward access router AR_3

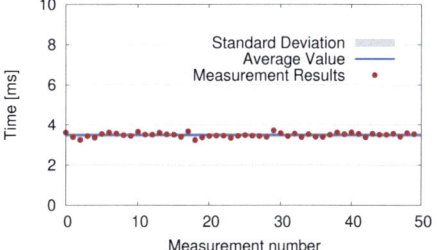

(d) Time to *activate* reservation after L3 handover to new access router AR_3 (phase ③)

Figure B.13: *Measurement results for mobility scenario M2 – MN acts as data flow sender and signaling responder*

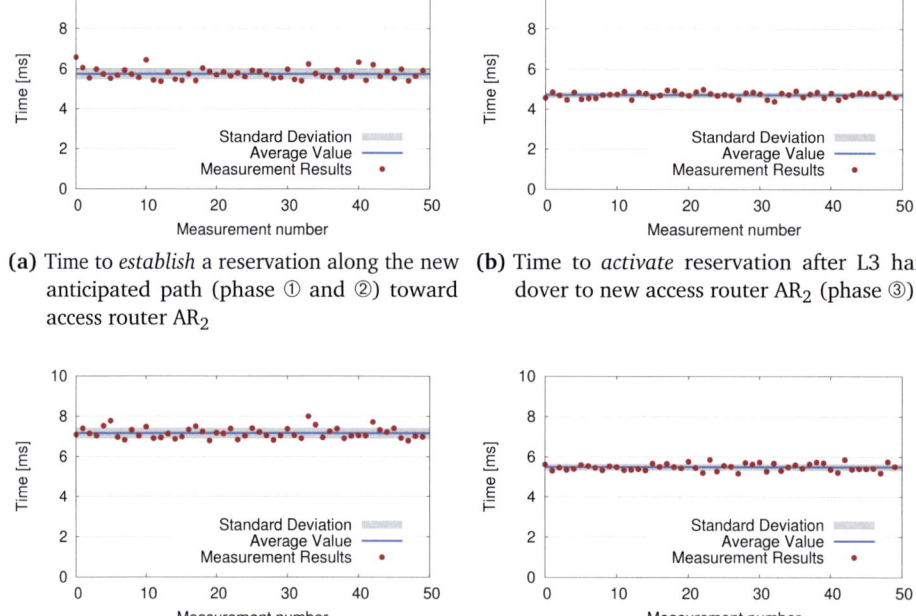

(a) Time to *establish* a reservation along the new anticipated path (phase ① and ②) toward access router AR_2

(b) Time to *activate* reservation after L3 handover to new access router AR_2 (phase ③)

(c) Time to *establish* a reservation along the new anticipated path (phase ① and ②) toward access router AR_3

(d) Time to *activate* reservation after L3 handover to new access router AR_3 (phase ③)

Figure B.14: *Measurement results for mobility scenario M3 – MN acts as data flow receiver and signaling initiator*

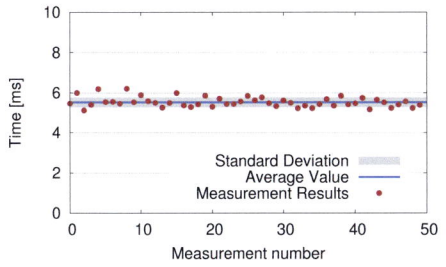

(a) Time to *establish* a reservation along the new anticipated path (phase ① and ②) toward access router AR_2

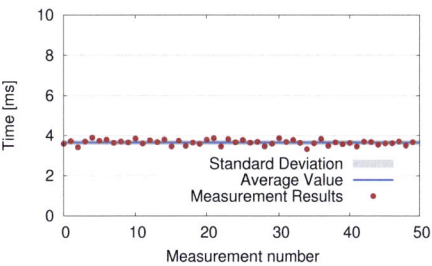

(b) Time to *activate* reservation after L3 handover to new access router AR_2 (phase ③)

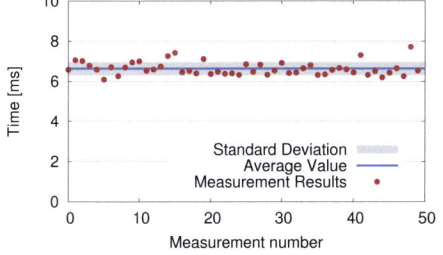

(c) Time to *establish* a reservation along the new anticipated path (phase ① and ②) toward access router AR_3

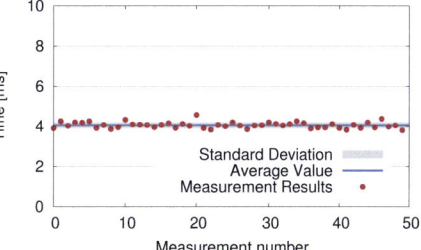

(d) Time to *activate* reservation after L3 handover to new access router AR_3 (phase ③)

Figure B.15: *Measurement results for mobility scenario M4 – MN acts as data flow receiver and signaling responder*

Appendix C

Evaluation Hard Handover Signaling

C.1 M3 – Mobile Node is Data Flow Receiver and Signaling Initiator

In case the MN is data flow receiver and reservation initiator, the MN must send a NOTIFY message directly toward the CN in order to trigger a QoS NSLP QUERY which is used to install reverse-path state in downstream direction and triggers a replacing RESERVE to be sent by the MN subsequently. The detailed message sequence diagram for this scenario is depicted in Figure C.1.

In order to send the NOTIFY message toward the CN a GIST three-way handshake between the MN and the CN must be performed by means of the EST-MRM. Since the path in downstream direction toward the MN's new location has not been established yet, a GIST three-way handshake precedes each QoS NSLP QUERY.

The time needed to establish a new reservation by means of a hard handover can then be expressed by

$$
\begin{aligned}
t_{\mathrm{HHO}} &= o + p + s + \left(\sum_{i=1}^{\beta+1} \frac{3}{2} \mathrm{RTT}_i \right) + \left(\sum_{i=1}^{\beta+1} o_i + p_i + r_i + \frac{3}{2} \mathrm{RTT}_i \right) + u + \frac{\mathrm{RTT}}{2} \\
&\quad + \left(\sum_{i=1}^{\beta} f_{RSV_i} + \frac{\mathrm{RTT}_i}{2} \right) + v + \frac{\mathrm{RTT}}{2} + \left(\sum_{i=1}^{\beta} f_{RSP_i} + \frac{\mathrm{RTT}_i}{2} \right) \\
&= o + p + s + u + v + \mathrm{RTT} + \left(\sum_{i=1}^{\beta} f_{RSV_i} + f_{RSP_i} + \mathrm{RTT}_i \right) \\
&\quad + \left(\sum_{i=1}^{\beta+1} o_i + p_i + r_i + 3 \times \mathrm{RTT}_i \right)
\end{aligned}
\tag{C.1}
$$

The time needed to tear down the old reservation along the old path can be expressed by

$$
t'_{\mathrm{HHO}} = z_{NOTIFY} + y + \left(\sum_{j=1}^{\gamma-1} f_{NOTIFY_j} + f'_{RSV_j} \right) + \left(\sum_{j=1}^{\gamma} \mathrm{RTT}_i \right)
\tag{C.2}
$$

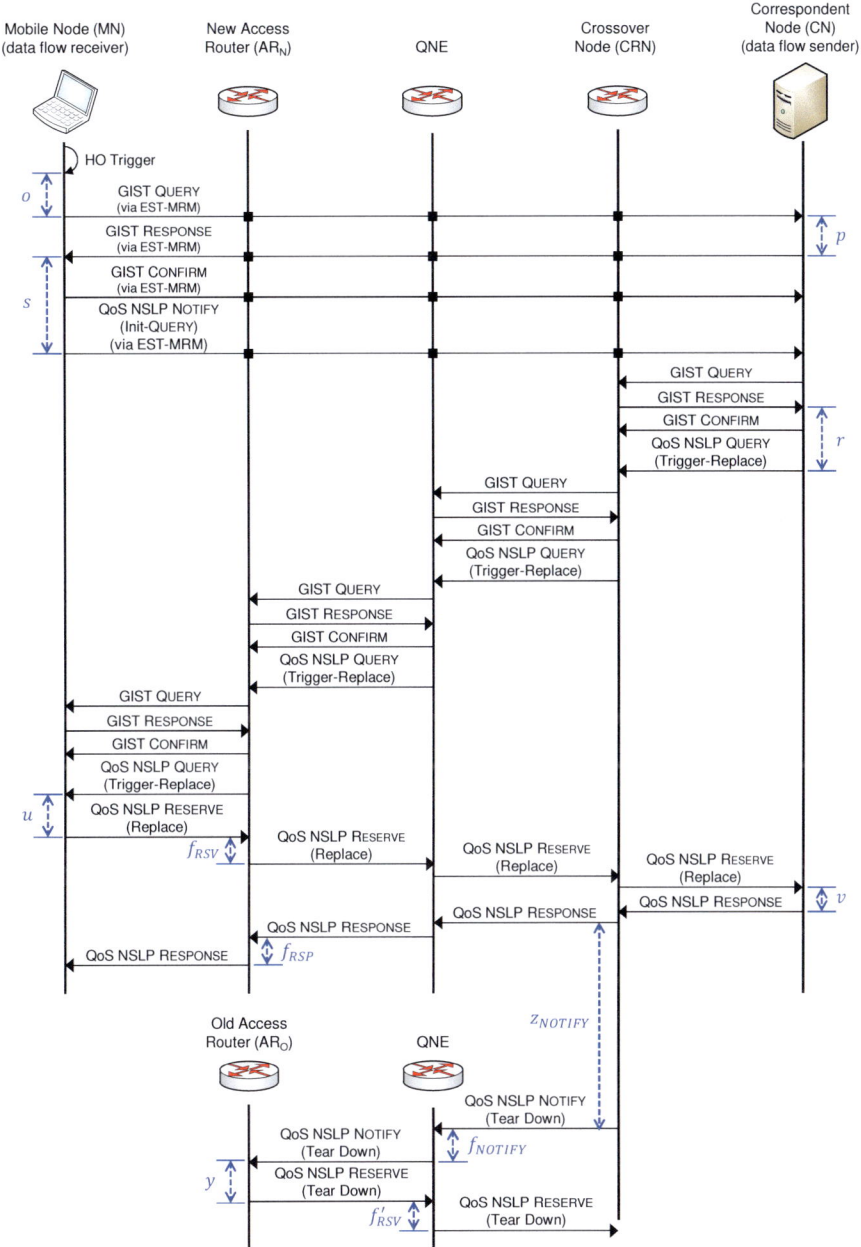

Figure C.1: *Processing times for a hard handover signaling procedure if MN is data flow receiver and reservation initiator*

C.2 M4 – Mobile Node is Data Flow Receiver and Signaling Responder

In case the MN is data flow receiver and reservation responder, it must send a NOTIFY message directly toward the CN in order to trigger a replacing RESERVE to be sent by the CN. The detailed message sequence diagram for this scenario is depicted in Figure C.2.

In order to send the NOTIFY message toward the CN a GIST three-way handshake between the MN and the CN must be performed by means of the EST-MRM. Since the path in downstream direction toward the MN's new location has not been established yet, a GIST three-way handshake precedes each replacing RESERVE.

The time needed to establish a new reservation by means of a hard handover can then be expressed by

$$
\begin{aligned}
t_{\text{HHO}} &= o + p + s + \left(\sum_{i=1}^{\beta+1} \frac{3}{2} \text{RTT}_i \right) + \left(\sum_{i=1}^{\beta+1} o_i + p_i + q_i + \frac{3}{2} \text{RTT}_i \right) \\
&\quad + v + \frac{\text{RTT}}{2} + \left(\sum_{i=1}^{\beta} f_{RSP_i} + \frac{\text{RTT}_i}{2} \right) \\
&= o + p + s + v + \frac{\text{RTT}}{2} + \left(\sum_{i=1}^{\beta} f_{RSP_i} + \frac{\text{RTT}_i}{2} \right) \\
&\quad + \left(\sum_{i=1}^{\beta+1} o_i + p_i + q_i + 3 \times \text{RTT}_i \right)
\end{aligned}
\tag{C.3}
$$

The time needed to tear down the old reservation along the old path can be expressed by

$$
t'_{\text{HHO}} = z_{RSV} + \left(\sum_{j=1}^{\gamma-1} f_{RSV_j} \right) + \left(\sum_{j=1}^{\gamma} \frac{\text{RTT}_i}{2} \right)
\tag{C.4}
$$

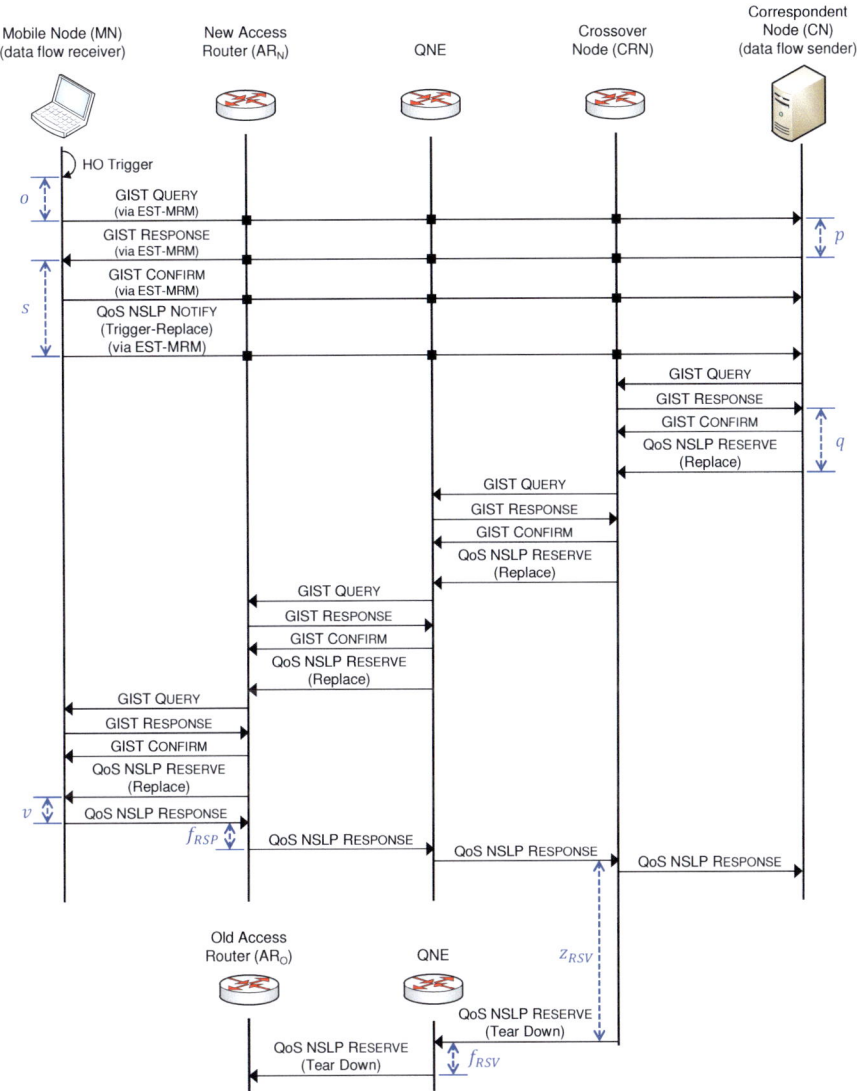

Figure C.2: *Processing times for a hard handover signaling procedure if MN is data flow receiver and reservation responder*

C.3 Detailed Measurement Based Evaluation Results

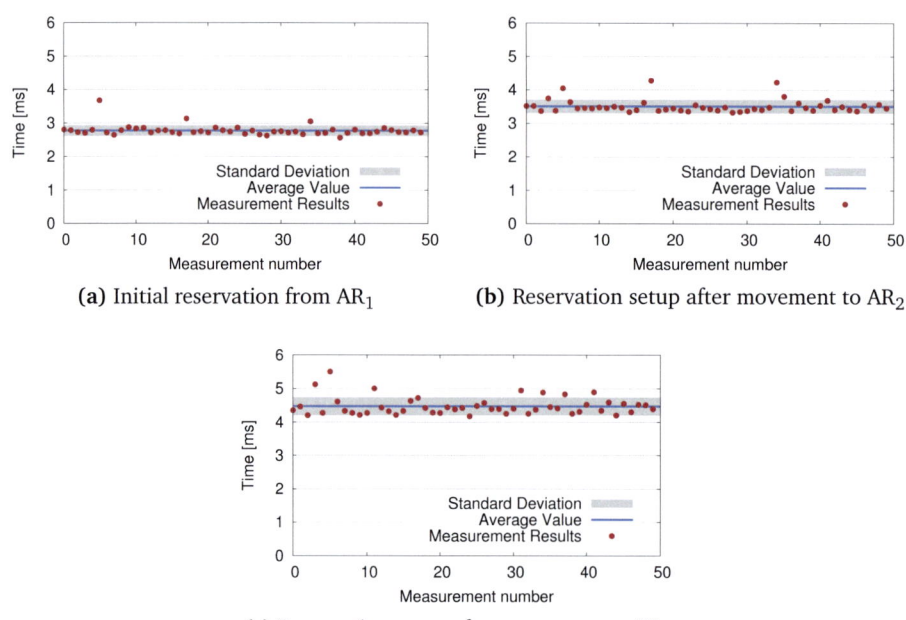

(a) Initial reservation from AR$_1$ (b) Reservation setup after movement to AR$_2$

(c) Reservation setup after movement to AR$_3$

Figure C.3: *Hard handover measurement results for scenario M1 – MN is data flow sender and signaling initiator*

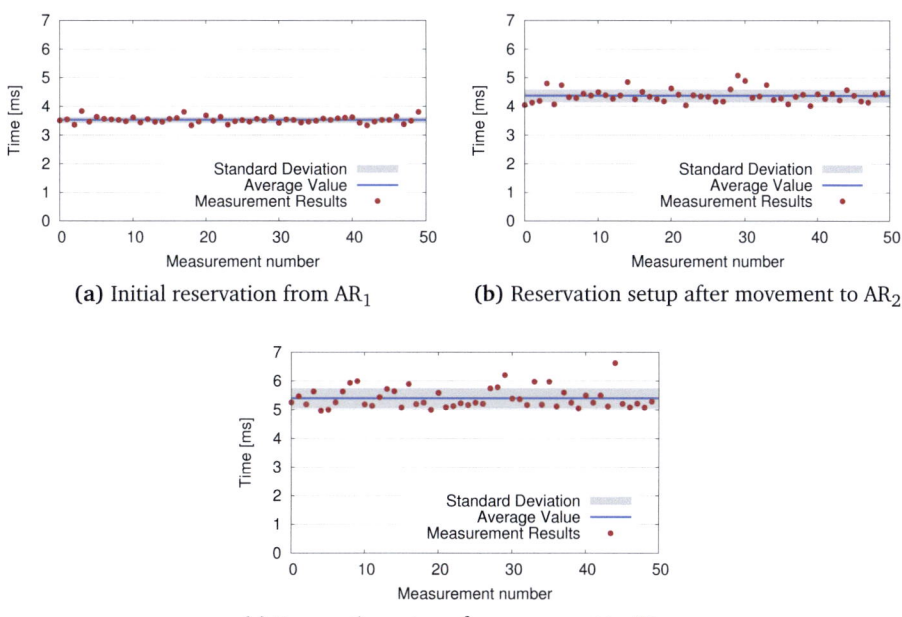

(a) Initial reservation from AR_1

(b) Reservation setup after movement to AR_2

(c) Reservation setup after movement to AR_3

Figure C.4: *Hard handover measurement results for scenario M2 – MN is data flow sender and signaling responder*

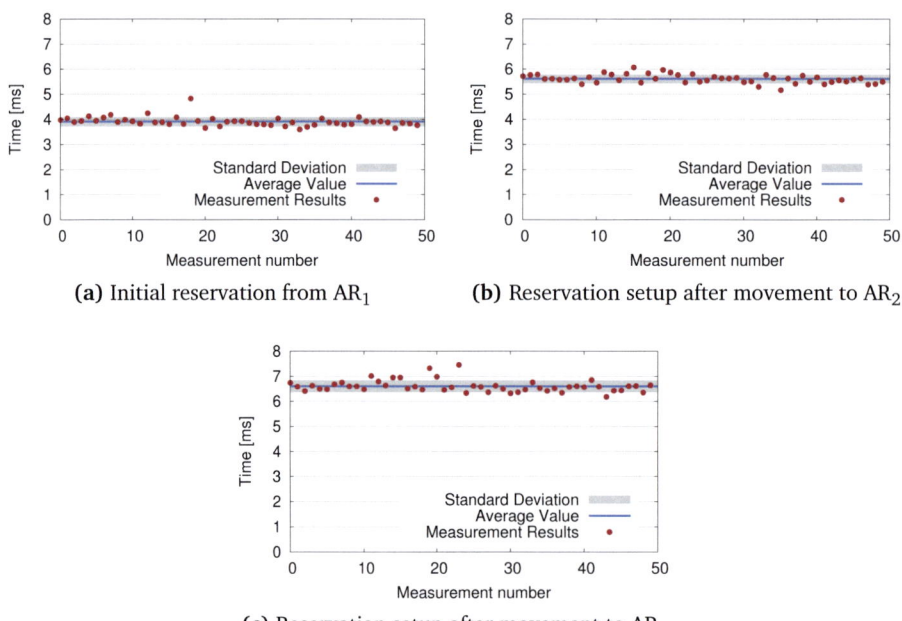

(a) Initial reservation from AR_1

(b) Reservation setup after movement to AR_2

(c) Reservation setup after movement to AR_3

Figure C.5: *Hard handover measurement results for scenario M3 – MN is data flow receiver and signaling initiator*

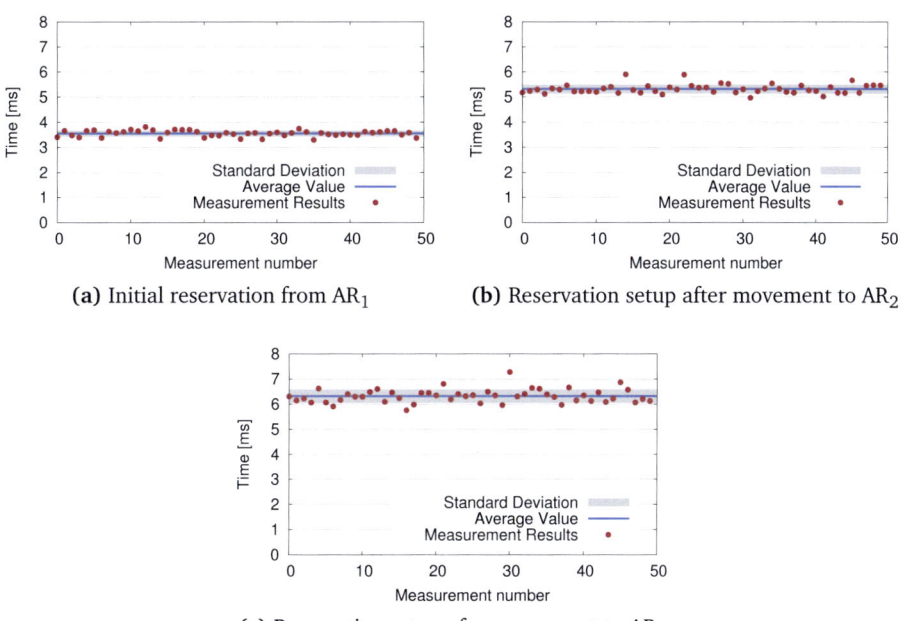

(a) Initial reservation from AR_1

(b) Reservation setup after movement to AR_2

(c) Reservation setup after movement to AR_3

Figure C.6: *Hard handover measurement results for scenario M4 – MN is data flow receiver and signaling responder*

Evaluation of QoS Signaling for IP Multicast

All QoS signaling experiments in an IP multicast environment were performed in a testbed consisting of 16 testbed PCs, each of which being equipped with an Intel Xeon X3430 quadcore CPU (2.40 GHz), 4 GB RAM, and four Intel 82580 Gigabit Ethernet network interfaces. All network interfaces were interconnected by a Cisco Catalyst Switch 6500 running CatOS. The resulting topology is illustrated in Figure 5.11 on page 184.

D.1 IP Multicast Configuration

This section describes how the different signaling entities being used in the multicast evaluations were configured. Testbed PC tb6 served as multicast tree root node and used the following static network configuration:

Listing D.1: *Network configuration on the multicast tree's root node tb6*

```
# This file describes the network interfaces available on your system
# and how to activate them. For more information, see interfaces(5).

# The loopback network interface
auto lo
iface lo inet loopback

# The primary network interface
auto eth4
iface eth4 inet dhcp

# Multicast Setup:
```

```
auto eth0
iface eth0 inet static
address 10.6.7.6
netmask 255.255.255.0
network 10.6.7.0
```

Since the Linux kernel sets the IP TTL value of IP multicast packets to 1 by default, the next hop along the path would discard this packet. Therefore, the following script was used on tb6 in order to increase a multicast packet's IP TTL value to 9:

Listing D.2: *Increase of IP TTL value for IP multicast packets leaving the multicast tree's root node tb6*

```
#!/bin/sh

# On the multicast tree's root node, no smcroute is necessary. Instead, increase
# the TTL for IP packets being destined toward the multicast address 224.7.7.7
iptables -t mangle -A POSTROUTING -d 224.7.7.7 -j TTL --ttl-inc 9
```

Intermediate signaling entities along the multicast distribution tree used one incoming and two outgoing interfaces. For instance, tb11's interfaces were configured as follows:

Listing D.3: *Network configuration on the intermediate signaling entity tb11*

```
# This file describes the network interfaces available on your system
# and how to activate them. For more information, see interfaces(5).

# The loopback network interface
auto lo
iface lo inet loopback

# The primary network interface
auto eth4
iface eth4 inet dhcp

auto eth0
iface eth0 inet static
address 10.8.11.11
netmask 255.255.255.0
network 10.8.11.0

auto eth1
iface eth1 inet static
address 10.11.16.11
netmask 255.255.255.0
network 10.11.16.0

auto eth2
iface eth2 inet static
address 10.11.17.11
netmask 255.255.255.0
network 10.11.17.0
```

Routing entries must also be statically configured in this testbed on the corresponding hosts. The following lists the routing commands used on tb11:

Listing D.4: *Routing commands used on tb11 in the file /etc/network/if-up.d/set-routes*

```
#!/bin/sh
echo 1 >/proc/sys/net/ipv4/conf/eth0/forwarding
echo 1 >/proc/sys/net/ipv6/conf/eth0/forwarding
echo 1 >/proc/sys/net/ipv4/conf/eth1/forwarding
echo 1 >/proc/sys/net/ipv6/conf/eth1/forwarding
echo 1 >/proc/sys/net/ipv4/conf/eth2/forwarding
echo 1 >/proc/sys/net/ipv6/conf/eth2/forwarding

ip route add 10.6.7.0/24 via 10.8.11.8
ip route add 10.7.8.0/24 via 10.8.11.8
ip route add 10.7.9.0/24 via 10.8.11.8
ip route add 10.8.10.0/24 via 10.8.11.8
ip route add 10.9.12.0/24 via 10.8.11.8
ip route add 10.9.13.0/24 via 10.8.11.8
```

The smcroute software[1] must be installed on all hosts except the multicast tree's root node (tb6). The following script was used on tb11 in order to activate IP multicast forwarding:

Listing D.5: *Configuration of the smcroute multicast forwarding rules on tb11*

```
#!/bin/sh

# Forward incoming multicast packets coming from 10.8.11.8 on eth0
# and destined to 224.7.7.7 on interfaces eth1 and eth2
sudo smcroute -k
sudo smcroute -d
sudo smcroute -a eth0 10.8.11.8 224.7.7.7 eth1 eth2
sudo smcroute -a eth0 10.7.8.7 224.7.7.7 eth1 eth2
sudo smcroute -a eth0 10.6.7.6 224.7.7.7 eth1 eth2
```

On all multicast tree leaf nodes (i.e., tb14 to tb21) the smcroute daemon had to be configured as follows:

Listing D.6: *Configuration of the smcroute multicast forwarding rules on the multicast tree's leaf nodes tb14 to tb21*

```
#!/bin/sh

# configure as multicast receiver
smcroute -k
smcroute -d
smcroute -j eth0 224.7.7.7

# enables multicast ICMP packets to be echoed back
# (disabled by default within Ubuntu)
echo 0 | tee /proc/sys/net/ipv4/icmp_echo_ignore_broadcasts
```

---

[1]The evaluations used version 0.94.1-1 from the Ubuntu 10.10 repository

D.2 NSIS Specific Configuration Parameters

All multicast extensions were implemented in a dedicated development branch.
The code can be retrieved from:

```
$ svn co https://svn.tm.kit.edu/nsis/dist/nsis-ka/branches/20090723-multicast
```

On all hosts GIST must be configured to be aware of the used multicast destination address. Furthermore, the newly introduced artificial GIST response delay
must be set accordingly in the signaling entity's etc/nsis-ka.conf files:

```
[gist]
# List of IP addresses that should be considered by GIST to be local (used for
# multicast)
local-equiv-addrs = "224.7.7.7"

# Artificial GIST Response delay for IP multicast in milliseconds
multicast-response-delay = 20
```

Additionally on all multicast tree's leaf nodes (i.e., tb14 to tb21) the QoS NSLP
instance must be aware that it acts as last signaling hop for corresponding multicast
signaling sessions. This can be accomplished by setting the following parameter in
the signaling entity's etc/nsis-ka.conf files:

```
[qos-nslp]
# Last signaling hops of a multicast address must be explicitly
# subscribed to this particular multicast address
subscribed-multicast-groups = "224.7.7.7"
```

A sender-initiated resource reservation can then simply be established by tb6 as
follows:

Listing D.7: *Establishing a sender-initiated resource reservation on the multicast tree's*
root node tb6

```
$ cd 20090723-multicast/qos-nslp/src
$ sudo ./client 10.6.7.6 224.7.7.7
```

And a receiver-initiated resource reservation can be established by tb6 as follows:

Listing D.8: *Establishing a receiver-initiated resource reservation on the multicast*
tree's root node tb6

```
$ cd 20090723-multicast/qos-nslp/src
$ sudo ./client 10.6.7.6 224.7.7.7 r
```

Evaluation Resource Reservation Aggregation

The evaluation of the aggregation concepts was performed on a testbed PC which was equipped with an Intel Xeon X3430 quadcore CPU running at 2.40 GHz and 4 GB RAM. A 32 bit Ubuntu Linux 10.10 served as operating system with Linux kernel 2.6.35 and OMNeT++ was used in version 4.0p1.

The topology being created by ReaSE consisted of four stub ASes and one transit AS as depicted in Figure 6.32. The router-level topology of stub AS sas2 is illustrated in Figure E.1, the one for stub AS sas3 is illustrated in Figure E.2, and the one used at stub AS sas4 is illustrated in Figure E.3.

The code used to evaluate the aggregation concept can be retrieved via subversion from

```
https://svn.tm.kit.edu/nsis/dist/qos-nslp-ka/branches/20111025-qos-nslp-
    resource-aggregations
```

Within this repository the topology's ned file is located at

```
oppNSIS/models/qos_nslp/resource_aggregations/ned/topologies/
    InternetLikeDiss/topology.ned
```

and the omnetpp.ini file is located at

```
oppNSIS/models/qos_nslp/resource_aggregations/eval/scenarios/internet-
    like-diss/omnetpp.ini
```

Once everything has been setup correctly, the simulation can be started via

```
$ cd oppNSIS/models/qos_nslp/resource_aggregations/
$ ./qos_nslp_resource_aggregations -u Cmdenv
```

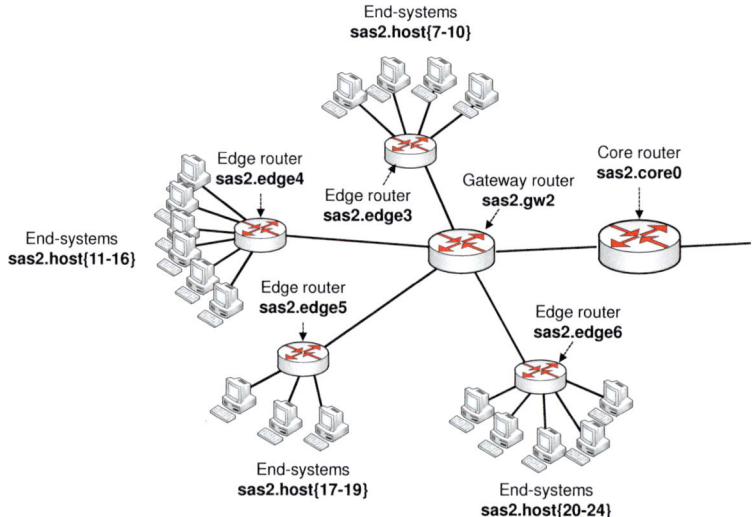

Figure E.1: *Topology used within stub AS sas2 for evaluation scenario*

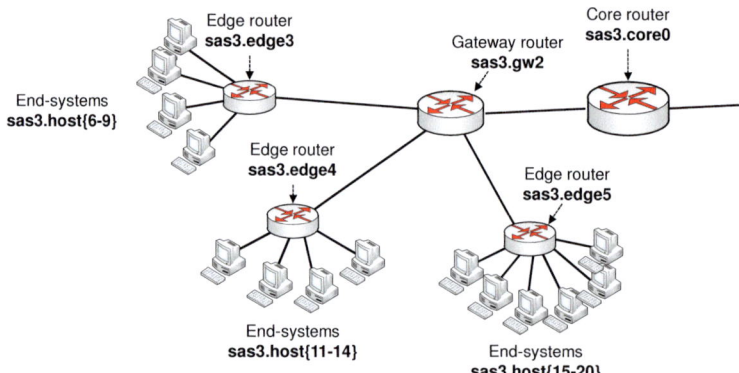

Figure E.2: *Topology used within stub AS sas3 for evaluation scenario*

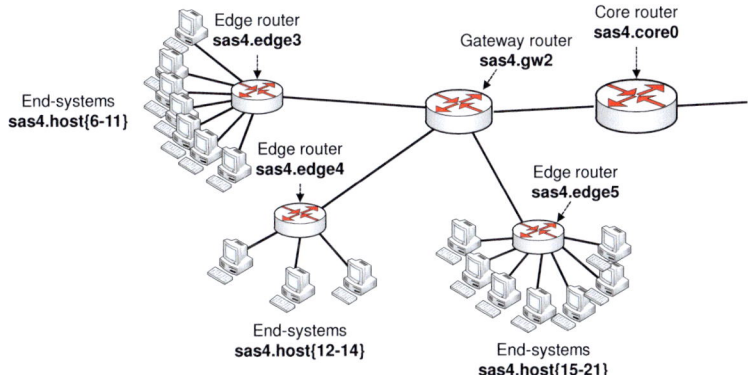

Figure E.3: *Topology used within stub AS sas4 for evaluation scenario*

Summary of Publications

Journal papers

- R. Bless, **M. Röhricht**. *Implementation and Evaluation of a NAT-Gateway for the General Internet Signaling Transport Protocol*. In: Scalable Computing: Practice and Experience, Vol. 11, No. 4, ISSN 1895-1767, pp. 329–343, December 2010

- R. Bless, **M. Röhricht**, and C. Werle. *Authenticated Quality-of-Service Signaling for Virtual Networks*. In: Journal of Communications, Vol. 7, No. 1, ISSN 1796-2021, pp. 17–27, January 2012

Peer-reviewed conference papers

- R. Bless and **M. Röhricht**. *QoS Support for Mobile Users using NSIS*. In L. Fratta et al., editor, Networking 2009, volume 5550 of Lecture Notes in Computer Science, pages 169–181, Aachen, Germany, May 2009. Springer.

- R. Bless and **M. Röhricht**. *Secure Signaling in Next Generation Networks with NSIS*. In IEEE International Conference on Communications (ICC 2009), 2009, pages 1–6, Dresden, Germany, June 2009. IEEE.

- R. Bless and **M. Röhricht**. *Integration of a GIST implementation into OMNeT++*. In Digital Proceedings of 3rd International Workshop on OMNeT++ (Hosted by SIMUTools 2010), pages 1–4, Malaga, Spain, March 2010. ICST.

- R. Bless and **M. Röhricht**. *End-to-End Quality-of-Service Support in Next Generation Networks with NSIS*. In IEEE International Conference on Communications (ICC 2010), 2010, pages 1–6, Cape Town, South Africa, May 2010. IEEE.

- R. Bless, **M. Röhricht**. *Quality-of-Service Signaling for Virtual Networks*. In proceedings of the 10th Würzburg Workshop on IP: Joint ITG, ITC, and Euro-NF Workshop "Visions of Future Generation Networks"(EuroView 2010), pages 1–2, Würzburg, Germany, August 2010.

- R. Bless, **M. Röhricht**. *Implementation and Evaluation of a NAT-Gateway for the General Internet Signaling Transport Protocol*. Proceedings of the 3rd IEEE International Workshop on Internet and Distributed Computing Systems

(IDCS 2010) (Hosted by HPCC 2010), pp. 659–664, Melbourne, Australia, September 2010

- R. Bless and **M. Röhricht**. *Advanced Quality-of-Service Signaling for IP Multicast* In ACM/IEEE International Workshop on Quality of Service (IWQoS 2011), San Jose, CA, USA, June 2011.

- R. Bless, **M. Röhricht**, and Christoph Werle. *Authenticated Setup of Virtual Links with Quality-of-Service Guarantees* In IEEE International Conference on Computer Communications and Networks (ICCCN 2011), Maui, HI, USA, July 2011.

- **M. Röhricht**, R. Bless. *Advanced Quality-of-Service Signaling for the Session Initiation Protocol (SIP)*. Proceedings of the first IEEE ICC 2012 Workshop on Telecommunications: from Research to Standards, Ottawa, Canada, June 2012

Bibliography

[AA97]   D. O. Awduche and E. Agu. "Mobile Extensions to RSVP." In: *Proceedings of the 6th IEEE International Conference on Computer Communications and Networks (ICCCN)*. IEEE. Las Vegas, NV, USA, Sept. 1997, pp. 132–136. ISBN: 0-8186-8186-1. DOI: `10.1109/ICCCN.1997.623302`.

[ABC99]   D. Ahlard, J. Bergkvist, and I. Cselenyi. *Boomerang Protocol Specification*. Internet-Draft draft-bergkvist-boomerang-spec-00. IETF, June 1999. URL: `http://tools.ietf.org/html/draft-bergkvist-boomerang-spec-00`.

[Akb09]   H. Akbaba. "Entwurf und Implementierung von Sicherheitsmechanismen für NSIS Protokolle." Advisor: Roland Bless, Martin Röhricht. Studienarbeit. Universität Karlsruhe (TH), Aug. 2009.

[AN97]   T. Aura and P. Nikander. "Stateless Connections." In: *Proceedings of the 1st International Conference on Information and Communications Security (ICICS)*. Ed. by Y. Han, T. Okamoto, and S. Qing. Vol. 1334. Lecture Notes in Computer Science. Beijing, China: Springer Berlin / Heidelberg, Nov. 1997, pp. 87–97. ISBN: 978-3-540-63696-0.

[Aru+08]   M. Arumaithurai et al. "Performance Study of the NSIS QoS-NSLP Protocol." In: *Proceedings of the IEEE Global Telecommunications Conference (GLOBECOM)*. IEEE. New Orleans, LA, USA, Nov. 2008. DOI: `10.1109/GLOCOM.2008.ECP.486`.

[BCA00]   J. Bergkvist, I. Cselenyi, and D. Ahlard. *Boomerang - A Simple Resource Reservation Framework for IP*. Internet-Draft draft-bergkvist-boomerang-framework-00. IETF, Nov. 2000. URL: `http://tools.ietf.org/html/draft-bergkvist-boomerang-framework-00`.

[BD04]   R. Bless and M. Doll. "Integration of the FreeBSD TCP/IP-stack into the discrete event simulator OMNet++." In: *Proceedings of the 36th Winter simulation conference (WSC)*. Washington, D.C., USA, Dec. 2004, pp. 1556–1561. ISBN: 0-7803-8786-4. DOI: `10.1109/WSC.2004.1371498`.

[BD07]   R. Bless and M. Doll. *Inter-Domain Reservation Aggregation for QoS NSLP*. Internet-Draft draft-bless-nsis-resv-aggr-01.txt (Work in progress). IETF, July 2007. URL: `http://tools.ietf.org/html/draft-bless-nsis-resv-aggr-01`.

[BL02]   B. Braden and B. Lindell. *A Two-Level Architecture for Internet Signaling*. Internet-Draft draft-braden-2level-signal-arch-01. IETF, Nov. 2002. URL: `http://tools.ietf.org/html/draft-braden-2level-signal-arch-01`.

[Ble+05]   R. Bless et al. *Sichere Netzwerkkommunikation: Grundlagen, Protokolle und Architekturen*. First. Springer Berlin Heidelberg, 2005.

[Ble+07]   R. Bless et al. "A quality-of-service signaling architecture for seamless handover support in next generation, IP-based mobile networks." In: *Wireless Personal Communications* 43.3 (2007), pp. 817–835. ISSN: 0929-6212. DOI: `10.1007/s11277-007-9260-9`.

[Ble+12a]   R. Bless et al. *NSIS-ka – A free C++ implementation of NSIS protocols*. `http://www.nsis-ka.org/`. Institute of Telematics, Karlsruhe Institute of Technology (KIT), Dec. 2012.

[Ble+12b]   R. Bless et al. *OppBSD – A FreeBSD Network Stack integrated into OMNeT++*. Dec. 2012. URL: `https://svn.tm.kit.edu/trac/OppBSD/`.

[Ble02]   R. Bless. "Integriertes Management qualitätsbasierter Internetkommunikationsdienste." PhD thesis. Universität Karlsruhe (TH), Dec. 2002.

[Ble04]   R. Bless. "Towards Scalable Management of QoS-based End-to-End Services." In: *Proceedings of the IEEE/IFIP Network Operations and Management Symposium (NOMS)*. Vol. 1. IEEE/IFIP. Seoul, Korea, Apr. 2004, pp. 293–306. DOI: `10.1109/NOMS.2004.1317668`.

[Ble10]   R. Bless. *An Explicit Signaling Target Message Routing Method (EST-MRM) for the General Internet Signaling Transport (GIST) Protocol*. Internet-Draft draft-bless-nsis-est-mrm-02.txt (Work in progress). IETF, June 2010. URL: `http://tools.ietf.org/html/draft-bless-nsis-est-mrm-02`.

[BR09a]   R. Bless and M. Röhricht. "QoS Support for Mobile Users using NSIS."
           In: *Networking*. Ed. by L. Fratta et al. Vol. 5550. Lecture Notes in
           Computer Science. Springer. Aachen, Germany, May 2009, pp. 169–
           181. ISBN: 978-3-642-01398-0. DOI: 10.1007/978-3-642-01399-
           7_14.

[BR09b]   R. Bless and M. Röhricht. "Secure Signaling in Next Generation Net-
           works with NSIS." In: *Proceedings of the IEEE International Confer-
           ence on Communications (ICC)*. IEEE. Dresden, Germany, June 2009.
           DOI: 10.1109/ICC.2009.5199441.

[BR10a]   R. Bless and M. Röhricht. "Implementation and Evaluation of a
           NAT-Gateway for the General Internet Signaling Transport Protocol."
           In: *Scalable Computing: Practice and Experience* 11.4 (Dec. 2010),
           pp. 329–343. ISSN: 1895-1767.

[BR10b]   R. Bless and M. Röhricht. "Integration of a GIST implementation into
           OMNeT++." In: *Proceedings of the 3rd ICST International Workshop
           on OMNeT++*. ICST. Torremolinos, Malaga, Spain, Mar. 2010. ISBN:
           978-963-9799-87-5. DOI: 10.4108/ICST.SIMUTOOLS2010.8698.

[BR11]   R. Bless and M. Röhricht. "Advanced Quality-of-Service Signaling for
           IP Multicast." In: *Proceedings of the 19th ACM/IEEE International
           Workshop on Quality of Service (IWQoS)*. ACM/IEEE. San Jose, CA,
           USA, June 2011. DOI: 10.1109/IWQOS.2011.5931345.

[BRW12]   R. Bless, M. Röhricht, and C. Werle. "Authenticated Quality-of-Service
           Signaling for Virtual Networks." In: *Journal of Communications* 7.1
           (Jan. 2012), pp. 17–27. ISSN: 1796-2021.

[CH00]   W.-T. Chen and L.-C. Huang. "RSVP Mobility Support: A Signaling Pro-
           tocol for Integrated Services Internet with Mobile Hosts." In: *Proceed-
           ings of the 19th Annual Joint Conference of the IEEE Computer and
           Communications Societies (INFOCOM)*. Vol. 3. IEEE. Tel Aviv, Israel,
           Mar. 2000, pp. 1283–1292. DOI: 10.1109/INFCOM.2000.832519.

[Che+00]   J.-C. Chen et al. "A QoS Architecture for Future Wireless IP Networks."
           In: *Proceedings of the 12th IASTED International Conference on
           Parallel and Distributed Computing and Systems (PDCS)*. Las Vegas,
           NV, USA, Nov. 2000.

[Cis12a]   Cisco Systems Inc. *Cisco Visual Networking Index: Forecast and Methodology, 2011–2016.* http://www.cisco.com/en/US/solutions/collateral/ns341/ns525/ns537/ns705/ns827/white_paper_c11-481360.pdf. May 2012.

[Cis12b]   Cisco Systems Inc. *Cisco Visual Networking Index: Global Mobile Data Traffic Forecast Update, 2011–2016.* http://www.cisco.com/en/US/solutions/collateral/ns341/ns525/ns537/ns705/ns827/white_paper_c11-520862.pdf. Feb. 2012.

[Cla88]   D. D. Clark. "The Design Philosophy of the DARPA Internet Protocols." In: *SIGCOMM Computer Communication Review* 18.4 (Aug. 1988), pp. 106–114. ISSN: 0146-4833. DOI: 10.1145/52325.52336.

[Cro+03]   J. Crowcroft et al. "QoS's Downfall: At the bottom, or not at all!" In: *Proceedings of the ACM SIGCOMM workshop on Revisiting IP QoS: What have we learned, why do we care?* RIPQoS '03. Karlsruhe, Germany: ACM, 2003, pp. 109–114. ISBN: 1-58113-748-6. DOI: 10.1145/944592.944594.

[DC90]   S. E. Deering and D. R. Cheriton. "Multicast Routing in Datagram Internetworks and Extended LANs." In: *ACM Transactions on Computer Systems* 8 (2 May 1990), pp. 85–110. ISSN: 0734-2071. DOI: 10.1145/78952.78953.

[Det10]   M. Dettling. "Nahtlose Dienstgüteunterstützung für mobile Knoten durch Anticipated Handover mit QoS NSLP." Advisor: Roland Bless, Martin Röhricht. Studienarbeit. Karlsruhe Institute of Technology (KIT), Feb. 2010.

[Det12]   M. Dettling. "Skalierbarkeit qualiatsunsutzter Internetkommunikation durch Aggregation von Ressourcen-Reservierungen mit QoS NSLP." Advisor: Roland Bless, Martin Röhricht. Diplomarbeit. Karlsruhe Institute of Technology (KIT), Mar. 2012.

[DR01]   J. Daemen and V. Rijmen. "The Wide Trail Design Strategy." In: *Proceedings of the 8th IMA International Conference on Cryptography and Coding (IMA).* Ed. by B. Honary. Vol. 2260. Lecture Notes in Computer Science. Cirencester, UK: Springer Berlin / Heidelberg, 2001, pp. 222–238. ISBN: 978-3-540-43026-1. DOI: 10.1007/3-540-45325-3_20.

[Feh+99]   G. Fehér et al. "Boomerang – A Simple Protocol for Resource Reservation in IP Networks." In: *Proceedings of the IEEE Workshop on QoS Support for Real-Time Internet Applications*. IEEE. Vancouver, Canada, June 1999.

[FJ93]   S. Floyd and V. Jacobson. "The Synchronization of Periodic Routing Messages." In: *ACM SIGCOMM Computer Communications Review* 23.4 (1993), pp. 33–44. ISSN: 0146-4833. DOI: 10.1145/167954. 166241.

[FKT02]   X. Fu, C. Kappler, and H. Tschofenig. *Analysis on RSVP Regarding Multicast*. Tech. rep. IFI–TB–2002–001. http://filepool.informatik. uni-goettingen.de/publication/tmg/2002/XF_CK_2002_01. pdf. Göttingen, Germany: Institut für Informatik, Georg-August-Universität Göttingen, Oct. 2002.

[FP01]   S. Floyd and V. Paxson. "Difficulties in Simulating the Internet." In: *IEEE/ACM Transactions on Networking* 9.4 (Aug. 2001), pp. 392–403. ISSN: 1063-6692. DOI: 10.1109/90.944338.

[FS07]   S. Felis and M. Stiemerling. "Securing a Path-Coupled NAT/Firewall Signaling Protocol." In: *IP Operations and Management*. Ed. by D. Medhi et al. Vol. 4786. Lecture Notes in Computer Science. Springer Berlin / Heidelberg, 2007, pp. 61–72. DOI: 10.1007/978-3-540- 75853-2_6.

[FTH06]   X. Fu, H. Tschofenig, and D. Hogrefe. "Beyond QoS signaling: A new generic IP signaling framework." In: *Computer Networks* 50.17 (Dec. 2006), pp. 3416–3433. ISSN: 1389-1286. DOI: 10.1016/j.comnet. 2006.01.006.

[Fu+05]   X. Fu et al. "NSIS: A New Extensible IP Signaling Protocol Suite." In: *IEEE Communications Magazine* 43.10 (Oct. 2005), pp. 133–141. ISSN: 0163-6804. DOI: 10.1109/MCOM.2005.1522137.

[Fu+09]   X. Fu et al. "Overhead and Performance Study of the General Internet Signaling Transport (GIST) Protocol." In: *IEEE/ACM Transactions on Networking* 17.1 (Feb. 2009), pp. 158–171. ISSN: 1063-6692. DOI: 10.1109/TNET.2008.926502.

[FV90]   D. Ferrari and D. C. Verma. "A Scheme for Real-Time Channel Estab-
            lishment in Wide-Area Networks." In: *IEEE Journal on Selected Areas
            in Communications* 8.3 (Apr. 1990), pp. 368–379. ISSN: 0733-8716.
            DOI: `10.1109/49.53013`.

[GDB03]   R. Greco, L. Delgrossi, and M. Brunner. "Towards RSVP Version 2." In:
            Quality of Service in Multiservice IP Networks. Ed. by M. A. Marsan
            et al. Vol. 2601. Lecture Notes in Computer Science. Springer Berlin
            Heidelberg, 2003, pp. 704–716. ISBN: 978-3-540-00604-6. DOI: `10.
            1007/3-540-36480-3_51`.

[GS08]   T. Gamer and M. Scharf. "Realistic Simulation Environments for
            IP-based Networks." In: *Proceedings of the 1st ICST International
            Workshop on OMNeT++.* ICST. Marseille, France, Mar. 2008. ISBN:
            978-963-9799-20-2. DOI: `10.4108/ICST.SIMUTOOLS2008.3079`.

[Han06]   M. Handley. "Why the Internet only just works." In: *BT Technology
            Journal* 24.3 (3 July 2006), pp. 119–129. ISSN: 1358-3948. DOI:
            `10.1007/s10550-006-0084-z`.

[Har09]   S. Hartte. "Integration einer NSIS-Implementierung in OMNeT++."
            Advisor: Roland Bless, Martin Röhricht. Studienarbeit. Universität
            Karlsruhe (TH), Aug. 2009.

[HC03]   N.-F. Huang and W.-E. Chen. "RSVP Extensions for Real-Time Services
            in Hierarchical Mobile IPv6." In: *Mobile Networks and Applications*
            8.6 (Dec. 2003), pp. 625–634. ISSN: 1383-469X. DOI: `10.1023/A:
            1026022325876`.

[Hil+05]   J. Hillebrand et al. "Quality-of-Service Management for IP-based Mo-
            bile Networks." In: *Proceeding of the IEEE Wireless Communications
            and Networking Conference (WCNC).* Vol. 2. IEEE. New Orleans, USA,
            Mar. 2005, pp. 1248–1253. DOI: `10.1109/WCNC.2005.1424688`.

[ITU91]   ITU. *Security architecture for Open Systems Interconnection for
            CCITT applications.* Recommendation X.800. Geneva, Switzerland:
            International Telecommunications Union, Mar. 1991.

[Ji+07]   P. Ji et al. "A Comparison of Hard-State and Soft-State Signaling
            Protocols." In: *IEEE/ACM Transactions on Networking* 15.2 (Apr.
            2007), pp. 281–294. ISSN: 1063-6692. DOI: `10.1109/TNET.2007.
            892849`.

[Lab+10]   C. Labovitz et al. "Internet Inter-Domain Traffic." In: *Proceedings of the ACM SIGCOMM 2010 conference*. New Delhi, India: ACM, Aug. 2010, pp. 75–86. ISBN: 978-1-4503-0201-2. DOI: 10.1145/1851182.1851194.

[Lai08]   M. Laier. "Analysis and Design of Mobility Support for QoS NSLP." Advisor: Roland Bless, Martin Röhricht. Studienarbeit. Universität Karlsruhe (TH), Dec. 2008.

[Lee+00]   S.-B. Lee et al. "INSIGNIA: An IP-Based Quality of Service Framework for Mobile ad Hoc Networks." In: *Journal of Parallel and Distributed Computing* 60.4 (2000), pp. 374–406. ISSN: 0743-7315. DOI: 10.1006/jpdc.1999.1613.

[Lee+99]   S.-B. Lee et al. *INSIGNIA*. Internet-Draft draft-ietf-manet-insignia-01. IETF, Oct. 1999. URL: http://tools.ietf.org/html/draft-ietf-manet-insignia-01.

[Len10]   M. Lenk. "Multicast-Erweiterung der NSIS-Protokollfamilie zur Dienstgütesignalisierung." Advisor: Roland Bless, Martin Röhricht. Diplomarbeit. Karlsruhe Institute of Technology (KIT), Mar. 2010.

[Li+04]   L. Li et al. "A First-Principles Approach to Understanding the Internet's Router-level Topology." In: *Proceedings of the ACM SIGCOMM 2004 conference*. Portland, Oregon, USA: ACM, Aug. 2004, pp. 3–14. ISBN: 1-58113-862-8. DOI: 10.1145/1015467.1015470.

[LM04]   Z. Li and P. Mohapatra. "QRON: QoS-Aware Routing in Overlay Networks." In: *IEEE Journal on Selected Areas in Communications* 22.1 (Jan. 2004), pp. 29–40. ISSN: 0733-8716. DOI: 10.1109/JSAC.2003.818782.

[LMD06]   S. Lai, Y. Ma, and H. Deng. "HO-RSVP: a protocol providing QoS support for seamless handover between wireless networks." In: *Proceedings of the 2nd ACM International Workshop on Quality of Service & Security for Wireless and Mobile Networks (Q2SWinet)*. ACM. Torremolinos, Malaga, Spain, Oct. 2006, pp. 103–110. ISBN: 1-59593-486-3. DOI: 10.1145/1163673.1163693.

[LSP08]   G. Lampropoulos, A. K. Salkintzis, and N. Passas. "Media-Independent Handover for Seamless Service Provision in Heterogeneous Networks." In: *IEEE Communications Magazine* 46.1 (Jan. 2008), pp. 64–71. ISSN: 0163-6804. DOI: 10.1109/MCOM.2008.4427232.

[MA04]   B. Moon and A. H. Aghvami. "Quality-of-Service Mechanisms in All-IP
            Wireless Access Networks." In: *IEEE Journal on Selected Areas in
            Communications* 22.5 (June 2004), pp. 873–888. ISSN: 0733-8716.
            DOI: 10.1109/JSAC.2004.826924.

[Man+02]   J. Manner et al. "Evaluation of mobility and quality of service in-
            teraction." In: *Computer Networks* 38.2 (2002), pp. 137–163. ISSN:
            1389-1286. DOI: 10.1016/S1389-1286(01)00255-9.

[MJV96]   S. McCanne, V. Jacobson, and M. Vetterli. "Receiver-driven Layered
            Multicast." In: *Conference proceedings on Applications, technolo-
            gies, architectures, and protocols for computer communications*. SIG-
            COMM '96. Palo Alto, California, USA: ACM, Aug. 1996, pp. 117–130.
            ISBN: 0-89791-790-1. DOI: 10.1145/248156.248168.

[MST07]   J. Manner, M. Stiemerling, and H. Tschofenig. *Authorization for NSIS
            Signaling Layer Protocols*. Internet-Draft draft-manner-nsis-nslp-auth-
            03. IETF, Mar. 2007. URL: http://tools.ietf.org/html/draft-
            manner-nsis-nslp-auth-03.

[MVZ11]   D. Martin, L. Völker, and M. Zitterbart. "A Flexible Framework for
            Future Internet Design, Assessment, and Operation." In: *Computer
            Networks* 55.4 (Feb. 2011), pp. 910–918. ISSN: 1389-1286. DOI: 10.
            1016/j.comnet.2010.12.015.

[Nah+11]   K. Nahrstedt et al. "QoS and resource management in distributed
            interactive multimedia environments." In: *Multimedia Tools Appl.* 51
            (1 Jan. 2011), pp. 99–132. ISSN: 1380-7501. DOI: 10.1007/s11042-
            010-0627-7.

[NIS08]   National Institute of Standards and Technology. *Secure Hash Stan-
            dard (SHS)*. Federal Information Processing Standard (FIPS) 180-3.
            Department of Commerce, Oct. 2008.

[Per02]   C. E. Perkins. "Mobile IP." In: *IEEE Communications Magazine* 40.5
            (May 2002), pp. 66–82. ISSN: 0163-6804. DOI: 10.1109/MCOM.2002.
            1006976.

[PHS00a]   P. Pan, E. Hahne, and H. Schulzrinne. *BGRP: A Framework for Scalable
            Resource Reservation*. Internet-Draft draft-pan-bgrp-framework-00.
            IETF, Jan. 2000. URL: http://tools.ietf.org/html/draft-pan-
            bgrp-framework-00.

[PHS00b]   P. P. Pan, E. L. Hahne, and H. G. Schulzrinne. "BGRP: Sink-Tree-Based Aggregation for Inter-Domain Reservations." In: *Journal of Communications and Networks* 2 (June 2000), pp. 157–167.

[PHS99]   P. Pan, E. L. Hahne, and H. Schulzrinne. *BGRP: A Tree-Based Aggregation Protocol for Inter-Domain Reservations*. Tech. rep. CUCS-029-99. Columbia University, Dec. 1999.

[PS07a]   S. G. Polito and H. Schulzrinne. "Authentication and Authorization Method in Multi-domain, Multi-provider Networks." In: *Proceedings of the 3rd EURO-NGI Conference on Next Generation Internet Networks (NGI)*. Trondheim, Norway, May 2007, pp. 174–181. ISBN: 1-4244-0857-1. DOI: 10.1109/NGI.2007.371213.

[PS07b]   R. Prior and S. Sargento. "Inter-Domain QoS Routing with Virtual Trunks." In: *Proceedings of the IEEE International Conference on Communications (ICC)*. IEEE. Glasgow, Scotland, June 2007, pp. 139–146. DOI: 10.1109/ICC.2007.31.

[PS99]   P. Pan and H. Schulzrinne. "YESSIR: A Simple Reservation Mechanism for the Internet." In: *ACM SIGCOMM Computer Communication Review* 29 (2 Apr. 1999), pp. 89–101. ISSN: 0146-4833. DOI: 10.1145/505733.505740.

[Rai+12]   C. Raiciu et al. "How Hard Can It Be? Designing and Implementing a Deployable Multipath TCP." In: *Proceedings of the 9th conference on Networked Systems Design and Implementation (NSDI)*. NSDI'12. San Jose, CA: USENIX Association, Apr. 2012.

[RB12]   M. Röhricht and R. Bless. "Advanced Quality-of-Service Signaling for the Session Initiation Protocol (SIP)." In: *Proceedings of the 1st IEEE ICC 2012 Workshop on Telecommunications: from Research to Standards*. IEEE. Ottawa, Canada, June 2012.

[RFC1112] S. Deering. *Host extensions for IP multicasting*. RFC 1112 (Standard). Updated by RFC 2236. Internet Engineering Task Force, Aug. 1989. URL: http://www.ietf.org/rfc/rfc1112.txt.

[RFC1190] C. Topolcic. *Experimental Internet Stream Protocol: Version 2 (ST-II)*. RFC 1190 (Experimental). Obsoleted by RFC 1819. Internet Engineering Task Force, Oct. 1990. URL: http://www.ietf.org/rfc/rfc1190.txt.

[RFC1321]   R. Rivest. *The MD5 Message-Digest Algorithm*. RFC 1321 (Informa-
            tional). Updated by RFC 6151. Internet Engineering Task Force, Apr.
            1992. URL: http://www.ietf.org/rfc/rfc1321.txt.

[RFC1633]   R. Braden, D. Clark, and S. Shenker. *Integrated Services in the Inter-
            net Architecture: an Overview*. RFC 1633 (Informational). Internet
            Engineering Task Force, June 1994. URL: http://www.ietf.org/
            rfc/rfc1633.txt.

[RFC1819]   L. Delgrossi and L. Berger. *Internet Stream Protocol Version 2 (ST2)
            Protocol Specification - Version ST2+*. RFC 1819 (Experimental).
            Internet Engineering Task Force, Aug. 1995. URL: http://www.ietf.
            org/rfc/rfc1819.txt.

[RFC1958]   B. Carpenter. *Architectural Principles of the Internet*. RFC 1958 (In-
            formational). Updated by RFC 3439. Internet Engineering Task Force,
            June 1996. URL: http://www.ietf.org/rfc/rfc1958.txt.

[RFC2104]   H. Krawczyk, M. Bellare, and R. Canetti. *HMAC: Keyed-Hashing
            for Message Authentication*. RFC 2104 (Informational). Updated by
            RFC 6151. Internet Engineering Task Force, Feb. 1997. URL: http:
            //www.ietf.org/rfc/rfc2104.txt.

[RFC2113]   D. Katz. *IP Router Alert Option*. RFC 2113 (Proposed Standard).
            Updated by RFCs 5350, 6398. Internet Engineering Task Force, Feb.
            1997. URL: http://www.ietf.org/rfc/rfc2113.txt.

[RFC2205]   R. Braden et al. *Resource ReSerVation Protocol (RSVP) – Version 1
            Functional Specification*. RFC 2205 (Proposed Standard). Updated by
            RFCs 2750, 3936, 4495, 5946, 6437. Internet Engineering Task Force,
            Sept. 1997. URL: http://www.ietf.org/rfc/rfc2205.txt.

[RFC2208]   A. Mankin et al. *Resource ReSerVation Protocol (RSVP) – Version 1
            Applicability Statement Some Guidelines on Deployment*. RFC 2208
            (Informational). Internet Engineering Task Force, Sept. 1997. URL:
            http://www.ietf.org/rfc/rfc2208.txt.

[RFC2210]   J. Wroclawski. *The Use of RSVP with IETF Integrated Services*. RFC
            2210 (Proposed Standard). Internet Engineering Task Force, Sept.
            1997. URL: http://www.ietf.org/rfc/rfc2210.txt.

[RFC2211]   J. Wroclawski. *Specification of the Controlled-Load Network Element
            Service*. RFC 2211 (Proposed Standard). Internet Engineering Task
            Force, Sept. 1997. URL: http://www.ietf.org/rfc/rfc2211.txt.

[RFC2212]   S. Shenker, C. Partridge, and R. Guerin. *Specification of Guaranteed Quality of Service*. RFC 2212 (Proposed Standard). Internet Engineering Task Force, Sept. 1997. URL: http://www.ietf.org/rfc/rfc2212.txt.

[RFC2386]   E. Crawley et al. *A Framework for QoS-based Routing in the Internet*. RFC 2386 (Informational). Internet Engineering Task Force, Aug. 1998. URL: http://www.ietf.org/rfc/rfc2386.txt.

[RFC2474]   K. Nichols et al. *Definition of the Differentiated Services Field (DS Field) in the IPv4 and IPv6 Headers*. RFC 2474 (Proposed Standard). Updated by RFCs 3168, 3260. Internet Engineering Task Force, Dec. 1998. URL: http://www.ietf.org/rfc/rfc2474.txt.

[RFC2475]   S. Blake et al. *An Architecture for Differentiated Services*. RFC 2475 (Informational). Updated by RFC 3260. Internet Engineering Task Force, Dec. 1998. URL: http://www.ietf.org/rfc/rfc2475.txt.

[RFC2597]   J. Heinanen et al. *Assured Forwarding PHB Group*. RFC 2597 (Proposed Standard). Updated by RFC 3260. Internet Engineering Task Force, June 1999. URL: http://www.ietf.org/rfc/rfc2597.txt.

[RFC2711]   C. Partridge and A. Jackson. *IPv6 Router Alert Option*. RFC 2711 (Proposed Standard). Updated by RFC 6398. Internet Engineering Task Force, Oct. 1999. URL: http://www.ietf.org/rfc/rfc2711.txt.

[RFC2747]   F. Baker, B. Lindell, and M. Talwar. *RSVP Cryptographic Authentication*. RFC 2747 (Proposed Standard). Updated by RFC 3097. Internet Engineering Task Force, Jan. 2000. URL: http://www.ietf.org/rfc/rfc2747.txt.

[RFC2750]   S. Herzog. *RSVP Extensions for Policy Control*. RFC 2750 (Proposed Standard). Internet Engineering Task Force, Jan. 2000. URL: http://www.ietf.org/rfc/rfc2750.txt.

[RFC2990]   G. Huston. *Next Steps for the IP QoS Architecture*. RFC 2990 (Informational). Internet Engineering Task Force, Nov. 2000. URL: http://www.ietf.org/rfc/rfc2990.txt.

[RFC2998]   Y. Bernet et al. *A Framework for Integrated Services Operation over Diffserv Networks*. RFC 2998 (Informational). Internet Engineering Task Force, Nov. 2000. URL: http://www.ietf.org/rfc/rfc2998.txt.

[RFC3031] E. Rosen, A. Viswanathan, and R. Callon. *Multiprotocol Label Switching Architecture*. RFC 3031 (Proposed Standard). Updated by RFC 6178. Internet Engineering Task Force, Jan. 2001. URL: http://www.ietf.org/rfc/rfc3031.txt.

[RFC3097] R. Braden and L. Zhang. *RSVP Cryptographic Authentication – Updated Message Type Value*. RFC 3097 (Proposed Standard). Internet Engineering Task Force, Apr. 2001. URL: http://www.ietf.org/rfc/rfc3097.txt.

[RFC3175] F. Baker et al. *Aggregation of RSVP for IPv4 and IPv6 Reservations*. RFC 3175 (Proposed Standard). Updated by RFC 5350. Internet Engineering Task Force, Sept. 2001. URL: http://www.ietf.org/rfc/rfc3175.txt.

[RFC3182] S. Yadav et al. *Identity Representation for RSVP*. RFC 3182 (Proposed Standard). Internet Engineering Task Force, Oct. 2001. URL: http://www.ietf.org/rfc/rfc3182.txt.

[RFC3246] B. Davie et al. *An Expedited Forwarding PHB (Per-Hop Behavior)*. RFC 3246 (Proposed Standard). Internet Engineering Task Force, Mar. 2002. URL: http://www.ietf.org/rfc/rfc3246.txt.

[RFC3247] A. Charny et al. *Supplemental Information for the New Definition of the EF PHB (Expedited Forwarding Per-Hop Behavior)*. RFC 3247 (Informational). Internet Engineering Task Force, Mar. 2002. URL: http://www.ietf.org/rfc/rfc3247.txt.

[RFC3260] D. Grossman. *New Terminology and Clarifications for Diffserv*. RFC 3260 (Informational). Internet Engineering Task Force, Apr. 2002. URL: http://www.ietf.org/rfc/rfc3260.txt.

[RFC3261] J. Rosenberg et al. *SIP: Session Initiation Protocol*. RFC 3261 (Proposed Standard). Updated by RFCs 3265, 3853, 4320, 4916, 5393, 5621, 5626, 5630, 5922, 5954, 6026, 6141, 6665. Internet Engineering Task Force, June 2002. URL: http://www.ietf.org/rfc/rfc3261.txt.

[RFC3290] Y. Bernet et al. *An Informal Management Model for Diffserv Routers*. RFC 3290 (Informational). Internet Engineering Task Force, May 2002. URL: http://www.ietf.org/rfc/rfc3290.txt.

[RFC3376]   B. Cain et al. *Internet Group Management Protocol, Version 3*. RFC 3376 (Proposed Standard). Updated by RFC 4604. Internet Engineering Task Force, Oct. 2002. URL: http://www.ietf.org/rfc/rfc3376.txt.

[RFC3439]   R. Bush and D. Meyer. *Some Internet Architectural Guidelines and Philosophy*. RFC 3439 (Informational). Internet Engineering Task Force, Dec. 2002. URL: http://www.ietf.org/rfc/rfc3439.txt.

[RFC3520]   L.-N. Hamer et al. *Session Authorization Policy Element*. RFC 3520 (Proposed Standard). Internet Engineering Task Force, Apr. 2003. URL: http://www.ietf.org/rfc/rfc3520.txt.

[RFC3521]   L.-N. Hamer, B. Gage, and H. Shieh. *Framework for Session Setup with Media Authorization*. RFC 3521 (Informational). Internet Engineering Task Force, Apr. 2003. URL: http://www.ietf.org/rfc/rfc3521.txt.

[RFC3550]   H. Schulzrinne et al. *RTP: A Transport Protocol for Real-Time Applications*. RFC 3550 (Standard). Updated by RFCs 5506, 5761, 6051, 6222. Internet Engineering Task Force, July 2003. URL: http://www.ietf.org/rfc/rfc3550.txt.

[RFC3564]   F. L. Faucheur and W. Lai. *Requirements for Support of Differentiated Services-aware MPLS Traffic Engineering*. RFC 3564 (Informational). Updated by RFC 5462. Internet Engineering Task Force, July 2003. URL: http://www.ietf.org/rfc/rfc3564.txt.

[RFC3726]   M. Brunner. *Requirements for Signaling Protocols*. RFC 3726 (Informational). Internet Engineering Task Force, Apr. 2004. URL: http://www.ietf.org/rfc/rfc3726.txt.

[RFC3748]   B. Aboba et al. *Extensible Authentication Protocol (EAP)*. RFC 3748 (Proposed Standard). Updated by RFC 5247. Internet Engineering Task Force, June 2004. URL: http://www.ietf.org/rfc/rfc3748.txt.

[RFC4066]   M. Liebsch et al. *Candidate Access Router Discovery (CARD)*. RFC 4066 (Experimental). Internet Engineering Task Force, July 2005. URL: http://www.ietf.org/rfc/rfc4066.txt.

[RFC4080]   R. Hancock et al. *Next Steps in Signaling (NSIS): Framework*. RFC 4080 (Informational). Internet Engineering Task Force, June 2005. URL: http://www.ietf.org/rfc/rfc4080.txt.

[RFC4081] H. Tschofenig and D. Kroeselberg. *Security Threats for Next Steps in Signaling (NSIS)*. RFC 4081 (Informational). Internet Engineering Task Force, June 2005. URL: `http://www.ietf.org/rfc/rfc4081.txt`.

[RFC4094] J. Manner and X. Fu. *Analysis of Existing Quality-of-Service Signaling Protocols*. RFC 4094 (Informational). Internet Engineering Task Force, May 2005. URL: `http://www.ietf.org/rfc/rfc4094.txt`.

[RFC4120] C. Neuman et al. *The Kerberos Network Authentication Service (V5)*. RFC 4120 (Proposed Standard). Updated by RFCs 4537, 5021, 5896, 6111, 6112, 6113, 6649. Internet Engineering Task Force, July 2005. URL: `http://www.ietf.org/rfc/rfc4120.txt`.

[RFC4124] F. L. Faucheur. *Protocol Extensions for Support of Diffserv-aware MPLS Traffic Engineering*. RFC 4124 (Proposed Standard). Internet Engineering Task Force, June 2005. URL: `http://www.ietf.org/rfc/rfc4124.txt`.

[RFC4230] H. Tschofenig and R. Graveman. *RSVP Security Properties*. RFC 4230 (Informational). Internet Engineering Task Force, Dec. 2005. URL: `http://www.ietf.org/rfc/rfc4230.txt`.

[RFC4270] P. Hoffman and B. Schneier. *Attacks on Cryptographic Hashes in Internet Protocols*. RFC 4270 (Informational). Internet Engineering Task Force, Nov. 2005. URL: `http://www.ietf.org/rfc/rfc4270.txt`.

[RFC4295] G. Keeni et al. *Mobile IPv6 Management Information Base*. RFC 4295 (Proposed Standard). Internet Engineering Task Force, Apr. 2006. URL: `http://www.ietf.org/rfc/rfc4295.txt`.

[RFC4949] R. Shirey. *Internet Security Glossary, Version 2*. RFC 4949 (Informational). Internet Engineering Task Force, Aug. 2007. URL: `http://www.ietf.org/rfc/rfc4949.txt`.

[RFC5380] H. Soliman et al. *Hierarchical Mobile IPv6 (HMIPv6) Mobility Management*. RFC 5380 (Proposed Standard). Internet Engineering Task Force, Oct. 2008. URL: `http://www.ietf.org/rfc/rfc5380.txt`.

[RFC5905] D. Mills et al. *Network Time Protocol Version 4: Protocol and Algorithms Specification*. RFC 5905 (Proposed Standard). Internet Engineering Task Force, June 2010. URL: `http://www.ietf.org/rfc/rfc5905.txt`.

[RFC5944]   C. Perkins. *IP Mobility Support for IPv4, Revised*. RFC 5944 (Proposed Standard). Internet Engineering Task Force, Nov. 2010. URL: http://www.ietf.org/rfc/rfc5944.txt.

[RFC5971]   H. Schulzrinne and R. Hancock. *GIST: General Internet Signalling Transport*. RFC 5971 (Experimental). Internet Engineering Task Force, Oct. 2010. URL: http://www.ietf.org/rfc/rfc5971.txt.

[RFC5973]   M. Stiemerling et al. *NAT/Firewall NSIS Signaling Layer Protocol (NSLP)*. RFC 5973 (Experimental). Internet Engineering Task Force, Oct. 2010. URL: http://www.ietf.org/rfc/rfc5973.txt.

[RFC5974]   J. Manner, G. Karagiannis, and A. McDonald. *NSIS Signaling Layer Protocol (NSLP) for Quality-of-Service Signaling*. RFC 5974 (Experimental). Internet Engineering Task Force, Oct. 2010. URL: http://www.ietf.org/rfc/rfc5974.txt.

[RFC5975]   G. Ash et al. *QSPEC Template for the Quality-of-Service NSIS Signaling Layer Protocol (NSLP)*. RFC 5975 (Experimental). Internet Engineering Task Force, Oct. 2010. URL: http://www.ietf.org/rfc/rfc5975.txt.

[RFC5979]   C. Shen et al. *NSIS Operation over IP Tunnels*. RFC 5979 (Experimental). Internet Engineering Task Force, Mar. 2011. URL: http://www.ietf.org/rfc/rfc5979.txt.

[RFC5980]   T. Sanda et al. *NSIS Protocol Operation in Mobile Environments*. RFC 5980 (Informational). Internet Engineering Task Force, Mar. 2011. URL: http://www.ietf.org/rfc/rfc5980.txt.

[RFC5981]   J. Manner et al. *Authorization for NSIS Signaling Layer Protocols*. RFC 5981 (Experimental). Internet Engineering Task Force, Feb. 2011. URL: http://www.ietf.org/rfc/rfc5981.txt.

[RFC5996]   C. Kaufman et al. *Internet Key Exchange Protocol Version 2 (IKEv2)*. RFC 5996 (Proposed Standard). Updated by RFC 5998. Internet Engineering Task Force, Sept. 2010. URL: http://www.ietf.org/rfc/rfc5996.txt.

[RFC6275]   C. Perkins, D. Johnson, and J. Arkko. *Mobility Support in IPv6*. RFC 6275 (Proposed Standard). Internet Engineering Task Force, July 2011. URL: http://www.ietf.org/rfc/rfc6275.txt.

[RFC6301]   Z. Zhu, R. Wakikawa, and L. Zhang. *A Survey of Mobility Support in the Internet*. RFC 6301 (Informational). Internet Engineering Task Force, July 2011. URL: http://www.ietf.org/rfc/rfc6301.txt.

[RSA78]   R. L. Rivest, A. Shamir, and L. M. Adleman. "A Method for Obtaining Digital Signatures and Public-Key Cryptosystems." In: *Communications of the ACM* 21 (2 Feb. 1978), pp. 120–126. ISSN: 0001-0782. DOI: 10.1145/359340.359342.

[San12]   Sandvine Incorporated ULC. *Global Internet Phenomena Report 2H 2012*. http://www.sandvine.com/downloads/documents/Phenomena_2H_2012/Sandvine_Global_Internet_Phenomena_Report_2H_2012.pdf. Nov. 2012.

[SCJ11]   R. Stankiewicz, P. Cholda, and A. Jajszczyk. "QoX: What is it Really?" In: *IEEE Communications Magazine* 49.4 (Apr. 2011), pp. 148–158. ISSN: 0163-6804. DOI: 10.1109/MCOM.2011.5741159.

[SGV03]   R. Sofia, R. Guérin, and P. Veiga. "SICAP, A Shared-segment Inter-domain Control Aggregation Protocol." In: *Proceedings of the IEEE Workshop on High Performance Switching and Routing (HPSR)*. IEEE. Torino, Italy, June 2003, pp. 73–78. DOI: 10.1109/HPSR.2003.1226683.

[Sig+03]   G. Siganos et al. "Power Laws and the AS-Level Internet Topology." In: *IEEE/ACM Transactions on Networking* 11.4 (Aug. 2003), pp. 514–524. ISSN: 1063-6692. DOI: 10.1109/TNET.2003.815300.

[Sof03]   H. R. E. C. Sofia. "SICAP, a Shared-segment Inter-domain Control Aggregation Protocol." PhD thesis. Universidade de Lisboa, Oct. 2003.

[Sol04]   H. Soliman. *Mobile IPv6: Mobility in a Wireless Internet*. Addison-Wesley, 2004. ISBN: 0-201-78897-7.

[SPF06]   N. Steinleitner, H. Peters, and X. Fu. "Implementation and Performance Study of a New NAT/Firewall Signaling Protocol." In: *Proceedings of the 26th IEEE International Conference on Distributed Computing Systems Workshop (ICDCS) Workshops*. IEEE. Lisboa, Portugal, July 2006. DOI: 10.1109/ICDCSW.2006.63.

[SRC84]   J. H. Saltzer, D. P. Reed, and D. D. Clark. "End-To-End Arguments in System Design." In: *ACM Transactions on Computer Systems* 2.4 (1984), pp. 277–288. ISSN: 0734-2071. DOI: 10.1145/357401.357402.

[Sta11]   W. Stallings. *Cryptography and Network Security: Principles and Practice*. Fifth. Prentice Hall International, 2011.

[Sub+04]   L. Subramanian et al. "OverQoS: An Overlay based Architecture for Enhancing Internet QoS." In: *Proceedings of the 1st conference on Networked Systems Design and Implementation (NSDI)*. NSDI'04. San Francisco, CA, USA: USENIX Association, Mar. 2004.

[Sun+11]   Y. Sun et al. "Fast RSVP: Efficient RSVP Mobility Support for Mobile IPv6." In: *Wireless Personal Communications* 60 (4 Oct. 2011), pp. 769–807. ISSN: 0929-6212. DOI: 10.1007/s11277-010-9973-z.

[TBA01]   A. K. Talukdar, B. R. Badrinath, and A. Acharya. "MRSVP: A Resource Reservation Protocol for an Integrated Services Network with Mobile Hosts." In: *Wireless Networks* 7.1 (Jan. 2001), pp. 5–19. ISSN: 1022-0038. DOI: 10.1023/A:1009035929952.

[TF06]   H. Tschofenig and X. Fu. "Securing the Next Steps In Signaling (NSIS) Protocol Suite." In: *International Journal of Internet Protocol Technology* 1.4 (2006), pp. 271–282. ISSN: 1743-8209. DOI: 10.1504/IJIPT.2006.010562.

[TLL01]   C.-C. Tseng, G.-C. Lee, and R.-S. Liu. "HMRSVP: A Hierarchical Mobile RSVP Protocol." In: *Proceedings of the 21st IEEE International Conference on Distributed Computing Systems Workshop (ICDCS)*. IEEE. Phoenix, AZ, USA, Apr. 2001, pp. 467–472. DOI: 10.1109/CDCS.2001.918746.

[TN00]   V. Talwar and K. Nahrstedt. "Securing RSVP For Multimedia Applications." In: *Proceedings of the 8th ACM International Conference on Multimedia (MULTIMEDIA)*. ACM. Marina del Rey, CA, USA, Nov. 2000, pp. 153–156. ISBN: 1-58113-311-1. DOI: 10.1145/357744.357916.

[TNN01]   V. Talwar, K. Nahrstedt, and S. K. Nath. "RSVP-SQOS : A SECURE RSVP PROTOCOL." In: *Proceedings of the IEEE International Conference on Multimedia and Expo (ICME)*. IEEE. Los Alamitos, CA, USA, Aug. 2001, pp. 579–582. ISBN: 0-7695-1198-8. DOI: 10.1109/ICME.2001.1237786.

[Tse+05] T. Tsenov et al. "Advanced Authentication and Authorization for Quality of Service Signaling." In: *Workshop of the 1st IEEE International Conference on Security and Privacy for Emerging Areas in Communication Networks (SecureComm)*. IEEE. Athens, Greece, Sept. 2005, pp. 224–235. ISBN: 0-7803-9468-2. DOI: `10.1109/SECCMW.2005.1588317`.

[TSZ99] A. Terzis, M. Srivastava, and L. Zhang. "A Simple QoS Signaling Protocol for Mobile Hosts in the Integrated Services Internet." In: *Proceedings of the 18th Annual Joint Conference of the IEEE Computer and Communications Societies (INFOCOM)*. Vol. 3. IEEE. New York, NY, USA, Mar. 1999, pp. 1011–1018. DOI: `10.1109/INFCOM.1999.751655`.

[USA07] USAGI Project – Linux IPv6 Development Project. *Mobile IPv6 stack for the GNU/Linux Operating System*. `http://www.linux-ipv6.org/`. Sept. 2007.

[Val+04] D. Vali et al. "A Survey of Internet QoS Signaling." In: *IEEE Communications Surveys Tutorials* 6.4 (2004), pp. 32–43. ISSN: 1553-877X. DOI: `10.1109/COMST.2004.5342297`.

[Var+12] A. Varga et al. *OMNeT++ Network Simulation Framework*. `http://omnetpp.org/`. Dec. 2012.

[VH08] A. Varga and R. Hornig. "An Overview of the OMNeT++ Simulation Environment." In: *Proceedings of the 1st ICST International Workshop on OMNeT++*. ICST. Marseille, France, Mar. 2008. ISBN: 978-963-9799-20-2. URL: `http://dl.acm.org/citation.cfm?id=1416222.1416290`.

[WC97] P. P. White and J. Crowcroft. "The Integrated Services in the Internet: State of the Art." In: *Proceedings of the IEEE* 85.12 (Dec. 1997), pp. 1934–1946. ISSN: 0018-9219. DOI: `10.1109/5.650176`.

[Wes+02] L. Westberg et al. *A Proposal for RSVPv2*. Internet-Draft draft-westberg-proposal-for-rsvpv2-01. IETF, Oct. 2002. URL: `http://tools.ietf.org/html/draft-westberg-proposal-for-rsvpv2-01`.

[WG06] C. B. Weinstock and J. B. Goodenough. *On System Scalability*. Tech. rep. MU/SEI-2006-TN-012. `http://www.sei.cmu.edu/library/abstracts/reports/06tn012.cfm`. Pittsburgh, PA, USA: Software Engineering Institute, Carnegie Mellon University, Mar. 2006.

[Wu+99]   T.-L. Wu et al. "Securing QoS: Threats to RSVP Messages and Their Countermeasures." In: *Proceedings of the 7th IEEE/IFIP International Workshop on Quality of Service (IWQoS)*. IEEE/IFIP. London, UK, June 1999, pp. 62–64. DOI: 10.1109/IWQOS.1999.766479.

[Zha+93]   L. Zhang et al. "RSVP: A New Resource ReSerVation Protocol." In: *IEEE Network* 7.5 (Sept. 1993), pp. 8–18. ISSN: 0890-8044. DOI: 10.1109/65.238150.